THE ENVIRONMENTAL PSYCHOLOGY OF PRISONS AND JAILS

This book distills 30 years of research on the impacts of jail and prison environments. The research program began with evaluations that documented the stunning success in reducing tension and violence of new jails created by the U.S. Bureau of Prisons, which had a novel design intended to provide a nontraditional and safe environment for pretrial inmates. This book uses assessments of this new model as a basis for considering the nature of environment and behavior in correctional settings, and more broadly in all human settings. It provides a critical review of research on jail environments and of specific issues critical to the way they are experienced and places them in historical and theoretical context. It presents a contextual model for the way environment influences the chance of violence.

Richard E. Wener is Professor of Environmental Psychology in the Department of Technology, Culture and Society at the Polytechnic Institute of New York University, where he codirects the Sustainable Urban Environments program, and is a faculty affiliate of the Rutgers University Center for Green Building. He is a Fellow of Division 34 of the American Psychological Association and has served as President of Division 34. In 2010, Professor Wener was a Fulbright Fellow at the Vienna University of Technology.

For more than 30 years, Professor Wener has studied the way correctional architecture affects facility operations and the behavior of staff and inmates. This work began in 1975 with evaluations of the first "new-generation jails" – federal Metropolitan Correctional Centers in Chicago and New York. He has since conducted evaluations of dozens of prisons and jails and several large nationwide surveys of correctional facilities. He has consulted in the area of facility design and planning for adult and juvenile detention and corrections facilities. He was also part of a team that studied conditions of confinement to support revisions of American Correctional Association standards for the design of jails and prisons. His writing has addressed design and management features that serve to reduce violence, vandalism, and stress in correctional settings by understanding the lessons of successful direct supervision facilities.

Professor Wener's articles have appeared in journals such as *Environment and Behavior, Journal of Environmental Psychology, Journal of Architectural and Planning Research, Criminal Justice and Behavior, Corrections Compendium, American Jails, Transportation Research (Part F), Transportation, Journal of Applied Social Psychology,* and *Psychology Today.* He has served on the editorial boards of *Environment and Behavior, Journal of Architectural and Planning Research,* and *Journal of Environmental Systems.*

Cambridge Series in Environment and Behavior

General Editors: Daniel Stokols
Irwin Altman
Terry Hartig

The Environmental Psychology of Prisons and Jails

Creating Humane Spaces in Secure Settings

RICHARD E. WENER

Polytechnic Institute of New York University

CAMBRIDGE
UNIVERSITY PRESS

CAMBRIDGE UNIVERSITY PRESS
Cambridge, New York, Melbourne, Madrid, Cape Town,
Singapore, São Paulo, Delhi, Mexico City

Cambridge University Press
32 Avenue of the Americas, New York, NY 10013-2473, USA

www.cambridge.org
Information on this title: www.cambridge.org/9780521452762

First published 2012

Printed in the United States of America

A catalog record for this publication is available from the British Library.

Library of Congress Cataloging in Publication Data
Wener, Richard.
The environmental psychology of prisons and jails : creating humane
spaces in secure settings / Richard E. Wener.
p.   cm.
Includes index.
ISBN 978-0-521-45276-2 (hardback)
1. Environmental psychology.   2. Prisons.   3. Jails.   4. Correctional institutions.   I. Title.
BF353.W46   2012
155.9′62–dc23   2012002709

ISBN 978-0-521-45276-2 Hardback

Contents

SECTION THREE. A MODEL AND CONCLUSIONS

Series Foreword

This book series was conceived at a time when the complex relations between human behavior and the sociophysical environment began to attract the attention of many people working in the social sciences and environmental design professions. The field of environment and behavior studies emerged from innovative conceptual and methodological approaches that directly addressed limitations in the ways that human-environment relations were previously understood. This multidisciplinary field brings together people working in psychology, sociology, geography, anthropology, and other academic disciplines with people active in architecture, landscape architecture, urban and regional planning, and other design professions. Although their combined efforts can yield valuable new insights on a great range of problems, they also entail challenges in communication and cooperation that stem from a diversity of intellectual styles and worldviews. Goals also differ. For some participants in the environment-behavior field, the primary goal is the resolution of a basic or theoretical problem, while for others the primary goal is the resolution of some real-world practical problem.

For almost 40 years, the Environment and Behavior series has offered a common meeting ground for those working in this important, exciting, and complex field. Coming from a variety of disciplines and so representing diverse perspectives, contributing authors have taken on problems of standing concern, the study of which had become relatively well established. These authors were asked to do more than simply summarize the work already done on the given problem; they were encouraged to advance the field intellectually by setting forth a particular point of view or theoretical standpoint. A key goal of the series was to make available books that would be useful to a broad range of students and other readers from different disciplines and with different levels of formal professional training, in hopes of providing points of entry into the field and facilitating its further development.

The present book is a fitting contribution to the Environment and Behavior series. Beyond summarizing the work done on a specific problem of lasting societal concern and putting forward a particular point of view about how to address that problem, it shares the humanitarian values and high aspirations that run through all of the previous contributions to this series. Like earlier books in the series, this volume by Professor Richard E. Wener expresses a strong conviction that the good of individuals and the public can be served by using the results of scientific inquiry to guide sensitive environmental design. More directly than any of the earlier books, though, it speaks to the unwarranted suffering that can follow when people are captive in poorly designed environments.

The present book brings to a dignified conclusion the long tenure of this series with Cambridge University Press. Research, environmental design, and publishing proceed together in a dynamic societal context that not only opens new possibilities but also presents challenges to long-standing practices. The challenges that the Press now face have led its representatives to decide not to extend this series further. Their decision saddens us, but we understand the reasons for it. We thank the Press for the generous support provided over the many years that it has served as publisher for the series. Our respect for the mission and espoused values of the Press remain undiminished, and we are confident that its reputation will continue to be well served by the excellent books that it has already published in the Environment and Behavior series, including the present one.

Conclusion of this book series, of course, does not signal the end of the field of environment-behavior studies, nor does it mean that there will no longer be a book series dedicated to environment and behavior studies. It remains to be seen whether a series like this one will be launched with a different publisher. In any case, we see no end to the need for creation, dissemination, and application of knowledge about problems involving human behavior and the environment.

Guest Editor
Terry Hartig

Founding Editors
Irwin Altman and Daniel Stokols

Foreword

If you expect to participate in the planning or design of a new correctional facility, this book is a gold mine of applied research findings about "what works" to create successful correctional facility environments. "Success" in this case is concerned with those physical environment conditions associated with positive behavior by inmates. Dr. Rich Wener wrote this career-long compendium of his findings and those of many others in search of the physical attributes and conditions of confinement that can make a correctional facility more than a human warehouse. Whether you are a corrections director, a planner, an architect, or another psychologist, this book will give you a wealth of hard evidence about how the physical environment can affect inmate behavior and staff–inmate interaction.

Dr. Wener's book looks beyond the usual focus on physical security to other factors in the physical environment supportive of desired behavioral change. He has given those who will be involved in developing the next generation of jails and prisons in the twenty-first century a tremendous variety of findings about how the built environment can support or inhibit human change.

When elected officials and the public get involved in the decision process about a new jail or prison project, this book may also prove to be valuable beyond the professions. The public image of the jail or prison is usually the old punishment fortress, which is assumed to be what corrections is about, the human warehouse. If we expect our correctional institutions to help reduce criminality, that old image must change. This first major collection of objective research and analysis demonstrates for politicians and the public that correctional institutions can be much more successful when their designers focus on the interaction of environment and behavior.

Although the work is primarily focused on the North American experience, its findings include principles with universal application that can be seen in correctional institutions in other regions. The first part gives an interesting history short course on corrections, which is a good lead-up to Wener's own candid history of his involvement, findings, and beliefs that "direct supervision" is a more successful model than "indirect" or "intermittent inmate supervision." The totality of results in all twelve chapters explain that supporting behavioral change through direct supervision principles and practices requires that the facility's design and staff's methods of inmate management work together consistently.

Having worked in the field of correctional facility planning since the 1970s, Professor Wener, through this book, gives us all a long-awaited solid evidence base for correctional planning and design that gives high priority to environment-behavior relationships.

Bob Goble,
Carter Goble Lee Companies
Columbia, South Carolina, USA

Acknowledgments

There are many people to whom I owe acknowledgment and thanks for providing support that led to this volume.

First, I would not have been able to finish this work without the help of several libraries and numerous librarians – both for the comfort of their space that allowed reflective and quiet writing time, and for their aid in finding resources. The former category includes the skilled and friendly though overworked and undercompensated librarians of the Maplewood Memorial Library in my hometown.

For resources, university libraries were, of course, critical. The librarians at Polytechnic University of NYU, in particular Nancy Byrne, were unfailingly supportive and helpful in digging up the many articles and books that I requested, and I very much appreciate their help. A special thanks, though, has to go to Phyllis Schultze, the Criminal Justice Librarian of the Don M. Gottfredson Library of Criminal Justice at the Rutgers School of Criminal Justice. She went far out of her way to help out with no obligation other than her personal desire to serve scholarship. She manages an incredible collection with grace and ease. I am only one of many whose work would be impossible without her support.

I would like to note several extraordinary people I have met who worked as administrators of some of the institutions we have studied, including W. R. (Ray) Nelson, Tom Barry, Larry Ard, Mike O'Toole, and Tom Allison. They are dedicated and intelligent men who have served their profession well. Because of this book, I have been able to be in touch with Ray Nelson and Mike O'Toole, after many years, and it has been a pleasure talking with them again.

I need to thank the many colleagues – architects and researchers – with whom I have worked on corrections research over the years and who have brought insight and creativity to many projects. These include Rod Miller,

Steve Carter, Craig Zimring, Rich Olsen, David Bogard, Chris Keys, Carol Knapel-Sanchez, Lisa Vigorita, Knut Rostat, Nate Clark, Melissa Farling, Bill Frazier, and Frank Schneiger. I have to save a particularly appreciative note for Jay Farbstein, who sought me out for a conversation about jail evaluations at an EDRA conference 35 years ago for what was the start of my longest continual working relationship. Jay has been a friend and most valued partner in much of this work. He, and many of the others, put up with my occasionally disorganized style and were invariably helpful and creative.

I also want to offer special thanks to Bob Goble, who has provided incredible moral support in past year, telling people about the book and encouraging me to finish it with the suggestion that architects were eagerly waiting for it.

I am lucky that a number of people with significant expertise in environmental psychology have been kind enough to read and comment on chapters, including Barbara Brown, Jennifer Veitch, Paul Paulus, Gary Evans, Dan Stokols, Arline Bronzaft, and Jay Farbstein.

Terry Hartig has served as guest editor for the Environment and Behavior series for this book, and I am lucky to have been able to work with him. His suggestions on the scope of this book, as well as on many details, have been invaluable, and he provided tremendously insightful, useful, and detailed comments. The blind reviewer provided by Terry and the Cambridge editors also offered a number of thoughtful comments, which I have tried to integrate into the final text.

There is no one to whom I owe as much as I do to my wife, and to say she was supportive does not cover it. She knows what she has meant to all this work, and that's all that really counts. And, on top of it all, when we first met, I didn't realize what a great copy editor she is. Thank you.

This book is dedicated to those I love, none of whom (I think) have ever seen the inside of the kind of places written about in this book, with special thoughts for Dor, Irv, Sam, Helen, Abe, and Rose, who aren't here to read it, and for Ginny, Rachel, Leah, and Rebecca, who are.

OVERVIEW

History of Correctional Design, Development, and Implementation of Direct Supervision as an Innovation

1

Introduction

It is often a curious experience for me to lecture about design and behavior in correctional settings because of the different groups of people with different kinds of expertise who may be in the audience. When I am speaking to criminal justice and corrections professionals, some of the concepts I discuss are well known (such as the history of prisons, the direct supervision system of design and management, the nature of prison crowding and isolation) but much of the psychology, especially environmental psychology – including research methodology, stress, post occupancy evaluation, personal space and territoriality, and psychology of crowding – is not. If I speak to psychologists just the opposite is true, and a meeting of architects presents a different set of competencies entirely. So it is with this book. Some topics will be well known to corrections people, others to psychologists, and still different ones to designers. The hard part is always in figuring out which elements of familiarity can be assumed and which need deeper background. I hope that parts of this book will be of interest to all of those groups – as well as others such as policy makers.

Put another way, I hope that criminal justice and corrections professionals will find the research on how correctional design affects staff and inmate behavior interesting. In particular, I think the perspective here on the nature of violence in institutions may be different from that usually encountered, as is the explanation of how and why direct supervision actually works. I hope psychologists can come away with a sense of these institutions as magnifiers of environmental impacts and, as such, as laboratories that can tell us things about human response to stress difficult to discern in other places. The message for architects is more value laden – correctional types and models are not the same and choosing one over another has significant and long-term consequences. It cannot be the role of the professional designer to simply build whatever the client requests ("and you want that torture chamber where?"), certainly not without exploring options and impacts. Most of the architects I know and with whom I have worked come to their clients with a strong set of values and ethics and have undoubtedly given up lucrative projects along the way because of their values. I hope the work herein can serve to support their discussions with clients. In the same way, I would hope this work would support correctional professionals, from administrators to unit officers, who, in my experience and contrary to media stereotypes, care deeply about doing a competent, ethical and humane job.

A JAIL OR PRISON BY ANY OTHER NAME

The names we use to label jails and prisons tell much about what those in charge are trying to do with them, or at least the image they want to portray. Prisons were called penitentiaries when the intent was to provide for solitary reflection and opportunities for penitence. Detention facilities are often called correctional centers, suggesting – at least at some point in time, or in some planner's mind – a goal to create change in behavior, correcting personality and behavioral problems. They may be simply called detention centers, jail (from the Latin for cave or hollow), or prison (from the Latin for to seize or arrest) when there is no overriding philosophic or ideological model other than detaining people, that is, keeping them off the streets.

Most, maybe all of these institutions are unpleasant places to spend a night, or many nights, even under the best conditions. That airplane coach seat that is tolerable for a 1-hour flight becomes claustrophobically tight when delayed on the tarmac for many uncertain hours. The jail tier or pod starts out measurably worse than the airplane, or than the institution itself looks in drawings or photos, and becomes even more so once the door slams closed for what may be an indeterminate amount of time.

The best of conditions are rare enough. I have been fortunate to observe and help document many jails that rate among the best environments of their kind, but I have never seen one that I wanted to study so closely as to stay overnight. Even where the inmates are unthreatening, the staff professional, and when designers have strived for "normalization" of the setting, the noise levels; odors; lack of access to light, air, and nature; the uncertain temperature control; and lack of privacy – for sleeping, sitting, using the toilet or shower – make these the kind of settings that few go to willingly. In 1974, during my first study of the brand-new Metropolitan Correctional Center in Chicago, Illinois, then clearly the top of the line in innovative, safe, and clean jails, an inmate said to me "sure this place looks nice, maybe like a motel, but how would you like to be locked inside a Holiday Inn room for three months?" I wouldn't, and the truth is that the place could never have been mistaken for a Holiday Inn (or even a much more budget-oriented hotel) then or now.

Prisons and jails are unique and extreme environments. They are what Goffman (1961) called "total institutions" – 24-hour settings where residents have no control over egress and are infantilized by the fact that they must depend on the staff for almost everything that is vital to their existence, including food, clothing, shelter, and contact with the outside. These are among the few places in our society where people are forcibly placed with no regard to their desire. Moreover, they are long-term environments. In psychology labs where crowding and isolation have often been studied, subjects (voluntarily) come and go in the space of an hour. By contrast, inmates may remain in crowded or isolated conditions, in small confined areas with little movement, all day, for days, weeks, months, and years. In jails they may stay on the small living unit all the time. In prisons, there is usually more variation of spaces – a yard, a work or class area – but there is still not much variety of place or behavior by noninstitutional standards. Where else do we invest so much time and money in a place for which the welfare and improvement of those housed there is often not the main, or often even a nominal goal?

For these reasons jails and prisons are bad places to live, and often not much better places to work. It is not uncommon to hear correctional officers grimly joke that although inmates get to go home eventually, officers are essentially sentenced for life. Over the decades some have argued that these institutions are so expensive, so inefficient, so irredeemably and irretrievably harmful, or so mistaken in approach that they should be closed, shut down, torn down, and replaced with a different, more effective, and more humane system (Ambrosio & Schiraldi, 1997; Elias, 1994; Nagel, 1977; Sommer, 1976; Warren, 2004; Witte, 1977). This is ironic given the beginnings of the American prison system (see Chapter 2) as a reform from more cruel options. In any case, there is no reason to think that the end of imprisonment is as imminent as some had hoped (Sommer, 1976). Nor does this book argue that point. That is a discussion for another time and place; here I will address issues of how the places that do exist impact those within them.

I should also note that as prisons and jails are difficult settings for living or working, they are also very difficult places in which to conduct research. This is important to point out because it helps explain the dearth of useful research in many areas, detailed in the chapters that follow. Many institutional administrations are acutely aware of the potential downside of research – real or imagined criticism of how well they do their job – and hence are often reluctant to provide access and support. Under the best circumstances access and security procedures make research in these places more time consuming and difficult than almost any other place. Without committed help, it is almost impossible.

Much of the research discussed in this book was only possible because of support from a committed high-level administrator (such as at the U.S. Bureau of Prisons (BOP), or the Civil Rights Division of the U.S. Department of Justice), or sometimes because of a court order to gather evidence in support of a legal action. Other studies were conducted by research offices of criminal justice agencies, such as the excellent research staff of the BOP, which seeks data to improve operations and to respond to congressional mandates for oversight.

This analysis is not remote and detached enough to pretend it is value free. My perspective is that some settings are better than others, and it is possible to build and run institutions that are safe, secure, and economically efficient without being tortuous or inhumane or eschewing human betterment as a goal. The values herein are simple: for those who have been declared by legitimate criminal justice and court systems to need forced detention, we should and can create places that are not toxic to the detainees or those who work there. There should be, at the very least, a kind of Correctional Hippocratic Oath to do no further harm. It is not inconceivable that well-planned, well-designed, and well-run institutions can leave people better off, less dangerous, and more likely to succeed than when they arrived. This is surely neither a radical nor an unreasonable goal.

The usefulness and ethics of doing research in jails and prisons should also be openly discussed and made clear. It is not ethical for the purposes of research to manipulate or extend conditions that may be presumed to be harmful. It is not ethical to use inmates or staff in experiments that test conditions without their informed consent. It should also be recognized that getting true informed consent from inmates is especially tricky, given the pressures and control over rewards and punishment that may be presumed to be connected to the research (Rachel Wener, 2007).

Our research[1] has always had the goal of increasing understanding of environment-behavior relationships in ways that would aid the system and support the people within it, including improving living conditions and reducing stress. We have studied conditions as they are and have occasionally conducted "natural experiments" in which we tried to measure the outcome of changes we did not and could not control. For example, in 1977, after we collected data in several living units of the New York Metropolitan Correctional Center, a court decision changed the way the institution dealt with overcrowding.[2] We went back and restudied the units that were affected, providing a useful assessment of the impacts of changes in population density (Wener & Keys, 1988; see Chapter 7, "Prison Crowding" for more information).

It is important at this point to restate what may be obvious: the conditions that make these settings special and that make them such useful platforms from which to observe the impact of environment on behavior also make them harsh and potentially damaging. In such extreme and total environments, every effect is magnified. Noise levels that one could tolerate for a brief exposure, such as on a street corner, in a subway car, or in a stadium, can be very stressful in a prison. The same is true for lighting, view, privacy, crowding, and isolation, as discussed in later chapters. People often work long hours without access to sun and nature, but to be involuntary shut away from these benefits for extensive periods is especially unpleasant, if not harmful for health.

The premise of this book is that the settings of these places, jails and prisons, represent more than just warehouses of bed space for arrested or convicted men and women. They are more complicated environments than just good or bad, comfortable or not. The design of a jail or prison is critically related to the philosophy of the institution, maybe even of the entire criminal justice system. It is the physical manifestation of a society's goals and approaches for dealing with arrested and/or convicted men and women, and it is a stage for acting out plans and programs for addressing their future. The bricks and mortar, glass and steel, cameras and screens of the institution may be the embodiment of a philosophy of corrections, and the design process can be the wedge that forces the system to think through its approach and review, restate, or redevelop its philosophy of criminal justice.

The setting of the jail or prison is part of an overt agenda that includes the kinds of spaces that are provided, the number of beds, the quality of space and programs for education, therapy, and training. But the setting is also part of a covert agenda. It is a manifestation of what or who inmates are in the minds of planners and designers, and what the designers imagine to be the job of correctional officers and other staff members.

In this book I review what is known about these settings from an environment-behavior perspective. The findings discussed herein are based on research, although the research, in many cases, is far from conclusive. The nature of research in institutions makes it very hard to make use of the kinds of controls and random selection that allow for rigor in methodology and certainty in findings.

The investment in the physical infrastructure of corrections over the past 30 years is vast, and new beds continue to be added to the inventory at astounding rates and frightening costs. It would be no less foolish to continue to build these institutions without a careful review of past practice (security, safety, programmatic success) as a guide to future construction than for a franchise to add new sites without looking at how well the last ones worked to sell product and satisfy customers. Yet that is what is most often done. Most jails in the United States, for instance, are "one-off" events – lone facilities built at the county level because most counties need one and only one. New jails often replace older ones that are closed because they are out of date, court-ordered to be closed, or just too small to support the inmate population and requisite programs. Each of the more than 3000 counties in the United States operates somewhat like an independent fiefdom, able to make significant decisions on its own. They often go forward with relatively little consideration given to experience in other jails, in spite of the best efforts of groups like the National Institute of Corrections Jail Center, a division of the U.S. Department of Justice.

There are many important questions related to corrections that are not addressed in this book: Should there be jails and prisons? Do they do more harm than good? What are the alternatives? What is their role in the overall criminal justice system – should it be to detain, to punish, to treat, to reeducate? Instead, in this book I use the perspective of environmental psychology to see how behavior and operations are affected by the environment, as broadly defined or in specific issues and features. This discussion is largely based on empirical studies that are usually conducted in the field, such as with post occupancy evaluations (POE). POEs have the stated intention of looking at buildings after they have been occupied, usually based on the responses of user groups, to see how well they work and what lessons can be learned. This approach sees design as a process of inquiry (Zeisel, 2006) and new buildings as, in essence, a complex of assumptions, estimates, and hypotheses for POEs to assess. Occasionally, instead of doing a POE as a one-off case study, large-scale surveys or quasi-experimental studies are possible, comparing facilities at one point in time or before and after change. These studies are part of a process that has recently become known as evidence-based design (Ulrich et al., 2008).

Environmental psychology takes a broad, holistic, and contextual view. It looks at the physical setting and the social and organization context, as well as economic and political aspects of the setting. No reasonable architect can begin to approach the design of a jail or prison without thoroughly understanding the management and operational system it is intended to support. Often the questions that arise in a good design process force planners and administrators to make implicit assumptions explicit, and this may cause clients to rethink strategies and approaches. The design process can be an opportunity for unfreezing organizational processes and assumptions. The design and operation – the physical, organizational and social environment – are experienced as a unity of place by the inmates. I discuss these connections throughout the book but make them most explicit in the chapter on violence and the conceptual model presented therein (Chapter 11).

This book does not present a deterministic view of the effect of design upon behavior. However powerful or striking the physical place may be, its impact is rarely felt directly and independently of other factors. Rather, the perspective is largely probabilistic; physical structures enable, influence, and change the likelihood of behaviors. The correctional model of direct supervision as discussed throughout the book and in detail in Chapters 3 and 4 is a great example of how and why this is true, but not the only example. The physical setting for this style of correctional design and management is important, but only to the degree it supports and fits within a larger approach to management.

THE ROLE OF DIRECT SUPERVISION IN THIS BOOK

One might reasonably read this book and wonder if it is a review of corrections in general or a paean to one specific model – direct supervision – in particular. Because one can find many recent and important books on prisons and jails that barely mention direct supervision, it is not unreasonable to ask why discussion of it should be dominant in a book that purports to be about broader concerns. The simplest answer is that direct supervision is what I know; it is the approach that represented my entrée into the study of correctional settings and a large part of my research conducted since. More importantly though, as I try to make clear in these pages, is what the operation and success of direct supervision systems say about the nature of incarceration, about institutional operations and living, and about environment-behavior impacts in general. It is for those reasons that we often refer to direct supervision in providing examples and descriptions of ways things can and have worked in institutions.

ORGANIZATION OF THIS BOOK

The first section, Chapters 1 through 5, presents an overview of correctional design and related issues. Chapter 2 provides an overview of several hundred years of history of prison and jail design. One chapter on this mammoth subject could not possibly be exhaustive. Rather this chapter tries to capture key trends and, more importantly, review them from the special perspective of environment and behavior. Chapters 3 and 4 are focused on specific elements of that history. Chapter 3 describes the development of the direct supervision model of correctional design and management, arguably one of the most important innovations in jail and prison design to evolve in the late twentieth century. In Chapter 4, I discuss our post occupancy evaluations of these first direct supervision jails. That is the most personal discussion, because it reviews my own early experiences in these sites when they were newly formed. Chapter 5 takes a longer view, reviewing literature on the impact and effectiveness of direct supervision across numerous studies and 30 years of history.

The next section, Chapters 6 through 10, addresses basic environmental psychology issues of interpersonal and group functioning in jails and prisons. Chapter 6 reviews privacy, territoriality, and personal space as they are viewed in these settings – how individual needs to claim and control space and for interpersonal interactions affect design and experience. Chapters 7 and 8 look at two common and critical conditions that represent opposite extremes of discrepancies between desired and achieved privacy: crowding and isolation. In them we review the literature and conceptual models that explain the impact of these conditions.

Chapters 9 and 10 extend this discussion to environmental conditions in general, and review issues relating to environmental stresses including noise, lighting (artificial and daylight), and views of nature. Issues of daylight and access to nature are garnering special attention in environmental psychology and are bolstered by work in neurology and the cognitive sciences. In some cases, relevant research has been done in correctional settings, but most often we must extrapolate from other settings to corrections.

The final section attempts to organize, conceptualize, and sum up the information previously presented. Chapter 11 ties much of this work together by focusing on the issue that in many ways drives much else of what happens in jails and prisons – violence and fear of it. In Chapter 11 I review perspectives on violent behavior and present my own environmentally based model addressing factors that influence violent acts and that may be used to reduce their frequency. Chapter 12 presents a conclusion and review, including suggestions for the directions of future work.

References

Ambrosio, T. J., & Schiraldi, V. (1997). *From Classrooms to Cell Blocks: A National Perspective.* Justice Policy Institute.

Bell v. *Wolfish,* 441 U.S. 520 (U.S. Supreme Court 1979).

Elias, R. (1994). A peace movement against crime. *Peace Review,* 6(2), 209–220.

Goffman, E. (1961). *Asylums.* New York: Anchor.

Nagel, W. G. (1977). On behalf of a moratorium on prison construction. *Crime & Delinquency*, 23(2), 154.

Preiser, W. F. E., Rabinowitz, H. Z., & White, E. T. (1988). *Post Occupancy Evaluation.* New York: Van Nostrand Reinhold.

Sommer, R. (1976). *The End of Imprisonment.* Oxford: Oxford University Press.

Ulrich, R. S., Zimring, C. M., Zhu, X., DuBose, J., Seo, H., & Choi, Y. (2008). A review of the research literature on evidence-based healthcare design. *Health Environments Research & Design*, 1(3), 61–125.

Warren, J. (2004). Shut down state youth prisons, experts say. *Los Angeles Times.*

Wener, R. E., & Keys, C. (1988). The effects of changes in jail population densities on crowding. *Journal of Applied Social Psychology*, 18, 852–866.

Wener, Rachel. (2007). Not situated to exercise free power of choice: Human subject research in prison settings. *Temple Journal of Science, Technology & Environmental Law*, 26, 365.

Witte, A. D. (1977). Work release in North Carolina – A program that works. *Law and Contemporary Problems*, 41, 230.

Zeisel, J. (2006). *Inquiry by Design: Environment/Behavior/Neuroscience in Architecture, Interiors, Landscape.* New York: WW Norton & Company.

2

Historical View

FROM THE PREHISTORY OF CORRECTIONS TO THE MODERN CRISIS

There is a considerable amount of literature describing the history of correctional philosophy, design, programs, and management (Evans, 1982; Johnston, 2000; Morris & Rothman, 1995). My intent is not to regurgitate, reinvestigate, or challenge those works. The purpose of this chapter is to provide historical context for the discussions that follow concerning the impact of design on behavior in correctional settings. This discussion is focused less on the details of who built what, when, and where, and more on some of the underlying forces that drove the designs.

The design of any building reflects the beliefs and assumptions of those creating it, whether there is a clear functional program that lays these out explicitly for all to see or the goals are subtle, presumed, and unstated. This is especially salient for correctional facilities that, as total institutions (Goffman, 1961), have a magnified impact on the lives of those who live or work inside. This book explores how correctional design reflects underlying beliefs about the nature of inmates as people and the job of overseeing them, as well as the nature of criminal behavior and the criminal mind.

Jails and Zoos

How much can we divine the intent, the presumptions about the occupants, and the underlying assumptions behind the design simply by looking at a building and its features? Imagine, for instance, an institution designed with small rectangular rooms, each sized to house one or several occupants. The rooms are visually porous at one end (usually by providing a fourth wall of metal bars) to facilitate viewing by caretakers or visitors.

FIGURES 1&2. "Obtained from Shutterstock.com"

The rooms and surrounding spaces are constructed of very hard materials (such as concrete, metal, or stone) that are largely impervious to attempts to mark, change, or destroy them. Physical barriers keep residents from having direct contact with one another, as well as with their caretakers or visitors.

This description could be said to accurately describe nineteenth-century prisons and jails, but it also reasonably portrays nineteenth-century zoological gardens. It is no accident that in design, materials, and layout, these early prisons and zoos resembled each other, although they are, to use biological terms, analogues rather than homologues. Their structure is similar, not because of common ancestors, but rather because of common functions. In both cases, the resident was seen as undomesticated, wild, and dangerous, lacking the moral compass attributed to civilized people. The purpose of the room or cage in each case was to prevent movement, to keep inhabitants separated, and to keep them from being able to reach and hurt keepers and, incidentally and occasionally, other residents. The bars, in both cases, were there to provide control by allowing for easy visual surveillance of all spaces, including spaces used for the most intimate and personal activities. Residents in both "have been stripped of almost all opportunities for the resident individual to gain any substantial control over their own environment" (Bukojemsky & Markowitz, 1999, p. 75).

In fact, like zoological gardens, the early model penitentiaries had visitors who came to observe these innovative experiments in moral reformation. "As an attraction for travelers, Cherry Hill [penitentiary] was said to rank with Niagara Falls and the U.S. Capitol. In one decade, 1862 to 1872, over 114,000 visitors paid to view the prison, presumably with no contact with the prisoners themselves" (Johnston, 2004, p. 25S). More than 14,000 people paid a quarter apiece for the privilege of standing in a dark, narrow corridor in Auburn (New York) Prison and peering through narrow slits in the wall to watch inmates as they worked in enforced silence (Lewis, 1922).

Of course, no one would argue that the prison and the zoo are the same. People did not advocate for the moral reform of animals in the zoo – by and large, the animals were viewed much more benignly. The fierce and stolid exterior image of the nineteenth-century prison was meant to provide a message to inmates and others about the harshness of their situation and the determination with which the state meant to punish them. It was not so with zoo design.

PERIODS OF CORRECTIONAL DESIGN

What I show in these chapters is that as the underlying assumptions about the nature of inmates and the purpose of incarceration have changed, so has the nature of the environment.[1] A case in point for corrections has been the development and evolution of the direct supervision design and management system, discussed in great detail in Chapters 3, 4 and 5. The designs of these institutions were radically different from their predecessors, but the most radically different thing about them was the underlying assumption of their planners that inmates (or most inmates, at least) were capable of normal and civilized behavior. This assumption led directly to the creation of living environments that resembled residential settings more than prisons.

Looking at corrections from this admittedly limited perspective suggests four distinct, if overlapping, periods of correctional design and approaches:

1. Prehistorical incarceration (up to the eighteenth century) – a period in which incarceration was mostly without a clear penological philosophy or goals, other than detention until the form of punishment was decided;
2. Early reformist-moralist institutions (late eighteenth to mid-twentieth century) – when institutions were created to change the nature of punishment, often with the goal of changing the behavior of the inmates;
3. Modern traditional institutions – twentieth-century modernizations of institutions intended to update and improve settings, but without any broad change in views of inmates or of the goals of facilities;

4. Modern reforms in corrections design and management (late twentieth century) – settings that are visibly different based on very different goals and views of the nature of inmates and detention.

In this chapter, we describe the first two of these eras with a focus on perceptions about inmates that underlay and drive design decisions. Who are they? How are they expected to behave and respond to treatment? These discussions provide context for more recent innovations in correctional planning and architecture, as discussed in Chapter 3.

Prehistory of Detention

Historians have not described an idyllic age when incarceration was not necessary. Indeed, there is no shortage of evidence of people being imprisoned for various reasons throughout human history (see Morris & Rothman [1995] and Johnston [2000] for detailed histories of penology and architecture), even though there was no formal, self-conscious philosophy of the nature of incarceration, especially for the purpose of correcting errant or antisocial behavior, until the late eighteenth and early nineteenth centuries. Only in the nineteenth century did a wide-scale agreement develop about the intent to use prisons as instruments of reform.

The history of imprisonment is a complicated story precisely because it intersects with the history of so many important social systems including, but not limited to, criminal justice, warfare, politics, religion, and moral philosophy. Because the jail and prison are, for the most part, instruments of the criminal justice system, their purpose, operational program, design, and internal conditions could not be addressed by the state until it was clear that the state was responsible for holding and punishing people who broke the civil and criminal law. That was not always the case. Until the eleventh or twelfth century, crime was often considered a matter between individuals or families. When the state became involved, punishment was largely a public spectacle meant to induce fear and shame. Imprisonment did not appear as a widely used systematic state-sanctioned function until the nineteenth century (Barnes, 1972; Peters, 1995; Spierenburg, 1995).

In the early history of imprisonment detention was used largely to hold people in one place until a decision could be made regarding their ultimate fate. If we accept that a jail is an institution that holds people until they are tried or sentenced and the prison is an institution where people are sentenced for punishment, then we can say that jails have a long history and the prison is a relatively recent invention. Until the nineteenth century, detention was, for the most part, not used *as punishment*, per se, or as part of any intended plan to change behavior (except, of course, the behavior of running away).

Jails were created and operated mostly for the purpose of the secure detention of suspected wrongdoers. They were intended to hold people in place until the real punishment could be administered for whatever stated purpose was intended (deterrence, punishment, elimination of a threat, and so forth). "Imprisonment was almost always an interlude between court appearance and ultimate punishment, usually torture or death" (Johnston, 2000, p. 1).

Prisoners were detained in whatever space was available and seemed secure. The varieties of mechanisms used to make sure people did not achieve freedom of movement might have been as simple as placing them in a pit or cage or tying them to a tree. Until the twelfth century, people were held in a large variety of adapted spaces (Johnston, 2000). Medieval English castles were designed for defense and had many of the elements we think of as the accoutrements of prisons – strong walls, secure perimeters (even including moats), and watch towers. It was easy, therefore, to use areas within castles as a kind of lockup, especially for political or military prisoners, although they may not have been more than storerooms deep within the fortress's keep or "donjon" (dungeon). Many castles contained oubliettes, a deep hole into which prisoners could be thrown to their death and forgotten. It was not until after the twelfth century, Johnston notes, that castles boasted areas specifically created to serve as detention spaces for prisoners.

Conditions of confinement in medieval prisons varied widely, largely depending on the social status of the inmate. Important wealthy prisoners might have servants with them and be free to roam throughout the castle, whereas lower-class inmates were likely to be chained in dungeons for long periods. "Privacy was a thing unheard of, except for rich prisoners of state, who lived on the inside (in the Tower, for example) in much the same state as on the outside, with their servants, their curtains, hangings and furniture and even their silver plate installed from their homes, their meals prepared by their own cooks, or brought in to them from the outside, with extra delicacies provided by friends and well wishers" (Johnston, 2000, p. 17).

In any event, Johnston (2000) notes that detention was not usually intended as a punishment in and of itself, and even if there was hope that harsh conditions might serve as a deterrent to others, reform of the inmate was certainly not a goal. It is not that no one had ever considered the possibility of

FIGURE 3. Noted in Johnston (2000) as "Cage in unidentified French chateau. Maurice Alhoy, Les Bagnes (1845), opposite 451" (page 9).

taking away someone's freedom as a punishment in and of itself; it simply was not heavily debated or practiced as a state policy for those who violated the law. There were cases in which persons were held in prisons for purposes other than pretrial detention, although, not surprisingly, reasons and conditions differed markedly for the lower classes (such as slaves) and upper classes (such as high-ranking political enemies) (Johnston, 2000). Prison facilities for slaves were common in the ancient world and were "used extensively in ancient Rome, Egypt, China, India, Assyria, and Babylon" (Morris, 1974, pp. 4–5).

When prisons were used to punish, their use was inverse to the severity of the crime (Morris, 1974; Johnston, 2000). That is, imprisonment might be used as punishment for petty crimes (debt, alcoholism, vagrancy, and so forth). Corporal punishment, capital punishment, and banishment were common sanctions for serious crimes. Persons accused and convicted of felonies were commonly sentenced to slavery, work, corporal punishment, or death rather than to time in prison (deFord, 1962). Branding was legal in England until 1829 (Andrews, 1899).

The increased use of detention, including new buildings created expressly for this purpose, was related to greater mobility of the population after the decline of medieval social structures (Irwin, 1985). With the Industrial

Revolution, the increase in trade and contact between communities and the growth of urban areas, people were less bound to specific villages. The various rounds of the bubonic plague in the fourteenth century and onward created a labor shortage that also made it easier for healthy workers to move where they wished to sell their labor (Boroda, 2008). These social forces created a growing class of people who were placeless, jobless and often seen as disruptive to the community. When members of this class were accused of a crime it was not clear that they would appear for trial, requiring some check on their movement, such as in a jail (Irwin, 1985).

Sixteenth-century workhouses (such as Bridewell in London) were another response to the rise of this class of vagrants whose offense did not justify corporal punishment (McKelvey, 1977). Even though workhouses (later generically called Bridewells) were a separate parallel system, their use overlapped with jails, and the two institutions merged by the nineteenth century. In the seventeenth and eighteenth centuries, the workhouses held mostly petty offenders while serious felons waited in the jail until their punishment was determined (McGowen, 1995), which might be transport to a distant colony, forced labor on a galley ship, doing public works or work in another setting, as well as corporal or capital punishment (Spierenburg, 1995). Walnut Street Jail discussed more in a later section, was built in Philadelphia in the late eighteenth century largely for the same reason, as a way to control the rootless rabble (Irwin, 1985).

The Environment of Gaols

The program for facilities into the eighteenth century was to "hold their inmates securely and to control any disorderly conduct" (Johnston, 2000, p. 28), with little discussion about the potential for deterrence. Little interest was evinced in the health or welfare of the inmates who were typically held – men, women, and children together – in large congregate spaces (Johnston, 2000

These *gaols* were created with little purpose other than to keep people from running away. There was no legal or moral imperative to provide safe or humane treatment. A jail might be expected to turn a profit on fees paid by inmates for food, clothing, or even leg irons. Guards were often expected to live on fees and bribes paid by inmates and their families (McKelvey, 1977; Johnston, 2000).

With this mix of inmates in common spaces, it is not surprising that many were victims of random acts of violence. Conditions were less harsh

FIGURE 4. "Inside Newgate," by George Cruickshank, 1845

for wealthy inmates, of course, who had greater control over their lives and conditions by virtue of their payments to guards and wardens. They could live in relative luxury by paying for their own services, while poor inmates might literally die of starvation. In fact, the poor inmates might incur debt for living expenses during their stay and wouldn't be allowed to leave until the debt had been paid (McKelvey, 1977).

The design criteria for these buildings were simple: heavy walls, with strong bars or doors. Care was even simpler: provide some basic amenities and don't let anyone escape. Beatings and torture in early jails and prisons were reported to be common, whether planned for political purposes or the natural result of using untrained and unsupervised guards.

The environment of early detention facilities was so stark that making comments on environmental quality seems almost petty, like donning a white glove to check the cleanliness of a barbecue pit. These earliest institutions might not have differed greatly from intended torture, with food deprivation, massive crowding, and lack of outside contact or access to sun and air or sanitation. In this kind of setting, with large congregate cells holding a mixed population, under the limited supervision of nonprofessional guards, one would expect that the area inside the cell would be "owned" and dominated by the most powerful inmates, that staff would tread there rarely and carefully, and that less powerful inmates would be abused and fearful.

THE EARLY REFORMIST/MORALIST INSTITUTIONS

The Roots of Change

Two elements that distinguish modern prison uses from the earlier period are (1) the notion of imprisonment itself as punishment, and (2) the intent to use the sentenced period (in some, if not all, cases) to change the behavior of the involuntary guest. Prison time as punishment is particularly appealing because of the ease with which time in prison lends itself to a seemingly rational and quantifiable metric of degree of punishment – the worse the crime, the longer the term. For instance, "the normal sentence for common crimes such as horse theft, larceny and burglary, from the time Eastern State opened through the 1870s, was two to two and a half years. The normal sentence for murderers and kidnappers was 21 years" (Phillips, 1996, para. 12).[2] That kind of social scaling has an air of precision, fairness, and objectivity no matter how arbitrary and subjective the decisions really are.

Other than simply removing people convicted of crimes from circulation, choosing imprisonment as a punishment for crime instead of corporal or capital sanctions begins to make sense if one believes that people are changeable, that their actions are not immutably stamped into them early in life or even before birth. For those who believe change is possible, the considerable control offered by a total institution appears to be a powerful tool for use in altering the behavior of criminals. Furthermore, if crimes are actions against the state and not an individual the state can be seen as having the right to change criminal behavior that is detrimental to society (Barnes, 1972).

The idea of using institutions to punish and change criminal behavior can be found in Plato's *Laws* (Saunders, 1991). Plato suggests using imprisonment as part of graduated punishments to fit the nature of the crime. In his prisons, no free man can visit, and food is brought by slaves. Longer sentences are given for different offenses or offenders (citizens vs. noncitizens). Plato advocated different kinds of prisons geared to the varying severity and ability to correct the behavior of the criminal (Peters, 1995).

One of the earliest movements toward corrections came in Amsterdam after a local court sentenced a 16-year-old boy to death for theft (Sellin, 1944). It appears that in the sixteenth century, as now, even people who might otherwise be skeptical about being able to change the behavior of adults had an easier time imagining the potential for reforming youthful offenders. City officials asked if there could not be a different, more productive way to address the problem of juvenile crimes. The result was the Amsterdam House of Correction, built in 1589 (Johnston, 2000).

Church Use of Imprisonment

Other early uses of imprisonment to change the offender came from the Catholic Church, the most powerful institution of the day. Notions of the potential for change and redemption came readily within the Church, which acted in some ways as a separate and parallel society with its own justice system to handle transgressions. Although the Church's response to misdeeds was not necessarily gentle (suffering was a necessary component of penitence), it was "the first institution in the West to use imprisonment consistently for any avowed purpose other than detention" (Johnston, 2000, p. 17).

The Church also provided the first structures resembling individual cells, anchorites, which were small rooms attached to church walls in which penitents might spend years, or even decades. Monasteries might include a series of small rooms for individual monks, each including a work area and small garden. Religious institutions maintained a separate, parallel institution in laws and facilities. Confinement of monks for crimes could be for both penitential and punitive purposes, as was common in the thirteenth century (Johnston, 2000).

Enlightenment and Reform

John Howard, the name most closely associated with British prison reform, pushed for the state to take responsibility for the quality of life and conditions of confinement in institutions of detention. In 1773, he was made High Sheriff of Bedfordshire and, quite unusually for the time, took seriously his responsibility to inspect the local prisons (Johnston, 2000; McGowen, 1995). He conducted a 3-year tour of British prisons and later expanded his travels to include many foreign sites. One facility he saw was the papal juvenile prison of San Michelle in Rome, built in 1704 specifically to support a program in which correction of bad behavior would come through discipline (including routine whippings). The builder created a design that was meant to provide for easy visual surveillance to maintain order, although Johnston notes that in the long halls constant observation of inmates from the staff room was difficult (2000). Howard's description of individual cells helped create awareness of this option for the modern prison.

On the whole, Howard was horrified by the conditions he found in almost every British jail. For Howard and other eighteenth-century reformers the jails and prisons were hotbeds of physical and moral disorder (Spierenburg, 1995). They drew an analogy between the spread of moral laxity and vice and the contamination of diseases. Moral and behavioral disease could be spread by contact between people across groups (that is, youth with older inmates, violent with nonviolent felons). His published accounts led to awareness and public concern for prison conditions and resulted in passage, in 1779, of the Penitentiary Act, which he coauthored. The bill proposed to construct two national penitentiaries for reform of inmates (one for men, another for women) and to abolish the widespread practice by which jailers lived on fees from inmates. The bill also provided for improved inspection, sanitation, and work programs, based largely on Howard's observations of Dutch houses of correction. The provisions of the act were costly and largely unimplemented, and the penitentiaries it called for were not built. Instead, England began to rely increasingly on transport to America and, later to Australia.³ Still, Howard's work had a huge impact on public opinion and laid the groundwork for the penological approach of Quakers in America.

The idea of the prison as an instrument of reform began in response to concerns about existing conditions, as "a reaction to the excesses and barbarisms of earlier punishments" (Morris, 1974, p. 4). Time as punishment and the prison as a place for reform and correction were to some degree responses to changing philosophical notions about the nature of evil, crime, punishment, and the public good. The reforms of the nineteenth century were largely based on the works of eighteenth century philosophers such as Beccaria, Bentham, Voltaire, and Howard who created a conscious approach to penology.

One of the most influential of these writers was Cesare Beccaria, who in 1764 published *On Crimes and Punishments* in which he applied the ideas of Montesquieu, Voltaire, and Rousseau to crime and justice (McKelvey, 1977). Beccaria argued that punishment was justified only in as much as it served the public good (as opposed to retribution or revenge). In making the focus of punishment the injury to the state, rather than the individual, he helped to change the underlying concept away from retribution for the injured party and toward restorative justice for society. He said that the severity of the punishment should be connected to the severity of the crime and suggested that the use of imprisonment *as* punishment was a humane alternative to corporal and capital punishment.

Others, such as Jeremy Bentham, spoke of the role of punishment in the law and its value as a deterrent, suggesting that the only justification for punishment was its effect on future actions (Parekh, 1993). A common thread may have been connecting the emerging idea of rehabilitation to more traditional Protestant notions of self-improvement through punishment and work, as well as behavior change spurred by fear of the alternative. Architects responded to this notion by creating prison facades intended to "convey dread and terror, hopefully leading to reform" (Johnston, 2000, p. 31). In Europe, by contrast prison architecture was expected to support reform by providing sanitary conditions, good visual surveillance, and opportunities for segregating inmates by gender, age, and seriousness of crime.

British workhouses and debtors' prisons were precursors to later penitentiaries (Hinkle & Henry, 2004; McKelvey, 1977). Debtors' prisons used loss of freedom as a punishment and workhouses explicitly used forced labor with the intent of bettering the character of the laborers (and not incidentally defraying the cost of the institution). Even so debtors were a very unusual class of prisoners, imprisoned by the will of the creditor more than the state and, as such, typically had the costs of their incarceration paid by the creditor. Also, because of their civil status, they enjoyed more rights than other inmates. For instance, they could see their family inside the jail (McGowen, 1995).

Bridewell workhouses began as institutions of reform, steeped in the Protestant notion of rehabilitation through work, but they remained as detention buildings after funds to support reform vanished (Tappan, 1960). This chain of events is common and pointed out repeatedly regarding buildings erected for a particular, sometimes even idealistic program of reform remaining in place, vestigially operating long after the program had died.

The Pennsylvania Experiment

As odd as it seems to modern sensibilities, the eighteenth-century American Quaker community played a significant role in the invention of the modern prison. A confluence of events and philosophies came together to create the prison as one of the most ambitious social experiments of its time. Quakers and other American reformers of the period were well aware of the work of Howard, Beccaria, and others. They were horrified by the common use of corporal and capital punishment as the only available sanctions for criminal acts, and sought a progressive response, a state sanction that could be both more humane and more effective in dealing with crime. This concern with a more humane approach to punishment goes back at least as far as the Quakers' earliest days in seventeenth-century America. British law had provided for capital punishment for more than a dozen offenses, and corporal punishment (stocks, lash, and so forth) for many more. Foucault (1979) reports that British law continued to add to the number of capital crimes – by 1760, there were 160 capital offenses, and the number rose to 223 by 1819. By contrast, Pennsylvania's Great Law of 1682 provided for death only for murder and treason, and substituted imprisonment in the House of Corrections or hard labor as the penalty for other crimes (Cadbury, 1894; Keedy, 1949).[4] William Penn had toured Europe and chose to model his House of Corrections after the one he saw in Holland that allowed for separation of males and females, debtors and vagrants, and where inmates were paid for their work and provided with seclusion for penitence and reflection (Teeters, 1955).

These laws were in effect until 1718 when the American colonies were forced to adopt British legal codes, with its reliance on fines and corporal and capital punishment (Tetters, 1955). After independence, the former colonies were especially eager to distinguish themselves from British approaches in as many walks of life as possible. It did not take long for support to build in the State of Pennsylvania to reject the British penal system in favor of one that seemed more distinctly American, with the most pressure coming from Quaker reformers in the Pennsylvania Prison Society. In 1788, the society proposed a law to substitute private or solitary labor for corporal punishment. The law, passed in 1790, was influenced by Howard's advocacy of single rooms and solitary confinement. It made the Walnut Street Jail available for all Pennsylvania inmates, and called for the erection of a new cellblock for hardened convicts, which served as the first penitentiary (McKelvey, 1977; Tetters, 1955).

The Walnut Street Jail was built in 1773 as a solution to overcrowding in the House of Corrections. It was typical for its time – a U-shaped building in which inmates were held in large, congregate rooms. A new small cellblock for hardened criminals was constructed within the jail yard in response to the 1790 law, and was known as "Penitentiary House." This jail within a jail contained 6 ft. by 8 ft. by 9 ft. individual cells made of stone. The walls were intended to be high enough to allow light but not communication (Johnston, 2000).

The most different and innovative quality of the new cellblock was its strict adherence to solitary confinement in the extreme, as had been suggested by European philosophers. Jean Mabillon, quoted in deFord (1962), had been among the first to see solitary confinement as a place for penitence. In the seventeenth century, he proposed much of what became the Pennsylvania model of confinement when he suggested that "'penitents might be secluded in cells . . . and there employed in various sortes of labor. To each cell might be joined a little garden, where at appointed hours they might take an airing and cultivate the ground. They might, while assisting in public worship, be placed in separate stalls'" (p. 46).

Eighteenth-century evangelicals had written about the value of solitary confinement as a necessary condition for reform through conversion (Jonas Harvey's "Solitude in Imprisonment," 1776, cited by McGowen, 1995). These reformist writers did not advocate prisons as places of comfort, although they did seek to change the worst abuses and conditions. The suffering that would come as part of imprisonment was not seen as something to be used in public display, as part of retribution or as a deterrence to others. Rather it was part of the religious ordeal necessary for conversion and inner change. Punishment could lead the prisoner to discover the "inner light" (McGowen, 1995, p. 96). As Foucault (1979) points out, the response to public executions was usually not the fear and awe for the majesty of the law that the code had intended, but rather raucous and often sympathetic with the prisoner and derisive of the state. The Quakers were looking for ways to avoid these public horrors. For Beccaria, Morris notes (1974), the prison was equivalent to a diversionary program from the evils of capital punishment.

These early penitentiaries were meant, quite literally, to be places for sinners to serve penance, to be penitent. The intent was to substitute "isolation, repentance, and the uplifting effects of scriptural injunctions and the solitary Bible reading" (Morris, 1974, p. 4) for capital and corporal punishment. Inmates might be brutish beasts, dangerous to the public, to other inmates, or to guards, but this was because they had lost contact with their spiritual nature. Through a kind of forced monasticism, living in total isolation, they could search their souls in self-reflection. The design was created "to produce by means of sufferings, principally acting on the mind and accompanied with moral and religious instruction, a disposition to virtuous conduct. The only sure preventive . . . [is] to impress so great a dread and terror, as to deter the offender from the commission of crime" (Hazard, 1829, p. 264).

The job of the staff was simply to keep inmates apart and to keep them from escaping or communicating. It was a job that called for total control of the inmate's environment with a minimum of interpersonal contact.[5] The cell has a mattress, toilet,[6] and a small window. "He sees the turnkey once a day, to receive a small pudding made of Indian corn, together with some molasses . . . during his whole confinement he is never allowed to walk out of his cell, even into the passage . . . In this situation, separated from every other individual, given up to solitude and reflection, and to remorse, he can communicate only with himself" (Duke of La Rochefoucauld-Liancourt, cited in Teeters, 1955, p. 40).

The construction of Eastern State Penitentiary (ESP) in 1829 was a response to the overcrowding experienced at Walnut Street Jail. It represented the first full expression of the Pennsylvania model of total solitary confinement and the world's first penitentiary intended to serve a broad region (Johnston, 2000). Architect John Haviland adopted a hub-and-spoke design, not uncommon in Europe. From their station in the rotunda at the hub, guards could view up to seven tiers by looking down the length of the hallways. The radial design, in addition to other advantages noted earlier, served as a physical representation

FIGURE 5. Eastern State Penitentiary, Courtesy of the Library Company of Philadelphia

of a well-ordered environment. Its symmetry and pattern demonstrated a logical and rational organization of space.

Every inmate was given his own individual cell, and a rather large one by standards then and now – 12 ft. by 8 ft. room, plus a 12 ft. by 8 ft. outdoor area. This arrangement allowed inmates space to live their lives in the cell and get fresh air without ever contacting another inmate – or a guard for that matter.

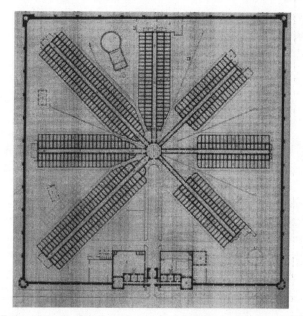

FIGURE 6. Eastern State Penitentiary, Courtesy of the Library Company of Philadelphia

FIGURE 7. Eastern State Penitentiary – From "Brief Sketch of the Origin and History of the State Penitentiary" by Richard Vaux, 1872 McLaughlin Brothers

The inmate ate alone, slept alone, and, when rules permitted, worked alone in the cell. From the moment they entered the prison and were brought to their cell wearing a hood, they saw no one except officials (and those rarely) and clergy for moral instruction (Phillips, 1996).

The more one reads about Eastern State Penitentiary, the more it becomes clear that its regime and design were characterized by two very different realities. First is the degree to which the intentions of its designers and organizers were truly benign and even idealistic. Although planners knew that the sentence of isolation would be difficult, it was not designed to cause pain, other than the degree to which they felt hardship was a necessary part of reformation and moral change. The plan was based on the desire to find a way to change the essential nature of the criminal toward becoming an upstanding citizen. It was truly unusual for the state to spend such large sums of money to deal with criminals for purposes other than retribution or punishment.

FIGURE 8. Eastern State Penitentiary – From "Brief Sketch of the Origin and History of the State Penitentiary" by Richard Vaux, 1872 McLaughlin Brothers

The second reality, though, is the harshness of the extreme measures taken to isolate inmates from human contact. The zeal of these well-meaning reformers can be seen in the degree of discipline used to enforce inmate isolation. No previous public institution had created such a harsh regimen to be imposed on involuntary subjects for their own good on such a large scale. It is hard to overstate the degree to which prisoners were stripped of their past and identity. "When any prisoners entered Eastern State or any other prison in the state of Pennsylvania, they were given a number and they were not to be called by their name until the day they were released" (Philips, 1996, para. 10), ostensibly to protect their privacy. They were brought to their cells blind-folded and were not allowed to communicate with other inmates or guards. Absolute silence was the rule of the institution. Guards walked their tours with socks over their shoes so that their steps could not be heard by inmates. Illicit noise-making by inmates was an infraction calling for discipline. "If they were caught whistling, singing or talking, they would either be deprived dinner every day for a week or taken to the cell block which was called the dungeon" (Philips, 1996, para. 14) where there would be no light, work, or exercise, and there would be restricted rations.

The uniqueness, strength, and purity of this grand experiment drew visitors from many countries, curious to see if such reform was possible. Most were greatly impressed by what they saw, possibly from the zeal of the reformers, possibly by the calm, quiet, and order in the institutions, a marked contrast to the atmosphere in most prisons of the time.

Thrown into solitude . . . [the prisoner] reflects. Placed alone, in view of his crime, he learns to hate it; and if his soul be not yet surfeited with crime, and thus have lost all taste for anything better, it is in solitude, where remorse will come to assail him. . . . Can there be a combination more powerful for reformation than that of a prison which hands over the prisoner to all the trials of solitude, leads him through reflection to remorse, through religion to hope; makes him industrious by the burden of idleness. . . . " (de Tocqueville, in Smith, 1983, p. 412)

Charles Dickens's oft-cited criticisms of Eastern State were in the minority. "In its intention, I am well convinced that it is kind, humane, and meant for reformation: but . . . very few men are capable of estimating the immense amount of torture and agony which this dreadful punishment, prolonged for years, inflicts upon sufferers" (Dickens, 1898, p. 117).

Auburn – The Alternative

The Pennsylvania system was idealistic and ambitious, but so drastic and revolutionary in concept that alternatives were bound to appear. Moreover, in spite of the many impassioned predictions, testimonials, and philosophical arguments made on its behalf, it was not an obvious or immediate success in reforming prisoners. Its most clear benefit was the calm, quiet, and order the system imposed on the prison environment, which, though no small thing, was not the striking achievement claimed by supporters.

The competing model that arose came from New York as embodied in the state penitentiary at Auburn. The Auburn model was developed, at least in part, in response to its own disastrous experience using the solitary system. In less than a year of total isolation in Auburn's tiny cells, five of the eighty-three prisoners had died and many of the rest were judged to be ill or insane (Toch, 2003). This was sufficiently disturbing to cause New York State officials to

FIGURE 9. Auburn State Penitentiary, Courtesy of the Cayuga Historical Museum

look elsewhere for options. The cost of the Pennsylvania system was another force that pushed New York officials to look for alternatives. The design and plan of ESP required large exterior cells, each accompanied by an individual outdoor space, making it costly in terms of the space required and also making it difficult to stack cellblocks to create huge multistory facilities. Moreover, Pennsylvania system institutions did not generate revenue to offset costs. They did not charge inmates for their own care and feeding, as had been the case in Howard's England, and the craft work produced by inmates in their cells was too small a cottage industry to have any impact on the bottom line.

The model that developed at Auburn tried to address these issues without removing the benefits of order achieved at ESP. They rejected the complete isolation of Pennsylvania. The philosophical approach they put forth instead stressed the curative powers of manual labor. Even though all inmates slept alone in the small cells, they were expected to spend their day working in large congregate spaces. Salvation came, proponents argued, not through penitence, but "through the development of industrious habits under strict discipline in congregate shops" (Mckelvey, 1977, p. 10).

Auburn shared with the Pennsylvania model an obsession about communication between inmates, but silence was made much more difficult to enforce because inmates at Auburn were often together. Silence, in the Pennsylvania model, was meant to help the inmate focus on internal issues and was considered necessary for moral change. More practically, silence also kept inmates from communicating, whether about plans for discord (assaults, riots, escapes) or exchanging information on criminal practices. Eastern State imposed silence by its rules and physical plan, whereas Auburn's congregate work system forced reliance on rules alone. Whenever inmates were together, at work or moving from space to space, they were expected to maintain total and absolute quiet. Military discipline was imposed in the extreme. Inmates were marched to and from work and meals in lockstep with eyes down, the only sound being footfalls and guards' commands. Auburn "replaced solitude with silence, introspection with labor" (Goldfarb & Singer, 1973, p. 28). The Auburn planners were not as optimistic about the possibility of the reformation of prisoners as were those in Pennsylvania. They considered the Philadelphia model of moral change "a pious wish" (Gettleman, 1961, p. 272). Their focus was on discipline, order, and the production of work.

The work system also allowed officials to rationalize the use of the small cells because they were occupied only at night for sleeping. Except for Sunday, inmates were expected to be working outside their cells during most waking hours. Also, because inmates were not permanently restricted to their cells, there was no need to decentralize all services, including access to sunlight and air. Auburn pioneered the use of inside cells (cells that did not run along an outside wall), providing back-to-back rows of 7 ft. by 7 ft. by 3.5 ft. rooms, none of which had direct access to outside light or views. The only light to cells came in through iron grating in the heavy oak doors (Johnston, 2000). These inside cells made it much easier to stack cellblocks for bigger (and more cost-efficient) institutions at Auburn and later Sing Sing.

Work was what filled the Auburn inmates' day, and proponents argued that it was reformative. But work on this scale (500 or more inmates engaged in organized production) was also profitable. The kinds of work the Auburn penitentiary could provide produced income that could significantly defray the cost of building and running the institution. In effect, Auburn officials had it both ways. They could argue that their system was better for inmates than

FIGURE 10. Inmates at Auburn State Penitentiary, Courtesy of the Cayuga Historical Museum

the system of isolation, and note that it was also much more cost-effective for the state.

Strict discipline was necessary to maintain silence and order because of the continual contact inmates had during their out-of-cell hours. The urge to communicate was strong, probably irresistible for many inmates. Only threat and use of harsh punishments could maintain silence. The initial warden of Auburn, for instance, made heavy use of flogging to maintain discipline. Some other prisons built on this model acted on the explicitly stated assumption that inmates must be humiliated in order to be reformed (Rothman, 1995).

Several writers have noted the similarity between Auburn-style prisons and mid-nineteenth-century factories (Johnson, 1987; Melossi & Pavarini, 1981). Both institutions were about efficiency, order, and maintaining a compliant and docile workforce. Melossi and Pavariini (1981) suggest that these two institutions supported each other, with the prisons providing the harsh consequence that helped factories to maintain order and discipline. Inmates made for a workforce that couldn't complain.

The two prison models spread in the United States and Europe. European countries for the most part adopted the Pennsylvania model (O'Brien, 1995). They focused on its reformative philosophy and worked to improve the system and reduce the level of distress the isolation caused inmates (as in the

Pentonville model prison in Britain – see Johnson, 1987). In America, where prison systems are decentralized and each state makes its own decisions, the Auburn model was widely adopted. Although the philosophical issues were discussed and debated, the income produced by inmate labor was the driving force in swinging states' decisions (McKelvey, 1977). Work as reform was largely replaced by work as a way to support the cost of the system. These were expensive facilities to build, in some cases the single biggest capital expenditure that a state would undertake. Any system that demonstrated a distinct cost saving had the advantage.[7]

Broader economic forces also played a role. In the United States there were chronic labor shortages, so the productive capacity provided by these institutions was significant. Europe, on the other hand, had no labor shortages and prison labor was seen as robbing free men of employment, and hence was politically much less attractive (Johnston, 2000).

DESIGN ISSUES OF EARLY JAILS

A defining characteristic of early jails and prisons was the lack of control over how inmates mixed with one another. Typically, inmates of all kinds were housed without regard to classification or threats they posed to one another. For prison administrators, safety and internal security were achieved by "constant inspection" (Johnston, 2000, p. 44), although the design of linear rows of congregate cells in most facilities left significant gaps in the line of sight between guards and inmates. Guards, looking down a long line of cells, could clearly see the front of the cells, and detect attempts at escape, but events inside the cells were out of view, except when the guard on patrol was near.

The lack of programs or other goals for early structures is reflected in the simplicity of their design, "usually consisting of a series of group cells, often arranged in no systematic pattern, or simply disposed around interior courtyards" (Johnston, 2000, p. 33). An example is London's Newgate Prison, built in 1769, where "most of the inmates were kept in a series of large rooms arranged around three courtyards, forming a central square and two smaller flanking squares. . . . Lax administration allowed prisoners to shake down one another and there was almost no supervision" (Johnston, 2000, p. 34).

Even when the guidelines for jail and prison design provided by sixteenth-, seventeenth-, and eighteenth-century architects were humane, the image presented to the community was of foremost concern. They typically suggested external facades that showed severity and evoked fear. One wrote that the ideal prison building was "short and massive, where the prisoners, humiliated, weighted down, are constantly before the eyes of other criminals who are confined there, offering a vision of the punishments that await them, in the repentance that must follow the dissoluteness of their past life" (Blondel, 1771, cited in Johnston, 2000, p. 31). These were structures "meant to keep the multitude in ... no visiting of friends, no education but religious education, no freedom of diet, no weavers' looms or carpenters' benches. There must be a great deal of solitude, coarse food, a dress of shame, hard, incessant, irksome, eternal labour, a planned and regulated and unrelenting exclusion of happiness in reading and writing inasmuch as free citizens had" (Sydney Smith, cited in Johnston, 2000, p. 44). Even so, some designers acknowledged the need to provide some comforts for the inmate, including sunlight and separation of different kinds of inmates[8] and the great Italian architect Palladio felt obligated to point out that inmates were being held in custody and not for punishment (Johnston, 2000).

Conditions inside these facilities were commonly very poor. They were crowded and unsanitary, and illness and death were common. The consistently deplorable conditions in eighteenth-century institutions led John Howard to crusade for more humane conditions of incarceration. Part of the reforms, as recommended by Howard and others, involved the need to separate inmates, especially so that older, more hardened inmates would not contaminate others. This idea was later carried to extreme levels in the Pennsylvania model for much the same reason. The goal of architecture for reformers was to provide a well-ordered environment that would regulate the conduct of inmates and make it easier to segregate them according to logical criteria (age, sex, and crime, for instance) (Spierenburg, 1995). Guidelines required providing adequate food and clothing and the employment of professional, salaried guards.

These reforms of the late eighteenth and early nineteenth centuries led to changes in the design and physical plant of prisons. The straightforward requirements for a prison, which had been simple, secure detention, multiplied as reformers focused on the institution's changing goals. Environments needed to provide adequate supervision to protect the safety of inmates. They needed to assure healthful conditions (clean and sanitary, adequate food and care) and offer the possibility of positive change by work, education, or prayer. The humanitarian writers of the day by no means proposed luxury, or even comfort. Conditions were kept marginal under the assumption that imprisonment needed to be unpleasant and at least offer fewer amenities than those present in the typical life of a free man. Maintaining inmate safety was largely to be accomplished through continual surveillance by guards, wardens, and visitors from reform societies; by isolation; and by classification and segregation of inmates by age, offense, risk, and gender. The goal of separating inmates led to the common use of single cells, but single cell policies were often overridden by the pressure of institutional population growth.

GEOMETRIES OF PRISONS

Johnston (2000) notes that there are three basic forms that the overall plan of a prison of the period could take: simple, regular, nonradial plans; circular or polygonal plans; or radial plans. These differences are not just variations of an architect's aesthetic sense or intention. Rather, the geometry and plan of the facilities both represent and are determined by differing concepts of the nature of institutional operations and, more specifically, the nature of security. The oldest facilities tended to use nonradial layouts, usually rectangular in shape, such as in London's Newgate Prison. These institutions were built with little formal attention to questions of classification or segregation of inmates, and so it is not surprising that they did not easily lend themselves to programs resulting from later ideas of separation by classification. The rectangular design largely depends on the strength of its barriers (stone walls, for instance) to maintain control. These suffice to keep inmates from harmful contact with staff, but do a poor job of protecting inmates from one another, especially given the widespread use of congregate cells. Additionally, these designs do not provide sight-lines that facilitate easy surveillance of the inmates by guards.

Bentham's Panopticon is the best known and most widely discussed of the proposed circular and polygonal shapes, because of the discussion by Foucault (1979), although few were actually built. Panoptic facilities rely, as the name suggests, on complete visual access of inmates' living areas by guards. The facility is circular with vertical floors of cells, stacked in a layer-cake fashion, visible to the guard station in the central core. The concept that drives the design is the notion that visual surveillance is the key element of security: bad behavior takes place out of sight, and any place that guards can see will be safe. The panoptic plan maximizes visibility of inmates by the guards (and, usually, vice versa) but comes with distinct limitations. Like the rectangular models, it does not easily support classification or segregation schemes and limits options providing inmates with secure access to fresh air (Johnston, 2000).

By the late eighteenth century, most prisons adopted a semicircular or radial plans (see Figure 11). The popularity of radial plans, linear tiers of cells that radiate from a central point, was spurred in the early nineteenth century by interest in the new Pennsylvania penitentiary model (Johnston, 2000). The radial plan provides a physical structure that supports a specific organizational scheme. It breaks cell areas into easy-to-identify and physically

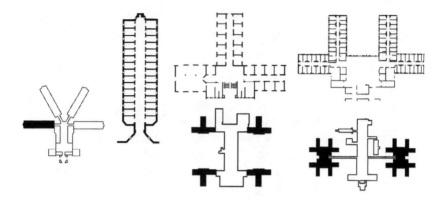

Radial plan   **Telephone pole plans**

FIGURE 11. Courtesy of L. Fairweather & S. McConville. Drawings adapted by Leah Wener from *Prison Architecture: Policy, Design, and Experience.* Oxford: Boston: Architectural Press, 2000.

separate entities. All spaces flow to and from a centralized area, making it easy to organize separate units to segregate different types and groups of inmates and provide for efficient use of staff and resources. These facilities were typically built as tiers in arms radiating out from a central area in a cross. The radial design also relies on strong barriers and surveillance by providing central staff areas with views down long straight corridors so that a few observers can easily tell if the site is in order.

There were also problems with radial designs. Although the radial designs were expected to provide for superior surveillance of inmates, they did so only in limited ways. Staff could easily see down the long hallways and into large rooms and yards, but the far corners of inmate areas and inmate cells were largely out of sight and sound, and hence control. Staff could only see inside the cells and other inmate areas by patrolling down the corridors or special separate hallways (catwalks) on regular, though intermittent, scheduled walking tours. This has been termed, in the modern context, *linear intermittent surveillance* (Nelson, 1988; see Figure 12). The inspection is not constant, and because it is predictable, inmates can often avoid detection as they have time and warning to change their behavior before the guard comes into sight. This is an important issue when inmates are alone in their cells because of the potential for suicide, fire-setting, or other undesirable behaviors, but is a particular problem when inmates are grouped in cells. An inmate who wants to assault another can simply wait until the guard is out of sight.

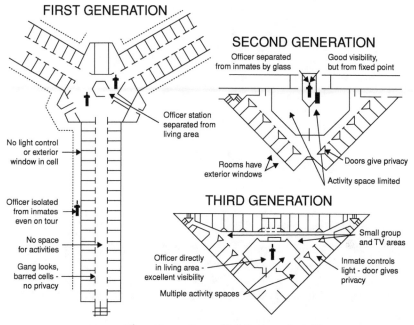

FIGURE 12. Three Generations of Jail Design – Leah Wener

Another unintended consequence of linear intermittent designs is that space becomes clearly, if unofficially, delineated into recognized territories. Staff members "own" all the areas outside of the living areas, but often the inmates have command of the inside space. That means that inmates control much of day-to-day life, usually through informal and coercive leadership structures, especially during gaps in staff tours when inmate areas are out of sight. In many such prisons, staff enter these inmate areas rarely, carefully, and only with backup.

In the twentieth century, form and layout changed, and in some ways became more efficient and effective. Johnston (2000) notes that prisons in the twentieth century were largely designed using rectangular plans (more common for small facilities), radial plans, or campus-like models with buildings dispersed over a broad field. The so-called "telephone pole plans" (one long central corridor with a series of intersecting, perpendicular buildings) became popular early in the twentieth century because they allowed for control of movement, made it easier to bring light into cells, and provided connections between programs and buildings (see Figure 11). They also provided for easier separation of inmates through classification, simpler supervision, and relatively easy expansion. The first such design was at Wormwood in

London, followed soon by several in the United States that were used for high levels of inmate control, including the federal correctional institution in Lewisburg, Pennsylvania. The biggest of these, however, had such long telephone pole spines that it was difficult to see from one end to the other. The same basic understanding of the relationship of architecture to inmate control was in place, however, through hard materials, strong barriers, and easy visual surveillance.

CRITIQUE

The Pennsylvania system as practiced at Eastern State Penitentiary provided an astonishingly restrictive environment that was, in spite of the best intentions of social reformers, highly stressful for inmates. It denied the essential social nature of human beings by removing them from all social contact (see Chapter 8, "The Psychology of Isolation in Prison Settings") and went to extraordinary lengths to strip people of their identities and individuality.

Indeed, there is little evidence of success in reforming criminals and many stories of damage to the health and psyche of inmates from living in these institutions. Penitentiaries around the country recorded dismay at the outcome of this great moral experiment. An 1837 report reviewing the Maryland Penitentiary, indicated that their outcome was "'similar to that of most others in the country; it has fallen far short, hitherto, of the sanguine hopes and expectations... of its founders and supporters and friends of humanity in general'" (Gettleman, 1961, p. 277). Moreover, an extraordinary amount of confidence and faith in the system was required for the state to maintain the organizational and fiscal discipline needed to keep the system going. It was a system that required the actions of true believers at the top and all the way through the organizational ladder. When successes did not pile up and after the Civil War when these institutions were confronted with deteriorating social conditions that led to extreme crowding, the Pennsylvania model of isolation was finally abandoned (McKelvey, 1977). It was a massive, extreme, and overreaching experiment in sensory deprivation and restricted environments based on theory and good intentions, but very little evidence.

The Auburn prison, on the other hand, eschewed idealism in favor of American industry and practicality. It provided a facade of reform but in reality its success in the American marketplace of ideas was driven largely by cost savings (McKelvey, 1977). The silent congregate system of Auburn, however, also required a high level of discipline, and the staff was able to maintain control only with harsh punishments. People are extremely resourceful in finding ways to communicate when easy channels are denied, as can be seen in prisoner-of-war stories from Vietnam.[9] In Auburn, even under constant threat of flogging, prisoners learned ways to communicate without guards hearing them through 2-inch ventilation ducts (McKelvey, 1977).

The Pennsylvania and New York systems, like others to come, resulted in many huge and expensive buildings that were created for a singular and specific program and system, but that remained in operation for many decades after those systems faded. These structures may have been ideal settings for their original, intended (even if misguided) uses, but their designs placed limitations on the ability of future wardens to try other approaches. As the physical models of these prisons proliferated in the United States and Europe, they were often run by people unaware of or unsympathetic to their original underlying philosophy. Many became human warehouses, where little "penitence" was expected or encouraged. Ultimately both systems gave way to other approaches for the treatment of criminals, with different demands on the architecture.

It is also worth noting that for all the reform zeal shown in creating prisons as a way to avoid the harsh corporal or capital punishments of the past, it is not clear that it was a lesser or more humane punishment for many. Rothman (1995) notes that even though many people were probably spared death or disfigurement in exchange for time in the penitentiary, for others the penitentiary system may have meant a more severe penalty. That is, because of the availability of what was viewed as a humane and even curative punishment, many people who otherwise might have received a light punishment or at least one that might be over quickly – a warning, a whipping, a fine, public humiliation – instead may have spent years in prison in isolation and/or in silence.

Rothman (1995) also observes the curious paradox that at a time when America was expanding and becoming more open socially, prisons were becoming more rigid. In Jacksonian America, crime was seen as a fundamental threat to the stability of the republic. Prisons were a positive invention, a way to improve society or to supplement failing social institutions by teaching basic moral values or a work ethic. With the increased mobility and social freedom of the period, some people felt schools and churches were failing to teach morals and obedience, leading to an increase in crime. However different the systems at Eastern State and Auburn might be, they were similar in their commitment to using the penitentiary to change the behavior of the criminal. As de Tocqueville noted, it was a grand social experiment designed to cure social ills and change the nature of people (Rothman, 1995).

For these institutions, architecture was a major part of the reform program. For example, the Boston Prison Discipline Society saw architecture as one of the "most important of moral sciences" (Rothman, 1995, p. 117). "Other things being equal, the prospect of improvement in morals, depends in some degree, upon the construction of buildings... (which were) monumental, as befit so noble an experiment" (p. 123). They were intended to impose a sense of social order and control as well as efficiency as symbolized, in part, in the regular and symmetrical design. Security in these facilities was maintained largely through separation and isolation, the use of thick walls and towers, as well as through the strict regime of silence.

These attempts at reformation of inmates and construction of facilities designed for that purpose continued through the first half of the nineteenth century. They were severely impaired, as many attempts at prison reform have been, by severe overcrowding that put a strain on resources and made maintenance of the strict philosophies of reform a luxury that could no longer be afforded. Placing several beds in cells became more common and adherence to the rules of silence was less strict. After the Civil War prisons were "characterized by overcrowding, brutality and disorder" (Rothman, 1995, p. 125), and administrators and guards (usually ex-soldiers) maintained routines with a military model of discipline.

Inmates' daily lives were less restricted in post–Civil War prisons than in the Pennsylvania or Auburn model penitentiaries, but the common practice of placing two men in a cell and regimes that allowed greater movement through the institution (such as in large congregate yards) increased opportunities for physical and sexual assault and hence placed a burden on staff to maintain order (McKelvey, 1977). The strict isolation and silence models may have been severe and inhumane, but they succeeded in reducing interpersonal violence.

A national study of prison conditions commissioned by New York State (Wines & Dwight, as reported in Rothman, 1995) reported that in 1867, for all practical purposes, there were no serious attempts at reform in penitentiaries in the United States. Common problems included poor physical conditions, inadequate training, and frequent use of corporal punishment. This and other reports pushed for changes in operations and physical plants, including larger cells, boards to oversee administration, better training of guards, and programs to prepare inmates for life after incarceration. There was also a movement for treatment that changed and progressed according to inmate behavior, resulting in indeterminate sentencing.

There were several renewed attempts at change in the second wave of nineteenth-century prison reform (deFord 1962), with agreement and consensus among penologists that "moral regeneration" (p. 101) of inmates was the primary goal of imprisonment. Here, as in many other nineteenth- and twentieth-century reform plans, there was a repeating cycle of "exposés, reports, proposals, then more exposés" (Rotman, 1995, p. 169).

For example, one response to these calls for change was the Elmyra, New York, reformatory opened in 1876 (Rotman, 1995). The plan was to enroll only first-time offenders, presumably those most amenable to change, in educational and vocational programs. The system broke down under heavy overcrowding, particularly with repeat offenders. It suffered from the classic problem of prison reforms – someone other than the reformer controlled who and how many people were sent to the institution.

The situation in late nineteenth- and early twentieth-century prisons in Europe was quite different. Although many penitentiaries had been built using the Pennsylvania system of solitary confinement, and often following the radial design as in Pentonville, this period in Europe represented one of declining prison populations (O'Brien, 1995). This was largely due to a movement toward alternatives in sanctions, such as parole and community-based punishments that focused on returning prisoners to society. In addition, European states took advantage of their colonies by transporting some of its worst offenders to distant lands.

Throughout the twentieth century, penologists used various models derived from science and behavioral science to describe and define criminal behavior and determine appropriate responses. As opposed to the models of the early nineteenth century, where crime was viewed as a moral or spiritual illness, now criminal behavior was often medicalized, and crime was seen an illness. More specifically, many focused on psychiatric models of crime as a mental illness, or used social learning models that viewed crime as inappropriate or socially deviant behavior. "Once crime has been diagnosed as an illness, it was logical to use the methods and language of medicine to 'cure' the offenders of their criminality.... By 1926, sixty-seven prisons employed psychiatrists, and forty-five had psychologists" (Rotman, 1995, p. 178).

One of the important early applications of social learning models was the self-government system applied at Sing Sing by Thomas Osborne in 1913 in which committees of inmates made decisions about important areas of inmate life, such as meals and recreational activities (Reich, 1994). Although the system was widely praised for improving the atmosphere and safety at Sing Sing, it was, like many such plans, opposed by some officers, inmates, and local politicians with vested interests in the old system and was ended by 1929. Another innovative program that foreshadowed the direct supervision models that are discussed in the next chapter, was the Norfolk Prison Colony, set up in 1927 by Howard Gill. His system was individualized and heavily treatment oriented. Inmates were housed in small groupings (fifty inmates), each with its own house officer. Psychological, social, educational, and physical treatment plans were developed for each inmate "for effective treatment and the promotion of social responsibility" (Rotman, 1995, p. 181). This program only lasted for 7 years, however, and closed in the face of conflicts between custodial and treatment goals, and charges of coddling. It was not clear, Rotman notes, that anyone had sufficient knowledge, skills, and techniques to successfully treat inmates at that time, but the programs in place were subverted, again, by overcrowding and by admission of inmates other than those originally intended for the facility.

Other changes in the U.S. prison system addressed the scale of living facilities in both extremes. Campus plans consisting of a series of small dispersed cottages were introduced mostly for women and juveniles. Around the same time, though, was the development of the "big house," huge prisons holding thousands of inmates – but professionally run (Johnston, 2000). The Federal Bureau of Prisons (BOP), founded in 1929, brought a more professional approach in its facilities.

Because the corrections system in the United States is, to a large degree, decentralized (at the federal and state level for prisons and county or city level for jails), many different kinds of approaches and facility types were and still are being used at the same time. For instance, in some places there was heavy economic exploitation – such as chain gangs and inmate labor – particularly in the South, well into the twentieth century (Lichtenstein, 1993).

After World War II, new attempts at establishing rehabilitative models included proposals for a variety of approaches, such as units supporting behavior modification (Rotman, 1995), some of which became discredited after misuses and abuses. The growth of prison populations, especially as the baby-boom generation approached adolescence and adulthood, led to conflicting ideas of how to proceed. These ideas are discussed more in Chapter 3.

The history of correctional design is based on various approaches to control through hard barriers. Designs, layouts, and geometries have changed, sometimes through the creativity of architects, sometimes to meet the goals of idealistic reformers. Reforms have come and gone, many lasting only a few years, until the reformer was discouraged or sent packing, or the reform was overwhelmed by overcrowding. Idealism fades, but its vestiges in physical structures remain long afterward. Many of these models started in the nineteenth century and endured through the twentieth century, and still have influence today. Some radically different approaches, though, appeared in the late twentieth century and are the focus of Chapter 3.

References

American Experience. "Vietnam Online" (1983, March 29, 2005). Retrieved December 1, 2010, from http://www.pbs.org/wgbh/amex/vietnam/series/pt.html.

Andrews, W. L. (1899). *Bygone Punishments.* William Andrews and Company: London.

Barnes, H. E. (1972). *The Story of Punishment.* Montclair, NJ: Patterson Smith.

Boroda, K. (2008). Plague and changes in medieval european society and economy in the 14th and 15th centuries. *The Journal of Arts and Science, 10*(1), 49–58.

Bukojemsky, A., & Markowitz, H. (1999). Environmental enrichment and exhibit design: The possibilities of integration. In A. B. Plowman & P. M. C. Stevens (Eds.), *Conference Centres for the New Millennium: Proceedings of the 5th International Symposium on Zoo Design.* Paignton, UK: Whitley Wildlife Conservation Trust.

Cadbury, S. (1894). Extracts from the diary of Ann Warder 1787. *The Pennsylvania Magazine of History and Biography, 81,* 61.

Coe, J. (1985). Design and perception: Making the zoo experience real. *Zoo Biology, 4*(2), 197–208.

Davies, J. D. (1955). *Phrenology: Fad and Science: A 19th-Century American Crusade.* London: Yale University Press.

de Beaumont, G., & de Tocqueville, A. (1833). *Du système pénitentiaire aux Etats-Unis et de son application en France.* Paris: H. Fournier Jeune.

deFord, M. A. (1962). *Stone Walls: Prisons from Fetters to Furloughs.* Philadelphia: Chilton Company, Book Division.

Dickens, C. (1898). *American Notes and Pictures from Italy.* New York: Charles Scribner and Sons.

Evans, R. (1982). *The Fabrication of Virtue: English Prison Architecture, 1750–1840.* Cambridge; New York: Cambridge University Press.

Foucault, M. (1979). *Discipline and Punishment: The Birth of the Prison.* New York: Vintage Press.

Gana, K., Deletang, B., & Metais, L. (2000). Is boredom proneness associated with introspectiveness? *Social Behavior & Personality: An International Journal, 28*(5), 499–505.

Gettleman, M. (1961). The Maryland penitentiary in the age of Tocqueville, 1828–1842. *Maryland Historical Magazine, 58*(3), 269–290.

Goffman, E. (1961). *Asylums.* New York: Anchor.

Goldfarb, R., & Singer, L. (1973). *After Conviction.* New York: Simon & Schuster.

Haines, M. R. (2002). Vital statistics. In S. B. Carter, S. S. Gartner, M. R. Haines, A. L. Olmstead, R. Sutch, & G. Wright (Eds.), *Historical Statistics of the United States, Earliest Times to the Present: Millennial Edition.* New York: Cambridge University Press.

Hazard, S. (1829). *Register of Pennsylvania.* Philadelphia: WF Geddes.

Hinkle, W. G., & Henry, S. (2004). Bridewell Prison and Workhouse. In M. Bosworth (Ed.), *Encylopedia of Prisons and Correctional Institutions* (pp. 82–84). Beverly Hills, CA: Sage.

Irwin, J. (1985). *The Jail: Managing the Underclass in American Society.* Berkeley, CA: University of California Press.

Johnson, R. (1987). *Hard Time: Understanding and Reforming the Prison.* Belmont, CA: Brooks Cole.

Johnston, N. B. (2000). _Forms of Constraint: A History of Prison Architecture._ Urbana; Chicago: University of Illinois Press.

Johnston, N. (2004). The world's most influential prison: Success or failure? _Prison Journal, 84_(4), 20.

Keedy, E. (1949). History of the Pennsylvania statute creating degrees of murder. _University of Pennsylvania Law Review,_ 759–777.

Lewis, O. F. (1922). _The Development of American Prisons and Prison Customs, 1776–1845: With Special Reference to Early Institutions in the State of New York._ Prison Association of New York.

Lichtenstein, A. (1993). Good roads and chain gangs in the Progressive South:" The negro convict is a slave." _The Journal of Southern History, 59_(1), 85–110.

Maple, T., & Finlay, T. (1989). Applied primatology in the modern zoo. _Zoo Biology, 8_(S1), 101–116.

McGowen, R. (1995). The well-ordered prison: England, 1780–1865. In N. Morris, Rothman, David J. (Ed.), _The Oxford History of the Prison: The Practice of Punishment in Western Society._ New York: Oxford University Press.

McKelvey, B. (1977). _American Prisons: A History of Good Intentions._ Montclair, NJ: Patterson Smith.

Melossi, D., & Pavarini, M. (1981). _The prison and the factory : Origins of the penitentiary system._ Totowa, N.J.: Barnes and Noble Books.

Morris, N. (1974). _The Future of Imprisonment._ Chicago: The University of Chicago Press.

Morris, N. (1976). _Presentation at Symposium at Chicago Metropolitan Correctional Center._ Chicago.

Morris, N. (1995). The contemporary prison: 1965 – present. In N. Morris & D. J. Rothman (Eds.), _The Oxford History of the Prison: The Practice of Punishment in Western Society_ (pp. 227–262). New York: Oxford University Press.

Morris, N., & Rothman, D. J. (1995). _The Oxford History of the Prison: The Practice of Punishment in Western Society._ New York: Oxford University Press.

Nelson, W. R. (1988). The origins of direct supervision: An eyewitness account. _American Jail, Spring,_ 8–14.

O'Brien, P. (1995). The prison on the continent: Europe, 1865–1965. In N. Morris & D. J. Rothman (Eds.), _The Oxford History of the Prison: The Practice of Punishment in Western Society_ (pp. 199–226). New York: Oxford University Press.

Parekh, B. C. (1993). _Jeremy Bentham: critical assessments._ London: Routledge.

Peters, E. (1995). Prison before the prison: The ancient and medieval worlds. In N. Morris & D. J. Rothman (Eds.), _The Oxford History of the Prison: The Practice of Punishment in Western Society_ (pp. 3–44). New York: Oxford University Press.

Phillips, B. (1996). _Eastern State Penitentiary: 140 Years of Reform._ Retrieved December 5, 2008, from http://www.geecoders.com/MollyMaguires/eastern.html.

Reich, I. (1994). _A Citizen Crusade for Prison Reform: The History of the Correctional Association of New York._ New York: The Association.

Rothfels, N. (2002). _Savages and Beasts: The Birth of the Modern Zoo._ Baltimore, MD: Johns Hopkins University Press.

Rothman, D. J. (1995). Perfecting the prison: United States, 1789–1865. In N. Morris & D. J. Rothman (Eds.), _The Oxford History of the Prison: The Practice of Punishment in Western Society_ (pp. 111–130). New York: Oxford University Press.

Rotman, E. (1995). The failure of reform: 1865–1965. In N. Morris & D. J. Rothman (Eds.), *The Oxford History of the Prison: The Practice of Punishment in Western Society* (pp. 169–198). New York: Oxford University Press.

Saunders, T. (1991). *Plato's Penal Code: Tradition, Controversy, and Reform in Greek Penology.* Oxford: Clarendon Press.

Sellin, J. T. (1944). *Pioneering in Penology: the Amsterdam Houses of Correction in the Sixteenth and Seventeenth Centuries.* Philadelphia: University of Pennsylvania Press.

Skinner, B. F. (1938). *The Behavior of Organisms.* New York: Appleton-Century-Crofts.

Smith, R. (Ed.). (1833). *The Friend: Religious and Literary Journal.* Philadelphia, PA.

Spierenburg, P. (1995). The body and the state: early modern Europe. In N. Morris & D. J. Rothman (Eds.), *The Oxford History of the Prison: The Practice of Punishment in Western Society* (pp. 44–70). New York: Oxford University Press.

Tappan, P. (1960). *Crime, Justice, and Corrections.* New York: McGraw-Hill.

Teeters, N. K. (1955). *The Cradle of the Penitentiary: The Walnut Street Jail in Philadelphia, 1773–1835.* Philadelphia: Philadelphia Prison Society.

Toch, H. (2003). The contemporary relevance of early experiments with supermax reform. *Prison Journal, 83*(2), 221–228.

Vincent, B. (1895). *Haydn's Dictionary of Dates and Universal Information Relating to All Ages and Nations.* New York: G.P. Putnam and Sons.

Woodham, C. (2008, April, 2008). Eastern State Penitentiary: A Prison With a Past. *Smithsonian.com* Retrieved 10/04/2010, 2010.

3

The Development of Direct Supervision as a Design and Management System

When the Chicago Metropolitan Correctional Center (MCC) opened in 1974, it was startlingly different from any jail seen before, certainly in the United States, and likely anywhere else (see Figure 12, page 37). The look and feel of the building from the outside was unusual – a sleek, white, twenty-six-storey, triangular structure with window slits that reminded people of a computer-punch card. It was even more unusual on the inside for its colors, textures, furnishings, and, most of all, its operational approach, which placed a single officer in the center of an open living area with forty-four inmates, without the protection of an enclosed office or control space. In this chapter, I trace the development of correctional concepts and design ideas that led to the development of this and other such innovative facilities.

THE FIRST DIRECT SUPERVISION JAILS

The three federal Metropolitan Correctional Centers (MCCs in New York and San Diego opened shortly after Chicago) were the first jails that were planned and designed to be operated under what the U.S. Bureau of Prisons (BOP) called its *functional unit management system*, using an approach that later became widely known as "direct supervision."[1]

It is hard for someone who has not seen these jails and their contemporaries to understand how truly revolutionary they were then and remain today. Visually and operationally they were light-years apart from other jails anywhere. "With their individual rooms featuring bright colors, carpeting, windows, water closets, shelving, reading lamps, and wooden doors, the three $10-to-$15-million facilities could easily be mistaken for modern college dormitories" ("Three Models for the Humane Prison that Satisfy the Critics," 1975, p. 52).

FIGURE 13. Chicago MCC, Courtesy of the US Bureau of Prisons

For novices to the field, and even many who were immersed in corrections, the concepts embraced in the creation of the MCC model represented innovations that were so totally different from other designs and approaches to detention that they seemed to come out of nowhere. A few correctional professionals, who felt that they violated understood concepts of security and safety, confidently predicted their failure (Anderson, 1983). A scan of the literature on direct supervision shows a great deal about its principles and how it works, but almost nothing about precedents before 1974. The thoughtful history by Nelson (1988) largely begins with the opening of the Chicago MCC.

Of course, no innovation is independent of its historical context. There is, however, little in the literature about where and how the ideas for direct supervision germinated and much early BOP documentation appears to have been lost. This lack of historical context is especially curious given that the MCC architectural programs made such strong statements about the ways

FIGURE 14. New York MCC, Courtesy of the US Bureau of Prisons

behavior would be affected by design, expectations, and supervision. One of the MCC architects noted, "They told us to move away from the cellblock, steel cage concept and to think more along the lines of a residential type of décor" ("Three Models for the Humane Prison that Satisfy the Critics," 1975, p. 53). The program document for the MCCs was explicit in its assumptions:

Planning for the new Metropolitan Complex is based on the assumption that pretrial detainees, being presumed innocent, should not be submitted to any restriction beyond those justified by the specific purpose of their detention... While a person is detained, the government is obliged to care for him and to protect him against dangers to his personal rights. These duties extend not only to proper feeding, clothing and health care, but also to treatment according to general American standards of decency and the full protection of human rights. . . . The functional unit concept will insure services and programs in close proximity to users and provide physical control over the prisoners with a minimum of effort. The independent nature of the functional unit permits relatively simple program alternatives. As the population characteristics change and need requirements change, programs may be individually altered, removed or added with minimum disturbance to the basic organization. (*Final Outline of the Architectural Requirements for Manhattan MCC of the Foley Square Court House Annex*, 1971)

Statements like this suggest that the U.S. Bureau of Prisons, an otherwise conservative organization, had a high level of confidence in a set of radical innovations, confidence that could have come only from past successful experiences. Some evidence for early inclinations toward the type of thinking that led to the creation of the MCCs can be seen in the collected writings of James Bennett, who was BOP director from 1937 to 1964. This is especially clear when he contrasts past and current approaches. For instance, Bennett cites a warden's comment that prisons had been traditionally constructed so "that even their aspect might be terrific... dark and comfortless abodes of guilt and wretchedness" (Bennett, 1964c, p. 255). He also recounts a visit to a state penitentiary so old, dark, crowded, and dirty that any rehabilitation there could have come about "only by accident" (Bennett, 1964a, p. 321). He notes with approval a change of correctional philosophy that began in the 1960s, moving the field away from models that led to excessive regimentation, mass treatment, and monotony.

It was clear to many in the 1960s, and through the 1970s, that new construction on a large scale was going to be required. The physical plants of county, state, and federal correctional facilities were poor. They were aging and in disrepair. Responses to the sorry state of prisons and jails in the United States went to opposite extremes, from calls for massive funding to rebuild the system to calls for a complete halt to construction. Meanwhile, the National Council on Crime and Delinquency promoted a moratorium on all prison construction until the impact of and needs for prison design could be better understood (Nagel, 1973). The moratorium call was largely ignored mostly because of the reality of a growing prison population and predictions of much more to come as the leading edge of the post-war baby-boom generation passed through childhood toward the years when contact with the justice system is most frequent (Keve, 1991).

The facilities that did exist were aging and increasingly seen as inappropriate, ineffective, and inhumane. The President's Task Force commented that "[t]he most glaringly inadequate institution on the American correctional scene is the one that affects more human lives than any other – the jail" (*The Criminal Offender*, 1970, p. 13).

In the early 1960s, U.S. Attorney General Robert Kennedy approached the Bureau of Prisons (BOP) with a mandate for them to develop innovative correctional programs and facilities (Keve, 1991). This led to the development of halfway house programs and several new juvenile facilities. Some changes worked their way through the legislative process, largely through the Senate Penitentiary Committee that was revived by Senator Roman Hruska in the mid-1960s after 30 years of dormancy. Hruska and his aide Richard Velde (later assistant director of the Law Enforcement Assistance Administration – LEAA) were given a tour of federal prisons by Norman Carlson (who later served as director of the federal Bureau of Prisons during the period when the MCCs were planned and built) and they were appalled at the age and deterioration of the system (personal communication, Velde, 2004).

They concluded that the level of disrepair in federal and state systems required a significant influx of funds. The Omnibus Crime Control and Safe Streets Act of 1968 established the Law Enforcement Assistance Administration, and the National Institute of Corrections, and led to the creation of congressional committees and presidential task forces to study problems in corrections. The crime bill provided that states had to conduct comprehensive surveys of facilities and were told to seek and follow the most advanced practice. To identify advanced practice a committee was appointed which lead to the creation of the National Clearinghouse for Criminal Justice Planning and Architecture, headed by professor of architecture Fred Moyer. The Clearinghouse was the early advocate for much of what later was seen as key to direct supervision design, including looking to non-correctional models (such as dormitories) for guidelines, and proposing use of normative environments with respect to module size, personal space, light, view and other elements (personal communication, Moyer, 2012).

Carlson noted there was a significant level of discontent among inmates that existed because of the sorry state of prisons and rehabilitation efforts, which culminated in the Attica riots of 1971. These helped to focus attention on the level of the problem and the need for change (personal communication, Carlson, 2004). There was a growing consensus indicated that something different had to be done, and funding from Congress in 1970 for new federal facilities brought the issue to the fore. A Presidential Task Force on Prisoner Rehabilitation was set up as an Ad Hoc Advisory Committee to LEAA, which included prestigious writers on criminal justice such as Norval Morris, Karl Menninger, and Vincent O'Leary, along with Carlson. This group "brainstormed what would be different in a new federal system" (personal communication, Carlson, 2004). The changes originally proposed by Kennedy were reflected in a 1969 statement outlining proposed corrections reform that was issued by the Nixon White House (Nixon, 1969). The "13-Point Program for Reform of the Federal Corrections System" called for a dramatic overhaul of rehabilitation programs and asked the Attorney

General to develop a 10-year master plan for reforming correctional activities (Woolley & Peters, 2010). W. R. Nelson, first warden of the Chicago Metropolitan Correctional Center, suggests that this order provided not only "license but a demand that the MCCs be daringly innovative and serve as models for local detention facilities" (personal communication, Nelson, 2004).

Among other things it provided for development of a federal correctional center for treatment of mentally ill offenders originally proposed years earlier and later constructed in Butner, North Carolina, as well as the creation of a center for training correctional officers. Former Bureau of Prisons Director James Bennett suggested that the new institution for mentally ill inmates was to be part hospital and part prison but "looks like neither. Its very design, intended to uplift the human spirit, is part of the therapy that has been conceived for its patients" (Bennett, 1964a, p. 379). He added that new construction of the past 10 years "has been accompanied by more concern for the needs of the prisoners than has been apparent in such construction for the past 200 years" (p. 379).

DEVELOPING THE PROGRAM FOR THE MCCS

The U.S. Bureau of Prisons and federal judges had long been unhappy with conditions in local jails where federal inmates were housed awaiting trial (Keve, 1991). When funding was approved for construction of three new federal detention centers in 1970, Carlson asked Gary Mote, chief architect for the Bureau of Prisons, to develop plans for these detention centers, as well as final designs for the long-awaited Butner facility and a new youth facility. Mote brought together three teams of designers and corrections professionals from inside and outside the bureau to work side by side on the projects for the "cross fertilization" of experience and ideas (personal communication, Mote, 2004). It was understood that these new facilities should be innovative and vastly different from existing places of pretrial detention.

For one thing, the team members were operating under the presumption that these pretrial detainees were innocent until proven guilty and therefore the environment should not be punitive.[2] Mote noted that when the detention team was having trouble agreeing on plans, John Minor, who had experience in the functional unit management system at the Morgantown, West Virginia, federal facility for juvenile offenders, was asked to work with them. Minor's input helped them realize the concept of unit management in the MCC architectural programs. Those involved recognized that the architectural programs and conceptual designs being prepared were unusual and innovative and uniformly agreed with Mote's sentiments that this experience was "the most exciting time of my life" (personal communication, Mote, 2004).

EVOLUTION OF KEY ELEMENTS OF THE DIRECT SUPERVISION MODEL

The precedents for the design and operational philosophy of what became known as direct supervision evolved from a series of changes and innovations over several decades or more, mostly within the BOP. The key innovative elements that arose from this evolution in thinking were:

1. Creating a new understanding of the role of the officer in the institution;
2. Taking officers out of control rooms and placing them in living areas where they would interact directly with inmates;
3. Implementing decentralized, small living units – functional unit management;
4. Promoting the use of noninstitutional – "normalized" environments;
5. Defining this new system and identifying its underlying management principles.

Several of these developments clearly overlap. Initial efforts at putting the officer in the living area, for instance, were closely connected with the evolution of unit management, which was deeply involved in the redefinition of the role of the officer. Still, it is useful to look individually at the development of each element that led toward significant change in the design and management of jails and prisons.

A NEW UNDERSTANDING OF THE ROLE OF THE OFFICER IN THE INSTITUTION

One important change in modern corrections has been the evolution of the basic institutional security job from that of "guard" to "corrections officer." More than a semantic nicety, this terminology reflects a change in the role of the security staff toward an increasing focus on the use of communication and counseling skills in dealing with inmates. It is not a progression that happened explicitly for or because of the development of the MCCs, unit management, or direct supervision, but it was supported by those developments and was an essential piece in their success. The officer's role in current corrections is nicely stated in a report on security made to Corrections Canada: "We believe that the Correctional Officer must be recognized as a professional in security procedures, people management, and conflict resolution" ("Report of the Task Force on Security," 2003, para. 24).

Security officers had often been poorly trained and held in low esteem. They were the brute force of prison systems. "Shabby facilities, lack of space, inadequate opportunities for work, and more profoundly still, an institutional routine under the eyes of guards in which security was the single most important consideration made life behind bars fundamentally different from life in the free society. In effect, custody prevailed over treatment.... Badly paid and incompetent personnel subverted the possibility of creating a rehabilitative prison environment" (Rotman, 1995, p. 183). As a warden commented in 1929, "the position of the guard was well-nigh intolerable; not only a meager salary but also long hours behind the walls that meant that he, no less than the inmate, was imprisoned" (Rotman, 1995, p. 183).

As far back as 1872 in France attempts were made to create training schools to develop a more skilled class of prison worker. Mostly correctional guards were trained on the job as apprentices to senior workers (O'Brien, 1995). O'Leary (personal communication, 2004) noted that there had been a number of attempts to involve officers in the rehabilitation of inmates via various kinds of treatment systems, corresponding to the development and popularity of the therapeutic community. The idea of a "therapeutic milieu" as a treatment mode arose after World War II in Britain and was most popularized by Maxwell Jones (Jones, 1956).

The therapeutic community overthrew the strict hierarchical organizations of most psychiatric settings in favor of a radically democratic plan. Patients became central to their own treatment and had full participation in decisions controlling the operations in their living area. An early therapeutic community in America was founded by Harry Wilmer whose observations are curiously reminiscent of later discussions of unit management and direct supervision:

I never found it necessary to isolate even one of the 939 patients with whom we dealt, despite the fact that almost every type of acute psychiatric disorder was represented in the group. This result was achieved largely because the staff, no longer free to use methods of control that brutalize both themselves and their patients, had to find new ways of dealing with patients. They found the new ways more effective and infinitely pleasanter than the old. (Wilmer, 1958, p. 42)

Levinson (1999) recognizes the similarities between unit management and therapeutic communities but notes that there are important differences. Responsibility and authority are not delegated to the staff of a functional unit in a jail or prison to the same degree as is done in therapeutic communities in a mental health facility, and certainly authority is not given to inmates in prisons or jails in the way therapeutic communities do for psychiatric patients. Although they have overlapping goals of providing a safe atmosphere and promoting growth and change among the residents, correctional settings emphasize the former and psychiatric settings focus on the latter.

As recently as the early 1960s, some authors in the field still saw case workers as professionals but not correctional officers (Blair & Kratcoski, 1992). Officers and other security staff, however, were increasingly being trained in communication and counseling skills and used as counselors or quasi-counselors in juvenile facilities in the early 1960s (personal communication, Gerard, 2004; personal communication, Levinson, 2004). Bennett (1964c) notes that officers had been successfully used in this fashion in experimental "open institutions" in the Seagoville, Texas, and Alderson, West Virginia, facilities for women. Officers there depended on their abilities as counselors and group leaders to keep control rather than on weapons or barriers. In 1961 the Bureau of Prisons began work on the development of the Demonstration Counseling Project, which was explicitly aimed at training corrections officers to be counselors (Keve, 1991). The professionalization of the officer's role was supported and promoted by unions and by the efforts of major American institutions, including the National Institute of Justice (NIJ), the National Institute of Corrections (NIC), and the American Correctional Association (ACA) (Morris, 1995).

This change in the officer's role, however, is neither universal nor has it been universally accepted. Hepburn (1989) comments that, although titles have changed (from guard to officer), there has not been, in many institutions and systems, a "substantive alteration in the duties of the traditional prison guard" (p. 191). Primary duties remain rule enforcement and custody. Moreover, he suggests that the new roles for officers have added to the uncertainty and ambiguity of the job, making work even more difficult for correctional officers.

These comments make the radical nature of the change embodied in the unit management–direct supervision approach even more impressive, as does their contrast with the views of Howard Gill. Gill was a noted American corrections reformer of the first half of the twentieth century. Nevertheless he argued that officers should not take on other roles. The institution, he said, was "best served when a special corps of prison guards is trained in security policies and practices as the police of the prison community . . . they will not fraternize with prisoners but at all times be firm, stern and authoritarian" (Gill, 1962, p. 314). To be fair, it has been noted that in practice Gill distinguished this group of officers who served as a kind of internal police force from others who served specifically as program staff, and whose functions resembled today's direct supervision officers (personal communication, Nelson, 2004).

TAKING OFFICERS OUT OF ENCLOSED CONTROL ROOMS

Taking officers out of control rooms and placing them in the living area with inmates was a much more difficult concept for state and county correctional departments to accept than it was within the federal system. Federal corrections officers were already being asked to place themselves in and among inmates, but officers in state and county facilities were almost always stationed in closed and locked control stations, physically separated from inmates except during movement or searches (personal communication, Levinson, 2004). Even with unit management, the federal system retained many facilities with linear designs in which officers spent their time touring long rows of cells (personal communication, Levinson, 2004). The federal "open institutions" of Seagoville and Alderson had successfully placed officers directly in living areas with inmates (Bennett, 1964b). Bennett noted that this "experiment is proving that our old criteria for determining that a prisoner is a dangerous and serious menace as long as he is under sentence needs a lot of revision. It also demonstrates that the time-honored belief that prisoners must be locked in tool-proof cells is the figment of a jail builder's imagination" (Bennett, 1964d, p. 279). "Moreover," Bennett also said, "it indicates that prisoners will respond to a program which actually carries out the oft-stated belief that there is a treasure in the heart of every man if you can but find it" (Bennett, 1964d, p. 279).

The MCCs and Butner Federal Correctional Institution were among the first facilities designed specifically for unit management and continual officer direct contact with adult inmates. Levinson (1999) notes that even though these concepts held sway with the BOP's leadership, many wardens were still concerned about this system and complained about the risk of serious violence and inmate takeovers. In the BOP central office, however, the idea of putting officers in living units with inmates was not controversial (personal communication, Mote, 2004). They thought that the biggest risk was in bringing inmate visitors to the living units, a problem eventually addressed in MCC designs by providing a separate secure elevator shaft for visitors.

Pulling officers out of secure control rooms was unnerving for some local jurisdictions. It was not as if officers in state and local facilities had never interacted with inmates without separation by bars. Such meetings had always occurred on occasion. The federal model differed by making such contact policy an important part of the management system, with support from

FIGURE 15. San Diego MCC, Courtesy of the US Bureau of Prisons

design, training, and supervisors. Some planners at the county level were so uncomfortable adopting the MCC model that they chose a half-way solution in which they created settings that resembled the living unit "pods" of the MCCs, but were smaller and set up so that several could be observed remotely from an enclosed officer station (Sigurdson, 1985). These kinds of settings have been termed podular remote supervision facilities (Nelson, 1983; see Figure 12, page 37).

Others chose the direct supervision model, but hedged their bets. When the Manhattan House of Detention (better known as "The Tombs") was gutted and renovated as a direct supervision jail, planners kept the living units unusually small (thirty-six beds) and created open officer stations, which could later be enclosed if the system failed. Clear partitions for turning the officers' stations into enclosed control rooms were purchased and stored in

FIGURE 16. Officer at Chicago Metropolitan Correctional Center, Courtesy of W. R. Nelson

a warehouse. The head of the local officers' union confidently predicted that inmates would destroy the space and attack the officers (Anderson, 1983). Quite to the contrary, the jail became a model of smooth and safe operations (Sigurdson, 1985; Wener, 1985).

DECENTRALIZED SMALL LIVING UNITS — FUNCTIONAL UNIT MANAGEMENT

Within the BOP, functional unit management was seen as the most important innovation in corrections management (Levinson, 1999). The goal was to decentralize management and reduce the scale of living units by dividing inmates into smaller groups. This would make it possible to maximize programming flexibility, provide consistent supervision, and bring services to the inmate. In functional unit management, those who had the most contact with inmates and knew them best were given increased authority to make decisions. It brought together the various people who provided inmate services (unit managers, case workers, and other social service staff) along with security officers who increasingly became part of the treatment team. Unit management, among other things, minimized transportation of prisoners, which was seen as the most dangerous situation for officers.

Unit management "incorporates the notion that cooperation is most likely in small groups that have lengthy interactions" (Levinson, 1999, p. 2). It is designed to "establish a safe, humane environment... which minimizes the detrimental effects of confinement" (Levinson, 1999, p. 10). A BOP publication points out that "Unit management gives inmates direct daily contact with the staff who make most of the decisions about their daily lives. These staff members (the unit manager, case manager, and correctional counselor) have offices in inmate living units. This results in improved inmate access to staff and greater staff access to inmates, providing staff with an awareness of significant inmate concerns and potential problems" (*About the Federal Bureau of Prisons*, 2001, p. 4).

The official BOP history indicates that the first attempts at unit management were made at the Federal Correctional Institution in Ashland, Kentucky, in the late 1950s (*60 Years of a Proud Tradition*, 2004), but there were many steps along the way. Levinson (1999) connects the development of unit management to progress in classification. Decisions about placement of an inmate within an institution had typically been made by personnel in a central office, far removed from the daily experience of the inmate's behavior. In the late 1950s institutions such as the Federal Correctional Institution in El Reno, Oklahoma, began to experiment with unit-based classification teams.

It makes sense that these ideas were first fully tested on juveniles. It is not that young inmates are easier to deal with than adults; often the contrary is true because of the impulsive quality of adolescents, especially those in the criminal justice system. Still, there is greater agreement and optimism among professionals and the general public on the need for educational and rehabilitative programs for juveniles, and on the ability of such programs to have a positive impact. Roy Gerard, a former BOP warden, noted that housing units at the juvenile institution in Englewood, Colorado, were subdivided into smaller living groups in a proto-unit management system (personal communication, 2004). This system progressed to a demonstration counseling program at the National Training School for Boys (NTS) where all the cases connected to one team were placed in one living space (Levinson, 1999).

In 1961 this evolved into a full-blown unit management system at NTS, which ran for several years.

A study conducted by the Bureau of Prisons compared students in a unit management cottage with those traditional cottages (*Rational Innovation*, 1964). The unit management cottage included additional staffing (correctional, programmatic, and counseling) and programming. The youth in that cottage were released earlier on parole, had higher academic achievement, exhibited more prosocial behavior, and committed less misconduct and disciplinary offenses, and although overall rates of recidivism were not different, they committed less serious offenses when they were released and had longer periods before re-offending. These results helped to lead to the implementation of unit management in all of the NTS living areas and eventually to its dissemination to other institutions (Levinson, 1999).

The Robert F. Kennedy Center for Youth at Morgantown, West Virginia, became the first institution designed around unit management as a central programmatic philosophy (personal communication, Gerard, 2004; personal communication, Levinson, 2004; personal communication, Minor, 2004). Research there showed positive staff and inmate responses to unit management and accelerated its use in other institutions. Levinson reports that by 1978 unit management had been implemented in some fashion in almost every BOP juvenile and adult facility.

Unit management was a bold, novel idea because of the historic division between treatment and security staff (DiIulio, 1994). There was some staff resistance to decentralized management ideas, which is not surprising given the slow nature of institutional change, especially in large, tradition-bound organizations such as the Bureau of Prisons (personal communication, Mote, 2004). Unit management came to be seen within the BOP as an important part of facility operations, even by those who had initially been skeptical. By 1970, when planning for the MCCs was getting started, the concept was fully entrenched in BOP plans. For the MCC "the best idea was building unit management into the architecture [which] protected it from being changed when [administrators] changed. The very walls argue for unit management" (personal communication, Levinson, 2004).

THE USE OF A NON-INSTITUTIONAL, NORMALIZED ENVIRONMENT

In addition to changing officers' roles, pulling officers out of locked stations, and implementing decentralized functional unit management, the other striking element of the design of the new MCCs was the use of non-institutional fixtures, furnishings, and materials. In many ways, these designs represented

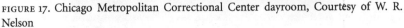

FIGURE 17. Chicago Metropolitan Correctional Center dayroom, Courtesy of W. R. Nelson

an application of concepts from social and environmental psychology. These facilities were overtly and consciously created to maximize the power of expectations to encourage positive behavioral norms, as set through social as well as physical symbols. They provide soft, flexible materials and furnishings to encourage caretaking among users. The designs are, in many cases, bright and colorful. They have carpets on floors and use light, upholstered furniture. Many fixtures are not hardened and vandal proof, but sometimes quite light and breakable.

These design elements did not inherently follow from the implementation of unit management, but do logically derive from other trends. In particular, there had been a push in the late 1960s for reintegration of prisoners after incarceration. The presidential task force (*The Challenge of Crime in a Free*

FIGURE 18. New York Metropolitan Correctional Center dayroom, Courtesy of W. R. Nelson

Society, 1967) promoted reintegration as did the White House memorandum on prison reform (1969). These reports suggested that in order to promote the reintegration of prisoners, programs have to fight the tendency of inmates to become acclimated to a new norm within the corrections setting, a process that has been termed *institutionalization* or *prisonization* (Clemmer, 1958). This could be accomplished, in part, by re-creating the prison environment using symbols of non-institutional housing environments. It also involves providing increased levels of privacy through the use of single rooms, and decreasing the regimentation of institutional life. The publications and dissemination efforts of the Clearinghouse helped turn these ideas into design guidelines, disseminating them broadly among states and counties. Such an approach led planners to create settings that looked and felt less institutional, with bright colors on walls and furniture, carpeted floors, lightweight soft chairs, doors instead of bars, and windows to the outside.

The architect for the New York MCC adopted the idea that unbreakable objects only challenge inmates to try to break them. Something more home-like – like the small tensor lamp used in New York MCC cells – offers no challenge. Breaking it provides no gratification and only leaves the occupant without light (personal communication, Jordan Gruzen, 2004). Similarly, Sommer (1974) suggested that design that attempts to resist vandalism by being impervious to human impact ("hard architecture") actually evokes

FIGURE 19. San Diego Metropolitan Correctional Center dayroom, Courtesy of W. R. Nelson

such behavior, whereas design that is malleable to human needs, even fragile ("soft architecture"), promotes caretaking. He noted that "the architecture of the isolation cell is based on a variant of Murphy's Law – if something can be destroyed, it will be destroyed" (p. 2). If designers "challenge people to destroy something... they will find a way to do it" (p. 10). Hard architecture is "costly, dehumanizing, and it isn't effective" (p. 11). Inmates usually do not destroy objects indiscriminately in riots, Sommer observed, and often televisions purchased with inmate funds and art produced by inmates are left untouched, suggesting such valued things are likely to be treated more respectfully. All three MCCs made special efforts to include bright colors and non-institutional fixtures, furniture, and materials.

DEFINING THE SYSTEM AND IDENTIFYING UNDERLYING MANAGEMENT PRINCIPLES

The MCC designs were clear successes by almost any measure (Wener, 2006), as is discussed in detail in Chapter 4. They were not, however, immediately copied. The design and operation were just too radical and too different for many, especially in state and local jurisdictions. These jails were seen by some as special cases because they were in the federal system, which, some argued, held a different (that is, less aggressive) kind of inmate. This attitude changed markedly after several local direct supervision facilities came on line, including the Contra Costa Main Detention Facility and the Manhattan House of Detention. Many, however, credit the "selling" of the MCC concept to the work of W. R. Nelson, who after serving as warden of the Chicago MCC became chief of the National Institute of Corrections Jails Division.

Nelson and Davis (1995) also identified a series of management principles that were critical to the successful operation of this approach. These principles (see Nelson, 1990 for a detailed discussion) are a mixture of elements that are basic to good management in any correctional setting (or most other administrative situations, for that matter) and issues that are particularly critical to making this unique correctional approach work. They include: maintaining "effective control" (being completely in charge of the environment and eliminating areas of "de facto" inmate control); providing "effective supervision" with personal interaction as well as surveillance; selecting and training competent staff; maintaining safety for staff and inmates; operating cost-effectively; teaching and practicing good communications between staff and inmates and among staff; correctly classifying inmates and orienting them to the new situation; and enforcing rules in a fair and impartial manner.

Experiences Outside the United States

In the mid- to late twentieth century, Western Europe experienced problems similar to those in the United States in jail and prison facilities. That is, most countries were dealing with aging infrastructure and overcrowding, although levels of incarceration in absolute numbers and in rates per capita were much lower than those in the United States (Bailey, 2000; Brody & Zuberty, 2000; Dunbar & Fairweather, 2000; Hulten, 2000; McConville, 2000). As in the United States this was driven in part as a response to increased crime even though "for all this enormous expenditure, the nature of the connection between rates of imprisonment and crime rates is far from certain" (McConville, 2000, p. 2). A British prison that opened in Blundeston, Suffolk, in 1963 served as a model of a facility based on an ideal of treatment, with workshops and facilities for education (Dunbar & Fairweather, 2000). This was "a major departure from the long open cell blocks of radial prisons. The layout was more spread out and less monolithic, smaller cellblocks at the four corners of the central nucleus of communal facilities" (p. 22). When prison construction began again, motivated by continued crowding and a series of riots, about two decades later, the British home office visited and studied new facilities in the United States (*New Directions in Prison Design*, 1985) and expressly

FIGURE 20. Justizzentrum, Leoben, Austria R. Wener

FIGURE 21. Justizzentrum, Leoben, Austria R. Wener

FIGURE 22. Justizzentrum, Leoben, Austria Richard Wener

modeled a number of their new designs on the direct supervision system. Facilities using this model include those built in Doncastor in 1993, Woodhill in 1992, and Lancaster Farms in 1993. For the most part, these British facilities used the triangular floor plan based on the Chicago MCC. Dunbar and Fairweather (2000) comment that "the most fundamental design change in the last 30 years has been the switch from radial layouts to direct supervision 'new generation' designs, where a greater degree of staff-inmate contact has been encouraged. This had far-reaching psychological and security implications for both inmates and staff"(p. 31).

Both France and The Netherlands experienced similar issues and building programs (Brody & Zuberty, 2000; Hulten, 2000). Although both made use of high-rise construction and living units that were smaller in scale, there is no evidence that they also copied direct supervision models.

FIGURE 23. Visiting Centre, Belmarsh Prison, Thamesmead, London, Courtesy of L. Fairweather & S. McConville. From *Prison Architecture: Policy, Design, and Experience.* Oxford; Boston: Architectural Press, 2000.

Similar designs can, however, develop independently. A new justice complex in Leoben, Austria responded to some of the same concerns that drove the MCC designs, but in this case within a different historical, legal and cultural context. In addition to space for over 200 inmates, the complex contains local courts and justice ministry workers. Its striking glass facade was intended to provide a layer of transparency so that criminal justice workers would remain aware of the connection of their efforts to the penal system (Hellmayer, 2005).

Like the MCCs, the complex at Leoben was created in response to an aging prison infrastructure and a desire to demonstrate that something better and more socially useful could be done with imprisonment. The result is a prison with some elements in common with the MCCs, but also some very different design features and solutions. Designers were apparently unaware of MCCs and direct supervision designs in United States, but their similar aims and goals are reflected in programmatic statements. Architects noted that a critical goal was to improve the quality of the experience in the prison for both inmates and staff, by creating living conditions much like that outside the prison so that inmates would not need to be resocialized at the end of their term of incarceration.

The layout was "determined by demands of security and humanity" (p. 112), providing "maximum security outside; maximum freedom inside" (Lewis, 2009). A quotation from the first article of the 1948 UN Declaration of Human Rights is carved into the wall next to the prison entranceway.

There was a strong emphasis on making art part of the environment and paintings, murals and sculpture were dispersed throughout the prison setting. In addition, they sought to increase the sense of personal control and independence among inmates by giving them the ability to reach many areas and services without staff escort.

Inmate housing areas are small, created to be apartment like. Living areas typically house fifteen inmates and include a modest kitchen (where inmates could cook their own meals and snacks), a small exercise area, dayroom, and balcony with exterior access to courtyards, significant use of daylight and heavy soundproofing. Inmates can personalize their bedrooms which are typically for one inmate and includes a toilet, sink, and shower. The Leoben design also includes space for conjugal visiting – both as a reward and as a rehabilitation function – with overnight privacy for family visits – something that is politically very difficult to argue for in the United States.

The institution is still, on the inside at least, recognizable as a prison, with its use of hard barriers, tight boundaries, and heavy hardware. Like the MCCs, though, one visitor noted that "in the three or four hours we spent roaming all through the place, I hadn't seen a single example of vandalism" (Lewis, 2009, p. 2). The Leoben design appears to be receiving a close look from other European criminal justice systems and already some are copying the plan, even though there is also criticism that it is too soft.

CONCLUSION

It is clear, then, that the concepts of the MCCs, even though radical in the context of 1970s jail design and management, evolved from a series of operational and design changes that took place over several decades, driven by the U.S. Bureau of Prisons and the Clearinghouse for Criminal Justice Planning and Architecture. These changes began in small steps that addressed how inmates were classified and grouped, how officers were used and trained, and eventually how spaces were organized. As important as some of the individual steps were, however, the whole became much more than the sum of the parts. The most radical aspect of unit management and direct supervision was that they ultimately challenged and changed the underlying assumptions that served as the basis of correctional operations. They altered the essential understanding of who inmates are, how they can be expected to behave, and how they will respond to treatment. In so doing, these jails have created opportunities for better, more humane, and more effective correctional systems. These opportunities have not always been fulfilled but there are now many examples of institutions that successfully operate on notions that many people once thought of as naive. They were created on the idea that if you provide inmates with humane settings and expect civil behavior from them, the result will be a better and safer environment. This remains one of the most hopeful aspects of modern correctional design.

References

60 Years of a Proud Tradition: An historical perspective of the Federal Bureau of Prisons. Retrieved March 4, 2004, from www.bop.gov/ipapg/sum9ofp5.pdf.
About the Federal Bureau of Prisons. (2001). Washington, DC: Federal Bureau of Prisons.
Anderson, D. C. (1983, 10/25/1983). The editorial notebook: New York's new generation jail. *New York Times*, p. a34.
Bailey, E. (2000). Building for growth. In L. Fairweather & S. McConville (Eds.), *Prison Architecture: Policy, Design, and Experience* (pp. 72–84). Oxford, UK: Architectural Press.
Bennett, J. V. (1964a). Look again John Howard. In J. V. Bennett (Ed.), *Of Prisons and Justice: A Selection of Writings of James V. Bennett* (pp. 378–383). Washington, DC: U.S. Government Printing Office.
Bennett, J. V. (1964b). Of prisons and justice. In J. V. Bennett (Ed.), *Of Prisons and Justice: A Selection of Writings of James V. Bennett* (pp. 317–327). Washington, DC: U.S. Government Printing Office.
Bennett, J. V. (1964c). Penology and architecture. In J. V. Bennett (Ed.), *Of Prisons and Justice: A Selection of Writings of James V. Bennett* (p. 255). Washington, DC: U.S. Government Printing Office.
Bennett, J. V. (Ed.). (1964d). *Of Prisons and Justice: A Selection of Writings of James V. Bennett.* Washington, DC: U.S. Government Printing Office.
Blair, R., & Kratcoski, P. C. (1992). Professionalism among correctional officers: A longitudinal analysis of individual and structural determinants. In P. J. Benekos & A. V. Merlo (Eds.), *Corrections: Dilemma and Directions* (pp. 97–120). Cincinnati, OH: Anderson Publishing Company.
Brody, J. F., & Zulberty, M. (2000). Prisons in Europe: France. In L. Fairweather & S. McConville (Eds.), *Prison Architecture: Policy, Design, and Experience* (pp. 109–117). Oxford, UK: Architectural Press.
Clemmer, D. (1958). *The Prison Community.* New York: Rinehart.
DiIulio, J. (1994). The evolution of executive management in the Federal Bureau of Prisons. In J. W. Roberts & N. Morris (Eds.), *Escaping Prison Myths: Selected Topics in the History of Federal Corrections* (pp. 159–174). Washington, DC: American University Press.

Dunbar, I., & Fairweather, L. (2000). English prison design. In L. Fairweather & S. McConville (Eds.), *Prison Architecture: Policy, Design, and Experience* (pp. 16–29). Oxford, UK: Architectural Press.

Final Outline of the Architectural Requirements for Manhattan MCC of the Foley Square Court House Annex. (1971). Washington, DC: U.S. Bureau of Prisons, Department of Justice.

Flynn, E., Moyer, F. D., Powers, F. A., & Plautz, M. J. (1971). *Guidelines for the planning and design of regional and community correctional centers for adults.* Urbana, IL: University of Illinois Press.

Gill, H. (1962). Correctional philosophy and architecture. *Journal of Criminal Law & Criminology, 53*(3), 312–321.

Hasenlechner, A. (2006). *Justizzentrum Leoben.* Löcker.

Hellmayer, N. (2005). Heterotopia and Humanity: Leoben Judicial Complex, Austria. *architektur.aktuel.*

Hepburn, J. R. (1989). Prison guards as agents of social control. In L. Goodstein & D. Mackenzie (Eds.), *The American Prison: Issues in Research and Policy* (pp. 191–208). New York: Plenum Press.

Hulten, P. V. (2000). Prisons in Europe: The Netherlands. In L. Fairweather & S. McConville (Eds.), *Prison Architecture: Policy, Design, and Experience* (pp. 118–122). Oxford, UK: Architectural Press.

Jones, M. (1956). The concept of a therapeutic community. *American Journal of Psychiatry, 112*(8), 647–650.

Keve, P. (1991). *Prisons and the American Conscience: A History of U.S. Federal Corrections.* Carbondale, IL: Southern Illinois University Press.

Levinson, R. B. (1999). *Unit Management in Prisons and Jails.* Lanham, MD: American Correctional Association.

Lewis, J. (2009, June 14). Behind Bars . . . Sort Of. *New York Times Magazine,* Retrieved from www.nytimes.com/2009/06/14/magazine/14prisons-t.html?pagewanted=all.

McConville, S. (2000). The architectural realization of penal ideas. In L. Fairweather & S. McConville (Eds.), *Prison Architecture: Policy, Design, and Experience* (pp. 1–15). Oxford, UK: Architectural Press.

Morris, N. (1995). The contemporary prison: 1965 – present. In N. Morris & D. J. Rothman (Eds.), *The Oxford History of the Prison: The Practice of Punishment in Western Society* (pp. 227–262). New York: Oxford University Press.

Nagel, W. (1973). *The New Red Barn: A Critical Look at the Modern American Prison.* Philadelphia: The American Foundation, Inc.

Nelson, W. R. (1983). New generation jails. *Corrections Today, April,* 108–112.

Nelson, W. R. (1988). The origins of direct supervision: An eyewitness account. *American Jail, Spring,* 8–14.

Nelson, W. R. (1990, May 20). *Revisiting the Principles of Direct Supervision.* Paper presented at the 5th Annual Symposium on Direct Supervision, Reno, Nevada.

Nelson, W. R., & Davis, R. M. (1995). Podular direct supervision: The first twenty years. *American Jails, 9*(3), 11–22.

New Directions in Prison Design: Report of a Home Office Study of New Generation Prisons in the USA. (1985). London: HMSO.

Nixon, R. M. (1969). *Statement Outlining a 13-Point Program For Reform of the Federal Corrections System.* Washington, DC: White House.

O'Brien, P. (1995). The prison on the continent: Europe, 1865–1965. In N. Morris, Rothman, David J (Ed.), *The Oxford History of the Prison: The Practice of Punishment in Western Society* (pp. 199–226). New York: Oxford University Press.

Rational Innovation: The Cottage Life Intervention Program. (1964). Washington, DC: U.S. Bureau of Prisons, Department of Justice.

Report of the Task Force on Security. (2003, Aug. 8, 2008). Retrieved Nov. 12, 2010, from http://www.csc-scc.gc.ca/text/pblct/security/security-05-eng.shtml.

Rotman, E. (1995). The failure of reform: 1865–1965. In N. Morris & D. J. Rothman (Eds.), *The Oxford History of the Prison: The Practice of Punishment in Western Society* (pp. 169–198). New York: Oxford University Press.

Sigurdson, H. (1985). *The Manhattan House of Detention: A Study of Podular Direct Supervision.* Washington, DC: National Institute of Corrections.

Sommer, R. (1974). *Tight Spaces: Hard Architecture and How to Humanize It.* Englewood Cliffs, NJ: Prentice-Hall, Inc.

The Challenge of Crime in a Free Society: A Report by the President's Commission on Law Enforcement and Administration of Justice. (1967). Washington, DC: United States Government Printing Office.

The Criminal Offender: What Should Be Done? The Report of the President's Task Force on Prisoner Rehabilitation. (1970). Washington, DC: The White House.

Three models for the humane prison that satisfy the critics. (1975). *Building Design and Construction, 16*(3), 52–54.

Wener, R. E. (1985). *Environmental Evaluation: Manhattan House of Detention.* New York: NYC Department of Corrections.

Wener, R. E. (2006). The effectiveness of direct supervision correctional design and management: A review of the literature. *Criminal Justice & Behavior, 33,* 367–391.

Wener, R. E., & Clark, N. (1977). *User Based Evaluation of the Chicago Metropolitan Correctional Center – Final Report.* Washington, DC: U.S. Bureau of Prisons.

Wilmer, H. (1958). Toward a definition of the therapeutic community. *American Journal of Psychiatry, 114*(9), 824–833.

Woolley, J. T., & Peters, G. (1969). *The American Presidency Project* [online]. Retrieved Nov. 10, 2010, from http://www.presidency.ucsb.edu/ws/?pid=2316.

4

Post-Occupancy Evaluations of the Earliest DS Jails

EVALUATION OF THE FEDERAL METROPOLITAN
CORRECTIONAL CENTERS

The previous chapters established the historical, architectural, and organizational context for the Federal Metropolitan Correctional Centers (Mccs) in New York, Chicago, and San Diego as the first attempts to design facilities expressly for unit management and direct supervision. In this chapter, I describe the program and design of these jails in more detail and present the results of post occupancy evaluations my colleagues and I conducted that sought to learn whether or not these designs were successful in providing a safer and less stressful environment. These evaluations studied the earliest direct supervision jails with multiple goals: understand how and how well these new approaches worked, and identify successes and problems to be addressed in future designs.

In many ways the MCC designs represented an application of concepts from social and environmental psychology, even if not expressly referenced as such by early planners and designers. The success of these facilities depends in part upon the power of expectations (set through social as well as physical symbols) to create positive behavioral norms. It relies on interpersonal communications to defuse potentially dangerous situations, and on expectations that officers will proactively identify and deal with problems before they explode. The designs also provide "soft," flexible materials and furnishings to encourage caretaking among users (Wener, 1977; Wener & Olsen, 1978).

The initial support for design research in the first MCCs was motivated by plans of the Federal Bureau of Prisons (BOP) to build several more jails based on the same program. Though the Federal Bureau of Prisons had a strong and active research office, it had never conducted design research per se – that is, social science–based studies of the impact of design on behavior. It is, in a way, odd that design research was not an integral part of the MCC plans from the start, because these buildings represented a conscious attempt at doing something new and revolutionary. In effect, they were experiments in concrete and steel, and in management – urban-scale hypotheses awaiting a test. Design research of the sort we proposed offered the ability to complete the plan-design-build-test loop (Zeisel, 2006) and test these hypotheses.[1] It also offered a systematic way to learn lessons that could improve future iterations of the same building type.

We set out to conduct thorough evaluations of the Chicago and New York MCCs, along with a briefer "walk-through" assessment at the San Diego MCC. The goals of the studies were to:

- Document the degree to which basic assumptions upon which the facility was planned held true. Did these facilities work as hoped? If so, how well?
- Identify which features should be retained for future facilities and which needed change or improvement.
- Learn what staff, management, and inmates thought about the facility.
- Find out how the facility is used. What do staff and inmates do, and how well does that match expectations?
- Compare the three new MCC buildings, identifying common successes or problems and assessing the value of their different design solutions to the program requirements.

THE MCC PROGRAM

An architectural program (sometimes called a "brief") is a statement of requirements that the client has for the proposed building. These documents can be simple or can be long and detailed and may include spatial requirements, adjacency needs, and various technical needs for the facility. The program may also include broad statements of philosophy and goals as well as specific behavioral intentions – how the design is expected to promote critical user activities and attitudes. The program for the MCCs was explicit in the broad goals and expectations for these new jails (*Final Outline of the Architectural Requirements for Manhattan MCC of the Foley Square Court House Annex*, 1971).

Our first task in developing an evaluation strategy was to review planning documents and interview the BOP personnel and private architects who were responsible for the MCC plan and design. The notion of the MCC as an experiment became even clearer when we discovered the way in which the Bureau of Prisons had handled the three design contracts. When seeking architects to design the MCCs in New York, Chicago, and San Diego, the

Bureau of Prisons included firms with little correctional experience, who might be free of the assumptions and biases inherent in earlier approaches to building correctional facilities (only the New York firm had ever designed a correctional facility before).[2] In addition, the Bureau of Prisons asked the three firms to avoid contact with one another. They wanted three unique, untainted design solutions for the same program.

The document that was given to the architects was not extremely detailed – a great deal was left to each of them to work through and develop as part of their design process. The broad philosophical underpinnings, however, were clear and, as noted in the last chapter, stressed presumption of innocence of inmates in a pretrial facility, and the goal of normalization of the environment. The basic programmatic principles outlined by the Bureau of Prisons for the designers were to:

- Create a setting that would be secure from escape and safe for both staff and inmates.
- Create a humane setting based on the notion that this facility was to be for pretrial detention and thus inmates are presumed innocent until proven guilty. This included allowing for reasonable privacy with provision of single bedrooms.
- Create a design that supported "functional living units" to house inmates. These living units should be small in scale (forty to fifty inmates) and be largely self-contained. Most services (including dining and visiting) should be decentralized to eliminate the regimentation of regular inmate movement. The units should be based on the notion of direct supervision,[3] providing no enclosed officer stations. Inmates should be able to move freely within the secure boundaries of the living unit.
- Create a physical setting that would help reduce some of the "trauma" of incarceration by:
  - providing a "normalized" environment, free of the symbols, colors, and materials that traditionally identify total institutions.
  - locating the site in prime downtown areas to be close to transportation, making for easy visiting, and allowing for work-release programs.
  - providing a design that was open, with high visibility and clear sight lines, to promote officer awareness of activities and contacts with inmates.
  - allowing some measure of unescorted inmate movement through the setting to reduce regimentation and the sense of confinement. The high degree of perimeter security afforded by high-rise facilities in down-town sites allowed for greater freedom of movement within the secure boundaries.

Designers were told to plan space and services for a pretrial detention population that would likely stay no more than 30 days and hence would need few long-term programs and services. They assumed that the small-scale living units would allow for greater flexibility in classifying and separating inmates. They expected that the normalized setting, privacy, and increased staff presence would reduce tension and stress among inmates and result in reduced assaults and vandalism.

THE ARCHITECTURE OF THE MCCS

The design of these jails reflected both the program they were given and the individual interpretations provided by the three teams of architects. All three building sites were in prime center-city locations near courts and services and therefore the architects chose high-rise plans, ranging from eleven to twenty-four stories. All had attractive facades that did not connote "jail" from the exterior.

There were other common elements in the final designs. All of the designers decided to use split-level plans for the living units, as the best way to group from forty-four to forty-eight rooms in a modest footprint. In each the bedrooms were a half flight up or down from a central dayroom level. In all cases subgroupings of rooms were along wings or hallways. All made extensive use of nontraditional materials, including indoor-outdoor carpeting and soft, upholstered furniture, as well as mixtures of bright colors on walls. In all cases, fixed officer stations were eliminated. Planners hoped that by leaving out a home base for corrections officers, they would be encouraged to spend more of their time in motion, observing and interacting with the inmates.

In each facility, cells were designed for one occupant – each was approximately 70 square feet and had a single bed, a sink and toilet, and a desk with a lamp and chair. Cells had wooden doors with small viewing windows and switches operable by the occupant for overhead lights (though night-lights were left on and officers could switch on a light for easier security viewing). Showers were available on each floor. The main floor, in all cases, had tables and chairs for dining, along with some recreation facilities – Ping-Pong or pool tables, and a room with exercise equipment.

There were some important differences among the jails. New York and San Diego each had sites with wider footprints, allowing two units side by side on each floor – reducing interior travel time for members of the same management unit and team. In Chicago, they chose to use only a small part of the site for the building itself to reduce the "oppressive" institutional quality that came with long corridors of horizontally spread out buildings (personal communication, J. Hartray, August 2, 2010). The rest of the site was given over to a plaza and low-rise garages. This narrow building allowed just one living unit per floor, with all internal transport by elevator.

Chicago had by far the most unusual plan – an equilateral triangle. This shape gave all rooms an outside view, while providing for an efficient use of interior space. It also allowed for more complete visibility of inmates than either of the other two designs. Within the triangle, almost all space outside of the bedrooms could be viewed from a single, central location. The New York living unit, by comparison, had several spaces that could not be viewed from one location, including a class area that was around a corner and out of sight on the upper level of each unit. In the Chicago triangle, however, interior dayroom space was closed off from daylight except for that which filtered in from cell windows. It also provided the least amount of available floor space per unit.[4] Both New York and San Diego had more room for seating, dining, and recreation.

The intent to use "normalized" furnishings and fixtures was seen by some as a gamble. Typically, correctional settings seek furnishings with some of the same qualities as those found in public parks – such as indestructibility – on the presumption that anything that can be damaged will be. As Sommer (1974) described, however, the actual impact may be just the opposite, because hard architecture challenges and encourages destructive behavior. Moreover, in addition to unpleasant appearance, such hardness comes at a high price. Steel toilets cost many times more than porcelain ones. The same is true for the choice of steel over wooden doors and secure versus normal light fixtures. In each of these cases, and in many others, the MCCs chose to use the more ordinary and less expensive option. They hoped that the facility operations and norms would lead to reduced breakage. At any rate, with the lower cost of the fixtures they chose they could suffer considerable damage and replacement of furnishings and still be financially ahead. The most extreme example of an inexpensive and fragile fixture was the light chosen for use in cells in the Chicago MCC – a bare, half-frosted bulb that simply protruded horizontally from the bedroom walls.

The facilities also differed in the distribution of an important resource, televisions. The Chicago and San Diego MCCs provided four mini-TV lounges for each living unit. Jails are sedentary places and much time is spent sitting, waiting for legal procedures, so television is an important resource. In Chicago, the TV areas were laid out like small living rooms, in four corners of the triangle (two upper and two lower). The New York design provided only two TV areas, one in the central living area and the other in an enclosed solarium.

FIGURE 24. Light in inmate room, Chicago MCC. Courtesy of W. R. Nelson

RESEARCH METHODS FOR STUDYING THE MCCS

The two evaluations (in Chicago and New York) were planned as extended and detailed case studies. The research instruments, used first in Chicago and then in New York, evolved and changed throughout. The most important data for this study were those that came from surveys of users. These were "bottom-up" studies in that they concentrated on information from the most basic level of users – officers and inmates. Higher-level administrators were interviewed, but most time and effort was spent getting information from those who were directly and continually affected by the living unit environment.

In both MCC studies, several kinds of data were collected:

- *User opinions and perceptions.* Inmates and officers were surveyed through the use of closed-ended questionnaires and individual structured interviews.
- *Behavioral observations.* Both studies also made use of systematic and detailed observations of behavior, known as behavior mapping (Ittelson,

Rivlin, & Proshansky, 1967). The purpose of behavior mapping is to get a picture of how people use a space. Trained observers toured living units, recording behavior at regular intervals with codes indicating where it occurred (the living unit was divided into more than fifty predefined areas), who was involved (number of officers and/or inmates), and its kind (several dozen behaviors were recorded from a list of predefined behavior categories).

In Chicago, 126 inmates (about one-third of the population) and 74 staff members (about one-half the total) completed questionnaires. In addition, 35 structured interviews were conducted with inmates as well as many informal interviews with staff and administrators. Behavioral mapping was conducted over 6 days in three different living units from 9:00 A.M. through 9:00 P.M. In the New York MCC, 13 corrections officers and 111 inmates were given structured interviews. Observations were completed on two living units for 4 days each. In all, over 20,000 observations were made.

Respondents ranged from 20 to 74 years of age (average = 30 years), and had been in the institution for between 1 to 45 weeks (average = 13 weeks). Staff member average age was 31 years, ranging from 21 to 61 years; the average time at the MCC was 30 weeks, with a range of 1 to 78 weeks.

No formal data was collected at the San Diego MCC, although a walk-through tour was completed over 2 days, including informal interviews with inmates, staff, and administrators. In all three cities, interviews were conducted with members of the architectural teams.

RESULTS – EVALUATION OF THE MCC MODEL[5]

The reports describe how the facilities were viewed by their users and discuss successes and remaining problems with the designs.

MCC Successes

On many of the most essential points, data from the two case studies concurred. In fact, the similarity of results between the two jails is an important finding in itself, representing a kind of intersite replicability as a validity check for the MCC model. In spite of floor plans, which look very different, the conceptual approaches to incarceration were the same, and the broad response of inmates and staff to the institutional environments were very similar.

Another interesting though unexpected finding was the degree to which inmates and staff agreed about significant issues in both facilities. Staff and inmates not only agreed about the general performance of the facility (low levels of stress and threat, well cared for), they also tended to agree on design preferences. Both indicated that the private rooms were good in helping to reduce stress, and that the open setting was an important factor in encouraging staff–inmate communication, resulting in reduced tension and violence. Traditionally, staff and inmates are seen as having opposing goals and needs, in direct competition with one another. For instance, restrictive movement may help staff to maintain control but is a negative aspect of the environment for inmates. What was unexpected and fascinating at the MCCs was the degree to which staff seemed to feel that what was good for inmates was, for the most part, also in the best interest of officers. If privacy, easy access to TV and phones, or less restricted movement helped reduce inmate tension and anger, then it also served to make the staff's job easier and safer.

This is not to say that staff viewed inmates in a positive light. In fact, some officers volunteered that conditions in these facilities were "too good" for people who had committed serious crimes, and that the MCC environment "coddled" inmates. Value statements aside, though, most officers agreed that the setting met its important goals for security and safety.

That, in fact, was the single most important finding. In the broadest sense, the MCCs worked as buildings, as an inmate management system, and as a concept. Inmates were housed securely (that is, without escapes) in an atmosphere in which there was stunningly little tension, fear of assault, or vandalism. One observer suggested, only half in jest, that the New York MCC might have been one of the few buildings in New York City in 1974 without significant vandalism.

The level at which the buildings "worked" is demonstrated in the survey data. In response to our questions, inmates and staff agreed that the institution was safe and that inmates treated it well. Most inmates had at least some experience in other jails and prisons, and almost all agreed that this was an easier place to be detained than other institutions. For many of the most significant issues, the impact of the setting was immediately obvious to even the casual observer. In a typical living unit at the Chicago or the New York MCC, inmates and staff appeared remarkably calm and relaxed. Inmates and staff moved about the unit freely, often engaging in casual conversations with one another. There were no visible signs from officers of fear of assault, even though no backup officer was present and no hard barriers separated them from the inmates. During their first year of operation, neither of these jails experienced sexual assaults or any serious physical assaults by inmates upon other inmates or upon staff.

The unusual nature of the Chicago MCC was demonstrated to me the first time I visited a living unit. Upon being "buzzed" into the unit, I was greeted by the officer, who almost immediately said that I should make myself comfortable while he handled a chore. With that he left the unit, leaving me alone with forty-four inmates for several minutes. My initial apprehension was contrasted by the behavior of the inmates – they ignored me completely and went about their business, even though I suspected that some enjoyed my obvious discomfort. After a few moments, it became clear to me that I was not at risk.

Living units were staffed by both male and female officers, and the female officers who worked on male units seemed every bit as safe and effective as male officers. This made sense because the primary job of the officer was to use managerial and communication skills, not physically overpowering strength. The success of female officers is supported by other reports (Adler, 1998; Bowersox, 1981; Boyd & Grant, 2005; Cross-Gender Supervision, 2000; Farkas, 1999; Jenne & Kersting, 1996; Kissel, 1980).

The units were kept remarkably clean and in good repair. There was no visible graffiti and no reported cases of intentional breakage of the porcelain toilets. Even the extraordinarily fragile light bulbs in bedrooms at the Chicago MCC were rarely broken, and then invariably by accident. In fact, the distinction between accident and vandalism was less clear than we had expected (as is discussed further in Chapter 11). Several times when we spoke to an administrator or a maintenance staff member, we were told that a damaged TV or broken bulb had been the result of vandalism. Most often, when we looked into the incident further and talked to the responsible unit officer and/or the inmates involved, we found that the damage had been accidental or the result of normal wear and tear.

A common phenomenon in the MCCs, and later in direct supervision jails, has been the conversion of hardened skeptics. The first warden of the Chicago MCC, William R. Nelson, had already served as warden at the federal prison in Danbury, Connecticut, when he came to this position. He was dubious that inmates would refrain from damaging the relatively fragile furnishings, or that staff would be safe without more protection. He quickly became a believer in this system of design and inmate management and for decades after was one of its chief advocates.

The BOP research staff was concerned that our final report might overemphasize minor problems at the MCCs because we lacked experience in other jails to see how far these jails had truly progressed beyond earlier environments. They suggested that we collect some comparative data in a more traditional jail to provide perspective – a benchmark against which we might compare the MCC. The Wayne County Jail was chosen for comparison because Detroit was expected to be the site for a future MCC. Initial planning for a new federal jail there had already begun.

The Wayne County Jail was an older, crowded, "linear intermittent" style jail, not atypical of many big-city jails. There were differences between Wayne County and the MCCs in a number of respects, including jurisdiction (county versus federal). Still, many federal inmates had been housed at Wayne County Jail and other similar local facilities where local federal detention was not available. Inmates interviewed in Wayne County showed broad differences from those at the NYMCC about privacy (10 percent at the NYMCC said privacy was not adequate, versus 84 percent in Wayne County), crowding (33 percent said they were bothered by crowding at the NYMCC, versus 83 percent at Wayne County), and noise (74 percent said the MCC was less noisy than other jails, 81 percent said Wayne County was more noisy). Almost three-quarters of the inmates at Wayne County said they felt that there was a significant chance of being attacked while there (71.4 percent) and 50 percent said fights there were frequent, whereas inmates at the NYMCC said fights were rare and virtually no one thought the chances of being attacked were high.

Problems at the MCCs

This is not to say that these new facilities were without problems. Problems that did exist, however, were not of the sort that were most devastating to inmates or staff (such as assault) or institutional functioning (such as damage). Fears for safety are so paramount that when they exist, other issues may become muted or hidden. When the risk of assault has been removed, attention and energy can be turned to other concerns. The most ubiquitous complaint among inmates in both MCCs, for example, was that they were constantly bored. The functional units were small and, by design, self-contained. Inmates rarely left the unit to visit other areas of the jail. Their range of environmental variety, and hence the richness of behavioral options, was extremely limited. Access to outdoors was further reduced because of the need for staff escort. Those activities on the living units were easy and common; those that required use of an off-unit, centralized space were difficult and rare. Inmates regularly complained of going long stretches without outdoor access, especially in the Chicago winter when the twenty-sixth floor roof-top gym could be windy and unbearably cold. The roof was, in fact, the only large exercise and recreation space in the building, so recreation was extremely limited during poor weather. In many jails, the commissary or library might provide an opportunity to leave the unit, but at the MCCs these functions were brought to the inmates in their living area.

In addition, many inmates were detained at the MCC for longer periods than the designers had been led to believe. Architects had assumed a maximum stay of 3 months. Instead, many inmates stayed as long as a year. The small on-unit exercise room, which seemed sufficient for several weeks, became clearly inadequate as the months stretched on. The behavioral mapping data reflected inmate boredom in the inordinate amount of time they spent sleeping (sleep accounted for 20 percent of all daytime behavior). As we discuss in Chapter 8, "The Psychology of Isolation in Prison Settings," boredom can be more than just an annoyance and has recently been viewed as an important stressor (Moser et al., 2004; Vodanovich, 2003).

A few isolated areas in the MCCs experienced environmental damage but these often seemed to be exceptions that proved the rule. Prime among these areas were the intake holding rooms where one found broken fixtures and names carved into wooden benches – the kinds of things expected in other settings but not otherwise found there. Interestingly enough, the intake areas were unique in being the only inmate contact spaces in the MCCs that did not hold to the design principles created for the living areas. In these areas, inmates were kept locked in barren, confined group holding rooms away from staff stations. Intake staff members were not in a position to freely, continually, and casually observe and be in contact with the inmates. These areas were, in effect, mini-linear intermittent jails. Moreover, inmates in jail intake areas are often experiencing the greatest level of stress. They may have been free and on the street just hours before, and now they sit facing unpleasant and uncertain prospects, locked in a small room with other people they do not know and may not trust. The need for staff contact may have been highest there, even though its availability was the lowest. A similar phenomenon was observed at the renovated Manhattan House of Detention.

Other concerns reflect differences in the Chicago and New York designs. A major concern for Chicago MCC staff was the time and frustration spent using elevators. There, with only one unit per floor, any movement between units required elevator travel, whereas in the New York MCC most trips between units required just a short walk. Officers in New York expressed much less concern about time spent waiting for elevators.

New York inmates were also less likely to say that they felt cooped up and cramped, reflecting the significantly larger size of that living unit. Chicago inmates complained more about their inability to look out the windows. The tall thin slits in Chicago bedrooms were uncomfortable viewing ports, compared to the wide rectangular windows of the New York building. The

FIGURE 25. Bench in intake cell, Manhattan House of Detention. R. Wener

degree to which Chicago inmates would go to gain a more panoramic view was demonstrated by the number of times we found chairs against the wall of the exercise room. Inmates, we learned, would stand on those chairs for long periods looking out of the wide – but high off the floor – windows in that space.

An advantage of the Chicago design was in its provision of four small TV areas, which seemed to be a good match for the natural divisions among inmates for viewing. They became natural territorial gathering points for groups as defined by interest, language, race, or ethnicity. At the New York jail where there were only two TVs per unit, one was usually reserved for Spanish-language programs, and the other was on English-language channels. This meant that the groups competed for access to the TVs, and a considerable number of arguments (usually verbal) ensued.

FIGURE 26. Exercise room, Chicago MCC. Courtesy of W. R. Nelson

The TVs were largely responsible for another common complaint – noise. Even with the use of carpeting and other soft materials, noise levels were often bothersome. The four TVs in Chicago were in open areas and near inmate rooms. Further, the inmate culture made it unlikely one person would ask another to reduce the TV's volume. Rather, others were more likely to increase their volume to compensate. When we used decibel meters, we found that ambient noise levels in the Chicago MCC were regularly above the recommended maximum level of 70 DBA.[6]

In both jails, officers complained about the lack of an officer station. Their interest was not in getting a closed and protected office, but rather in finding a place where they could fill out and store paperwork in privacy.[7] The original goal of the design was to eliminate the officer station entirely in order to encourage the officer to keep on the move throughout the unit for an entire shift. This proved to be unrealistic. In fact, most officers ended up "claiming" a dining table in the multipurpose area as their own, as a place to fill out forms, to find moments to rest, and to meet with inmates.

Crowding became an issue within a few years of the opening of these jails. The New York MCC was, at the time of our studies, much more crowded than Chicago. Its only dormitory had increased its capacity from 60 to 120 inmates,[8] and one other unit had more inmates than designed capacity (see Wener & Keys, 1988, for a study of the impact of this increased density, discussed in Chapter 7). Our survey showed that the New York dormitory unit was perceived as the most unpleasant living space, with the least privacy, the most crowding, and the highest levels of stress.

In summarizing staff and inmate response to the design of the MCCs, we identified several issues that seemed most critical in determining their success:

1. The constant and casual level of contact and communication between staff and inmates, and between staff and administration, fostered by the open design and the unit management system.
2. The quality of the physical space in setting positive behavioral expectations for inmates.
3. The privacy available to inmates through their ability to enter their room as needed.
4. The degree to which the design allowed inmates to exert some level of control over their exposure social and physical stressors.
5. The availability of needed resources.

Chapter 6 (privacy), Chapters 7 through 10 (stressors), and Chapter 11 (causes of violent behavior) discuss these issues in more detail.

EVALUATION OF CONTRA COSTA COUNTY MAIN DETENTION CENTER

In the first years after the MCCs were opened, many state and local officials reviewed but rejected the direct supervision model, often arguing that it worked in the MCCs only because the BOP housed a special class of inmates (federal) who were, some thought, less violent than those in state and local institutions. The opening of the new Contra Costa County Main Detention Facility (CCMDF) (Martinez, California) in 1981 represented an important next step in the development of the direct supervision model. It took the risk of being the first nonfederal agency to design, build, and operate a jail based on this new model, largely because of its visionary director, Larry Ard. Ard's team visited the MCCs and consciously copied many of their features. They also obtained a copy of the Chicago MCC evaluation report (Wener & Clark 1977) and used it in reviewing its design and as a training document for officers.

The CCMDF was probably the most visited and studied jail of its time. Shortly after it opened, William Frazier (1985), working with Jay Farbstein and me, conducted an evaluation of the facility as part of his Ph.D. thesis in criminal justice. A few years later, Zimring (1989) reevaluated the building.

FIGURE 27. Contra Costa County Main Detention Facility – Courtyard. Courtesy of W. R. Nelson

In 1992, Contra Costa County opened a second jail (the West Country Adult Detention Facility), which was evaluated by Jay Farbstein and myself (1993).

Frazier compared operations in the new jail to those in Contra Costa's previous linear intermittent facility. Among his most striking findings was a 90 percent reduction in the number of assaults when comparing the last 6 months in the old jail to the first 6 months in the new facility. He also found that some of the features Contra Costa had installed to improve on the Chicago design had been successful, such as decentralized access to outdoors and recreation by providing a small patio and recreation space as part of each unit. These features were well used, secure, and appreciated by both staff and inmates.

For the most part, staff and inmates were very satisfied with the new facility. Most of the concerns that were elicited were related to heating, ventilation, and air-conditioning (HVAC) problems, and to the crowding that rapidly occurred. The evaluation noted that the "traditional jail complaints from both staff and inmates revolving around lack of space, exercise areas, phones, and the like are conspicuous by their absence" (Wener, Frazier, & Farbstein, 1985, p. 87).

One important design innovation by the Contra Costa designers was the creation of an intake area that used the basic principles of direct supervision that had been applied to the rest of the institution. In this new facility, incoming inmates waited in a lounge space (called "open booking") that looked much like an oversized doctor's waiting room, rather than in a series of closed holding rooms. The space had television and magazines to address boredom, and were openly and constantly supervised by the staff members who worked in the area and were stationed at the processing desk. As a result, this space had none of the vandalism common to the intake areas in the MCCs. The success of this space surprised many. Even though a few intoxicated or assaultive inmates were placed in holding cells, the vast majority waited their turn for processing quietly and calmly in a space that had little tension. Open booking areas have been widely copied in newer direct supervision jails. The one area where inmates were kept in a hard and isolated space was the court holding room. Frazier reported that this room was the only one that was regularly "trashed" by inmates (Frazier, 1985).

One recommendation from the Wener and Olsen report not followed was the suggestion that control louvers be placed on cell ventilating grills so that inmates could adjust airflow. A colleague reported that before the new jail was officially opened, they held a VIP night, when local officials were invited to visit and spend a night in the facility. In the morning, our colleague observed that many of the VIP guests had stuffed the air vent with towels to keep the cold draft off them while they slept – a behavior called vandalism by facility managers when it occurred in the Chicago MCC.

Frazier also noted an increased sense of staff competence in the new building, which he related to the direct supervision operation. Staff members in this facility were more likely to see themselves as professionals, rather than as custodians.

Zimring's re-evaluation of the CCMDF (1989) found that the facility had fared well in the intervening years, in spite of heavy crowding. At the time of his POE, the facility was operating at 250 percent of original rated capacity. Even so, the staff and administration rated the facility as a building that was effective to operate and had a low level of stress. Staff and inmates perceived the level of openness and the amount of staff-inmate contact as highly positive. It was also seen as a very cost-effective design, especially by allowing a significant amount of self-escorted movement of inmates, eliminating the need for several additional staff positions. Even with significant levels of overcrowding, the rate of assaults and vandalism remained low.

CONCLUSIONS

The MCCs and the Contra Costa Main Detention Facility represented a sharp break with traditional design and practice. The plans for design and operation of these jails involved significant risks and leaps of faith, as described in Chapter 3, which were justified by the outcomes. These facilities changed long-held understandings of many corrections professionals regarding how institutions worked. It is not that operators and planners had been unsure about the nature of correctional operations. Most are very sure indeed. As an academic on the outside looking in, one thing that has been most interesting to me has been the degree to which premises – the foundations of correctional management that were taken as axiomatic for decades – have been stood on their head by experiences in new facilities. Can staff freely and safely interact with inmates? Can they do so without backup staff observing their every move? Can inmates be trusted with breakable materials? The quick and sure answer of earlier times ("of course not") has changed to "certainly" for many modern jail managers. The reversal of traditional concepts was so striking that it led to particular problems in transition for middle-level managers. Many of these professionals (often at the rank of captain or lieutenant) came up through the ranks and spent years working on the line in corrections. The switch to direct supervision meant a rejection of their understanding of what correctional work was all about, and an implied diminution of the value of their experience. Not all became converts to the direct supervision philosophy, and some retired.

These case studies provided lessons learned for future planners. These included observations on problems in these facilities, such as with ventilation systems, or with vandalism in the intake areas. They also showed that subtle differences in how design responds to the program had important effects, such as the impact of having two versus four television areas. These post occupancy evaluations offered a verification of proof of concept, documenting a level of success many had thought unlikely. They were case studies and did not provide the kind of multifacility cross-sectional or longitudinal data that most social scientists would require as evidence of success. Studies that provide data that better approximates those criteria are presented in Chapter 5.

References

Adler, J. R. (1998). Cross gender supervision and control in male prisons in England: A prisoners' perspectives. *Criminal Justice Policy Review, 9*(3–4).

Bowersox, M. S. (1981). Women in corrections: Competence, competition, and the social responsibility norm. *Criminal Justice & Behavior, 8*(4), 491–499.

Boyd, E., & Grant, T. (2005). Is gender a factor in perceived prison officer competence? Male prisoners' perceptions in an English dispersal prison. *Criminal Behaviour & Mental Health, 15*(1), 65.

Cross Gender Supervision (Writer) & A. C. Association (Director). (2000). In C. C. Inc. (Producer), *JOB Video Series*. Lanham, MD: American Correctional Association.

Farkas, M. A. (1999). Inmate supervisory style: does gender make a difference? *Women-and-Criminal-Justice, 10*(4), 1–24.

Final Outline of the Architectural Requirements for Manhattan MCC of the Foley Square Court House Annex. (1971). Washington, DC: U.S. Bureau of Prisons, Department of Justice.

Frazier, W. (1985). *A Postoccupancy Evaluation of Contra Cost County's Main Detention Facility.* Golden Gate University, San Francisco.

Ittelson, W. H., Rivlin, L. G., & Proshansky, H. M. (1967). The use of behavioral maps in environmental psychology. In H. Proshanksy, W. Ittleson, & L. Rivline (Eds.), *Environmental Psychology: Man and His Physical Setting* (pp. 658–668). New York: Holt, Rinehart and Winston.

Jenne, D. L., & Kersting, R. C. (1996). Aggression and women correctional officers in male prisons. *Prison Journal, 76*(4), 442–460.

Kissel, P. J. (1980). *A Study of Role Balancing: Female Corrections Officers on the Job.* Washington, DC: Federal Bureau of Prisons.

Moser, D. J., Arndt, S., Kanz, J. E., Benjamin, M. L., Bayless, J. D., Reese, R. L., et al. (2004). Coercion and Informed Consent in Research Involving Prisoners. *Comprehensive Psychiatry, 45*(1), 1–9.

Performance-Based Standards for Adult Local Detention Facilities (4th ed.). (2004). Lanham, MD: American Correctional Association.

Sommer, R. (1974). *Tight Spaces: Hard Architecture and How to Humanize It.* Englewood Cliffs, NJ: Prentice-Hall, Inc.

Vodanovich, S. J. (2003). Psychometric measures of boredom: A review of the literature. *Journal of Psychology: Interdisciplinary & Applied, 137*(6), 569–595.

Wener, R. E. (1977). *User Based Assessment of the New York Metropolitan Correctional Center: An Initial Overview and Summary.* Washington, DC: U.S. Bureau of Prisons.

Wener, R. E., & Clark, N. (1977). *User Based Evaluation of the Chicago Metropolitan Correctional Center – Final Report.* Washington, DC: U.S. Bureau of Prisons.

Wener, R. E., Frazier, W., & Farbstein, J. (1985). Three generations of evaluation and design of correctional facilities. *Environment & Behavior, 17*(1), 71–95.

Wener, R. E., & Keys, C. (1988). The effects of changes in jail population densities on crowding, sick call, and spatial behavior. *Journal of Applied Social Psychology, 18*, 852–866.

Wener, R. E., & Olsen, R. (1978). *User Based Assessment of the Federal Metropolitan Correctional Centers – Final Report.* Washington, DC: U.S. Bureau of Prisons.

Wener, R. E., & Olsen, R. (1980). Innovative correctional environments: A user assessment. *Environment & Behavior, 12*(4), 478–493.

Zeisel, J. (2006). *Inquiry by Design: Environment/behavior/neuroscience in Architecture, Interiors, Landscape, and Planning.* New York: W. W. Norton & Company.

Zimring, C. (1989). Post occupancy evaluation: Contra Costa County Main Detention Facility. *Atlanta: Environment/Behavior Inquiry.*

5

Effectiveness of Direct Supervision Models

This chapter reviews extant research assessing the impact and effectiveness of direct supervision design and management – what we know, and how confident we are in making conclusions.

By the mid-1980s, there was a growing acceptance by many in the community of correctional professionals that the direct supervision model was neither foolish nor reckless but was, in fact, a viable, safe, and effective way to manage inmates. Decisions about what kind of jail to build and operate were not being made by a community of scientists waiting for the results of key experiments. Rather, the spread of this model followed classic patterns of diffusion of innovations, as practitioners and agency heads made use of their own observations and the testimonials of respected colleagues (Rogers, 1995).

Jails and prisons are large, expensive undertakings to build and operate. In a federal system such as the United States, jails are typically built at the local level – by counties. There are over 3,000 counties in the United States, and most build only one jail, often the single biggest capital expense the county makes. It is, therefore, an investment undertaken with considerable caution. In the 1980s, many counties needed to replace their aging jails, and in more than a few cases, were under court order forcing them to do so. Administrators and designers learned about direct supervision from articles in trade publications, word of mouth from colleagues, presentations at professional meetings, and site visits to new facilities. This process was made significantly more thorough and efficient when the National Institute of Corrections (a division of the federal Department of Justice) began its PONI (Planning and Opening a New Institution) program. Professional tour groups streamed through the MCCs and Contra Costa MDF and often were convinced by what they saw. One jail administrator commented after visiting CCMDF that his attitude had changed from one of skepticism and disbelief to acceptance. "The lack of tension could be felt.... Some (in our visiting team) thought the prisoners were tranquilized ... they were instead reacting to the environment" (Wener, Frazier, & Farbstein, 1985, p. 92).

The direct supervision model was adopted and promoted by correctional organizations including the American Jail Association (AJA) and the American Correctional Association (ACA) as well as the National Institute of Corrections (NIC), which sponsored regular national symposia for the exchange of design and management information. Many localities chose to build direct supervision jails. In 1995, the NIC directory listed 199 direct supervision jails. In 2001, that number had grown to 293, and in the latest edition of 2006, 349 direct supervision jails are listed (Direct Supervision Sourcebook, 2006).

The questions of interest to researchers and policy makers went beyond outcomes ("Does the direct supervision model work?") to issues of process and operations ("How does it affect operations?" "What are its limits?" "What are its key tenets?"). For instance, several writers have suggested that this model works because it addresses the social and psychological needs of inmates and staff by assuring personal safety, providing privacy for inmates, making it clear the officer is in charge of the living area, and setting positive behavioral expectations (Bottoms, 1999; Gettinger, 1984; Wener, 2000; Wortley, 2003). Not unreasonably, though, some researchers and practitioners in the 1980s pointed out that the research evidence to support decisions that led to billions of dollars of construction was far from air tight, consisting as it did of testimonials, personal visits, and a few case studies. Wells (1987), in particular, noted the lack of rigorous research and wondered how fragile the direct supervision model might be when exposed to conditions of serious crowding and "double-celling" (putting a second inmate in cells originally designed for single occupancy).

In 1987, this criticism was both valid and necessary, and it was heeded by researchers and funding agencies. Now, over 25 years later, more than three dozen research reports have, in some fashion or other, attempted to assess the success of direct supervision correctional institutions. The quality, depth, and scope of these studies vary greatly. I don't include in this count a number of anecdotal reports (usually made by facility administrators and printed in publications of professional organizations) giving personal perspectives on the experience of managing or working in a direct supervision jail. Most discuss differences between direct supervision and traditional jails, or describe changes in atmosphere and behavior before and after a change to a direct supervision facility, and some refer to or directly cite data from institutional archives or reports concerning assaults, vandalism, and so on.

More importantly, for this discussion, a number of formal studies address issues of efficacy. These include detailed post occupancy evaluations and other case studies[1] as well as cross-sectional or longitudinal studies[2] that make comparisons among multiple correctional settings or within one setting across a period of time (such as pre-post change studies).

These studies focus on critical issues including:

- Quality of the living environment, including safety and security (inmate–inmate assaults, sexual assaults, inmate–staff assaults, suicide, vandalism, escape), tension, stress, and recidivism.
- Management and staff issues, including stress, job satisfaction, job enrichment, staff turnover, and management style.
- Cost, including construction and furnishing cost, staffing, and operating cost.
- Design features, including the success of various design features associated with direct supervision.
- Specific topics such as crowding and smoking.

These studies have several things in common, beyond the fact that each involves a search for understanding of the impact and dynamics of direct supervision design and management. Almost all recognize methodological limitations in their research designs and therefore make limited claims for their findings. Often, for instance, the direct supervision facility is the replacement jail constructed by a county, and therefore it is significantly newer and has more resources than the traditional one to which it is being compared. It is often difficult or impossible from the description provided to assure that inmate populations among the facilities in a study are truly comparable. Similarly, it is clear that there are variations in design, management style, and training among facilities that call themselves "direct supervision." As this model has gained acceptance, places with an increasingly wide range of designs and operating styles are defining themselves as "direct supervision" facilities (Farbstein & Wener, 1989; Tartaro, 2002).

The studies reviewed here cover hundreds of jails and prisons, including direct supervision and traditional facilities.[3] In spite of their methodological limitations, what is most impressive is the degree of agreement in the results of these studies. Taken as a whole, the studies are strikingly consistent in supporting the claim that the new generation direct supervision model is successful and is a more effective jail design and management system. This is particularly true in the degree to which these facilities are perceived as safer and less stressful, with fewer incidents of violence, and are less expensive to build and operate.

All of the anecdotal or personal reports were highly supportive of direct supervision, although many, as personal testimonials, could naturally be expected to be so. Of the eighteen case studies, the fifteen studies that made direct comparisons between direct supervision and more traditional facilities, and five longitudinal studies that compared systems before and after a new facility was built, almost all reported positive effects for the use of direct supervision. Only a few studies showed small or negligible differences between correctional facility types, and none showed direct supervision to be inferior to other models of design and management.

Those studies with nonconfirmatory findings were typically limited to special circumstances or issues, such as the effects of nonsmoking policies on aggression (Leone & Kinkade, 1994) or the impacts of moving to a new direct supervision institution on female inmates (Jackson & Stearns, 1995). The most significant and consistent exceptions to positive findings come from the several studies that found small or no improvements for staff (in satisfaction, motivation, and so forth) in direct supervision facilities (Houston, Gibbons, & Jones, 1988; Stohr, Lovrich, Menke, & Zupan, 1995; Zupan & Menke, 1991). One comparative study found direct supervision facilities to be more expensive to run than traditional institutions (Bigelow, 1993).

Aside from the one comparison of operating cost (Bigelow, 1993), **there is not one report** we have found (among the anecdotal reports, archival data, detailed case study descriptions, direct, cross-sectional comparisons between or among facilities or longitudinal comparisons across time) that has argued that direct supervision is in any way inferior to traditional means of designing and supervising jails and prisons. There is no study with data condemning direct supervision operations or showing them to be less effective than traditional facilities in any significant way. The overwhelming sense of the research is that direct supervision is, in fact, a better way of designing and operating a jail or prison. This is especially important when one considers the degree of skepticism among professionals that greeted the introduction of this system. Most thought it might lead to damage, injury, and loss of control of the detention environment; however, the opposite has proven to be the case.

Several authors of more recent studies commented that the evidence supporting the superiority of direct supervision, though present, was not as strong as might have been expected given the very wide differences and broad claims for superiority described and in some cases documented by early reports (Senese, Wilson, Evans, Aguirre, & Kalinich, 1997). These more modest differences may have occurred for several reasons. First, it may be that in some way the early use of this new style, like first applications of a new drug, may have been the most potent, particularly when it was being implemented by founders of the approach who were "true believers." It is also possible that the comparison group has improved. Traditional institutions in many jurisdictions were run by the same systems and administrators as the direct supervision facilities. It is not unreasonable to think that management in these traditional facilities was affected and improved by training and experience in the management principles of direct supervision facilities. Traditional institutions may, in fact, be better run than they were 25 years ago.

Evidence also shows that direct supervision facilities may experience more overcrowding than traditional ones. Several studies found that some direct supervision institutions were operated further beyond rated capacity than traditional jails (Farbstein & Wener, 1989; Stohr, Lovrich, Menke, & Zupan, 1994; Zupan & Stohr-Gillmore, 1988). It has been suggested that courts are more ready to incarcerate when the facilities in question are considered to be safe and humane. Direct supervision facilities may attract additional inmates, and hence overcrowding, because judges are less reluctant to use that sanction (Lund, Morrise, & Jordan, 1998; Morris, 1976).

RESEARCH EVIDENCE

Operational Issues

Safety and Security
As direct supervision facilities came online, particularly during the 1980s and 1990s, many managers used their professional organization publications (such as *American Jails* and *Corrections Today*) to share their experiences with their colleagues. The anecdotal reports that appear in the literature are typically descriptions of new facilities provided by their designers or administrators. As such, they might be viewed as the equivalent of bragging by a proud new parent. Still, even though one must accept that these reports lack scientific distance and objectivity, they are interesting in their reports of striking differences between the new and old facilities. A number of managers and designers commented on improved staff and inmate safety and reduced number of incidents through the use of direct supervision (Conroy, 1989; Heuer, 1993; Kibre, 1991; Mueller, 1998; Nelson, 1976, 1983b; Pellicane, 1990; Wallenstein, 1987). For example, Conroy (1989) reported that in the year after opening the direct supervision jail in Santa Clara County, California, corrections officers almost universally felt "an absence of fear and reduced stress as compared to the traditional jail environment" (p. 64). There had been, he noted, few weapons and no serious staff or inmate assaults. Nelson (1976, 1983a), as the first warden of the Chicago MCC, noted that vandalism in this

new direct supervision jail was "virtually non-existent" and that staff and inmates were safe from physical assault. "There have been few if any murders, sexual assaults, or aggressive assaults. Suicides, contraband weapons, disturbances, escapes, vandalism, and graffiti are rare" (p. 110). He also indicated that the calm atmosphere supported the innovation of using female officers on all living units, including those with male inmates.

Wallenstein (1987) reported that after 18 months of operation in the direct supervision jail in Bucks County, Pennsylvania, graffiti and vandalism was nonexistent, and inmate–inmate assaults were rare and invariably minor, and were less than half as frequent as in the previous facility. Use of disciplinary segregation was reported to be down by 30 percent. He said that staff felt much safer – there had been only two serious assaults in 18 months.

As noted in Chapter 4, staff and inmates felt the threat of assault was low at the Chicago and New York Metropolitan Correctional Centers (MCCs). The New York MCC was compared to the older and traditionally designed Wayne County Jail, which also held federal inmates. The MCC was perceived as much safer than the Wayne County Jail, where inmates felt that fighting was a problem and risk of attack was very high and unpredictable (Wener & Olsen, 1980).

Similar findings came from assessments of the Manhattan House of Detention (MHD). Inmates reported remarkably low levels of tension and minimal risk of violence or sexual assault (Sigurdson, 1985; Wener, 1985). Staff indicated that the risk of assault was much lower than in other New York City Department of Correction facilities and that racial tensions were also reduced.

These findings were supported by National Institute of Corrections (NIC) audits of other direct supervision jails (Farbstein, Liebert, & Sigurdson, 1996; Sigurdson, 1987a, 1987b). The audits involved surveys of staff and inmates and review of archival data. They reported what the authors considered to be extraordinarily low levels of institutional assaults and other disturbances. In the reporting period (1 year for the Manhattan House of Detention; over 2 years for Pima County, Arizona; over 3 years for Larimer County, Colorado), none of these direct supervision sites had experienced a homicide, suicide, sexual assault, inmate disturbance, or court-ordered judgment. The Manhattan House of Detention and Pima County Jail had no aggravated assaults, and the Larimer County Jail had only four. The Manhattan House of Detention had found four contraband weapons (plastic razors), Pima County had found one contraband weapon, and Larimer County had found five. There were similarly low numbers of incidents at audited direct supervision jails in Norfolk, Massachusetts; Dakota County, Minnesota; and Hillsborough County, Florida (Farbstein, Liebert, & Sigurdson, 1996). The authors described these rates as strikingly low and enviable for any detention facility. In other evaluations that we conducted of direct supervision jails, inmates and staff also agreed that the risk of violence or sexual assault was remarkably low (Wener & Farbstein, 1994a, 1994b; Wener, Knapel, & Vigorita, 1996).

Farbstein and Wener (1989) along with Zimring (1989) conducted a mail survey of administrators at fifty-two institutions (thirty-eight prisons and fourteen jails) followed by on-site case studies of seven of these settings (four prisons and three jails). The direct supervision (DS) and non-direct supervision (NDS) facilities in the large sample did not differ on age of facility or average capacity. DS institutions, however, reported an average of 12.99 violent incidents over a 12-month period compared to 32.04 for the NDS institutions ($t = -1.70$, $p < .10$) and had improved levels of perceived safety. DS facilities offered better surveillance and had lower response times to emergency calls. Inmates in DS settings felt that staff did a better job of protecting them.

Knapel, Wener, and Vigorita (1986) surveyed 160 administrators of new DS and NDS facilities, all of which had received commendations for their design. Not surprisingly, most (80 percent) rated their design as successful and saw their institutions as safe or very safe (91 percent). The DS facilities in the sample, though, were rated significantly better for perceived safety.

Other studies that directly compared DS and NDS facilities also found DS environments safer. Nelson, O'Toole, Krauth & Whitemore (1983) reported that the six NDS jails studied averaged fifteen times more assaults (154.3 and 141.5) for a 2-year period than did the five DS jails of similar capacity (10.4 and 8.7), and more than four times the number of escapes (39 to 9).

A comparison of two jails in the same complex – one DS and the other NDS – found that more inmates in a DS jail felt safe than did so in the NDS (81 percent to 47 percent) (Williams, Rodeheaver, & Huggins, 1999). Staff felt safe in both places and saw no differences in the level of fights, but the DS jail had lower levels of inmate–inmate assaults (12 versus 33), inmate–correctional officer assaults (0 versus 3), and incident reports (61 versus 97).

Senese, Wilson, Evans, Aguire, and Kalinich (1997) compared a DS jail and an NDS facility in the same county, along with two NDS jails in other states, using archival sources. The DS jail performed much better on safety and rules violations and had significantly lower levels of inmate–inmate violence and inmate–staff violence, far fewer written warnings issued to inmates, and not as many instances where inmate privileges were revoked. The total number of incident reports over two 6-month periods was 50 percent lower in the DS jail compared to the NDS jail (211 versus 333), but there were no differences in verbal threats.

Frazier (1985) reported that from 6 months before to 6 months after the move to a new jail in Contra Costa County, California, the level of assaults dropped by 90 percent. A later study of the same institution (Zimring, 1989) confirmed that, although the jail experienced significant crowding in the 14-year period between studies, a high level of perceived safety continued among inmates and staff. Similarly, after the transition from an old to new DS facility in Sonoma County, California, overall assaults were down by 50 percent (Jackson, 1992). Assaults on staff were down by 25 percent, there were 90 percent fewer inmate–inmate assaults, criminal disciplinary infractions were reduced by half, there was 68 percent less inmate fighting, and the use of disciplinary isolation was reduced 33 percent. Both male and female inmates felt safer in the new jail.

Bayens, Williams, and Smykla (1997) reviewed archival records from a period 5 years before to 5 years after a move to a DS jail. Even though population demographics were very much the same in both periods, fifty-one of seventy measures of behavior and institutional functioning improved in the 5 years after the move. Overall, serious safety infractions (such as fighting, inmate or staff assault) were down 58 percent. Minor infractions, however, such as insubordination, were up 129 percent in the post-move period. Tartaro (2002, 2003), on the other hand, analyzed a dataset from 646 jails and found no significant relationship between design and supervision style and the number of infractions. She noted, however, that there had been no external checks to assure the quality of direct supervision operations in many of the jails labeled as DS.

Liebert, Knabel, and Davis (1993) studied a new DS jail that had experienced a number of high-profile incidents, including escapes, serious assaults, and an inmate death. The authors concluded that problems in the institution were related to poor design decisions and inadequate implementation of the DS model, including officer training.

Tension and Stress
A number of studies have reported lessened levels of tension and stress among inmates and staff in DS institutions (Knapel, Wener, & Vigorita, 1986; Wener, 1985; Wener & Clark, 1977; Wener & Farbstein, 1994b; Wener, Farbstein, & Knapel, 1993; Wener & Olsen, 1980; Zimring, 1989; Zupan & Stohr-Gillmore, 1988). None reported increased tension in DS institutions.

Vandalism and Maintenance
Administrators have commented on the lack of graffiti and other forms of vandalism in DS institutions (Nelson, 1983a; Wallenstein, 1987), a finding

supported by case studies (Nelson, 1986; Wener & Olsen, 1980) and comparisons among DS and NDS institutions (Farbstein & Wener, 1989; Senese & Kashem, 1997; Williams, Rodeheaver, & Huggins, 1999). The old Contra Costa County jail had seen high levels of vandalism – 150 incidents of damaged mattresses per year, an average of two TVs needing repair per week, an average of ninety-nine sets of inmate clothes destroyed per week. When measured again after the new DS jail was opened, the levels of vandalism were much lower – in the 2-year period, no mattresses had been destroyed, only two TV sets had needed repair, and fifteen sets of inmate clothes had been destroyed (Wener, Frazier, & Farbstein, 1987, p. 42). In addition, several studies suggested that DS facilities are perceived to be cleaner and better maintained than NDS institutions (Farbstein & Wener, 1989; Knapel et al., 1986; Wener & Olsen, 1980; Williams et al., 1999).

Contraband and Minor Violations
Several studies found particularly low levels of contraband in DS facilities (Senese et al., 1997; Sigurdson, 1985, 1987a, 1987b). Jackson (1992) reported contraband up slightly in DS institutions, even though he suggested this might be because correctional officers had more time to search in the new facility.

Wener and Olsen (1980) reported that inmates in DS jails felt that property theft was not a problem, but two studies found that theft and other minor violations increased as major violations decreased in DS facilities (Bayens et al., 1997; Senese et al., 1997). The authors of these studies suggested that this might be the result of closer reporting and more aggressive enforcement of rules by officers in these DS settings.

Suicide

Administrators have suggested that DS institutions experience fewer suicides than NDS facilities (Nelson, 1983a; Saunders, 1995). Sigurdson (1985, 1987a, 1987b) reported no suicides in National Institute of Corrections audited DS jails and Senese et al. (1997) and Bayens et al. (1997) reported fewer suicides in DS than NDS institutions. Tartaro (2003), however, found no effect of design and management style on suicides.

Rehabilitation and Recidivism
Many writers have observed that the philosophy of direct supervision and the level of control and improved atmosphere it affords makes it possible for them to offer more in the way of rehabilitative and supportive programs than would be otherwise available (Arbiter, 1988; Ard, 1991; Bordenaro, 1992;

Saxton, 1990; Wallenstein, 1987). The new jails we studied in Contra Costa County (West County), Orlando (Genesis), and Massachusetts (Dedham) had been designed to take advantage of the level of safety and control afforded in direct supervision facilities by offering a range of therapeutic and educational programs – very unusual in the short-term detention environment of jails (Wener & Farbstein, 1994a, 1994b; Wener, Knapel, & Vigorita, 1996). The goal was to see if they could have an impact on inmate lives (and conceivably on recidivism) even in the short interim of jail stays. Many inmates in these programs reported that they had, indeed, felt that the experience had improved their lives and chances for staying out of jail.

Only one study has looked closely at the impact on rates of recidivism of being incarcerated in a DS jail that made heavy use of such programs (Applegate, Surette, & McCarthy, 1999). All inmates in this direct supervision housing had daily involvement in one of several educational, counseling, or training programs. Archival records were reviewed from the entire 3,100-bed, Orange County, Florida, system, which included DS and NDS facilities (Applegate, Surrette, & McCarthy, 1999). Rearrest rates of 600 inmates were analyzed for 18 months post release and classified by time of incarceration (less than 5 days, 6 to 45 days, or 45 days or more). Fifty-three percent of all released inmates had been rearrested at least once within the 18-month period (mean number of rearrests = 1.54; mean time to rearrest = 193 days). The rearrest rate was significantly related to gender, age, and prior record. Further, when the inmate had spent 23 days or longer in the DS facility, the rearrest rate was significantly correlated with time served. "Longer terms of confinement reduced recidivism only when the offenders were housed in new generation facilities for a substantial portion of their sentence" (p. 545). By way of caution, it should be noted that inmates were not randomly assigned to the DS jail, but rather transferred there based on a willingness to engage in the program, suggesting possible selection and self-selection bias in the sample.

In sum, the predominance of research evidence indicates that DS design and management fosters more perceived safety among officers and inmates, reduced levels of serious and violent incidents, fewer inmate assaults on staff, and a diminished number of inmate–inmate assaults. There is also some evidence for lower levels of vandalism, better staff–inmate interactions, reduced levels of stress, decreased escapes or risk of escape, a drop in the rate of fires, cleaner and better maintained settings, and improved recidivism. At the same time, there is some evidence of increases in minor offenses in DS institutions, which may have to do with higher levels of activity and engagement by staff.

Institutional Costs

Advocates have argued that the DS model results in lower construction costs, presumably because high-strength, high-impact, vandal-resistant materials are less necessary. Administrators have, indeed, reported reduced construction costs with the use of wood or metal swinging cell doors instead of sliding solid metal doors, and instead of steel toilet fixtures (DeWitt, 1987; McKenzie, 1997; "Modern prisons can reduce costs and stress," 1992; Mueller, 1998). Farbstein and Wener (1989) and Nelson (1988a) also reported that DS institutions reduced construction costs by using less expensive materials. National Institute of Corrections audits of DS jails noted that the commercial-grade furniture seemed to be holding up well, leading to very low repair costs (Sigurdson, 1985, 1987a, 1987b).

Because of their previous successes with direct supervision, officials in Contra Costa County, California, experimented with lower-cost "dry cells" (cells without toilets) and drywall construction in their new West County jail (Ard, 1991). There have been concerns about wear and tear of the dry wall in West County, although vandalism in these cells has not been reported as a problem (personal communication, V. Persons, National Institute of Corrections Jail Center, November 5, 2003).

Additionally, it is contended that one officer can oversee many more inmates in a direct supervision facility than with traditional models, consequently resulting in lower operations costs (DeWitt, 1987; Pellicane, 1990). A comparison of actual operational costs for the new DS Dade County Stockade to those that had been previously projected for a traditional jail found significant savings (Atlas, 1984). The DS staffing for 1,000 inmates was 172 positions leading to an annual operating cost of $6.2 million per year, compared to the projected staffing for a traditional jail of about the same size of 295 positions at $9.3 million per year. Atlas argued that further cost savings might result from reduced sick call rates, reduced time lost to injury, and less turnover of officers. Another DS jail provided a movable wall between two 64-cell living units that could be opened each night allowing the two units to be supervised by a single officer, reducing staffing costs (Ard, 1991; Wener & Farbstein, 1994a). McNamara (1992) also claimed that DS allowed officers to supervise more inmates, and indicated that one officer could reasonably supervise as many as eighty inmates in a properly designed DS setting.

Sigurdson (1985) reported that officers in the Manhattan House of Detention claimed 1,810 fewer sick days than officers at equivalent New York City system facilities, resulting in a savings of $250,000 in overtime pay. Nelson

(1986) also found that DS jails required fewer staff and had less sick leave and staff turnover.

Farbstein and Wener (1989) found that DS facilities reported that fewer staff were needed to operate living units and were more likely to rate soft (presumably less expensive) materials as appropriate for use in their institution. They also found that DS jail managers were less concerned about inmates initiating lawsuits claiming poor treatment or "cruel and unusual punishment"[4] because of confinement conditions.

However, Williams et al. (1999) saw no savings in staffing levels or costs in a DS facility that was compared to other institutions. Also, Bigelow (1993) reported that staffing costs in three DS facilities were much higher (60 percent) than for three NDS institutions, mostly because of higher staff-to-inmate ratios. The author noted (personal communication, T. Bigelow, January 15, 2003) that the staffing disparities could be the result of differing facility goals that might, for instance, lead to greater use of program staff at the DS jails.

In short, there is evidence that DS can result in reduced operational costs with respect to staffing, as well as lessened maintenance costs, even though a few studies did not support that finding. There is also some support for the contention that DS can also result in lower construction costs, although assuring comparability of situations and measures for assessing construction costs is particularly difficult.

Staff and Management Impacts

An important aspect of the direct supervision model is the delegation of authority to correctional officers, who are expected to enforce rules closely and make decisions about infractions as events occur, with less need to "bump" every infraction to a higher-ranking officer or infractions committee (Zupan, 1991). The intended result is increased job satisfaction and professionalism and an enriched working environment.

Administrators and planners have commented, for instance, that staff members like to work in these settings (Kibre, 1991) and that direct supervision improved the possibilities for cross-gender staffing (Cross gender supervision, 2000; Wallenstein, 1990). The MCCs, for example, were pioneers in using female officers on male units where females were shown to be as effective as male officers in maintaining order, and at no more risk of assault ("Cross Gender Supervision," 2000; Wener & Clark, 1977).

Job Satisfaction/Enrichment

Results of research on job satisfaction are inconsistent. Zupan and Menke (1988) conducted a longitudinal study of work perceptions among officers

6 months before and after the transition from an NDS to a DS jail. Some improvements were reported in job satisfaction, but changes were fewer and more modest than had been predicted. The authors hypothesized that staff were negatively affected by reduced inmate distance and their limited ability to withdraw from contact with inmates. Conroy, Smith, and Zupan (1991) also found that compared to officers in traditional jails, officers in DS jails were more satisfied with their jobs.

On the other hand, a study comparing four DS with three NDS facilities (Zupan & Menke, 1991) found no differences in job enrichment and motivating potential. DS officers were more satisfied with some aspects of their job (environment, pay, promotion possibilities) but less so with others (the character of work, the quality of supervision). The authors suggest that this latter result may be because the officers in traditional jails are less independent and get more supervision. Jackson (1992) also found a split response. Correctional officers were more satisfied with their jobs in DS jails and were more positive about people and pay, but less happy with job feedback, possibly due to more isolation from other officers. Correctional officers felt they had more space and freedom in the DS facilities, and had less-crowded conditions, but they also felt they had experienced less teamwork in the new jail.

Taking a different tact, Stohr, Lovrish, Menke, and Zupan (1994) compared several DS facilities according to their fit with DiIulio's control and investment models of inmate management (1987). DiIulio had proposed that prisons and jails would operate best if they use highly centralized management, rigid rule enforcement, and tight oversight and control to maintain order. Stohr, Lovich, Menke, and Zupan (1994) suggest that well-functioning DS jails use, instead, the "employee investment model" that tempers strict control with the use of interpersonal skills to guide and counsel as well as supervise inmates. Contrary to DiIulio's predictions, their data indicated increased job satisfaction, motivation, and organizational commitment in the two DS jails that better approximated an employee investment model than in those that more closely approximated control models of management.

Professionalism

Wallenstein (1987) claimed that although the roles of correctional officers had largely been in opposition to inmates and based on coercion and self-survival, in DS jails, they were seen and saw themselves as professionals who were competent to maintain control of the setting. Officers in the first DS jails, including some who had been skeptical about working in such close proximity to inmates, commented that in these new jails they felt less like guards and more like professionals (Wener, Frazier, & Farbstein, 1987). Social climate was found to be better in a DS jail than in a comparable NDS institution

(Houston, Gibbons, & Jones, 1988). Similarly, improvements were noted in the organizational climate among staff after a move from a traditional to a DS jail (Zupan & Menke, 1988).

Officers have been reported to feel an increased sense of control in DS environments (Williams et al., 1999). In contrast to the staff in traditional jails, DS officers are more career oriented (Menke, Zupan, & Lovrich, 1986; Zupan & Menke, 1987). Officers saw interpersonal skills as the key to successfully managing their job and felt that problems were inherent in the nature of the correction officer's work. The authors indicated that a "lack of coherent philosophy linking officer practices with detention facility goals" (Zupan & Menke, 1987, p. 15) could lead to operational problems, and concluded that there was a need to redefine tasks and responsibilities to significantly enrich the officer's job.

Staff Stress

Several case studies reported that the staff experienced generally low levels of tension in DS jails (Wener, 1985; Wener & Olsen, 1980). Other research has reported that staff in DS institutions had lower levels of stress than those in NDS facilities (Conroy et al., 1991; Farbstein & Wener, 1989; Knapel et al., 1986). Conroy, Smith, and Zupan (1991) pointed out that the most important issue for officers was not the amount of job-related stress, but job effectiveness and the quality of work. Compared to NDS officers, DS officers had fewer instances of on-the-job hassles and stress-inducing events.

Not all were so positive, though. One study found very high levels of stress in several DS jails (Stohr, Lovrich, & Wilson Gregory, 1994). The authors suggested that some DS jails manage stress better than others and that good management can increase job satisfaction and reduce stress. Another study found that turnover, an indicator of stress, was high (13.8 percent) in several DS jails (Stohr, Self, & Lovrich, 1992). Some staff left because they were simply uncomfortable with the level of inmate interaction required in a DS setting.

Several case studies focused on situations or settings that were less than ideal. Knapel, Wener, and Vigorta (1995) conducted a POE of a 20-year-old jail that was built for indirect supervision but was being run as direct supervision in some living areas (a new direct supervision jail was to open in less than a year). Trying to implement direct supervision in this facility was seen as a struggle because of poor surveillance offered by the physical layout and because of severe overcrowding. Even though rates of actual assaults were low, inmates indicated concern about the potential for assault. Noise levels and high levels of damage to the facility were problems. The DS units were generally rated better and safer than were the NDS units.

Another evaluation (Leone & Kinkade, 1994) addressed an issue of growing concern in correctional settings – the impact of new no-smoking policies. Traditionally, smoking has been common in institutions because it was seen as an outlet for the stress and boredom of incarceration. Concern for liability over inmate and staff health has led many institutions to ban smoking in many or all areas. Leone and Kinkade (1994) studied the impact of a non-smoking policy on aggression (predicted to increase) and staff health (predicted to improve) in a DS jail. They found that the new policy resulted in increased inmate–inmate and inmate–staff assaults, although there was not a concomitant increase in use of disciplinary segregation, because they presumed that staff attributed the events to cigarette deprivation. Staff health, as measured by sick days, did not improve as predicted.

Liebert, Knabel, and Davis (1993) conducted an assessment of a new DS jail that was experiencing serious problems with a number of high-profile incidents, including escapes, serious assaults, and an inmate's death. They concluded that the problems in the institution were related to poor implementation of the DS model, including a design that "stuck" correctional officers at the work station, and insufficient emphasis on providing a vision, mission, and training for supervisors and officers.

In sum, there is mixed evidence that officers in DS jails are more satisfied with their jobs and the quality of their working environment. It appears that DS officers have reduced sick time, a greater sense of professionalism, are more career-oriented, feel less hostility and more in control of their environment, and experience improved organizational and social climate. Even though several studies indicated reduced levels of stress for officers in DS institutions, others found no stress differences and no significant differences in job enrichment or motivating potential.

CONCLUSION

Methodological Issues

There are methodological problems inherent in the kinds of field research efforts required to study jails and prisons in situ, and these can limit claims for the generality of findings that might emanate from any individual study (see Cook & Campbell, 1979). Many reports must be considered anecdotal in nature, often written by those with significant investment in the DS model. Others are individual case studies that do not directly compare DS and NDS settings. Those that do make direct comparisons across settings or time are at best quasi-experiments, although some of these have strong designs.

Often the DS institution being studied is a replacement facility and therefore significantly newer, and possibly has more resources than the traditional facility to which it is being compared. In addition, comparability across institutions of types of inmates, training and level of staffing, or number and quality of programs and other resources is often unknown. Moreover, it can be difficult to know how well institutions claiming to use the DS model have actually adhered to the tenets and principles of that system based on survey data alone. There is evidence of great variability of practice among institutions purporting to use direct supervision (Farbstein & Wener, 1989; Tartaro, 2002). Whatever the supervision system, much variance in facility operation depends on the quality of institutional management, something that is not easy to measure and experimentally or statistically control. Studies that look at multiple institutions under a single management team, such as Williams et al. (1999), have a significant advantage in this respect.

Effectiveness of Direct Supervision

The research reviewed here (in spite of any methodological limitations) and decades of professional practice show that the DS model is neither a dangerous nor risky proposition, as some once feared. It is an effective means of inmate management that has been accepted as best practice by agencies at the federal, state, and local levels and by accrediting organizations. DS facilities are consistently perceived by staff and inmates to have safer living environments and, in fact, experience fewer violent or security-related incidents. The emerging pattern indicates that serious and major infractions are much less common in DS facilities, whereas minor infractions and property theft may occur at the same or higher levels (Bayens et al., 1997; Senese et al., 1997). It is too soon to know if this latter result is a real difference in behavior or an artifact of closer observation, reporting, and recording of events. Officers in DS settings are expected to closely attend to small infractions and are freed to do so by the relative infrequency of larger and more dramatic events.

Staff working in these living units appear to be clearly in control of the institutional environment, allowing DS jails to offer a range of programs that directly address the reasons for incarceration. The evidence from a study of one DS institution emphasizing these kinds of programs suggests that recidivism may be reduced (Applegate et al., 1999), although rigorous cross-sectional and longitudinal studies are needed to provide process as well as outcome evaluations of these efforts. It also would be useful to see if similar results extend to DS prisons, where rehabilitation programs are more common.

The least clear and most mixed results concern management and staff issues. For instance, some studies found staff in DS jails to be more satisfied (Conroy et al., 1991) and less stressed, whereas others found no differences in important measures (Zupan & Menke, 1991) and high levels of stress (Stohr, Lovrich, & Wilson Gregory, 1994). This may indicate that working in a DS institution is a mixed blessing in which officers have more control and authority but less immediate contact with other staff, and lack the comfort of a hard barrier between themselves and potentially violent individuals. It is, arguably, both a more professional and rewarding job and a more demanding one, as well. This reality may be reflected in the conflicting results of some studies. Further investigation should follow Zupan and Menke (1988) and Stohr-Gilmore et al. (1994) by emphasizing independent assessments of actual operational and management style.

It would also be useful to pay more attention to gender differences in the way inmates respond to traditional and DS settings. Because most correctional facilities have largely male inmate populations, women in many settings are far more restricted in access to spaces and facilities (Wener & Farbstein, 1994b). Several studies have suggested that women experience the loss due to incarceration differently and more severely than men, including in DS facilities (Jackson & Stearns, 1995; Pogrebin & Dodge, 2001).

Some evidence supports the claim that DS institutions are less expensive to build and operate. Operational cost savings are difficult to judge because they are dependent on staffing assumptions and programmatic goals. Early DS institutions extended the understood limits for the number of inmates one officer could effectively supervise on living units, and these ratios have been stretched even further in light of growing jail populations. Newer facilities have added staff to run habilitative programs, in the hope that these increased staffing costs will result in long-term gains by reducing incarceration rates. Other potential operational cost savings may result from reduced staff sick days and turnover and lowered repair costs, although these savings have not been consistently documented. Research in the future needs to carefully measure costs but at the same time look at institutional goals, level of control provided over inmate behavior, and quality of operations.

There are a few studies (Senese et al., 1997; Zupan & Menke, 1988) in which the superiority of DS was not as large as might have been expected given the more striking findings in early reports, such as 90 percent reductions in violence reported by Frazier (1985). There are several possible explanations for these differences. It is possible, of course, that early reports in some ways overstated the benefits of direct supervision because of the stark comparisons that were made between new facilities with the earlier jails that were old, in poor repair, and had insufficient space. More recent studies have compared DS jails to newer and better serviced alternatives, including several studies that compared NDS and DS institutions operated by the same agency. Administrators in these systems may have learned lessons in implementing direct supervision that transferred to the operation of the NDS institutions (Houston et al., 1988; Senese et al., 1997; Williams et al., 1999). In effect, traditional institutions may be better than they were 25 years ago, at least in part as a result of learning from the implementation of the DS model.

On the other hand, there are several reasons research may actually understate the success of direct supervision. A number of studies found that DS facilities experienced significantly more crowding than traditional ones (Farbstein & Wener, 1989; Stohr, Lovrich, & Wilson Gregory, 1994; Zupan & Stohr-Gillmore, 1988). Though DS facilities have performed well in spite of overcrowding, issues such as safety, stress, program implementation, staff–inmate communication, and social climate may still be affected (Liebert, 1996; Senese et al., 1997; Zupan & Menke, 1991). Although considerable attention has been given to individual impacts of institutional crowding (Paulus, 1988), more research on ecological and system-wide effects is needed (Gaes, 1994).

Paradoxically, this level of overcrowding may occur, at least in part, because DS facilities are seen to operate so well. Judges may be less reluctant to use the sanction of incarceration to places seen as safe and humane (Lund et al., 1998; Morris, 1976).

The positive effects of direct supervision may also be understated, because, as noted earlier, not all of the institutions classified as such adhere to the principles advocated by its originators (Liebert, 1996; Nelson, 1988c; Tartaro, 2003). Implementation of DS without sufficient staff training, for instance, can lead to operational problems (Hughes, 2003; Liebert et al., 1993). It is important for future research to independently verify application of the DS model so that comparisons can be made on the basis of actual institution design and operation, rather than from self-applied labels.

Direct supervision seems to be a robust model, then, but one with limits. It appears able to survive overcrowding, environments harder than originally proposed, fixed (though open) officer stations, dormitories instead of private cells, and high inmate–officer ratios. DS facilities may have difficulties, though, when the level and quality of training is insufficient (see the model described in Chapter 11 for a more detailed description of factors that are likely to affect DS outcomes). Research should study more closely how these limitations affect operation.

Direct supervision was a radical departure from accepted practice in a field known for conservative thought. It is often difficult for significant innovations to spread (Rogers, 1995), and even more so when change requires a commitment to significant capital costs in ways that may be politically unpopular. Here was an approach that took environments where violence was endemic, at a time in the 1970s when problems of urban violence seemed intractable, and created a calm and safe atmosphere. Moreover it did so in a way that eschewed the hard-edged "big-house" approach in favor of improved communications and social contact. Although more restrictive housing is used for inmates who are expected to be violent in the correctional setting, it is not correct to assume that it is a model only fit for "easy" or minimum security inmates. Quite the contrary, many jail managers point out that most jail units are considered high-security settings, because of the variety of inmates placed there and, frequently, the lack of information about their histories.

The success of direct supervision that seemed so improbable at first says something about management and design beyond the purely correctional experience. Direct supervision is, significantly, a management system, and as such it has been discussed and studied for how it implements important management principles and how these lessons might be applied to different settings, including other kinds of institutions or work environments (Davis, 1987; Zupan & Menke, 1991). The accumulated experiences of the use of direct supervision in jails and prisons are also important to architecture and social and environmental psychology. The case of direct supervision offers a dramatic demonstration of how change in the physical and social environment can work to change behavior. The difference in appearance and atmosphere between older traditional facilities and DS jails and prisons is apparent and palpable. In research fields that often measure important change in terms of a few percentage points of variance, the broad changes in levels of aggression and in social relationships between inmates and officers can be striking.

References

Applegate, B. K., Surette, R., & McCarthy, B. (1999). Detention and desistance from crime: Evaluating the influence of a new generation jail on recidivism. *Journal of Criminal Justice, 27*(6), 539–548.

Arbiter, N. (1988). Drug treatment in a direct supervision jail: Pima County's Amity Jail Project. *American Jails, Summer,* 35–40.

Ard, L. (1991). Fifth generation jail: Contra Costa's West County justice facility. *Large Jail Network Bulletin, 2*(4), 2–8.

Atlas, R. (1984). *Dade County Stockade Expansion: The Future of the American Jail.* Unpublished manuscript.

Bayens, G. J., Williams, J. J., & Smykla, J. O. (1997). Jail Type and Inmate Behavior: A Longitudinal Analysis. *Federal Probation, 61*(3), 54–62.

Bigelow, T. (1993). *Comparing the cost of direct supervision with traditional jails.* The Florida Criminal Justice Executive Institute, Associates.

Bordenaro, M. (1992). Direct supervision reforms correctional facilities. *Building Design and Construction, August,* 30–35.

Bottoms, A. E. (1999). Interpersonal violence and social order in prisons. In M. Tonry & J. Petersilia (Eds.), *Prisons* (Vol. 26, pp. 205–283). Chicago: University of Chicago Press.

Conroy, R. (1989). Santa Clara County direct supervision jail. *American Jail,* 3(3), 59–67.

Conroy, R., Smith, W. J., & Zupan, L. L. (1991). Officer stress in the direct supervision jail: A preliminary case study. *American Jails,* 5(5), 34–36.

Cook, T. D., & Campbell, D. T. (1979). *Quasi-Experimentation: Design & Analysis Issues for Field Settings.* Chicago: Rand McNally College Publishing Co.

Cross gender supervision. (2000). In American Correctional Association (Producer), *JOB Video Series.* Alexandria, VA: American Correctional Association.

Davis, R. (1987). Direct supervision as an organization management system. *American Jails, Spring,* 50–53.

DeWitt, C. B. (1987). *Building on Experience: A Case Study of Advanced Construction and Financing Methods for Corrections.* Washington, DC: U.S. National Institute of Corrections.

DiIulio, J. (1987). *Governing Prisons: A Comparative Study of Corrections Management.* New York: Free Press.

Direct Supervision Jails: 2006 Sourcebook, National Institute of Corrections Information Center (3rd ed.). (2006). Longmont, CO: National Institute of Corrections Information Center.

Farbstein, J., Liebert, D., & Sigurdson, H. (1996). *Audits of Podular Direct-Supervision Jails.* Washington, DC: National Institute of Corrections.

Farbstein, J., & Wener, R. E. (1989). *A Comparison of "Direct" and "Indirect" Supervision Correctional Facilities.* Washington, DC: National Institute of Corrections – Prison Division.

Frazier, W. (1985). *A Postoccupancy Evaluation of Contra Cost County's Main Detention Facility.* San Francisco: Golden Gate University.

Gaes, G. (1994). *Prison Crowding Research Reexamined.* Washington, DC: Federal Bureau of Prisons.

Gettinger, S. H. (1984). *New Generation Jails: An Innovative Approach to an Age-Old Problem.* Washington, DC: U.S. National Institute of Corrections.

Heuer, G. F. (1993). Direct supervision. *American Jail,* 57–60.

Houston, J., Gibbons, D., & Jones, J. (1988). Physical environment and jail social climate. *Crime & Delinquency, 34,* 449–466.

Hughes, D. (2003). The new generation jail: Ten years after. *American Jails, May/June,* 39–45.

Jackson, P. (1992). *Detention in Transition: Sonoma County's New Generation Jail.* Boulder, CO: National Institute of Corrections Jail Center.

Jackson, P. G., & Stearns, C. A. (1995). Gender issues in the new generation jail. *Prison Journal, 75*(2), 203–221.

Kibre, J. (1991). New approach to minimum security at San Joaquin County Men's Facility. *Corrections Today, 53*(2), 116, 118–119.

Knapel, C., Wener, R. E., & Vigorita, L. M. (1986). *Post Occupancy Evaluation: AIA/CAJ/ ACA Justice Facility Citation Winners.* Washington, DC: Justice Facilities Research Program of the American Institute of Architectural Research and Committee on Architecture for Justice.

Leone, M. C., & Kinkade, P. T. (1994). New designs, new ideas, and new problems: An analysis of the effects of non-smoking policies on a "new generation" jail. *The Justice Professional, 8*(2), 1–21.

Liebert, D., Knapel, C., & Davis, R. (1993). *San Joaquin County Stockton, California: Jail Operations and Physical Plant.* Washington, DC: National Institute of Corrections Jail Center.

Liebert, D. R. (1996). Direct supervision jails – The second decade: The pitfalls. *American Jails, 10*(4), 35–37.

Lund, L. J., Morrise, M. J., & Jordan, A. (1998). Civil liabilities, unconstitutional jails and planning of new institutions part v. *Nebraska Jail Bulletin, 139 January/Feb.*

McKenzie, D. (1997). Walworth County Jail tests direct supervision model by integrating its concepts into "superpod" design. *American jails, 11*(4), 59–52.

McNamara, M. (1992). *Better Than A Mexican Jail: Post-Occupancy Evaluation of A Direct Supervision Detention Facility Dormitory.* Paper presented at the Annual Conference of the Environmental Design Research Association, April 9–12 Boulder, CO.

Menke, B., Zupan, L., & Lovrich, N. (1986). *Research Note: A Comparison of Work-Related Attitudes between New Generation Correction Officers and Other Public Employees.* Paper presented at the Annual Meeting of the Academy of Criminal Justice Sciences, Orlando, Florida.

Modern prisons can reduce costs and stress. (1992). *Civil Engineering. Civil Engineering J1 – Civil Engineering* (Vol. 62, p. 14). Reston, VA: American Society of Civil Engineers.

Morris, N. (1976). Presentation at Symposium at Chicago Metropolitan Correctional Center. Chicago, IL.

Mueller, J. (1998). Contra Costa revisited: A lasting program innovation. *American Jails, 12*(1), 30–33.

Nelson, W. R. (1976). *U.S. Metropolitan Correctional Centers: An Operational Perspective.* Paper presented at the American Correctional Association, New Orleans.

Nelson, W. R. (1983a). New generation jails. *Corrections Today, April,* 108–112.

Nelson, W. R. (1983b). *New Generation Jails: The Development of a Trend for the Future of the American Jail.* Boulder, CO: National Institute of Corrections Jail Center.

Nelson, W. R. (1986). Can cost savings be achieved by designing jails for direct supervision inmate management (pp. 13–20). In J. Farbstein & R. E. Wener (Eds.), *Proceedings of the First Annual Symposium on New Generation Jails.* Boulder, CO: National Institute of Corrections.

Nelson, W. R. (1988a). Cost savings in new generation jails: The direct supervision approach. *NIJ Construction Bulletin, July.*

Nelson, W. R. (1988b). The origins of direct supervision: An eyewitness account. *American Jail, Spring,* 8–14.

Nelson, W. R. (1988c, April 24). *The Origins of the Direct Supervision Concept: A Personal Account.* Paper presented at the Third Annual Symposium on Direct Supervision Jails, Los Angeles.

Nelson, W. R. (1990, May 20). *Revisiting the Principles of Direct Supervision.* Paper presented at the 5th Annual Symposium on Direct Supervision, Reno, Nevada.

Nelson, W. R., O'Toole, M., Krauth, B., & Whitemore, C. (1983). *New Generation Jails*. Rockville, MD: National Institite of Corrections.

Paulus, P. B. (1988). *Prison Crowding: A Psychological Perspective (Research in Criminology)*. New York: Springer-Verlag.

Pellicane, A. (1990). *Direct Supervision Management: A Case Study*. Paper presented at the 5th Annual Symposium on Direct Supervision, Reno, Nevada.

Pogrebin, M. R., & Dodge, M. (2001). Women's account of their prison experiences: A retrospective view of their subjective realities. *Journal of Criminal Justice, 29*, 531–541.

Rogers, E. M. (1995). *Diffusion of Innovations* (4th ed.). New York: The Free Press.

Saunders, S. (1995). *Direct Supervision Jails: A Management Model for the 21st Century*. The Florida Criminal Justice Executive Institute Associates, Inc. – Senior Leadership Research Papers. Retrieved Feb. 17, 2003, 2004, from the World Wide Web: http://www .fcjeia.org/Corrections_issues_in_criminal_Justice.htm and http://www.fdle.state.fl. us/FCJEI/SLP%20papers/Saunders.htm.

Saxton, S. (1990). *Reintegration: A Strategy for Success*. Paper presented at the 5th Annual Symposium on Direct Supervision, Reno, Nevada.

Senese, J. D., Wilson, J., Evans, A. O., Aguirre, R., & Kalinich, D. B. (1997). Evaluating jail reform: A comparative analysis of podular/direct and linear jail inmate infractions. *Journal of Criminal Justice, 25*, 61–73.

Sigurdson, H. (1985). *The Manhattan House of Detention: A Study of Podular Direct Supervision*. Washington, DC: National Institute of Corrections.

Sigurdson, H. (1987a). *Larimer County Detention Center: A Study of Podular Direct Supervision*. Washington, DC: National Institute of Corrections.

Sigurdson, H. (1987b). *The Pima County Detention Center: A Study of Podular Direct Supervision*. Washington, DC: National Institute Corrections.

Stohr, M. K., Lovrich, N. P., Menke, B. A., & Zupan, L. L. (1994). Staff management in correctional institutions: Comparing DiIulio's "control model" and "employee investment model" outcomes in five jail settings. *Justice Quarterly, 11*(3), 471–479.

Stohr, M. K., Lovrich, N. P., & Wilson Gregory, L. (1994). Staff stress in contemporary jails: Assessing problem severity and the payoff of progressive personnel practices. *Journal of Criminal Justice, 22*(4), 313–327.

Stohr, M. K., Self, R., & Lovrich, N. (1992). Staff turnover in new generation jails: An investigation of its causes and prevention. *Journal of Criminal Justice, 20*, 455–478.

Stohr, M. K., Lovrich, N. P., Menke, B. A., & Zupan, L. L. (1995). Staff management in correctional institutions: Control model and employee investment model outcomes in five jail settings, part II. *American Jails, 9*(3), 28–29, 31–36.

Tartaro, C. (2002). The impact of density on jail violence. *Journal of Criminal Justice, 30*(6), 499–510.

Tartaro, C. (2003). Suicide and the jail environment: An evaluation of three types of institutions. *Environment & Behavior, 35*(5), 605–620.

Wallenstein, A. (1987). New generation/direct supervision correctional operations in Bucks County, Pennsylvania. *American Jails, Spring*, 34–36.

Wallenstein, A. (1990). *Cross-Gender Inmate Supervision: Notes on an Evolving Staffing/ Labor Relations Issue*. Paper presented at the 5th Annual Symposium on Direct Supervision, Reno, Nevada.

Wells, J. (1987). Direct supervision: Panacea or fad? Does it warrant full acceptance? *American Jails, Spring*, 46–49.

Wener, R. E. (1985). *Environmental Evaluation: Manhattan House of Detention.* New York: NYC Department of Corrections.

Wener, R. E. (2000). Design and the likelihood of prison assaults. In L. Fairweather & S. McConville (Eds.), *Prison Architecture* (pp. 49–54). Oxford: Architectural Press.

Wener, R. E. (2005). The invention of direct supervision. *Corrections Compendium, 30*(2), 4–7, 32–34.

Wener, R. E., & Clark, N. (1977). *User Based Evaluation of the Chicago Metropolitan Correctional Center – Final Report.* Washington, DC: U.S. Bureau of Prisons.

Wener, R. E., & Farbstein, J. (1994a). *Genesis Facility: Post-Occupancy Evaluation, Final Report* (154459). Washington, DC: National Institute of Corrections.

Wener, R. E., & Farbstein, J. (1994b). *Post Occupancy Evaluation: West County Detention Facility, Richmond, California.* Washington, DC: National Institute of Corrections Jail Center.

Wener, R. E., Farbstein, J., & Knapel, C. (1993). Post occupancy evaluations: Improving correctional facility design. *Corrections Today, 55*(6), 96–103.

Wener, R. E., Frazier, W., & Farbstein, J. (1985). Three generations of evaluation and design of correctional facilities. *Environment & Behavior, 17*(1), 71–95.

Wener, R. E., Frazier, W., & Farbstein, J. (1987). Building better jails. *Psychology Today, 21*(6), 40–49.

Wener, R. E., Knapel, C., & Vigorita, L. M. (1996). *Post Occupancy Evaluation of Norfolk County Correctional Center.* Dedham, MA: AIA.

Wener, R. E., & Olsen, R. (1980). Innovative correctional environments: A user assessment. *Environment & Behavior, 12*(4), 478–493.

Williams, J. L., Rodeheaver, D., & Huggins, D. (1999). A comparative evaluation of a new generation jail. *American Journal of Criminal Justice, 23*(2), 223–246.

Wortley, R. (2003). *Situational Prison Control: Crime Prevention in Correctional Institutions.* New York: Cambridge University Press.

Yin, R. (1994). *Case Study Research: Design and Methods* (2nd Ed.). Beverly Hills, CA: Sage Publishing.

Zimring, C. (1989). *Post Occupancy Evaluation of the Contra Costa County Main Detention Facility.* Atlanta: Environment/Behavior Inquiry.

Zupan, L. L. (1991). *Jails: Reform and the New Generation Philosophy.* Cincinnati, OH: Anderson Publishing Co.

Zupan, L., & Menke, B. (1987). *Job Enrichment and Direct Supervision Correctional Officers: The Role of Management.* Paper presented at the Second Annual Conference on New Generation Jails, Clearwater, FL.

Zupan, L. L., & Menke, B. (1988). Implementing organizational change: From traditional to new generation jail operations. *Policy Studies Review, 7,* 615–625.

Zupan, L. L., & Stohr-Gillmore, M. K. (1988). Doing time in the new generation jail: Inmate perceptions of gains and losses. *Policy Studies Review, 7*(3), 626–640.

Zupan, L., & Menke, B. (1991). The new generation jail: An overview. In J. Thompson & G. Mays (Eds.), *American Jails: Public Policy Issues* (pp. 131–147). Chicago: Nelson-Hall Publishers.

SECTION TWO

ENVIRONMENT-BEHAVIOR ISSUES IN CORRECTIONS

6

Correctional Space and Behavior – Privacy, Personal Space, and Territoriality in Institutions

In this chapter I address theory and research related to issues of physical space, interpersonal distances, and control thereof. At a larger scale and at a distance, a correctional institution can be considered in terms of broad macro-organizational issues of design and management – how a facility is created, how space is organized, and how rules are devised and maintained. Day to day and moment to moment, however, the social ecology of a place is experienced on the smaller scale of interpersonal relations involving privacy, personal space, and territoriality. These are central to the way the correctional space is seen and felt. This chapter considers each of these issues in turn, first addressing privacy as a model that helps to place in context personal space and territoriality, as well as crowding and isolation, which are considered in Chapters 7 and 8.

PRIVACY

Privacy plays a central role in this discussion and, especially as viewed through the lens of Altman's model (Altman 1981), is central to both the concepts of territoriality and personal space in institutions. For this discussion, we do not address the legal dimensions of privacy (although they are conceptually related to the spatial ones), but, instead, focus on social interpersonal and environmental aspects. Altman's model provides a way to place these notions into a unified conceptual context as opposed to viewing them as freestanding, independent, and disconnected phenomena of the way people use space.

In this sense, privacy is all about interpersonal boundary regulation and control – how much contact does one have with others, where, when, how, and by whose choice? Privacy concerns the ability to make adjustments to a place to match as closely as possible available and the desired levels of contact with others.

Altman's (1981) model presumes that people everywhere share a dynamically changing need for social contact, ranging from the desire to be absolutely alone, with no interaction with or information about others, to the need for broad and intense interaction with one, several, or many other people. Optimal privacy, as Altman describes it, represents a match or goodness of fit between the level of contact wanted and the contact available, allowed and achieved. This is a dynamic process in that the desired levels of social interaction and information access fluctuate over time, moment to moment, age to age, just as the levels that are afforded by the social, organizational, and physical circumstances vary. Typically, the individual needs control over the situation in order to achieve privacy. He or she has to be able to operate on and change the situation to fit changing desires for greater or lesser contact. For Altman, then, optimal privacy does not necessarily mean being alone. Rather it is to be alone when being alone is desired, to be with several others sometimes, or with many people at other times. This model also generates definitions of *crowding* and *isolation* (both of which are discussed further in later chapters). *Crowding* is the state in which attempts at privacy fail because a person has no choice but to be in contact with more people than wanted, whereas *isolation* is the opposite – privacy fails because the person wants to interact with more people but is kept from doing so by architectural, social, or organizational limitations. By this definition, of course, correctional settings are intensely poor places for privacy. The very nature of the legal and social contract that creates the right to incarcerate someone (Foucault, 1979) transfers control over these choices from the individual to the organization. Being in a jail or prison inherently limits privacy.

Even in a correctional facility people will try to display some level of control over interactions. They use a variety of means to regulate interactions in order to maintain privacy, including verbal statements, nonverbal behavior, and physical arrangements of space. In Altman's model, territoriality and personal space are two tools used to affect physical and social distance in regulating levels of contact and access to help achieve the desired degree of being open or closed. They are related, albeit different, nonverbal tools for affecting level of social contact.

Several writers have focused on the specific ways in which we use privacy to meet various personal needs and goals (Pederson, 1999; Westin, 1967). They address specific kinds of privacy and the emotional and social functions that privacy serves. These discussions make it especially clear where and how the lack of privacy impacts inmates in correctional settings.

Pederson and Westin have suggested that there are various types of privacy, including solitude, the state of being alone by choice. *Solitude*, in this case, is distinguished from *isolation,* which refers to being alone at the directive of others (see Chapter 8). Privacy is also experienced in *intimacy* – close contact with others for emotionally charged interchange; in *anonymity* – achieving aloneness by not being recognized in a crowd; and through *reserve* – withdrawing into one's self. In a jail or prison, opportunities for solitude are highly prized but almost impossible to achieve, except for fleeting moments. Fewer and fewer institutions have individual cells for economic reasons, and space and site-line limitations further reduce or eliminate other opportunities for physical separation.

In addition, in most total institutions, intimacy among inmates is actively discouraged, if for no other reason than to reduce the opportunities for sexual exploitation. Similarly, correctional managers in well-run institutions work hard to assure that inmates are not anonymous and fall between the cracks. Much of the focus of direct supervision and unit management (see Chapter 3), for example, is in creating a scale and level of contact between inmates and officers that eliminates anonymity and makes it possible for staff to get to know the inmates. Given the inability to have access to physical supports for privacy regulation, the most common strategy for privacy that is available to inmates is to demonstrate reserve and turn inward to avoid interactions and to establish self-control.

These different kinds of privacy, both Pederson and Westin observe, serve important social and psychological needs. For example, solitude and intimacy can play important roles in achieving emotional release, often seen when one needs to deal with strong emotions such as fear, grief, or anger. People often seek space away from strangers when they have to confront these feelings and need to receive the comfort of others. This option is generally unavailable in correctional settings, not just because isolated space is difficult to find, but also because any display of strong emotions is likely to be discouraged. There are few good places to go for an emotional outlet when an inmate receives bad news about a job, a relationship, or a court proceeding. As Gifford (2002) noted, we may need to get off the public stage before we can reflect and make sense of what is going on. Privacy allows reflection, understanding, and sometimes personal growth to emerge from events, once we can take a step back in order to review and make sense of them. The lack of such privacy options in a correctional setting may, then, be more than an inconvenience. It may reduce an inmate's ability to accept, understand, and maturely deal with bad news.

Privacy also plays an important role in self-evaluation and rejuvenation. As noted in Chapter 2, the extreme solitude of the first penitentiaries was provided expressly (although in a misguided way) to allow inmates to have both space and time for reflection and self-evaluation in the unrealized hope that it would lead to moral change. Even though self-evaluation is often actively encouraged by prison programs as part of the rehabilitation process, most institutions lack spaces where contemplation and attention to inward assessment is possible without constant interruption by other people and activities.

Though desires for privacy are, as Altman (1981) describes them, universal and powerful, they may be especially relevant in the context of a total institution. Privacy, we have said, expressly involves the ability to exert control over place and interaction as a way of limiting access to self. Being an inmate in a correctional institution specifically and intentionally entails loss of the right and the ability to exert such control. Becoming an inmate means handing over to the authorities the ability to determine the "where," the "when," and the "with whom" of your day – time and space are controlled by others. Privacy or lack thereof becomes one of the defining concepts of incarceration. Foucault (1979) stressed that maintaining a high degree of control over inmate social contacts is a key to understanding the heart of the correctional experience. In the extreme, as presented in the Panopticon, the prison was intended to make the inmate aware of the omniscience of the authorities that comes from never being certain if, at any particularly moment, he or she is being observed (Semple, 1993).

It is the job of the prison or jail staff to know about the inmate at all times, where they are, what they are doing, how they are feeling, and with whom they are angry. Privacy, as used in the outside world to protect personal communication or as part of the creative process, does not exist for inmates in the total institution. Indeed, "[s]ome judges and others have asserted that...prisoners have no right or expectation of privacy while they are incarcerated" (Ingram, 2000, p. 3). As Altman (1981) and Goffman (1961) have noted, for these very reasons, loss of privacy becomes a large part of the stress of being incarcerated.

Loss of privacy can also be an important part of the total institution's ability to strip the individual of his or her sense of self (Jiménez, 2000). Of course, the one aspect of daily institutional life that makes the loss of privacy in correctional settings especially clear, salient, and unpleasant has to do with personal hygiene – use of the toilet and shower. The inability to avoid being watched, even for these activities, is emblematic of the loss of normal levels of social and spatial control. Kira, in his classic human factors study of the bathroom (1976), discussed the power of cultural norms for modesty in bathrooms, related to the perception that evacuative functions are dirty and need to be out of view. He commented that privacy deprivation for

FIGURE 28. Orange County Jail, Orlando, Florida. R. Wener

bathroom use is, in Western cultures at least, particularly stressful. He also noted that people use, and sometimes exploit, the privacy norm that exists for bathroom use to support other activities – such as using the privacy of a bathroom for uninterrupted reading time. Even in the best institutions, privacy for these basic functions is lacking. In most jails and prisons, cells serve as both sleeping and toilet spaces. Even within the confines of a one-person cell, privacy is limited by open bars or windows in cell doors that exist expressly to reduce visual privacy and make views of the inmate available to staff making their rounds.

Privacy Control and Stress

By defining *privacy* in terms of control or lack of control over the degree of openness to interaction, we are also able to connect it to the broader literature on environmental stress. *Control* – the ability to regulate the level of exposure to environmental events – has been linked to the degree to which people experience stress and have lasting effects from exposure to stressors (see Evans, 1982; Evans & Stecker, 2004). This appears to be the case for a variety of stressors that are relevant to the correctional context, including noise (Cohen, Evans, Krantz, & Stokols, 1989; Cohen, Evans, Stokols, & Krantz, 1986; Glass & Singer, 1972), heat and cold (Bell & Greene, 1982), as well as isolation and crowding (Baron & Rodin, 1978; Baum & Valins, 1977; Epstein, 1982; Evans & Wener, 2007).

Unpredictable, intermittent stressors appear to have the most negative and lasting impacts (Evans, 1982; Glass & Singer, 1972). As Foucault (1979) indicated, the correctional setting stands out above almost all others as one in which individuals are, often expressly and purposely, placed in unpredictable settings where they are denied the ability to choose or effect when, where, how, and with whom they will be in direct contact. Add to that the fact that in correctional settings, more than any other kind of place, undesired contact brings with it an element of risk and danger from assault, and one would expect the stress that results from lack of privacy to be especially high.

Baron and Rodin (1978) discuss control as the central mediating concept of environmental experiences. They note that control is not just the physical ability to manipulate settings, but also the ability to predict events. One common response to experiencing lack of control is an exaggerated attempt to reassert it – reactance. People may adjust to reduced decisional freedom, for instance, with aggressive behavior – especially if they feel forced into a physically or psychologically cramped situation – what Baron and Rodin call "deprivation of onset control" (1978, p. 171) and cannot leave the situation – "lack of offset control" (p. 171).

How people respond may be determined, in part, by the attributions they make about the cause of their problem. Individuals may try to reduce the stress of loss of privacy by increasing territorial behavior – acting to assert a claim over a specific area or object. In a prison situation, this might be seen in dominant individuals claiming a prized seat by the TV, for example. Such territorial behavior may enable prisoners to avoid conflicts. Violence is more likely to erupt when dominance hierarchies are unstable and the territorial claim is challenged, which is more common in times of high turnover of inmates (Sundstrom & Altman, 1972). High turnover is the normal condition in jails.

Expectations of Control

One of the pains of imprisonment is that inmates come to expect little in the way of control over information and access they had in their former lives. They learn that aspects of control taken for granted outside the institution are rare inside:

Locked up alone in a cell, the prisoner is subjected to permanent supervision by guards, who practice silent surveillance through a hatch in the cell door or via a video camera. South African poet Breyten Breytenbach explained in an interview why this surveillance is so oppressive: One of the strongest impressions of prison is that you're never alone. You're always alone – I was in solitary confinement – but whatever you do, every word you say, is completely known to the authorities. In most countries, several prisoners share a cell, and are never alone for even a moment. Thus the stress of imprisonment, paradoxically, consists of forced community. (Wouterloot, 1995)

Smith (1982) found that jail inmates who moved from a more to a less restrictive setting, where increased levels of personal control were possible, had increased expectancy levels for privacy and isolation. In Moore's study of sick-call rates (1980), the cellblocks with the lowest levels of visual privacy had higher levels of heath care utilization than did those with more visual privacy.

Goffman's (1959) descriptions of front and back stage elements in the social presentation of self and social interaction add another dimension to an analysis of the correctional situation. In normal life, when at work, shopping, or social gatherings, we are "onstage," where we present ourselves to the public as we wish to be seen. Other times and places – back stage – we are out of the public eye and can relax and worry less about how we are seen by others. In the prison or jail, though, there is no such distinction. All activity, including behavior that is normally out of public view (such as sleeping, dressing, using the toilet), is onstage. There is no place to be off-stage, off-camera, away from scrutiny, and able to relax from social structures and rules.

In the 1970s, when direct supervision was a new concept and when many new jails were being built to replace an aging infrastructure, single cells were considered important for security and privacy. Today, however, in most jails and prisons, the privacy offered by single cells is seen as a luxury that can no longer be afforded. The vast majority of inmates are in multiple occupancy rooms – doubles, triples, or more, as the numbers of incarcerated inmates have regularly outstripped initial population projections (see Chapter 7 – "Prison Crowding").

When several inmates share a cell, the problems that are created go beyond physical closeness. Sharing toilet facilities within a cell violates basic privacy norms regarding sight, sound, and odor. It is stressful to most inmates, even though they have no choice but to adjust and accommodate because the situation is so common in many correctional settings that it is seen by administrators as the norm and not as a problem in great need of repair.

We studied a jail that used alternating access to the dayroom as a way to adjust to overcrowded conditions (Bogard & Wener, 2007). The facilities and congregating spaces (showers, dayroom, and dining tables) had been sized for an expected capacity of one inmate in each of the thirty-six single cells. At the time of our visit, however, all cells had two inmates and the dayroom was too small to be used by all seventy-two inmates at one time. In response, procedures were changed so that inmates were kept locked in cells, except for the periods when half were allowed into the dayroom at any one time. This was accomplished by allowing alternating access from upper and lower tiers: those whose cells were on the upper tier of the living unit were allowed out of their cells for 90 minutes, after which time they returned to their cells and those whose cells were on the lower tier were allowed out.

From the perspective of privacy, the inmates "lose" in either instance in such a regime. When they are in their rooms, they are locked in with a cellmate and have no ability to be alone to read, sleep, dress, or use the toilet. When they are out of the cell, they are locked out of access to their "stuff" in the cell. Another option might be to alternate groups differently. Instead of rotating access between upper and lower tier inmates, officers might let one person from each cell out to the dayroom for these alternating periods. In such a case, both the "out time" (for TV, phone, exercise, and so forth) and the "in time" (solitude for toilet, sleep, reading, thinking) become positive conditions. Accepting the absence of privacy as a prison norm is so common, however, that the idea of taking such an approach simply does not occur.

Wolfe and Golan (1976) discussed privacy and behavior in terms of the way space use changed in a psychiatric institution as social density increased. They noted that as the number of people in a bedroom increased, there was a reduced range of behaviors in that bedroom, and that passive behaviors moved from the bedroom to public areas. Wener and Olson (1980) also found that as a number of people in a jail cell increased, the focus of isolated passive behavior (sit, read, sleep) shifted from the bedroom to public places. Single cells provide options, then, for private behaviors that are lost in multiple cells, with ramifications for institutional living.

For example, Zimring, Weitzer, and Knight (1982) showed that when residents in total institutions have private bedrooms with closable, lockable doors, they are more social and less withdrawn. These private spaces allow for opportunities to retreat when desired and hence to have freedom to be more social otherwise. They suggest that the lack of private space encourages "more eager boundary control behaviors in public" (p. 158) – that is, more aggressive territorial behavior. In this pre- and post-change study of an institution for the developmentally disabled those designs that increased control over social interaction as well as of physical systems (light, heat, noise) positively impacted stress and interaction.

The correct design helped reduce social stress because it gave a wider choice of spaces that were better defined as true ownership and helped reduced direct physical stress by means of improved mechanical controls (p. 159).

These results are also supported by studies in college dormitories. Students who had more effective privacy regulation mechanisms – especially those who communicated "keep out" – were less likely to leave the university before graduation (Vinsel, Brown, Altman, & Foss, 1985). In addition, dormitory architecture that increases levels of uncontrollable, unpredictable social interaction made residents less sociable, less likely to engage in cooperative versus competitive social interactions, and more likely to withdraw from contact (Baum & Valins, 1977).

PERSONAL SPACE

Personal space refers to the minimal or optimal interpersonal distances regularly used during social interactions. It is usually discussed in terms of dyadic interchange, but it can be relevant for interactions of more than two people. Within a given culture, the distances people use for the same functions of social interaction are typically consistent. Altman (1981) describes personal space, along with territoriality, as a privacy regulation mechanism people use to control or regulate contact with others. There have been a great many studies of the way people use interpersonal spacing during interaction (see Aiello, 1987, for a full review), and a number that have focused specifically on inmates with aggressive or violent histories.

Although some early discussions of personal space have referred to "body buffer zones" (Curran, Blatchley, & Hanlon, 1978; Hildreth, Derogatis, & Mccusker, 1971; Horowitz, Duff, & Stratton, 1964; Rubinstein, 1975; Stratton & Horowitz, 1972; Wilds, 1973) and "personal space bubbles" (see Little, 1965; Patterson, 1975; Sommer, 1969), these terms are somewhat misleading. The concept of interpersonal distance only has meaning as it relates to interaction with other people. As Hall (1959, 1969) has discussed at length, use of space serves as a form of communication and can have significant meaning in terms of the kind and quality of relationships.

Two findings emerge from research conducted over the past several decades that have looked at interpersonal distancing of residents in total institutions. First, people with violent or aggressive histories tend to require larger interpersonal distances than others. This was first reported by Kinzel (1970), who noted not only that violent inmates had larger personal space distances than nonviolent inmates, but also that the distance was particularly large when approached from the rear. These findings have been supported in part or whole by other studies (Curran et al., 1978; Hildreth et al., 1971; Roger & Salenkamp, 1976), although the first two did not find differences in rear approach between aggressive inmates and others. Walkey and Gilmour (1984) developed a video rating method for measuring interpersonal distance.

They found that this measure predicted which inmates were likely to engage in fighting better than any of sixteen other measures, except current offense (Gilmour & Walkey, 1981; Walkey & Gilmour, 1984).

Personal space invasions of institutionalized patients may be a significant cause of aggressive behavior. Invasions result in anger (O'Neal, Brunault, Marquis, & Carifio, 1979) and have been found to evoke aggressive responses from cognitively impaired nursing home residents (Ryden, Bossenmaier, & McLachlan, 1991), dementia patients in an Alzheimer unit (Bridges–Parlet, Knopman, & Thompson, 1994), and psychiatric in-patients (Fagan–Pryor et al., 2003). Patients in a forensic psychiatry unit who were not able to retire to their rooms when irritated and who experienced intrusions into their personal space had higher rates of aggressive behavior (Daffern, Mayer, & Martin, 2004).

Rago, Parker, and Cleland (1978) also found that increasing space available on a unit for the profoundly retarded reduced aggressive incidents, which they attributed, in part, to reduced sense of crowding. Reduced levels of personal space is one consequence of crowding in a correctional institution. In those conditions, forced closeness may serve as a trigger for aggressive responses.

TERRITORIALITY

Territoriality differs from personal space in that it refers to the way in which we behave vis-à-vis a specific piece of space – a geographical entity – rather than the relative distance between people. It is reflected in concepts like identification, marking, personalization, defense, and ownership, which have meaning to the individual and also affect how other people think about and act toward others.

Individuals in institutions may try to reduce their level of exposure to social or physical stimuli by creating filtering mechanisms. They may, for instance, use territories and boundaries as control mechanisms to allow space for withdrawal, or reduce the intensity of stimuli such as by engaging in less intense, personal interactions (Aiello, 1987).

Brown (1987), in her comprehensive review of the literature, noted that there were two different lines of thought in defining *territoriality*. The first comes from the animal literature and has a biological orientation in the way it refers largely to defense of space and how space is marked. The second stream addresses human territoriality and focuses on the organizational benefits of territorial behavior, such as psychological identification with space, personalization of settings, and the symbolic value of place. Space, for instance, is used for recognition and status. Defining and organizing interaction by territories serves, among other things, as a way to regulate access to critical resources and in that way it can reduce conflict over scarce resources.

Personalization and signs of territorial claim may serve as symbols that clarify ownership and reduce risks of intrusions in residential settings (Abu-Ghazzeh, 2000; Brown & Altman, 1983). Bobbitt (1995) studied youth correctional boot camps and concluded that higher levels of privacy and personalization were related to lower levels of aggression. Nevertheless, boot camp proponents often argue against allowing inmates to personalize their individual spaces.

Territorial behavior in the form of personalization may reduce aggression in settings for patients with dementia (Day, Carreon, Stump, & Greene, 2000; Faygan-Prior et al., 2003). "Residents in facilities with more privacy, more rooms that are individual, and more opportunities for personalization generally scored lower on . . . anxiety and aggression" (Zeisel et al., 2003, p. 708).

Commonly, three kinds of human territoriality have been identified: primary territories (such as homes), secondary territories (including work places), and public territories (such as cafeteria tables and park benches) (Brown, 1987). The distinctions between these kinds of territories depend on the amount of time spent in them (a great deal of time is spent in primary territories versus little time in public spaces), the amount of perceived and/or legal ownership (primary territories are clearly designated and owned, secondary territories less so, and public territories very little), the degree and manner in which the space is marked, how strongly the space is defended, and the ability people have to deny access to others.

The correctional setting magnifies these differences as it does other environmental issues. Bedrooms serve as primary territories in that the occupant has significant control over who can enter. People often add elements of personalization to the bedroom décor. It is, psychologically, a central location – the place to which, when all else fails, someone can withdraw. The space in a jail or prison that most closely resembles the bedroom is the cell, but there are important differences. Because this space is likely to be shared, and because staff always have the ability to view in and enter, inmates' means of controlling access and personalization is limited no matter how much time they spend there. Cells are, in some ways, then, more like shared secondary or even public territories.

In a dormitory-style unit, the level of control and ownership of space is even less – territory is limited to the bunk itself and the small standing space around it. Access to person and property is almost impossible to limit. This may help to explain the extraordinary finding by Paulus (1988) that the mere addition of a low partition around an otherwise open bunk in a dormitory reduced perceptions of crowding and stress in that dorm, on some measures to levels near those of single cells.

In humans, as with animals, many territorial markings are largely symbolic. Even though a low wall does little or nothing to limit visual access or support confidentiality of conversations, it serves this symbolic function quite well. A person crossing that boundary is well aware that they are entering another's territory – and can be seen by others (inmates and staff) around them.

Others have observed that territorial activity seems particularly strong in 24-hour institutional living environments. In such settings, Brown (1987) has said, there is a common relationship between territorial behavior and social dominance. There are some who "act as overlords, who claim territory that encompasses the territorial borders of lower status members of the group" (p. 516). Higher status, more dominant residents are more likely to occupy the largest and most desired spaces.

Paluck and Esser (1971) suggest that such territorial behavior is biologically based and is a more primitive way of regulating social interaction and strategies based on complex social organization. They argue that the use of territoriality becomes most prominent for people who are lacking the capability for complex cognitive action, such as those who have been institutionalized and labeled as severely retarded. The function of this kind of territorial behavior, they also suggest, is to reduce the stress that can come from interpersonal contact by organizing behavior in space in such a way as to reduce the likelihood of social contact, at least temporarily. This results "in more order in the environment through establishment of consistent spatial patterns between individuals" (p. 231).

Whether biologically based or not, however, territorial behavior seems to be pronounced in institutions for all kinds of residents, not just those who are cognitively impaired. It may be particularly likely to emerge in a total institution as a response to reduced levels of resources and reduced personal control in a confined space (Sossin, Esser, & Deutsch, 1978).

Territoriality and Aggression

One of the issues often discussed with respect to territoriality, especially in institutional settings, is its relationship to the level and kind of aggressive behavior. In these discussions, territorial activity has been identified both as a mechanism that incites and increases the level of aggression and as one that can serve to modulate or decrease the level of aggression. Ardrey (1967), for example, argued that a great deal of aggressive behavior in animals and in humans can be related to instinctive territorial behavior. He suggests that we are driven by instinct to identify and mark borders, and the desire to defend those boarders helps to trigger conflict with neighbors. Territorial defense is one of the most common forms of aggression, particularly when borders are indistinct and in dispute. Human aggression in terms of resource competition (is) mediated through territoriality and hierarchy (Van den Berghe, 1974, p. 777).

Territorial behavior may be related to reductions in the level of aggression by helping to physically separate parties in dispute. Territorial separation helps to organize space and reduce potential conflicts when access to resources is uncertain and ambiguous. It also helps to support and maintain dominance hierarchies. Indeed, one of the most common observations in the empirical literature on territoriality is the degree to which territoriality relates to dominance within the social group.

Even though territorial behavior clearly can occur in many different kinds of settings (Brown 1987), it may be, as Paluck and Esser (1971) indicate, particularly apparent and most strongly played out in total institutions. There, as made clear by Goffman (1961), social interactions are compressed into small and bounded spaces and the ability to avoid others is greatly reduced, with the result that the remaining options for regulating and formalizing interactions become more critical. A number of researchers have observed significant territorial behavior of residents in a variety of different kinds of institutions. Paluck and Esser (1971), for instance, saw a great deal of territorial activity in severely retarded institutionalized boys in the form of consistency of use in playground spaces and equipment, which was established by fighting and aggressive gestures. This territorial behavior, they noted, was particularly strong in relation to other behaviors and was resistant to change by verbal punishment or reinforcement. Similar kinds of territorial behavior were also observed in institutionalized retarded girls (Paslawskyj & Ivinskis, 1980), profoundly retarded adults (Rago, 1977), schizophrenic patients (Horowitz et al., 1964), adults in a psychiatric setting (Cooper, 1984), adolescent girls in a psychiatric facility (Sossin et al., 1978), and with school children (O'Neal, Caldwell, & Gallup, 1977; O'Neal et al., 1979). Territorial behavior has also been observed in prison inmates by Boudouris and Brady (1980), Cooley, Jewitt and Oren (1973), Roth (1971), Austin and Bates (1974), Wener and Olsen (1980), and Sundstrom and Altman (1972).

Some of these studies have noted the relationship between territoriality and dominance–submissive behavior, undoubtedly spurred by numerous ethological studies with animals that show the relationship between territoriality and dominance hierarchies (for detailed reviews, see Brown, 1987; Kaufman, 1983). Territoriality allows the holder – the dominant member – improved access to critical resources. In total institutions, dominant residents are likely to regularly use, lay claim to, and overtly or subtly mark and defend space, take over more desirable or more prominent space and important objects, and are more likely to transgress into the territories of others (Austin & Bates, 1974; Deutsch, Esser, & Sossio, 1978; Esser, Chamberlin, Chapple, & Kline, 1965; Esser, 1968; Paluck & Esser, 1971; Paslawskyj & Ivinskis, 1980; Sossin et al., 1978; Sundstrom & Altman, 1972).

The relationship between territorial behavior and dominance hierarchies has been connected to levels of aggressive behavior in institutional settings. A particularly clear demonstration of this connection was provided by Sundstrom and Altman (1972) in a longitudinal series of observations made in a cottage-style juvenile detention facility. They found that during periods of population stability, when there was no significant turnover in the boys residing in the cottage, the level of territorial behavior as measured by consistency of people in places (such as seeing the same boy regularly sit in the same chair) was quite high, and was strongly related to dominance hierarchies, while at the same time the level of aggression was quite low. That is, there was a clear demarcation of which boys were at the top and which were at the bottom of the pecking order. Those at the top had their clear choices of spaces – where to sit, where to eat, and so on. These territories seemed well established and were well known to the residents, and there was little conflict over the spaces or over the hierarchy.

When there was a great deal of turnover in the population, however, the hierarchy was in flux. In that condition, there was, the authors noted, a great deal of conflict among the boys as a new hierarchy sorted itself out. During this time, there was much less territorial behavior; that is, there was less consistency in who used what space. After a time, when a new hierarchy was established, the level of aggression decreased and the level of territoriality again increased.

Another study of young inmates also looked at the relationship between territorial behavior and aggression (Fleishing, 1973). The unit studied had eighteen young men (16 to 22 years of age), many of whom had a history of aggressive behavior. The inmate population was in flux during this period. The most dominant individuals seemed free to move through the institution, wherever or however they wanted. Less dominant individuals were somewhat restricted in range of movement, and the least dominant were very restricted and secluded in their use of space. The architecture of the space "was probably a controlling factor in the expression of aggression" (p. 193), especially if inmates had single rooms. In such a case, they were more able to use the room as an escape, which reduced violence. There was also an "edge effect" in which the variety and density of behaviors was greatest at community junctions – where territories of different groups intersected. Other studies of correctional settings have also noted the importance of having a space to which one can retreat from noise, stress, or danger for reducing the likelihood of aggression (Nijman et al., 1999; Wener & Olsen, 1980).

Roth (1971) reported an interesting, though disturbing, relationship between territoriality and aggression among homosexual prison inmates. He found that those who had been labeled by the staff as sexual predators, and indeed, rapists, established non-overlapping territories within the facility. In this minimum security institution, where inmates had a great deal of choice of where they were housed, these sexually aggressive inmates tended to separate themselves so that they did not occupy the same housing area. In this manner, the authors indicated, these predators were able to establish spaces where they could dominate others and yet where they would have a reduced chance of coming into conflict with each other.

Early research on territoriality by Altman and Haythorn (1967), conducted for the Navy on the psychology of dyads held in isolation for long periods of time, may be instructive here, even though it was done in a very different context. They found that over time, as sailors were jointly kept in isolation, their levels of territorial behavior gradually increased. At the same time, the sailors showed evidence of social withdrawal. The earliest and greatest amount of territorial possessiveness was over fixed geographic areas and personal objects. The authors also noted a connection between territoriality and dominance in that those sailors who scored highest on dominance scales showed the greatest amount of territorial behavior. They also found that those pairs who showed territorial behavior early in the isolation period (clearly identifying who used what space, bureau drawers, closet area, and so forth) had reduced conflict in the long run.

The function of human territoriality lies in its ability to help regulate interpersonal interaction. There has been discussion and some empirical evidence supporting the notion that the amount and nature of territorial behavior can have an impact on the amount and quality of interactions among inmates and between inmates and staff. Cooley et al. (1973), for instance, looked at the extent of territorial behavior in three Canadian correctional facilities. They noted that staff–inmate interaction that took place in inmate territories (such as living areas and courtyards) tended to be brief, infrequent, usually initiated by staff members and negative in tone and quality.

Staff spaces, on the other hand, were areas where inmates could not enter without express permission. Interaction there was typically highly formalized. The only places in which interactions were common, of long duration, and not hostile were those places that were seen as public territories and not "owned" by any one group, that is, areas that were not seen as "ours" or "theirs," but rather were open to everyone. These were more likely to have positive and more frequent social interaction.

Based on these observations, the authors argued that part of the purpose of design and programming in correctional facilities should be to "break down" territories and create more open spaces. This positive outcome is also supported, they said, by providing inmates with greater freedom of movement and more choice in spaces and activities. Facilities should provide greater spatial flexibility in options for the kinds of rooms inmates and staff use. This was particularly true and deemed appropriate for facilities that were open and similar to direct supervision institutions.

In a similar way, as discussed earlier in Chapter 3, direct supervision plans were meant in part to break down territorial divisions that, in other jails, created spaces that housed inmates to the exclusion of staff. As Nelson (1988) pointed out, linear intermittent and podular indirect supervision systems resulted in distinct staff and inmate territories. In DS jails, staff and inmates share the same space, staff are available in all areas, and their specific charge is to ensure that there are no inmate spaces that are "owned" and free of staff access. The reverse, of course, is not true – there are spaces for staff where inmates cannot go. Such is the power relationship in institutions.

Not all territorial behavior in prisons and jails is problematic, however, and even with staff–inmate divisions reduced, territorial behavior is still in evidence in DS jails. Observations in the Metropolitan Correctional Centers (Wener & Olsen, 1980), discussed earlier, showed that small social spaces within dayrooms became territorialized, often by a race, ethnicity, or some other group affinity. In these settings, large dayrooms were broken up into smaller subspaces. Each living unit in the Chicago MCC, for instance, had four small TV lounges. Typically, one of these TV areas would become known as the space for Spanish-language channels, another for sports, a third for cartoons, and so forth. These small spaces enhanced group formation and identity. In addition, these differentiations seemed to reduce potential for conflict between racial or ethnic groups, which otherwise might be vying for control of a TV. Similar design, however can have other consequences when the level of resources is insufficient. In the New York MCC there were only two TV areas for a similar number of inmates on a living unit. There conflicts (usually verbal) over choice of channel were much more common.

Territorial behavior is often characterized by marking. Marking of spaces is, in fact, often used as part of the definition of territoriality. Spaces must be marked – identified – in order to be recognized by others and defended.

In many institutions, clear, formal, and overt personalization is severely limited. They exist in staff spaces – locks, signs, and official papers are all statements of staff ownership and usually indications that residents must stay away. Inmates are typically not allowed to formally mark group spaces and often such indications are only made very subtly, through verbal or nonverbal warnings. The occasional exception is the inmate room and even there some institutions have rules against hanging pictures, posters, and the like in rooms. In other settings, such personalization of a shared living space has been shown to have positive effects (Gifford, 2002) by softening the institutional quality and adding an element of familiarity to an otherwise hard and impersonal space. Personalization may improve the social atmosphere of an institution (Holahan, 1976) or a dormitory (Vinsel et al., 1980).

Direct supervision management was designed to function with one officer per living area. In the earliest DS jails, the administration even removed the officer's desk, hoping to keep him or her on the move, roaming throughout the living area. These desks were eventually returned to the unit, because officers needed a space for paperwork. In addition, officers indicated a level of discomfort at being completely without a space of their own, even if it was one at which they spent little time. Again, both the real and symbolic aspects of having a territory are important in how individuals relate to their environment. In some instances, two officers have been assigned to a DS living unit, usually as an attempt to compensate for overcrowding. When that happens, space, to some degree, re-territorializes, when officers tend to "hang out" near each other at the control station and may spend less time roaming the living area (Bogard & Wener, 2007; Farbstein & Wener, 1989).

CONCLUSIONS

Territorial behavior may be particularly potent in the socially intense, low resource atmosphere of total institutions, with both negative and positive implications for life there. In total institutions, the level of territorial behavior is a response to the nature of the situation and the design of the space – intentionally or otherwise – and can be a two-edged sword. Territorial behavior is difficult, problematic, and even dangerous when design and management style result in spaces that function as independent staff and inmate territories, each largely off limits to the other group. In the worst cases, it can be a sign of loss of control by authorities as staff and inmates divide into exclusive territories and dominant inmates rule over people and spaces. Such can be the case in linear intermittent facilities where cells and day areas often function as inmate territories, informally managed by inmate hierarchies.

These hierarchies can maintain order but at a heavy price for those lower down on the dominance pecking order and for staff control. In some cases, these inmate-run spaces were even official policy. A classic example is that of the "inmate tenders" – inmate groups given the nod and power to establish order in the Texas prison system, until eliminated by court order in *Ruiz v. Estelle*, 1980 (Marquart & Crouch, 1985).

Territories also have their benefits. The predictability and stability that comes with informal ownership – not having to test anew each day to see who has what seat in dining area or at the TV – reduces potential conflict. Territoriality is reflected in the level of stability of population and the social order. Territoriality can also serve as a way to provide natural separation of otherwise potentially conflicting groups, and through personalization of space, a way of reducing the impersonalized and alienating nature of institutional life. "Designers," Painter (1991) indicated, "can help reduce friction caused by territoriality by clearly defining boundaries" (p. 25). So, even if it was possible to use design to totally eliminate inmate territories, as suggested by Cooley et al. (1973), it might not be beneficial, given the other positive impacts of territorial behavior.

Privacy as a central and organizing concept addresses what makes incarceration a special and difficult experience. Privacy concerns reducing stress and maintaining quality of life through choice and control, whereas incarceration is all about removing choice and control from the inmate and placing it in the hands of the institution. This is, as Foucault (1979) noted, the very heart of the experience. Any efforts to maintain a sense of self deal with sensitive personal and emotional situations, or adapt to stressful conditions that are daunting in the face of this essential reality. Both territoriality and personal space are mechanisms that inmates use to try to create a structure that provides some measure of control, at least over the quantity and quality of human interaction. Territoriality, such as clear understandings of who sits where, helps to provide a measure of order to reduce chaos and support social hierarchies. When social hierarchies are destabilized, such as by heavy turnover of populations, opportunities for confrontation and discord increase. No design, however sensitive, can change the basic truth of power and control in a correctional institution, but design features and sensitivities, such as private space in cells, have been useful in helping inmates cope with the stress of incarceration.

References

Abu-Ghazzeh, T. M. (2000). Environmental messages in multiple-family housing: Territory and personalization. *Landscape Research, 25*(1), 97–115.

Aiello, J. R. (1987). Human spatial behavior. In D. Stokols & I. Altman (Eds.), *Handbook of Environmental Psychology* (pp. 359–504). New York: John Wiley & Sons.

Altman, I. (1981). *Environment and Social Behavior: Privacy, Personal Space, Territory, and Crowding.* New York: Irvington Press.

Altman, I., & Haythorn, W. W. (1967). The ecology of isolated groups. *Behavioral Sciences & the Law, 12*(3), 169–182.

Ardrey, R. (1967). *The Territorial Imperative: A Personal Inquiry into the Animal Origins of Property and Nations.* London: Collins.

Austin, W. T., & Bates, F. L. (1974). Ethological indicators of dominance and territory in a human captive population. *Social Forces, 52*(4), 447–455.

Baron, A., & Rodin, J. (1978). Personal control as a mediator of crowding. In A. Baum, J. E. Singer, & S. Valins (Eds.), *Advances in Environmental Psychology.* Hillsdale, NJ: Lawrence Erlbaum Associates.

Baum, A., & Valins, S. (1977). *Architecture and Social Behavior: Psychological Studies of Density.* Hillsdale, NJ: Lawrence Erlbaum Associates.

Bell, P., & Greene, T. (1982). Thermal stress: Physiological comfort, performance, and social effects of hot and cold environments. In G. Evans (Ed.), *Environmental Stress* (pp. 75–104). Cambridge: Cambridge University Press.

Bobbitt, T. H. (1995, January 1995). *Correctional Boot Camps: Fact or Fad.* Retrieved July 4, 2005, from http://www.fdle.state.fl.us/FCJEI/SLP%20papers/Bobbitt.PDF.

Bogard, D., & Wener, R. E. (2007). *Assessment of Strategies Used to Manage Crowding in Direct Supervision Jails.* Washington, DC: National Institute of Corrections Jail Center.

Boudouris, J., & Brady, H. J. (1980). Attitudes of prison inmates. *Journal of Offender Counseling Services and Rehabilitation, 5*(1), 67–77.

Bridges-Parlet, S., Knopman, D., & Thompson, T. (1994). A descriptive study of physically aggressive behavior in dementia by direct observation. *Journal of American Geriatric Society, 42*(2), 192–197.

Brown, B. (1987). Territoriality. In D. Sotkols & I. Altman (Eds.), *Handbook of Environmental Psychology* (Vol. 1, pp. 505–531). New York: Wiley.

Brown, B. B., & Altman, I. H. (1983). Territoriality, defensible space and residential burglary: An environmental analysis. *Journal of Environmental Psychology, 3*, 203–220.

Cohen, S. (1980). After effects of stress on human performance and social behavior: a review of research and theory. *Psychological Bulletin, 88*, 82–108.

Cohen, S., Evans, G. W., Krantz, D. S., & Stokols, D. S. (1980). Physiological, Motivational, and Congitive Effects of Aircraft Noise on Children: Moving from the Laboratory to the Field. *American Psychologist, 35*(3), 231–243.

Cohen, S., Evans, G. W., Stokols, D. S., & Krantz, D. S. (1986). *Behavior, health, and environmental stress.* New York: Plenum.

Cooley, D., Jewitt, B., & Oren, E. (1973). *Territoriality – Its Effects on the Correctional Environment* (NCJ Number: 28207). Canadian Solicitor General.

Cooper, K. H. (1984). Territorial behavior among the institutionalized: A nursing perspective. *Journal of Psychosocial Nursing & Mental Health Services, 22*(12), 6–11.

Curran, S. F., Blatchley, R. J., & Hanlon, T. E. (1978). The relationship between body buffer zone and violence as assessed by subjective and objective techniques. *Criminal Justice & Behavior, 5*(1), 53–62.

Daffern, M., Mayer, M. M., & Martin, T. (2004). Environment contributors to aggression in two forensic psychiatric hospitals. *International Journal of Forensic Mental Health*, 3(1), 105–114.

Day, K., Carreon, D., Stump, C., & Greene, V. L. (2000). The therapeutic design of environments for people with dementia: A review of the empirical research. *The Gerontologist*, 40, 397–416.

Deutsch, R. D., Esser, A. H., & Sossin, K. M. V. (1978). Dominance, aggression, and the functional use of space in institutionalized female adolescents. *Aggressive Behavior*, 4(4), 313–329.

Epstein, J. (1982). Crowding stress and human behavior. In G. Evans (Ed.), *Environmental Stress* (pp. 133–148). New York: Cambridge University Press.

Esser, A. H. (1968). Dominance hierarchy and clinical course of psychiatrically hospitalized boys. *Child Development*, 39(1), 147–157.

Esser, A., Chamberlain, A., Chapple, E., & Kline, N. (1965). Territoriality of patients in a research ward. *Recent Advances in Biological Psychiatry*, 7, 37–44.

Evans, G. W. (Ed.). (1982). *Environmental Stress*. New York: Cambridge University Press.

Evans, G. W., & Stecker, R. (2004). Motivational consequences of environmental stress. *Journal of Environmental Psychology*, 24(2), 143–165.

Evans, G. W., & Wener, R. E. (2007). Crowding and personal space invasion on the train: Please don't make me sit in the middle *Journal of Environmental Psychology*, 27(1), 90–94.

Fagan-Pryor, E. C., Haber, L. C., Dunlap, D., Nall, J. L., Stanley, G., & Wolpert, R. (2003). Patients' views of causes of aggression by patients and effective interventions. *Psychiatric Services*, 54, 549–553.

Farbstein, J., & Wener, R. E. (1989). *A Comparison of "Direct" and "Indirect" Supervision Correctional Facilities*. Washington, DC: National Institute of Corrections – Prison Division.

Fleising, U. (1973). The social and spatial dynamics of a prison tier: An exploratory study. *Man-Environment Systems*, 3(3).

Foucault, M. (1979). *Discipline and Punishment: The Birth of the Prison*. New York: Vintage Press.

Gifford, R. (2002). *Environmental Psychology* (3rd ed.). Vancouver: Insight.

Gilmour, D. R., & Walkey, F. H. (1981). Identifying violent offenders using a video measure of interpersonal distance. *Journal of Consulting & Clinical Psychology*, 49(2), 287–291.

Glass, D., & Singer, J. (1972). *Urban Stress*. New York: Academic Press.

Goffman, E. (1959). *The Presentation of Self in Everyday Life*. New York: Anchor.

Goffman, E. (1961). *Asylums*. New York: Anchor.

Hall, E. T. (1959). *The Silent Language*. New York: Doubleday.

Hall, E. T. (1969). *The Hidden Dimension: Man's Use of Space in Public and Private*. Garden City, NY: Doubleday.

Hildreth, A. M., Derogatis, L. R., & Mccusker, K. (1971). Body buffer zone and violence: A reassessment and confirmation. *American Journal of Psychiatry*, 127(12), 1641–1645.

Holahan, C. J. (1976). Environmental change in a psychiatric setting: A social systems analysis. *Human Relations*, 29(2), 153.

Horowitz, M. J., Duff, D. F., & Stratton, L. O. (1964). Body-buffer zone. *Archives of General Psychiatry*, 11(6), 651–656.

Ingram, J. D. (2000). Prison guards and inmates of opposite genders: Equal employment opportunity versus right of privacy. *Duke Journal of Gender Law & Policy*, 7, 3.

Jiménez, M. d. P. M. (2000). Psychosocial Intervention with Drug Addicts in Prison. Description and Results of a Programme. *Psychology in Spain*, 4(1), 64–74.

Kaufmann, J. H. (1983). On the definitions and functions of dominance and territoriality. *Biological Reviews*, 58(1), 1–20.

Kinzel, A. F. (1970). Body-buffer zone in violent prisoners. *American Journal of Psychiatry*, 127(1), 59–64.

Kira, A. (1976). *The Bathroom.* New York: Viking Press.

Little, K. B. (1965). Personal space. *Journal of Experimental Social Psychology*, 1(3), 237–247.

Marquart, J. W., & Crouch, B. M. (1985). Judicial reform and prisoner control: The impact of *Ruiz* v. *Estelle* on a Texas penitentiary. *Law & Society Review*, 19, 557.

Moore, E. O. (1980). A prison environment: Its effect on healthcare utilization. *Dissertation Abstracts International*, 41(2), 437.

Nelson, W. R. (1988). The origins of direct supervision: An eyewitness account. *American Jail, Spring*, 8–14.

Nijman, H. L., Campo, J., Ravell, D., & Merckelbach, H. (1999). A tentative model of aggression on inpatient psychiatric wards. *Psychiatric Services*, 50(6), 832–834.

O'Neal, E. C., Brunault, M. A., Marquis, J. F., & Carifio, M. (1979). Anger and the body-buffer zone. *Journal of Social Psychology*, 108, 135–136.

O'Neal, E. C., Caldwell, C., & Gallup, G. G. (1977). Territorial invasion and aggression in young children. *Environmental Psychology & Nonverbal Behavior*, 2(1), 14–25.

Painter, S. (1991). Personal space and privacy: Implications for correctional institutions. *Forum on Corrections Research*, 3(2), 21–26.

Paluck, R. J., & Esser, A. (1971). Controlled experimental modification of aggressive behavior in territories of severely retarded boys. *American Journal of Mental Deficiency*, 76(1), 23–29.

Paslawskyj, L., & Ivinskis, A. (1980). Dominance, agonistic and territorial behaviour in institutionalized mentally retarded patients. *Australian Journal of Developmental Disabilities*, 6(1), 17–24.

Patterson, A. (1975). Personal space – Time to burst the bubble? *Man-Environment Systems*, 5, 67.

Paulus, P. B. (1988). *Prison Crowding: A Psychological Perspective (Research in Criminology).* New York: Springer-Verlag.

Pederson, D. (1999). Model for types of privacy by privacy functions. *Journal of Environmental Psychology*, 18(4), 397–405.

Rago Jr., W. V. (1978). Stability of territorial and aggressive behavior in profoundly mentally retarded institutionalized male adults. *American Journal of Mental Deficiency*, 82(5), 494–498.

Roger, D. B., & Schalekamp, E. E. (1976). Body-buffer zone and violence: a cross-cultural study. *Journal of Social Psychology*, 98, 153–158.

Roth, L. H. (1971). Territoriality and homosexuality in a male prison population. *American Journal of Orthopsychiatry*, 41(3), 510–513.

Rubinstein, E. S. (1975). *Body Buffer Zones in Female Prisoners.* University Microfilms International.

Ryden, M. B., Bossenmaier, M., & McLachlan, C. (1991). Aggressive behavior in cognitively impaired nursing home residents. *Research in Nursing & Health*, 14(2), 87–95.

Semple, J. (1993). *Bentham's Prison: A Study of the Panopticon Penitentiary*. New York: Oxford University Press, USA.

Smith, D. E. (1982). Privacy and corrections: A reexamination. *American Journal of Community Psychology*, 10(2), 207.

Sommer, R. (1969). *Personal Space: The behavioral basis of design*. Englewood Cliffs, NJ: Prentice-Hall, Inc.

Sossin, K. M., Esser, A. H., & Deutsch, R. D. (1978). Ethological studies of spatial and dominance behavior of female adolescents in residence. *Man-Environment Systems*, 8(1), 43–48.

Stratton, L. O., & Horowitz, M. J. (1972). Body buffer zone: A longitudinal method for assessing approach distances and patterns of psychiatric patients. *Journal of Clinical Psychology*, 28(1), 84–86.

Sundstrom, E., & Altman, I. (1972). *Relationships Between Dominance and Territorial Behavior: Field Study in a Youth Rehabilitation Setting – Technical Report* (Grant No. 70-065-PG-21). Washington, DC: Law Enforcement Assistance Administration.

Van den Berghe, P. L. (1974). Bringing beasts back in: Toward a biosocial theory of aggression. *American Sociological Review*, 39(6), 777–788.

Vinsel, A., Brown, B. B., Altman, I., & Foss, C. (1980). Privacy regulation, territorial displays, and effectiveness of individual functioning. *Journal of Personality and Social Psychology*, 39(6), 1104–1115.

Walkey, F. H., & Gilmour, D. R. (1984). The relationship between interpersonal distance and violence in imprisoned offenders. *Criminal Justice & Behavior*, 11(3), 331–340.

Wener, R. E., & Olsen, R. (1980). Innovative correctional environments: A user assessment. *Environment & Behavior*, 12(4), 478–493.

Westin, A. (1967). *Privacy and Freedom*. New York: Atheneum.

Wilds, C. E. (1973). Evaluation of a method of predicting violence in offenders. *Criminology*, 11, 427–436.

Wolfe, M., & Golan, M. B. P. (1976). Privacy and Institutionalization. *EDRA 7*. Vancouver, BC.

Wouterloot, L. (1995). At Home in Prison. *Mediamatic*, 8(2,3). Retrieved from http://www.mediamatic.net/5919/en/at-home-in-prison.

Zeisel, J., Silverstein, N. M., Hyde, J., Levkoff, S., Lawton, M. P., & Holmes, W. (2003). Environmental correlates to behavioral health: Outcomes in Alzheimer's special care units. *The Gerontologist*, 43(5), 697–711.

Zimring, C., Weitzer, W., & Knight, R. C. (1982). Opportunity for control and the designed environment: The case of an institution for the developmentally disabled. In A. Baum & J. Singer (Eds.), *Advances in environmental psychology, Volume 4: Environment and Health* (Vol. 4, pp. 171–210). Hillside, NJ: Lawrence Erlbaum.

7

Prison Crowding

WHY IS CROWDING IN PRISON AN ISSUE?

Probably more has been written about crowding than any other environmental issue affecting prisons. Many authors presume that the negative impacts of prison crowding are important, demonstrated, and obvious. Haney (2006), for instance, suggests that "the overcrowding that has plagued our nations prison system has changed the nature of imprisonment, altered correctional norms, placed the well-being of many prisoners and correctional staff in jeopardy, and contributed little or nothing to the worthy goal of reducing crime rates" (p. 293). Others are more skeptical and suggest that crowding impacts have not been well demonstrated by empirical research (Gaes, 1991).

The attention paid to crowding is not surprising given that prison population levels almost always seem to be on the rise towards and past capacity, and that administrators often complain that increased populations are a problem for safe and effective prison management. The social, political, legal, and bureaucratic forces that push for increasing the numbers of people in detention have always been stronger and more enduring than those that work toward lessening rates of incarceration, or that act to provide adequate levels of resources for those who are incarcerated. Events that push large numbers of people into lower social and economic strata, and/or increase levels of social disorganization, such as the end of slavery, returning soldiers after wars, surges in immigration, or increased use of drugs like crack cocaine, tend to increase crime, arrests, and, in turn, the number of people in jails and prisons.

The reality is, then, that prison populations tend to rise faster than the general population or than the number of available institutional beds, and that overcrowding and the inability to provide services (such as educational programs) are the constant companion of most correctional systems

(Blumstein & Beck, 1999). Certainly the recent history of corrections in the United States is one of regular and expensive spurts of construction that serve as (usually unsuccessful) attempts to catch up to burgeoning levels of jail and prison populations (see Chapter 2, "Historical View"). Recent reviews suggest that, though not universal, rapid increases in prison populations are seen as problematic in many countries and are widely viewed as having negative economic and social consequences (Buckley, 2001; Cabral, 1991; Cabral & Stangenhaus, 1992; Cui, 2007; *Commentary: The H.M. Northward Prison Report – The Reception of Inmates*, 2001; Hill, 2001).

Prison population growth kills thoughtful programs. There are many examples in the history of American corrections in which facilities created to support specific innovative operational or programmatic concepts were stifled by a population that grew well beyond the capacity for which it was designed. One classic example was the prison colony at Norfolk, Massachusetts, started by Howard Gill in 1927. Gill implemented many innovative classification and treatment approaches, but the new policies were overwhelmed by the admission of a large number of inmates, and in particular, inmates who did not fit the profile that the prison was designed to address (Rotman, 1995). The federal Metropolitan Correctional Centers are not immune to this trend. They were created with the specific intent of providing private rooms for each inmate (see Chapter 5, "Effectiveness of Direct Supervision Models"). Within a few years of opening, however, many or most rooms had double bunks (Davis, 1990; Wener & Keys, 1988). More recent direct supervision jails have been built on the assumption of two inmates per room. It may be that direct supervision as a philosophy and system has survived and flourished for more than three decades because it seems to handle crowding better than other approaches, as is discussed in detail in this chapter.

Prison officials have to deal regularly with the impacts of overcrowding, and it is not uncommon to see journalistic or other anecdotal accounts that blame crowding for disturbances and even riots (Barnes, 2003; Buckley, 2001; Firestone, 2001; Lieber, 1981; Stevens, 1986). Recent crowding in prisons is, in part, a function of changes in the demographics of the larger society. Prison growth in the United States had its largest jumps during the period when the huge post-war baby-boom cohort reached their teen years, an age when young males are more likely to commit crimes (Blumstein & Beck, 1999). Prison population growth, though, can also be a function of social policy. For example, prison populations have grown precipitously in the United States in the past several decades because of laws that created stiff and often mandatory penalties for drug possession and sale, such as "the three strikes and you're out" and the Rockefeller drug laws (DiIulio, 1999).

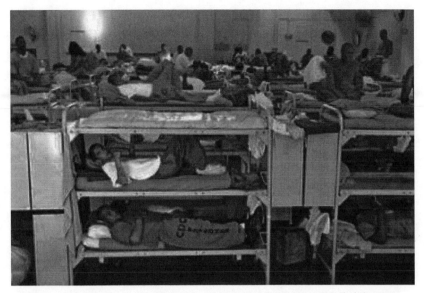

FIGURE 29. Courtesy of California Department of Corrections & Rehabilitation

In this chapter I review basic terms, definitions, and meanings of crowding for correctional as well as research settings; discuss research approaches to studying crowding in these settings; compare conceptual models of psychological responses to human crowding; and review research findings and their implications for institutional life and management.

WHAT PRISON CROWDING MEANS

When policy makers and researchers talk about prison crowding, they are not always speaking about the same thing. Specifically, two different conditions have been called *crowding* in correctional literature. The first addresses population levels that rise above the intentions of managers and the planned, rated, and designed capacity of institutions. This is crowding in the classic sense – an institution designed and rated to hold 500 inmates, for instance, finds itself with a population of 800 or more, almost inevitably causing double- or triple-bunking in cells.

As prison populations increase beyond designed and planned levels, the increase in density affects settings on both the macro scale (number of inmates to clothe, feed, treat medically, enter programs, run through intake and release, classify, and place in the correct housing unit) and the micro scale (number of people sharing cells, using showers, waiting for telephones, standing in line

FIGURE 30. Courtesy of California Department of Corrections & Rehabilitation

for meals, and so on). Increased density affects the immediate experiences of inmates when they use institutional living spaces, as well as the balance of resources available to people in all parts of the institution. It affects staffing levels, the ability to provide programs and services (such as counseling and training), and the adequacy of space for visiting, recreation, and education.

The second use of *crowding* with regard to prisons and jails is seen in studies that make comparisons among situations in which cell sizes and/or the number of inmates per cell vary, even though they may fit the intended design and use. Researchers interested in the impact of varying social or spatial densities, for example, might focus on and make comparisons of inmate responses in units that have single, double, triple, or dormitory living spaces – even if they do not exceed planned or rated capacity.[1]

These two situations may yield conditions that appear objectively the same – comparing one, two, or three inmates in a room, for instance – but treating them as the same fails to take into account the context in which these conditions exist and the level of stress for the overall institution. For instance, in institutions operating at designed and rated capacity, there is a far greater chance that other resources have been scaled to meet the needs of the population, from staffing levels to the size of the dayroom and the size and distribution of program spaces. Institutions operating well above planned levels are much more likely to have serious shortages of a broad variety of spatial and other resources.

Crowding Terms

Several concepts that come from crowding research in other kinds of settings are useful and potentially instructive. For instance, a distinction is often made between density and crowding. *Density* describes the physical phenomenon of people and units of space (such as people per room or square feet per person), whereas *crowding* refers to the related experiential state ("feeling crowded") (Stokols, 1972). High density is seen as a necessary, but not sufficient, condition for the experience of crowding. This implies, of course, that other elements related to the context of the density can have an effect on perceived crowding. Perceived crowding might be affected, for instance, by whom one is with in a room, not just how many, and by the ability to exit that room when desired.

Further distinctions have been made between "social density" and "spatial density" (see Baum & Paulus, 1987). Although these terms are somewhat artificial, arising from the nature of laboratory manipulations, they have relevance for real-world situations, including total institutions. *Social density* is usually used to refer to the number of individuals per unit space. In a laboratory study, a researcher might increase the absolute number of people in a room while holding the space per person constant, for example, doubling the number of people in a room while increasing room size so that the number of square feet per person remains the same. *Spatial density*, by contrast, refers specifically to the amount of space per person. Increasing this kind of density means restricting space, making the room smaller, while leaving number of people in the room constant. The issue is, most simply put, between difficulties caused by having to interact with increasing numbers of people versus the problems caused by having to interact with people in a very constricted space.

Research in laboratories and various settings has generally shown that, although high densities of both kinds can be problematic, increases of social density are more likely to be especially aversive and have important behavioral consequences, particularly as they relate to aggressive behaviors (Baum & Paulus, 1987). Constricting space can affect one's ability to engage in activities, but adding to the number of people in the immediate proximity causes an important increase in the amount, kinds, and quality of social interactions, situations, group relations, and possible conflicts.

Some studies of crowding in prisons have misused or at least altered the meanings of *social* and *spatial density*. For instance, some prison researchers have used *social density* to mean the percentage of people in dormitories versus single rooms, without presenting information on the relative differences in the amount of space per person in each. For this discussion we will refer specifically to the independent variables themselves to reduce confusion among definitions. These variables are of two sorts – those that address the number of inmates in rooms (particularly bedrooms or cells) and those that address the number of inmates in the institution as a whole. There are exceptions, of course, with some studies referring to living unit size rather than or in addition to institution size.

Others have distinguished between the concepts of *inside* and *outside density*. These terms originally appeared in large-scale correlational studies, usually carried out using census data, which attempted to determine if there was a connection between urban density and problems such as crime and delinquency. *Outside density* refers to the density of people per large-scale measurement of space (people per acre, per square mile or kilometer, for instance), whereas *inside density* denotes the number of people per room or apartment. It is not hard to see the potential connection of these terms to situations in prisons and jails. For instance, *outside density* might be viewed as analogous to living unit size or the level of the overall institutional population, whereas *inside density* could refer to the number of inmates in a cell. Research has generally found that inside density is a more powerful predictor of outcome measures than outside density (Baum & Paulus, 1987).

APPROACHES TO THE STUDY OF PRISON CROWDING

It is against this background that I consider studies that have addressed various kinds of high-density situations in prisons. Correctional crowding has been studied for many different reasons. In some cases, social and environmental psychologists, like Paulus and his colleagues at the University of Texas, turned to prisons as research settings because they recognized that issues of ecological validity limited the usefulness of university laboratory research on crowding. They saw prisons, in effect, as the best possible laboratory for understanding the effects of crowding on humans (Paulus, 1988). Conditions in prisons directly addressed all of the restrictions experienced by psychologists in other settings.

Exposure to a crowded situation could be measured only in minutes in laboratories, whereas people in prisons are exposed regularly to high densities for days, weeks, months, or even years. Also, ethical standards severely limit manipulation of levels of volition and control over exposure that are available to laboratory subjects. Students can leave if the level of stress is too high or if the situation is too uncomfortable. Prisons are, by definition, involuntary settings in which inmates have no such options. Naturally occurring levels of long-term, involuntary, high density make prisons attractive options for research and theory development. Ethical standards are not breached where the researcher does not create or prolong the condition. If there is a common human condition that can approximate the living conditions of rats in Calhoun's famous behavioral sink (Calhoun, 1962), it is most likely to be found in prisons.

The Civil Rights Division of the U.S. Department of Justice was actively involved in prison litigation addressing a variety of prison conditions, including racial integration as well as crowding (Trulson & Marquart, 2002). As a result, it supported research (like that of Paulus and his colleagues) that might provide objective assessments of conditions. Other prison crowding research, however, originated from the very different perspective of correctional bureaucracies and administrators who long considered crowding to be a problematic condition that leads to violence and even riots (*Commentary: The H.M. Northward Prison Report – The Reception of Inmates*, 2001; Cooke, 1992; Dillingham & Montgomery Jr., 1983; "Woolf warns of prison riot risk to staff and agencies," 2002). Administrators are interested in finding ways to predict and ameliorate conditions that can lead to disturbances. Some research (such as that sponsored by the Federal Bureau of Prisons in the 1970s) had as its major focus, then, to understand the impact of crowding on institutional operations.

These differences can go to the heart of what is important and worth observing. For instance, a social psychologist might be interested in discovering whether and why double or dormitory rooms cause more stress and behavioral change than do single rooms. Research funded by the institution, on the other hand, may consider inmate stress or discomfort to be of lesser importance and focus instead on other issues. Gaes (1991) and Ruback and Innes (1988), for instance, have suggested that social psychologists have focused too much on individual inmate responses and not paid enough attention to the issues that administrators see as important. For them, the threshold of concern may include the much higher bar set by court interpretation of constitutional protections against cruel and unusual punishment, or broad institutional and organizational impacts such as disruption, violence, program effectiveness and efficiency, as well as operating costs. Somewhere between may come the auditing and standard setting agencies charged with identifying the minimal or ideal conditions that institutions should provide for good, safe, and efficient operations.

CONCEPTUAL MODELS

A number of conceptual models have been suggested to explain the impact of high density on human behavior (Baum & Paulus, 1987), some of which are relevant to the prison situation. These range from perspectives that focus on conditions affecting levels of personal space (Hall, 1959; Knowles & Bassett, 1976; Sommer, 1969) to ones addressing privacy, such as Altman's model (1981) discussed in Chapter 6. For Altman, choice and control is critical. Feelings of crowding exist when the individual is exposed to more social interaction than desired.

Crowding has also been viewed as resulting from an overload of stimuli bombarding the senses. This view presumes that individuals have a limited cognitive and attentional capacity for dealing with information. When that capacity is reached or exceeded, individuals react adaptively by selectively tuning out stimuli, and by feeling overloaded and crowded (Milgram, 1970). Although overload could be a response to any stimuli, some writers have focused on the special impact of social overload. Saegert, for instance, suggested that social stimuli were a special case and that inundation with excessive, unwanted, and unpredictable social interactions led to stress and discomfort (Langer & Saegert, 1977; Saegert, 1975). This model received support from the dormitory studies of Baum and Valins (1977), which found that living arrangements that increased resident options for control over contact with many others reduced perceived crowding, even without changing actual living density.

Another approach, drawn more directly from social psychological research, is the cognitive neo-association model, based in part on attribution theory, suggested by Lawrence and Andrews (2004). They propose that, under conditions of increased crowding, individuals are likely to attribute negative responses to the presence of others, see others as hostile, and interpret their behavior and intent as hostile, increasing the likelihood of aggressive reactions.

Paulus (1988) has offered an integrated social interaction–demand model. Crowding has, he says, its "primary impact through its influence on social interaction" (p. 78) rather than by direct effect on individual perception of the situation. Even though crowding can come about in a variety of ways, the level of uncertainty, the amount of cognitive load produced, and the degree with which it interferes in reaching goals are critical in determining how crowded an individual will feel. In this perspective, social density is a more powerful predictor of crowding than spatial density because of the increased unpredictability produced by interactions with others. Merely having less space may be uncomfortable, but it does not inherently change the dynamics of the social situation or the level of uncertainty, unpredictability, goal blocking, and so on. This model also supports the notion that turnover can be an important element in producing crowding and stress, because of the increase in unpredictability that results when less familiar people enter the setting, as demonstrated by Sundstrom and Altman (1972).

Ecological models of crowding (Wicker, Kirmeyer, Hanson, & Alexander, 1976) may also be relevant for the prison situation, but have received comparatively little attention. In this case, the absolute number of people or amount of space is less critical than the balance of people and resources, suggesting a tipping point where too many people throw a system out of balance. This notion also relates to a classic ecological finding that scarcity breeds competition, which increases the likelihood of aggression (Mesquida & Weiner, 1996). For prisons and jails, this can include the balance of staffing resources (staff–inmate ratio), as well as the relative scarcity of other resources (telephones, televisions, food, and so on). Haney (2006), for instance, responded to resource scarcity in noting that there are fewer medical screenings in crowded prisons and that "many prisons systems have increased their rated 'capacity' ... without commensurate increase in programming, medical and mental health resources" (p. 266).

LEVELS OF ANALYSIS

As Gaes (1994) has said, different levels of analysis are relevant to an assessment of the impact of prison crowding, which can affect research methods, presumed causal factors, outcome measures, and the statistical techniques used in studies. Micro-level studies focus on the individual response to environmental conditions. Such studies view the crowding phenomenon as part of the province of social and environmental psychology and environmental cognition. They are largely concerned with how factors relating to social and spatial density bear on the individual's experience in that setting. Conceptual models that apply include those that emphasize personal space or that stress the impacts of interpersonal interactions – such as overstimulation and social overload and social interaction–demand models (Baum & Paulus, 1987). These models address the way in which the individual perceives, interacts with, and responds to the others around him or her and what the negative impact may be of that experience. The research literature on crowding, and broader studies of environmental stress in general, have often cited predictability and perceived control as predictors and mediators of stress (Evans, 1982).

Such studies gather data to address responses at the individual level to social or spatial density variations. Measures that have been used include inmate perceptions of the situation, level of felt crowding, stress, mood, motivation, discomfort, and predictability and control. They also involve psychological and physiological measures of stress effects and health, including blood pressure, stress hormones (such as cortisol, catecholamine), and symptom checklists (see Paulus, 1988; Ray, Wandersman, Ellisor, & Huntington, 1982; Ruback, Carr, & Hopper, 1986, among others). Crowding studies have also looked at inmate behavior and, in some cases, related these to archival measures of presumed responses to stress, such as levels of sickness complaints (Wener & Keys, 1988).

Another approach looks at macro-scale issues addressing the impacts of density on the broader institutional environment. In this case, the critical unit of analysis is the institution rather than the individual. For this kind of study, a broader ecological model that stresses person–system interactions and balances of resources to population may be more appropriate. Data collection in these studies is large scale (often analyzing data that cover whole institutions or many institutions at one time) and therefore necessarily eschew direct measurement of individuals in favor of analysis of information from archival sources. Independent variables in these studies are likely to be mined from existing data sets, such as overall institution size; living unit size; the balance and ratio of staff to inmates; the percentage of inmates in rooms of various sizes (singles, doubles, dorms, and so on); the balance of various kinds of key resources to the number of inmates, including space and materials; and the availability of programs and classes. Dependent variables typically include institutional rates of incidents, disturbances, violent acts, recidivism, sickness, psychiatric commitments, and deaths (such as Farrington & Nuttall, 1985; Gaes, 1994; Tartaro, 2002).

Measurements of the density of inmates per institution usually take several forms, so that the measure is less a reflection of large versus small facilities and instead reflects overpopulation, such as the ratio of average daily population levels to the rated capacity. All of these measures have potential drawbacks, however, no matter how careful the investigator. Rated capacity, for instance, does not necessarily reflect the original design capacity of the institution, or even general agreement of administrators on the optimal maximum population. For example, when bunks are added to rooms to turn single rooms into doubles, the rated capacity of the setting may be changed to reflect this new arrangement, making it "legal." In this respect, cross-sectional studies are more problematic than longitudinal ones, which at least have the advantage of observing response to changes in density in the same setting.

STUDIES ADDRESSING CROWDING IN PRISON
AT THE MICRO SCALE

Some studies have looked at the effects of prison crowding on individuals, largely using direct measurement from interviews, survey instruments, and psychophysiological measurements. Most of these studies made comparisons between or among inmates living in single cells, doubles, triples, multiple cells, and/or dormitories (which are usually large areas in which ten or more inmates share space). Several studies have also found significant effects of the amount of space provided to inmates (Cox, Paulus, McCain, & Schkade, 1979; McCain, Cox, & Paulus, 1976; McCain, Cox, & Paulus, 1980; Paulus, Cox, McCain, & Chandler, 1975; Paulus, McCain, & Cox, 1978). In general, these studies have supported the conclusion that increased density has significant negative effects. The most consistent result has been that the number of inmates per cell has been the best predictor of negative responses.

The most significant source of information about the impacts of variation in room densities on individual inmates comes from the research program conducted by Paulus, McCain, and Cox (1978). These studies are important because of the scale of the work (dozens of institutions over many years); their methodological care, effort, and rigor in the selection of inmates; their careful measurement of independent variables (distinguishing social and spatial density, for instance) and the dependent variables (using a variety of experiential, psychophysiological, and archival measures); their focus on issues of conceptual importance; and the consistency of their results. Even so, this body of work has not gone without critique (see Bonta & Gendreau, 1993; Gaes, 1985; Ruback & Innes, 1988).

Although the results of such a large research program are hard to summarize briefly (see Paulus, 1988, for a detailed discussion of their research), there have been some remarkably consistent findings. They have found that increasing the number of inmates per room generally worsens the quality of the rating inmates give to their environment, as well as perceived crowding, tolerance for crowding over time, perceived control, ratings of stress and psychophysiological measures of stress (such as blood pressure and catecholamines), the number of inmates seeking or getting medical services, and the level of reported incidents. In general, the amount of space per person was not a strong predictor of these effects.

More specifically, the most powerful effects came from comparisons of open dormitories with single rooms. Dormitories typically had more perceived crowding and higher levels of reported illness complaints. Inmates there experienced more negative moods. In many respects, double rooms also rated more poorly than single rooms, although mostly on the experiential measures and not on the illness complaints. In some cases and in some facilities, even when inmates indicated a preference for dormitories, the rating on crowding and stress scales was worse in dormitories.

Not all dormitories were the same, however. Their data showed surprisingly positive responses from inmates in dormitories that had larger spaces, single beds (as opposed to double bunk beds), and partitions (usually less than 6 feet high) segmenting them into cubicles, providing multiple differentiated spaces. These partitioned dorms were rated better than regular dormitories and performed almost as well as single rooms on most measures of inmate psychological and psychophysiological responses, although not on measures of illness complaints (Paulus, 1988).

Even though the data from Paulus, McCain, and Cox are the most comprehensive, other studies support some of these findings. Research has compared inmates living in single and multiple bed rooms, for instance, and found that the increased number of inmates in a room was related to increased escapes (Bruehl, Horvat, & George, 1979, cited in Paulus) and recidivism (Farrington & Nuttall, 1985). D'Atri and Ostfield (1975) conducted a particularly notable study because they were able obtain longitudinal data. Blood pressure was obtained from inmates in single rooms, after the same inmates were transferred to dormitory spaces, and, in some cases, after a return back to single rooms. They observed that blood pressure increased after the move to the dormitory and then decreased upon return to the single room. In a study that looked at space available per inmate, Megargee (1976) found that infractions increased as space decreased.

Two other studies collected longitudinal data on density changes. Ray, Wandersman, Ellisor, and Huntington (1982) looked at changes in the population in two dormitories of a juvenile facility. They obtained self-report and blood pressure data at three points in time over a 6-month period during which the population levels of the dorms varied widely. They found that blood pressure correlated highly with density, and reported that students who were leaders and doing the best in school were the most adversely affected. Illness complaints also increased in the higher density, but only for the dorm that housed the clinic. Hostility and expression of anger also increased with the rise in density. The social climate of the facility declined as density increased, with a greater sense of disorganization, and more hostility and disruption of treatment programs.

We were able to observe changes in two living areas that experienced relatively small changes in population levels (Wener & Keys, 1988). One unit saw an increase in the number of inmates, and the other had a concomitant decline. The two living units were, in fact, closely connected – they were on the same floor, were physically identical, and were run by the same team of managers and officers, and the inmates were randomly assigned to one unit or the other. When the population level first exceeded capacity, the administration chose to place the entire overflow on one of the units, leaving the other at the designed capacity. Later, by court order,[2] the population was leveled between the two units.

We found that perceived crowding and sick-call rates increased as populations levels increased and fell as populations fell. We also noted, however, a contrast effect – that these measures responded, to some degree, to the previous condition. That is, identical population levels in the two units were rated differently, depending on whether the previous condition was one of higher or lower density. Where the density had gone from sixty-four inmates per unit to fifty-six, crowding rating levels were lower than where density had changed from forty-eight inmates to fifty-six. Sick-call levels showed a similar pattern. Inmates were responding to whether conditions improved or got worse, as much as to the absolute density levels.

Other studies found that increased density led to reduced perception of safety among inmates (Roush, 1989). Increased perceived crowding was also related to greater perception of hostile intention of others (Lawrence & Andrew, 2004). In addition, administrators felt that crowding hurt the level of security they were able to provide (Kinkade, Leone, & Semond, 1995).

MACRO-SCALE STUDIES

Studies that have looked at the impact of crowding at the broader, macro level of overall institution size and density have had mixed results. Data sources in these studies are almost always archival. Even though use of these archival sources is necessary given the scale and focus of these studies, it also can be problematic because potential differences among living units, institutions, managers, or management systems can be covered over, as can differences in the quality and care with which institutions collect and archive their data. In general, these measures of density and outcomes tend to be less sensitive and more global (Paulus, 1988).

Overall, there is less clear support in these macro-scale studies for concluding that increased density leads to negative effects, although several suggest a significant impact of density, including studies conducted by BOP researchers who looked at very large data sets representing many institutions in the federal system. For example, Nacci, Teitelbaum, and Prather (1977), in a cross-sectional survey of federal institutions, found that increased institutional density was related to increased assault rates, although the relation was most significant for young inmates. Older inmates, they said, were more likely to withdraw under crowding pressure. Gaes (1985), taking a cross-sectional look at the federal system, also found a positive correlation between increased institution population and violence. Both crowding levels and the proportion of the population that resided in dormitories predicted assault rates.

A study by Jan (1980) is of note because it is one of the few to measure the changes in positive behaviors of the institution (such as program utilization) as well as negative behaviors (such as incidents). He found an increase of negative behaviors as population levels increased, but the increase was no larger than the growth of the population itself. There was, however, a significant decline in positive functions, such as class attendance, graduation from school and programs, and achieving parole as density levels increased. Jan also found that the strongest effects of crowding were on young inmates. Other studies also showed crowding effects only for some populations such as young (Ruback, Carr, & Hopper, 1986) or black inmates (Clayton & Carr, 1987).

Several studies had mixed effects in that density did not clearly predict negative events. Pellissier (1991) reported no significant increases in assaults, even after a rapid doubling of population in a federal prison, which he attributed to care taken to maintain programs. Sechrest (1989) found a positive relationship between density (actual population versus rated capacity) and assaults, but only for male inmates. Sechrest (1991) also reported relationships between density and assaults that were not simple or linear. Assaults increased as density did, but they were highest at levels somewhat below rated capacity. When population exceeded rated capacity, he found, assault rates declined. He suggested that other issues (such as classification and management) may be as or more important in these outcomes as density. Wooldredge and Winfree (1992) found that the suicide rate declined as crowding decreased, and that this was connected most importantly to improved staff–inmate ratios and the implementation of suicide prevention programs. Ekland-Olson (1986) reported that density was positively related to assault rates but negatively related to homicides, and suggested that violent acts were more related to other issues concerning the design of the institution and the nature of the population than to the level of crowding.

Clayton and Carr (1987) also found a relationship between density and recidivism, although Gaes (1994) suggests that this might be a spurious effect related to early release policies during times of overcrowding. Unlike Wooldredge and Winfree (1992), Fruehwald, Frottier, Ritter, Eher, and Gutier-rez (2002) noted a decline in suicides with increased density and suggested that this was because there were reduced opportunities for suicides when inmates were no longer alone in single cells. Huey and McNulty (2005) found that when overcrowded, minimum security institutions saw suicides increase to the levels of medium and maximum security sites.

Porporino and Dudley (1984) and Innes (1986) saw no relationship between density and violence, whereas Tartaro (2002) reported that violence decreased with crowding, as defined as an increase in the ratio of actual daily population to the rated capacity of the institution, although there was no correlation with the number of inmates in a cell. She suggested this might be due to a feedback loop in which staff members focus more attention on inmate behavior when crowding levels grow. Franklin, Franklin, and Pratt (2006) conducted a meta-analysis of institution-level studies, noting that a significant number of studies had, counterintuitively, found positive changes (declines) in misconduct reports as crowding increased. Some researchers suggest that this is because institutions develop tighter controls and pay more attention to operational details under crowded conditions. Their analysis concluded that there were no significant effects of institutional crowding on misconduct rates overall, even though for younger inmates crowding did lead to significantly higher levels of misconduct.

ADAPTATION TO DENSITY

Some have also asked about the issue of adaptation to density. That is, does the response to density change or modulate over time? Research on other stressors, such as noise, indicates that people often adapt rapidly to exposure to noise in laboratories (that is, the negative response abates over time) but less so to exposure outside the laboratory, such as community responses to airplane noises (Cohen & Weinstein, 1982). There is also evidence for adaptation to stress from temperature (Bell & Greene, 1982) and air pollution (Evans & Jacobs, 1982). In some situations, negative responses to stressors may be reduced because neurophysiological sensitivity is reduced or uncertainty lessened (Bell, Fisher, Baum, & Green, 1996).

Lessened severity of responses to crowding over time makes sense if the problems of crowding are due to heightened arousal levels or stimulus overload (Milgram, 1970). Other models, such as social overload (McCarthy & Saegert, 1978), suggest that adaptation is less likely. Paulus (1988) notes that at the start of their prison research program, his team expected to see adaptation to crowding effects over time, particularly in the form of increased tolerance for high-density situations. They found, instead, that inmates were somewhat less tolerant of high density over time, which they interpreted as increased value for privacy when living in high-density settings.

Over the course of many studies, Paulus and his colleagues concluded that adaptation did occur on some measures of inmate response. For instance, the rise in illness complaints tended to subside over time. Measures of inmate experience (such as ratings of crowding), however, do not decline. D'Atri

(1981), with the advantage of longitudinal measurements, found that systolic blood pressure declined over time for inmates in dormitories, and also saw a decline in clinic use (Ostfeld, Kasl, D'Atri, & Fitzgerald, 1987).

Gaes (1994) points out that there are alternative explanations for some of these presumed adaptation effects. For instance, reduced illness rates later in sentences could also occur if inmates enter the institution with physical problems that are addressed by the treatment they receive there. He also cautions researchers to be aware of living unit assignment bias. Inmates in some institutions may be assigned to single cells as a reward for good behavior, leaving more difficult inmates in dormitories. Of course, the opposite bias is also possible – the least troublesome and most minimal security inmates may be placed in less expensive dormitories, whereas higher-security single-room units are used for riskier, higher-security populations.

Gaes (1985) reviewed and extensively critiqued the state of prison crowding research. He noted appropriately the need to disentangle impacts on the ecological (institution or system-wide) level from those at the individual scale. The U.S. courts, he said, have used the Eighth Amendment proscription of cruel and unusual punishment to set a very high bar for judging the seriousness of crowding impacts, and an important distinction has been made between legal and psychological concepts. Like the notion of insanity, which is a legal term that serves as a backdrop against which psychologists discuss mental status, "cruel and unusual" has no psychological definition. To be fair, neither Paulus, McCain, Cox, and Chandler (1975) nor most other crowding researchers were focused on legal meanings of crowding, although some have testified as expert witnesses in court cases. Rather, they were seeking to determine as cogently as possible what the consequences of high density were for inmates, leaving it to the courts to interpret these findings against legal guidelines.

Gaes (1985) also urged researchers to look at the impact of other factors, beyond density, on inmate and organizational responses. These factors, he suggests, might, in fact, have a bigger effect than crowding on behavior and at the very least might be easier for administrators to address and ameliorate. Such an approach would be in keeping with Stokol's (1972) density-crowding distinction, which emphasized that factors other than density could have an important influence on perceived crowding, as well as with contextual approaches discussed by other environmental psychologists (see Altman, 1981). The studies by Paulus and his colleagues (1988) have addressed at least some of these issues, such as the effect of dormitory configurations on stress. Other design factors are likely to be important, such as openness, access to spaces and services, and use of direct supervision design and management systems, discussed in the next section. Age, gender, past behavior, and gang affiliation are also among the candidates for review.

Gaes (1985) also appropriately urged researchers to study the underlying mechanisms behind any crowding effects. Paulus's social interaction–demand model is a start, but for a detailed assessment of the causes of crowding effects, further research using direct assessment of inmate behavior (rather than relying on archival data) is needed. Similarly, assessments of system- and institution-wide effects are important and have the potential for improving conditions for all involved – administration, staff, and inmates.

Crowding in Direct Supervision Facilities

Direct supervision (discussed in detail in Chapters 3, 4, and 5) is an important innovation in American jails and prisons and has been adopted as the state of the art by most U.S. standards-setting bodies. It differs from traditional corrections models in relying heavily on direct contact and interaction between officer and inmates as the primary means of assuring safety and security (see Chapter 4, "The Development of Direct Supervision as a Design and Management System"). These management and design models have been unusually effective in reducing stress and violence within the institution (see Chapter 5, "Effectiveness of Direct Supervision Models").

Direct supervision institutions may be more likely to be crowded than other jails and prisons (Farbstein & Wener, 1989; Stohr, Lovrich, Menke, & Zupan, 1994; Zupan & Stohr-Gillmore, 1988), possibly because courts are less inhibited about incarcerating people in settings perceived as safe (Civil liabilities, unconstitutional jail and planning of new institutions, part I, 1997). Several reports suggest, however, that direct supervision facilities might do a better job of maintaining safety and security within the context of crowding than non-direct supervision settings (Farbstein & Wener, 1989; Sigurdson, 1985).

In a recent assessment (Bogard & Wener, 2007) we looked at different approaches to managing extreme overcrowding in three direct supervision jails. In all three cases, significant crowding was managed without overwhelming problems. But the increased population levels did result in serious changes to operating procedures. In one case, a second officer was added to the living unit. Although this may have made the staff more comfortable, it appeared to do little to increase security or safety. Another approach was to restrict half the inmates at a time to their rooms, reducing effective supervision and severely constricting inmate movement and opportunities. It was difficult to find examples of jails that responded to crowding in the way we thought might be most effective, by increasing programming options.

CONCLUSIONS

As with many issues in real and complicated settings, the relationship between crowding and behavior in a prison or jail setting is not simple. Studies have not always found a relationship between crowding, as defined by the degree to which the population is over the built or rated capacity, with rates of incidents or disturbances. There are several possible explanations for this lack of a positive finding. Of course, one could argue that it shows that overcrowding – such as adding a second or third person to a cell or increasing the overall institution population by 20 or 30 percent or more – is not a critical factor in institutional life. This seems an unlikely explanation, though, given the data from individual-scale studies, anecdotal experience of administrators, crowding research in other settings, and logic suggesting that increased tension, goal frustration, and competition for tight resources will be problematic. Stress seems likely to follow when people are placed in tight quarters with others who have a greater than average propensity for unpredictable and violent behavior, in a setting that allows few options to withdraw or avoid contact. Density in jails and prisons can be, at times, extremely high and certainly higher than humans normally experience in any other setting for significant durations.

Alternatively, one might argue that crowding is problematic but that people adapt to it over time. There is, however, little evidence for such adaption, and some data and theory that argues otherwise. Another explanation is that the effect of density in prisons may be a step function rather than operating as a continuous function. That is, there may be critical threshold levels of density and overcrowding that trigger problems.

A more likely explanation is that the impact of crowding is muted by institutional responses. As some authors have noted (Franklin et al., 1998; Gaes & McGuire, 1985; Tartaro, 2002), institutions do not remain static in the face of problems. Even though people do not seem to adapt well to crowding, institutions may. Institutions are dynamic systems that should and do change operations subtly or broadly in response to conditions. Some parts of the system may adjust automatically, as in the way staff members will take extra precautions in a more tense setting. Any good manager is likely to make adjustments of policy and staffing to meet new challenges, such as increased density. The use of additional officers, additional programs, and additional attention may help to counter the effects of overcrowding, though we (Bogard & Wener, 2007) found few jails that responded to crowding by increasing programs and resources to meet the increased need and head off problems.

Even when these interventions work to reduce overt acts of aggression, the overcrowding may still take its toll. Several studies suggest that suicide may be related to staff–inmate ratios. Putting more officers on an inmate living unit, though, may not be the most effective counter to increased population. Whether there are one or two officers for seventy inmates, for instance, each officer will have seventy inmates to get to know and understand, to react to, and to be responsible for. Some duties can be split up but the overall scale of the setting is still the same.

Haney (2006) comments that the trend toward increasingly high densities in jails and prisons has led to ever more difficult and oppressive institutional environments, which have important negative effects on inmates, even if these effects are not reflected in higher misconduct rates. Double-celling, he points out, was once the temporary exception, used in a crunch. Now it is the accepted standard. Because of crowding, he indicates, inmates are less well classified and placed within institutions, have less opportunity to be adequately diagnosed and treated for physical and mental problems, and experience reduced chances of exposure to helpful educational or training programs.

The evidence from research and much experience is that, in the end, crowding resulting in more inmates per cell will increase stress, tension, and the likelihood of negative and aggressive behavior, especially among those inmates with the poorest impulse control and most aggressive tendencies – younger prisoners. Responses of the institution to attenuate these effects can be expensive and draining. Even where misconduct rates don't rise, one might expect to see evidence of effects on the physical setting (wear and tear), programs (loss of smooth and efficient operation), and people (burnout and turnover). Although organizational adaptations to crowding can be effective, crowding will still likely reduce access to medical services (Kupers, 2005), and program success (Jan, 1980). It is still likely to reduce the ability of a facility to have a positive impact on recidivism through educational, therapeutic, or training programs.

References

Altman, I. (1981). *Environment and Social Behavior: Privacy, Personal Space, Territory and Crowding*. New York: Irvington Press.

Barnes, S. (Oct. 3, 2003). National briefing Southwest: Arizona: Plan to fight prison crowding. *The New York Times*, p. A24.

Baum, A., & Paulus, P. (1987). Crowding. In D. Stokols & I. Altman (Eds.), *Handbook of Environmental Psychology* (pp. 533–570). New York: Wiley.

Baum, A., Singer, J. E., & Valins, S. (Eds.), *Advances in Environmental Psychology*. Hillsdale, NJ: Erlbaum.

Baum, A., & Valins, S. (1977). *Architecture and Social Behavior: Psychological Studies of Density*. Hillsdale, NJ: Lawrence Erlbaum Associates.

Bell v. Wolfish, 441 U.S. 520 (U.S. Supreme Court 1979).

Bell, P., & Greene, T. (1982). Thermal stress: Physiological, comfort, performance, and social effects of hot and cold environments. In G. Evans (Ed.), *Environmental Stress* (pp. 75–104). New York: Cambridge University Press.

Bell, P., Fisher, J., Baum, A., & Green, T. (1996). *Environmental Psychology* (4th ed.). Ft. Worth, TX: Holt, Rinehart & Winston.

Blumstein, A., & Beck, A., J. (1999). Population growth in U.S. prisons, 1980–1996. In M. Tonry & J. Petersilia (Eds.), *Prisons* (Vol. 26, pp. 17–62). Chicago: University of Chicago Press.

Bogard, D., & Wener, R. E. (2007). *Assessment of Strategies Used to Manage Crowding in Direct Supervision Jails*. Washington, DC: National Institute of Corrections Jail Center.

Bonta, J., & Gendreau, P. (1993). Commentary on Paulus and Dzindolet: Models of the effects of prison life. *Criminal Justice and Behavior, 20*(2), 167–173.

Bruehl, D., Horvat, G., & George, G. (1979). Population Density and Institutional Performance in a Treatment Unit at the Federal Correctional Institution at Terminal Island, California. Paper presented at the Academy of Criminal Justice Sciences Annual Meeting, Cincinnati, OH.

Buckley, S. (March 22, 2001). Riots point to overcrowding in Brazil's prison. *The Washington Post*, p. A23.

Cabral, M. A. (1991). Aspectos psicossociais mais relevantes de 62 historias de vida de presidiarios confinados em carceres superpopulosos. *Jornal Brasileiro de Psiquiatria, 40*(10), 515–520.

Cabral, M. A., & Stangenhaus, G. (1992). Analise da incidencia de doencas psicofisicas numa populacao de presidiarios confinados em carceres superpopulosos. *Jornal Brasileiro de Psiquiatria, 41*(2), 67–72.

Calhoun, J. B. (1962). Population density and social pathology. *Scientific American, 206*, 139–148.

Civil liabilities, unconstitutional jail and planning of new institutions, part I. (1997). *Nebraska Jail Bulletin, 135*(June–July).

Clayton, O., & Carr, T. (1987). An empirical assessment of the effects of prison crowding upon recidivism utilizing aggregate level data. *Journal of Criminal Justice, 15*, 201–210.

Cohen, S., Evans, G. W., Stokols, D., & Krantz, D. S. (1986). *Behavior, Health, and Environmental Stress*. New York: Plenum.

Cohen, S., & Weinstein, N. (1982). Nonauditory effects of noise and behavior and health. In G. Evans (Ed.), *Environmental Stress* (pp. 45–74). New York: Cambridge University Press.

Commentary: The H.M. Northward Prison Report – The Reception of Inmates. (July 2001). Cayman Net News.

Cooke, D. (1992). Prison violence: A Scottish perspective. *Forum on Corrections Research, 4*(3).

Cox, V., Paulus, P., McCain, G., & Schkade, J. (Eds.). (1979). *Field Research on the Effects of Crowding in Prisons and on Offshore Drilling Platforms*. New York: Plenum.

Cui, W. H. (2007). High prison population in Queensland, Australia: Its implications and public policy choices. *Criminology Research Focus, 213*.

D'Atri, D. A. (1981). Crowding in prison: The relationship between changes in housing mode and blood pressure. *Psychosomatic Medicine, 43*(2), 95–105.

D'Atri, D. A., & Ostfield, A. (1975). Crowding: Its effects on the elevation of blood pressure in a prison setting. *Preventive Medicine, 4*, 550–566.

Davis, R. (1990). *After All This, We Are Still Overcrowded! A Guideline for Managing the Overcrowded Facility.* Paper presented at the 5th Annual Symposium on Direct Supervision, Reno, Nevada.

DiIulio, J. (1999, March 12, 1999). *Two Million Prisoners Are Enough.* Retrieved July 6, 2004, 2004, from the World Wide Web: http://www.lplac.org/read.htm.

Dillingham, S., & Montgomery Jr., R. (1983). Prison riots: A corrections nightmare since 1774. *The Prison Journal, 63*(1), 32–46.

Ekland-Olson, S. (1986). Crowding, social control, and prison violence: Evidence from the post-Ruiz years in Texas. *Law & Society Review, 20*(3), 389–421.

Erlich, P. (1971). *The Population Bomb.* New York: Balantine Books.

Evans, G. W. (Ed.). (1982). *Environmental Stress.* New York: Cambridge University Press.

Evans, G. W., & Jacobs, T. (1982). Air pollution and human behavior. In G. W. Evans (Ed.), *Environmental Stress* (pp. 105–132). New York: Cambridge University Press.

Evans, G. W., & Wener, R. E. (2007). Crowding and personal space invasion on the train: Please don't make me sit in the middle. *Journal of Environmental Psychology, 27*(1), 90–94.

Farbstein, J., & Wener, R. E. (1989). *A Comparison of "Direct" and "Indirect" Supervision Correctional Facilities.* Washington, DC: National Institute of Corrections – Prison Division.

Farrington, D., & Nuttall, C. (1985). Prison size, overcrowding, prison violence, and recidivism. In M. Braswell, S. Dillingham, & R. Montgomery (Eds.), *Prison Violence in America* (pp. 113–132). Cincinnati, OH: Anderson Publishing Co.

Firestone, D. (2001, May 23, 2001). Alabama: prison crowding crisis. *The New York Times,* p. A12.

Franklin, T. W., Franklin, C. A., & Pratt, T. C. (2006). Examining the empirical relationship between prison crowding and inmate misconduct: A meta-analysis of conflicting research results. *Journal of Criminal Justice, 34*(4), 401–412.

Freedman, J. L. (1975). *Crowding and Behavior.* San Francisco: W.H. Freeman and Company.

Fruehwald, S., Frottier, P., Ritter, K., Eher, R., & Gutierrez, K. (2002). Impact of overcrowding and legislational change on the incidence of suicide in custody experiences in Austria, 1967–1996. *International Journal of Law & Psychiatry, 25*(2), 119–128.

Gaes, G. (1985). *The Effects of Overcrowding in Prisons.* Washington, DC: Federal Bureau of Prisons.

Gaes, G. (1991). Challenging beliefs about prison crowding. *Federal Prison Journal, Summer,* 19–23.

Gaes, G. (1994). *Prison Crowding Research Reexamined.* Washington, DC: Federal Bureau of Prisons.

Gaes, G., & McGuire, W. J. (1985). Prison Violence: The Contribution of Crowding Versus Other Determinants of Prison Assault Rates. *Journal of Research in Crime & Delinquency, 22*, 41–65.

Hall, E. T. (1959). *The Silent Language*. New York: Doubleday.

Haney, C. (2006). The wages of prison overcrowding: Harmful psychological consequences and dysfunctional correctional reactions. *Journal of Law and Policy, 22*, 265–203.

Hildreth, A. M., Derogatis, L. R., & Mccusker, K. (1971). Body buffer zone and violence: A reassessment and confirmation. *American Journal of Psychiatry, 127*(12), 1641–1645.

Hill, G. (2001). Prison crowding in Asian countries. *Corrections Compendium, 26*(8), 3.

Huey, M. P., & McNulty, T. L. (2005). Institutional conditions and prison suicide: Conditional effects of deprivation and overcrowding. *The Prison Journal, 85*(4), 490.

Innes, C. (1986). Population density in state prisons (Bureau of Justice Statistics Bulletin, No. NCJ-103204). Washington, DC: Bureau of Justice Statistics.

Jan, L. (1980). Overcrowding and inmate behavior: Some preliminary findings. *Criminal Justice & Behavior, 7*(3), 293–301.

Kinkade, P., Leone, M., & Semond, S. (1995). The consequences of jail crowding. *Crime & Delinquency, 41*(1), 150–161.

Knowles, E. S., & Bassett, R. L. (1976). Groups and crowds as social entities: Effects of activity, size, and member similarity on nonmembers. *Journal of Personality and Social Psychology, 34*(5), 837–845.

Kupers, T. A. (2005). How to create madness in prison. In D. Jones (Ed.), *Humane Prisons* (pp. 47–58). Abington, UK: Radcliffe Publishing.

Langer, E. J., & Saegert, S. (1977). Crowding and cognitive control. *Journal of Personality & Social Psychology, 35*(3), 175–182.

Lawrence, C., & Andrews, K. (2004). The influence of perceived prison crowding on male inmates' perception of aggressive events. *Aggressive Behavior, 30*(4), 273–283.

Levy L., H. A. (1974). Effects of population density and crowding on health on health and social adaptation in the Netherlands. *Journal of Health and Social Behavior, 15*(3), 228–240.

Lieber, J. (1981). The American prison: A tinderbox. *The New York Times Magazine, 130*, 26.

McCain, G., Cox, V., & Paulus, P. (1976). The relationship between illness complaints and degree of crowding in a prison environment. *Environment & Behavior, 8*(2), 283–290.

McCain, G., Cox, V., & Paulus, P. (1980). *The Effects of Prison Crowding on Inmate Behavior*. Washington, DC: National Institute of Justice.

McCarthy, D., & Saegert, S. (1978). Residential density, social overload, and social withdrawal. *Human Ecology, 6*(3), 253–272.

Megaree, E. (1976). Population density & disruptive behavior in a prison setting. In A. K. Cohen, G. F. Cole, & R. G. Bailey (Eds.), *Prison Violence* (pp. 135–144). Lexington, MA: Lexington Books.

Mesquida, C. G., & Wiener, N. I. (1996). Human collective aggression: A behavioral ecology perspective. *Ethology and Sociobiology, 17*(4), 247–262.

Milgram, S. (1970). The experience of living in cities. *Science, 167*, 1461–1468.

Nacci, P. I., Teitelbaum, H. E., & Prather, J. (1977). Population density and inmate misconduct rates in the federal prison system. *Federal Probation, 41*, 26–31.

Nelson, W. R. (1983). New generation jails. *Corrections Today*, April, 108–112.

Ostfeld, A. M., Kasl, S. V., D'Atri, D. A., & Fitzgerald, E. F. (1987). *Stress, Crowding, and Blood Pressure in Prison*. Hillsdale, NJ: Lawrence Erlbaum Associates.

Paulus, P. B. (1988). *Prison Crowding: A Psychological Perspective (Research in Criminology)*. New York: Springer-Verlag.

Paulus, P., Cox, V., McCain, G., & Chandler, J. (1975). Some effects of crowding in a prison environment. *Journal of Applied Social Psychology, 5*(1), 86–91.

Paulus, P. B., McCain, G., & Cox, V. C. (1978). Death rates, psychiatric commitments, blood pressure, and perceived crowding as a function of institutional crowding. *Environmental Psychology and Nonverbal Behavior, 3*, 107–116.

Pelissier, B. (1991). The effects of a rapid increase in a prison population: A pre- and post-test study. *Criminal Justice and Behavior, 18*, 427–447.

Porporino, F. J., & Dudley, K. (1984). *An Analysis of the Effects of Overcrowding in Canadian Penitentiaries.* Ottowa: Ministry of the Solicitor General of Canada.

Ray, D. W., Wandersman, A., Ellisor, J., & Huntington, D. (1982). The effects of high density in a juvenile correctional institution. *Basic and Applied Social Psychology, 3*, 95–108.

Rotman, E. (1995). The failure of reform: 1865–1965. In N. Morris & D. J. Rothman (Eds.), *The Oxford History of Prisons* (pp. 169–198). New York: Oxford.

Roush, D. (1989). *Far From the Maddening Crowd: The Relationship Between Crowding and Safety in Juvenile Institutions.* Paper presented at the Congress of Corrections of the American Correctional Association, Baltimore, MD.

Ruback, B., Carr, T. & Hopper, C. (1986). Perceived control in prisons: Its relation to reported crowding, stress, and symptoms. *Journal of Applied Social Psychology, 16*, 375–386.

Ruback, R. B., & Innes, C. A. (1988). The relevance and irrelevance of psychological research: The example of prison crowding. *American Psychologist, 43*(9), 683–693.

Saegert, S. C. (1975). *Effects of Spatial and Social Density on Arousal, Mood and Social Orientation.* Doctoral dissertation, University of Michigan.

Sechrest, D. K. (1989). Population density and assaults in jails for men and women. *American Journal of Criminal Justice, 14*, 87–103.

Sechrest, D. K. (1991). The effects of density on jail assaults. *Journal of Criminal Justice, 19*, (3), 211–223.

Sigurdson, H. (1985). *The Manhattan House of Detention: A Study of Podular Direct Supervision.* Washington, DC: National Institute of Corrections.

Sommer, R. (1969). *Personal Space: The Behavioral Basis of Design.* Englewood Cliffs, NJ: Prentice-Hall, Inc.

Stevens, W. K. (1986, Jan. 5, 1986). Relief at prison riot's end gives way to dispute on its causes. *The New York Times Magazine, 135*, 12.

Stohr, M. K., Lovrich, N. P., Menke, B. A., & Zupan, L. L. (1994). Staff management in correctional institutions: Comparing DiIulio's "control model" and "employee investment model" outcomes in five jail settings. *Justice Quarterly, 11*(3), 471–479.

Stokols, D. (1972). On the distinction between density and crowding: Some implications for future research. *Psychological Review, 79*, 275–277.

Sundstrom, E., & Altman, I. (1972). *Relationships Between Dominance and Territorial Behavior: Field Study in a Youth Rehabilitation Setting – Technical Report* (No. Grant No. 70-065-PG-21). Washington, DC: Law Enforcement Assistance Administration.

Tartaro, C. (2002). The impact of density on jail violence. *Journal of Criminal Justice, 30*(6), 499–510.

Trulson, C. R., & Marquart, J. W. (2002). Inmate racial integration: Achieving racial integration in the Texas prison system. *The Prison Journal, 82*(4), 498.

Wener, R. E. (2005). The invention of direct supervision. *Corrections Compendium, 30*(2), 4–7, 32–34.

Wener, R. E. (2006). The effectiveness of direct supervision correctional design and management: A review of the literature. *Criminal Justice & Behavior, 33*, 367–391.

Wener, R. E., & Keys, C. (1988). Effects of changes in jail population densities on crowding, sick call, and spatial behavior. *Journal of Applied Social, 18*(10), 852–866.

Wicker, A. W., Kirmeyer, S. L., Hanson, L., & Alexander, D. (1976). Effects of manning levels on subjective experiences, performance, and verbal interaction in groups. *Organizational Behavior & Human Decision Processes, 17*(2), 251–274.

Wooldredge, J., & Winfree, L. (1992). An aggregate-level study of inmate suicides and deaths due to natural causes in U.S. jails. *Journal of Research in Crime & Delinquency, 29*(4), 466–479.

Woolf warns of prison riot risk to Staff and agencies. (2002, June 20, 2002). Guardian Unlimited.

Zupan, L. L., & Stohr-Gillmore, M. K. (1988). Doing time in the new generation jail: Inmate perceptions of gains and losses. *Policy Studies Review, 7*(3), 626–640.

8

The Psychology of Isolation in Prison Settings

THE MEANING OF ISOLATION IN THE PRISON CONTEXT

Isolation, in some form or another, is basic and essential to all aspects of imprisonment. To be sentenced to a prison is, after all, to be isolated by the criminal justice system from community and family. Among the many cited purposes of incarceration are detention and incapacitation, the need to remove the individual from society so they cannot commit further offense, and punishment, often by placing the individual at a distance from the normal benefits of life such as contact with friends and family, work, and sources of interest and stimulation. Isolation, in some degree, goes hand in hand with the very basis of incarceration, which may be, in and of itself, harmful to inmates' physical and mental health (Bonta & Gendreau, 1990; Paulus & Dzindolet, 1993).

Usually, however, the imprisoned individual becomes part of the institutional society or a subgroup therein, for better or worse. An individual is, by judicial decision, isolated in the institution from society, but not typically isolated from others within the institution. The term *isolation* as used here refers to that further step in separation – removing a prisoner from the institutional community to a living situation in which he or she is largely or exclusively alone, with little, if any, contact with other inmates or even with staff. Isolation of this sort usually has the goal of maximizing the level of control exerted over the inmate (Arrigo & Bullock, 2008).

Extreme isolation is not new to prisons, especially in the United States, and, as discussed in Chapter 2 ("Historical View"), goes back to the very beginning of the prison system. Moreover, the use of extreme isolation seems to be growing as the number of very high-security institutions for high-risk inmates increases. The isolation of the Pennsylvania system penitentiaries was designed for the purpose of helping the prisoner, although it is unlikely that this benign intent was any comfort to those prisoners who lived without human contact for years at a time. The isolation that is becoming more common today can be made even more extreme by means of technology,[1] and its purposes often have more to do with the operation of an institution or system than with inmate welfare.

This chapter begins with a review of the many different kinds of conditions that use separation from other inmates as part of the prison regimen. I consider the definition and nature of isolation as it is used in correctional settings, and review research findings in prisons and other settings both through a historical view of early penitentiaries and in the current context. Many studies have shown that psychological damage can result from isolation, but some respected researchers argue that isolation is not necessarily damaging. I discuss conceptual models that may be useful in understanding the kind and level of impact that isolation can have on inmates. Some early assumptions about models for prison isolation – such as its presumed connection to early sensory deprivation research – now seem inappropriate. It may be more useful, for instance, to consider the impacts of isolation by looking at the importance and uses of social contact in stressful situations.

What Prison Isolation Is Called

Prison isolation goes by many different names. Although these include synonyms and euphemisms, some also carry somewhat different meanings or implications. Among the terms that have been used for forms of isolation in prisons and jails are *solitary confinement,* which may or may not be the same as solitary confinement in a special new maximum security (or "supermax") institution; *segregation; administrative segregation; administrative detention; disciplinary segregation; protective custody;* and *timeout.* Sometimes the use of these labels simply varies by jurisdiction or country. Other related terms are more likely to be used by psychologists either in laboratory or institutional contexts, such as *sensory deprivation* or *restrictive environmental stimulation.*

Solitary confinement typically refers to placing an inmate in an isolated cell with few or no amenities, often for 23 hours a day.[2] The inmate may be kept away from the general population for periods ranging from a few days to months or years. Solitary confinement is often used as a punitive measure ("punitive segregation"), as a response to serious infractions of institutional rules. In other situations, keeping inmates away from most or all contact with other inmates may itself be the goal (as with protective custody), even though it may also be a side-effect of other actions, such as when inmates are restricted to their cell in order to remove their access to various programs. A "supermax" or SHU (special housing unit) facility is a special case of solitary confinement. Supermax facilities are a relatively recent phenomenon (Arrigo & Bullock, 2008; Pizarro & Stenius, 2004), although Toch (2003) argues that they have precedents in the earliest penitentiaries. They are institutions built to house inmates who officials feel need the tightest security, These inmates are often called "the worst of the worst" and are placed in conditions with the most extreme levels of security, as can be seen in the many layers of barriers shown in Figure 33 for Pelican Bay (Shalev, 2009). Often this includes housing areas where the only option is placement in single, isolated rooms within which inmates are separated from most or all other inmates, most or all of the time.

Generally speaking, [Special Housing Unit] prisoners are not permitted any contact visits, and they are often required to talk with visitors via closed-circuit television. In addition, SHU prisoners do not benefit from any congregate activity, such as exercise, dining, or religious services. Access to personal belongings, including reading materials, is strictly limited. These convicts typically have no opportunity to work or participate in educational or therapeutic programming. Prisoners in control units are given insufficient room to exercise and often have no access to recreational or athletic equipment. Most SHUs lack windows, so incarcerates are not exposed to natural light. The cells are often illuminated by artificial light 24 hours per day, and prisoners have no means of controlling the brightness or dimness in their units. Under these conditions, convicts may have difficulty determining whether it is day or night. Prisoners are assigned to control units for indefinite periods of time, which typically last for months or years. (Arrigo & Bullock, 2008, p. 625)

SHU can also refer to a "prison within a prison," an area inside the walls of a medium- or high-security prison where inmates who cause disturbances in other living areas can be placed. These may be difficult to distinguish from administrative segregation units, spaces where inmates are removed from the general population for violation of rules. Such units may be in a special area of the institution and in a setting where inmates have a reduced set of privileges. Protective custody, on the other hand, is, at least from a policy perspective, very different. Even though the physical space may be the same as that in other segregation areas, inmates are usually placed in these cells for their own protection, such as when they are seen as particularly vulnerable to assault or the potential object of a vendetta. Inmates may also be placed in protective custody at their own request if they feel threatened by other prisoners. Protective custody is usually thought of as nonpunitive, at least by design and policy.

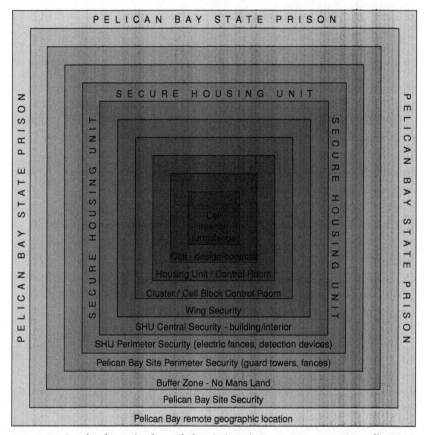

PELICAN BAY STATE PRISON

SECURE HOUSING UNIT

Cell interior furnishings
Cell - design controls
Housing Unit / Control Room
Cluster / Cell Block Control Room
Wing Security
SHU Central Security - building/interior
SHU Perimeter Security (electric fances, detection devices)
Pelican Bay Site Perimeter Security (guard towers, fances)
Buffer Zone - No Mans Land
Pelican Bay Site Security
Pelican Bay remote geographic location

FIGURE 31. Levels of security from Shalev, S. (2009). From *Supermax: Controlling Risk through Solitary Confinement*. Portland, OR: Willan Publishing. Courtesy of Sharon.

Timeout, more commonly used in juvenile detention settings, is a term that was derived in the 1960s from the development of operant-based approaches that applied reinforcement theory in so-called institutional "token economies" (Azrin, 1961). Timeout from reinforcement was designed to eliminate negative behavior and was achieved by placing a resident in a small room for very brief periods of time after emotional outbursts. Later on, the term became commonly and inappropriately used in other settings as a euphemism for more general and longer terms of isolation.

Sensory deprivation and *restrictive environmental stimulation* (REST) are expressions that come directly from psychological research (Suedfeld, 1982). *Sensory deprivation* refers to conditions in which subjects are placed in settings where they are cut off as much as possible from all external

FIGURE 32. Secure unit from Shalev, S. (2009). From *Supermax: Controlling Risk through Solitary Confinement.* Portland, OR: Willan Publishing, courtesy of Jason Oddy.

stimulation (Zubek, 1969). These settings may include flotation tanks, as well as extreme attenuation of light and sound (Lilly, 1956). REST reflects the uses of severely sensorially-restricted environments for therapeutic purposes. Following popularization of Lilly's work, flotation and isolation have become available to the general public for stress reduction and promotion of creativity (van Dierendonck & Nijenhuis, 2005).

RECENT RESEARCH IN ISOLATION

Many studies have explored the impact of isolation in prisons (see Haney, 2003; Suedfeld, Ramirez, Deaton, & Baker-Brown, 1982; Shalev, 2008 for good, even if contradictory, reviews). It is not always easy, however, to make comparisons

FIGURE 33. Secure cell, from Shalev, S. (2009). From *Supermax: Controlling Risk through Solitary Confinement.* Portland, OR: Willan Publishing, courtesy of Jason Oddy.

among the increasing number of studies in this area. These studies differ on many key factors, including the kind of institutions studied (such as prisons versus mental hospitals or training schools); the goal, purpose, and/or precipitating event to the isolation (such as protective custody versus disciplinary segregation, as noted earlier); the level of security and control in the isolated space; the amount of technology used to isolate or communicate with the inmate; the type of inmate being isolated (e.g., juveniles versus adults); the kinds of programs and activities available to inmates; the amount of contact possible with staff or other inmates; and the number, kinds, and level of access to environmental amenities available to inmates.

These settings probably vary significantly in the nature of the isolation space itself, although it is often not clear exactly how much because detailed descriptions of the physical setting are often lacking in these research articles. For example, it would be useful to know how much and what kind of contact is possible with staff or other inmates. How well appointed is the space? How barren or how clean is the cell area? What is the access to visitors (relatives or lawyers)? What other sources of information, stimulation, or communication are accessible, such as windows, telephone, TV, and radio? Further, the situations that have been reported may differ widely in the length of the restriction (ranging from several days to several years) and whether or not the isolation is, in the first instance or in an ongoing way, contingent on the actions and behavior of the inmate. They may also differ in the actions and reactions of the staff, ranging from appropriate and professional to hostile and brutal.

Moreover, there are also important variations among studies on some significant methodological issues that make it difficult to understand the true impact of the isolation. For instance, ethics and logistics usually make it impossible to collect longitudinal data that would allow assessment of inmate status, health, and other outcome variables before they enter isolation, for comparison with later periods. Post-test-only studies – as most are – often compare two groups, those who were sent to isolation and those who were not, even though there may be important a priori differences between these groups. The lack of experimental control in these studies makes it difficult to know which outcomes are due to the time spent in isolation and which, if any, are due to, or at least interact with, prior differences.

Isolation in Supermax Facilities

Issues concerning the impacts of isolation are today, in the United States at least, often framed with regard to the question of the use of so-called supermax institutions. Supermax conditions vary, but they tend to be highly restrictive in access and programs. Often inmates are significantly isolated with limited, if any, access to people or programs, sometimes for extremely long periods of time. A recent review comments that no good studies have examined the impacts of these facilities on individuals (Pizarro & Stenius, 2004). Still, given the extreme level of restriction and long sentences in supermax, the authors suggested that the likelihood of significant impacts on inmates is high (see also Arrigo & Bullock, 2008; Shalev, 2008, 2009). Lippke (2004) commented that the case for isolation in supermax-type facilities is based largely on the assumption that some inmates are too violent for other settings. He argues that other ways of confining such subjects are more cost-effective and less likely to have long-term negative effects.

Haney (2003), in his review of the literature on the psychological effects of prison isolation, also focused on solitary confinement in supermax facilities. For Haney, supermax facilities are a special case among institutions, because most of the variables considered relevant to the inmate experience are different there. The inmate population in these facilities is selected because they are viewed as high-security risks. Solitary confinement, in this instance, is not intended as a temporary measure in response to specific behavior problems, but is meant to be a permanent condition for the length of confinement. Length of time in solitary can often be counted in years. In addition, the newest supermax facilities often rely on technology to further monitor inmates and reduce human contact. In these facilities, inmate control over their isolation and over the environment they are in is further reduced, which in and of itself may increase the negative impacts of environmental stressors (Evans, 1982). Supermax facilities, Haney says, allow administrators to have a kind of isolation and control over inmate behavior that is "more total and complete and literally dehumanizing than has been possible in the past. The combination of these factors is what makes this . . . unique in the modern history of corrections" (p. 127).

Haney argues that the accumulated findings of research in these kinds of facilities show that isolation often causes a set of symptoms that includes sleep disturbance, anxiety, panic, rage, loss of control, paranoia, hallucinations, and self-mutilation. He states that "there are few if any forms of imprisonment that appear to produce so much psychological trauma and in which so many symptoms of psychopathology are manifested" (p. 125) and "there is not a single published study of solitary or supermax-like confinement in which nonvoluntary confinement lasted longer than ten days, where participants were unable to terminate their participation at will, that failed to result in negative psychological effects" (p. 133). Shalev (2008) agrees, stating "there is unequivocal evidence that solitary confinement has a profound impact on health and well-being, particularly for those with pre-existing mental health disorders, and that it may also actively cause mental illness" (p. 10).

The prevalence of psychological symptoms, Haney goes on, is extremely high, ranging from 50 percent to 90 percent in supermax-based studies. There were also very high rates of other symptoms such as anger, ruminations, and confused thoughts. Often, inmates suffer from what he calls *social pathologies*, such as changes in the ability to function socially as a result of the experience in isolation. These changes are not unlike the effects of prisonization (Clemmer, 1958), but more exaggerated. Symptoms include a high level of dependency and the inability to initiate behavior, further withdrawal from social contacts, and outbursts of anger. Haney concludes that the likelihood of psychopathological reactions from confinement "is broad, many of the reactions are serious, and existing evidence on the prevalence of trauma and symptomatology indicated that they are widespread" (p. 148).

Norval Morris was even harsher in his assessment of supermax facilities, calling them a "level of punishment close to that of psychological torture" (2000, p. 98). Prisoners in supermax prisons, he added, "are more isolated, observed and controlled, afforded less human contact and suffer more sensory deprivation than in earlier dungeons" (p. 107).

Not all agree, and a few have reached the opposite conclusion from reviews of the literature. Suedfeld (1982) suggests that researchers have a bias against solitary confinement, and Gendreau and Theriault (2010) conclude that research does not support claims of powerful effects, and "if there are outliers in the literature, it is from studies that claim segregation produced vivid negative psychological effects" (p. 5).

Impact of Isolation in Early Prisons

Are supermax prisons – and the reaction they engender – new? The psychological impact of isolation is one of the earliest issues to be addressed in the decades immediately after the invention of the modern prison in the United States. The history of prisons in the mid- and late nineteenth century (as discussed in Chapter 2) is, to a significant extent, one of the competitions between the Pennsylvania (isolation) and Auburn (congregate work) models of penitentiaries. The Pennsylvania model advocated the most extreme form of isolation. From the moment inmates left the outside world and passed through the doors of the institution (where they were hooded until they reached their cell), until the moment they exited the institution at the end of their term, inmates remained in isolation. They ate, slept, worked, and recreated alone. They had no conversations with other inmates or with guards, except for the occasional visit of a priest. There are many stories about powerful effects this isolation had on inmates, and Toch (2003) suggests that some of these reports were the equivalent of early program evaluation research in which impacts on inmates were carefully recorded. Some recorded high rates of madness and suicide. The Auburn Penitentiary, in fact, began as a prison that used the Pennsylvania model, but chose to change its operation after they experienced a number of inmate deaths and reported cases of insanity, which they attributed to the extreme levels of inmate isolation (Ignatieff, 1978; in Re: *Medley*, 1890).

Although most early observers were enamored with conditions such as those in penitentiaries that followed the Pennsylvania model, a few felt as

Charles Dickens did after his visit to Cherry Hill. "I believe that, in its effects, to be cruel and wrong... this slow and daily tampering with the mysteries of the brain to be immeasurably worse than any torture of the body" (Dickens, 1842, p. 39). In at least one case, a U.S. federal court decision was based on a presumption of the extreme and deleterious effects of solitary confinement on the human psyche. In this case (in Re: *Medley*, 1890), a convicted murderer was released because the court found that his time in solitary confinement while awaiting execution was unconstitutionally cruel and unusual. The court cited reviews of experiences in Pennsylvania-style penitentiaries, which found that solitary confinement produced mental illness, self-destructive behavior, rage, and antisocial behavior and other negative consequences. Other observations of isolation in nineteenth-century prisons in the United States and Europe made similar comments about devastating psychological effects of solitary confinement (Shalev, 2009).

It is important to place the conditions in these early Pennsylvania-style institutions, like Eastern State Prison, in some context. First, the level of isolation of these inmates was extreme by any standard. In addition, the social context of these conditions was different than in current prisons. In the early nineteenth century, the use of prison sentences as punishment was a new form of criminal justice. The invention of the penitentiary was a new and entirely unexpected condition in itself and Eastern State Prison's conditions were specific and unique. Prisoners there were the first to experience very long determinate sentences in total isolation. Application to current solitary confinement, therefore, should not be made casually.

Isolation and Health

Even though Suedfeld and Roy (1975) described positive therapeutic effects of isolation, some reports seem to show a connection between use of solitary confinement in prisons and deterioration of mental health. Arrigo and Bullock (2008) conclude that the negative effects of long-term prison isolation are manifest and clear. Nurse, Woodcock, and Ormsby (2003) cite isolation as a critical factor aggravating mental illness and violent behavior. Inmates who are placed in solitary confinement involuntarily (as opposed to having requested isolation) have a higher incidence of mental health problems than do non-isolated inmates. The incidence of inmates in isolation units who suffer from severe psychiatric disorders is very high – on the order of 30 percent and, in one study, one-third of the inmates reported that they had attempted suicide (Hodgins & Cote, 1991).

Even though isolation was seen as exacerbating these symptoms and was viewed by several authors as a condition that adds stress to these disorders, it is not possible in these studies to distinguish between selection effects and impact of the environment. It seems true that mentally ill inmates are much more likely to end up in isolation, and that isolation is likely to make mental disorders worse. Prisoners in isolation have been found to have lower levels of self-esteem than those in non-isolated settings or the general population out of prison (Blatier, 2000), increased anger, hostility, delusions, and hallucinations (Benjamin & Lux, 1975, 1977), rage, depression, withdrawal, for women (Korn, 2008), and loss of touch with reality (Kupers, 1999). The lack of contact with others and with the outside world (being cut off from many forms of contact and visiting) can be particularly devastating for mentally ill inmates (Benjamin & Lux, 1977; Cohen, 1998; Toch, 1992). These are the inmates who especially need this contact and the programs and job options offered in regular housing areas that are limited or denied in segregation. Moore (1980) found that inmates in segregation cells had the highest use of health care facilities, which he presumed to be connected to the stress of incarceration.

Toch (1992) suggests that isolation removes part of the normal coping mechanism used by inmates to survive institutional life and Cohen (1998) adds that even the use of double cells in some segregation areas may not make things better. Although a double cell eliminates some of the social deprivation of total isolation, having a cellmate in the context of isolation from others, programs, visitors, and the like can lead to paranoia, hostility, and violence.

Grassian and Friedman (1986) reviewed the literature on mental illness and isolation and concluded that there is evidence that isolation has negative psychological impacts, including what is known as "Ganser's syndrome," which includes anxiety and frequent ruminations (Andersen, Sestoft, & Lillebaek, 2001). They conclude that isolation carries major psychological risks, but they also suggest that restricted environmental stimulation can be useful for treatment, particularly in mental health settings (also see Suedfeld, 1982). Canter (2004), in an individual case study, describes an individual who committed suicide in jail, because, he surmises, the inmate had an extreme need to be in control of situations and isolation eliminated his ability to control his immediate environment.

Although most inmates feel safe in most spaces and for most of the time (O'Donnell & Edgar, 1999), segregation areas, along with showers, reception, and time in transit, are the areas where inmates feel most threatened. This is in some sense counterintuitive in that an inmate in isolation should, if nothing else, feel safe from attack. It may reflect the fact that there are many kinds of isolation, some kinds of which allow limited levels of contact. Like notions of safety on city streets (such as in discussions of "Defensible Space," Newman, 1973), inmates may feel most vulnerable when in high opportunity, low supervision settings. That is, an attack in a relatively isolated place is less likely to bring help from staff or other inmates. Inmates, in some institutions, moreover, may feel threatened by staff in isolated areas.

Another term that has been used for inmate response to isolation is Special Housing Unit Syndrome. Shalev (2009) lists a long set of psychological effects that make up this syndrome, including anxiety (from tension to panic attacks), depression, anger, cognitive disturbances, perceptual distortions, up to and including paranoia and psychosis.

Miller (1994) studied inmates living in three levels of restrictions in a federal institution – administrative detention (AD), disciplinary segregation (DS), and the general population. Inmates were given a general survey and symptom checklist. She found that, even though conditions in segregation were improved over early reports in terms of hygiene and care, the level of distress shown by inmates increased as the level of restriction increased (from the general population to AD to DS). In general, more restricted inmates had more intense symptomatology. Inmates in isolation (as well as on psychiatric units) are also more likely to engage in acts of self-mutilation (Jones, 1986).

Much research in this area relies on cross-sectional data, and few studies have used longitudinal measurements to demonstrate any negative effects of isolation. Several recent studies have attempted to do that, in spite of the logistical and ethical problems involved. The few who have used within-subject studies to observe longitudinal effects studied relatively short-term confinements. Zinger, Wichmann, and Andrews (2001) conducted a longitudinal study that looked at the impact of 60 days confinement in solitary in several high-security Canadian prisons. The solitary confinement group consisted both of inmates who were placed there involuntarily and of those who requested isolation. They were compared over the same period with a random sample of inmates from the general population. The authors argued that involuntary and voluntary subjects were not essentially different, because voluntary subjects opted for isolation under the coercion of threats of violence. No differences between voluntary and involuntary groups were found in their measure at either point in time.

Subjects in both groups were given interviews and a series of psychological inventories at the start and after 30 and 60 days. Those in segregation were in poorer mental health, more depressed, and less well adjusted than the comparison group. There was, however, no evidence of deterioration over time of subjects in either group. In a comment on this study, Roberts and Gebotys (2001) noted that the final data in the Zinger et al. study represented a population of which more than half was comprised of inmates who had requested isolation, because of attrition of subjects over time. Another commentary (Jackson, 2001) suggested that 60 days is not a long enough period to draw valid conclusions, in that the most significant impacts of isolation may come well after the actual time in isolation is complete.

Several recent Danish studies also looked at effects longitudinally. Andersen and colleagues (2001; Andersen, 2003) found that over a 2- to 3-month period, inmates in solitary confinement in a remand facility (pretrial) were unchanged in psychological functioning, whereas the psychological functioning of a comparison, nonsolitary confinement group improved. Moreover, the solitary confinement group did improve in functioning when transferred to normal housing. They also found that inmates in solitary confinement had higher risk of hospitalization for psychiatric reasons and that the risk increased with time in isolation (Sestoft, Andersen, & Lilleboek, 1998). They recommended changing Danish law to eliminate the use of solitary confinement.

On the other hand, Weinberg (1967) found no difference between short-term isolation in very severe or less severe situations on cognitive tests. Gendreau and Bonta (1984) concluded that solitary confinement is not necessarily harmful to mental health, although, they noted, isolation can be accompanied by harsh treatment, which can be harmful. One author (Rogers, 1993) even goes so far as to suggest that, since no severe impacts of solitary have been definitively shown, inmates should be housed in solitary confinement on a large scale, to reduce abuse and assault and to save staffing costs.

Suedfeld (1982), who is known for his work on sensory deprivation and restricted environmental stimulation therapy, argued that most of the data available on the effects of isolation in prison was of poor quality. Reports often made use of unique anecdotal accounts or analogous situations such as prisoners of war, which, he points out, are not really analogous to inmates in American prisons, because of differences in conditions, motivation, and background. He also argued that laboratory sensory deprivation research was not an appropriate comparison because of significant differences in the amount of environmental restriction, the amount of time subjects actually spend in that setting, the amount of control the subject has over the situation, the purpose of the isolation, and because of the real and/or perceived benevolence of the persons controlling the situation.

Suedfeld also argues that the prior assumptions and anti-solitary confinement bias of most researchers led to assumptions that solitary confinement was more negative than it is. He notes that there are also anecdotal stories indicating positive reactions to isolation by inmates such as reading, writing, and education. The potential positive aspect of solitary confinement is shown, he suggests, by the fact that in some situations inmates ask for solitary confinement as a way of removing themselves from the stresses of institutional life. Suedfeld and Roy (1975) noted improvements in the behavior of four young inmates who spent time in isolation, supported by significant psychotherapeutic intervention.

Suedfeld and his colleagues (1982) studied the impact of isolation on inmates in several maximum security institutions. Inmates who had been in isolation for rule breaking, for periods ranging from 5 days to 42 months, were interviewed. Although subjects reported unpleasant aspects of the time in seclusion, including boredom and a distorted sense of time, most developed coping mechanisms, and only a very few reported extreme problems (claustrophobia, anxiety ruminations). No hallucinations or delusions were reported. There were some negative effects after the isolation was over, including difficulty sleeping, as well as positive effects, such as a more serious attitude or increased participation in programs. Most complaints related to treatment by guards and the quality of food. Suedfeld, in fact, argues that the worst of the problems attributed to solitary confinement come from other aspects of the situation such as harassment by guards, bad food, and sanitation.

In their second study (Suedfeld et al., 1982), over 100 inmates in isolation in three institutions (some with no previous experience in solitary confinement) were interviewed using a battery of psychological tests. They found few negative effects that could be attributed to time spent in solitary confinement. More subjects complained to the interviewers about the guards than about sensory deprivation in this post-only study.

In a recent study, O'Keefe et al. (2010) compared inmates who had mental illness with those without mental illness in administrative segregation and in the general population over a 1-year period to look at impacts and changes over time due to extreme confinement. They used a large battery of mental health and observational scales and found that strong detrimental effects did exist and inmates in isolation developed symptoms consistent with past reports. They were not, however, able to confirm most of their major hypotheses, especially that these effects were special to administrative segregation because the effects there were not significantly greater than for those in the general population. Inmates with mental illness did show more elevated scores on the variety of measures of functioning and pathology, but they did not deteriorate faster in isolation than non-mentally ill inmates, also contrary to expectations. This article, it should be noted, has attracted significant controversy and methodological critiques on the National Institute of Corrections and Mental Health website (http://community.nicic.gov/blogs/mentalhealth/archive/2011/06.aspx).

SUMMARY OF RESEARCH

Inmates who go into solitary confinement seem more likely to have psychological problems, including severe mental illness. Whatever the disagreement among studies, it is likely that most forms of isolation are not good environments for inmates with significant psychiatric problems. The impact of isolation on inmates without prior mental problems is less clear. Some studies show problems (in adjustment, hospitalization), and others show no differences. Certainly anecdotal evidence and conventional wisdom argue that isolation is aversive and harmful, and few therapies recommend forced isolation for persons with severe disorders, even though voluntary isolation is accepted in some instances. Why, then, is there disagreement and so much difficulty showing significant impacts in more rigorous research?

It is possible, of course, that the anecdotal data is biased, that the conventional wisdom is wrong, and that isolation may be less likely to cause significant effects than thought, especially when other harsh circumstances are eliminated (assaultive staff, poor hygiene, and so forth). It is also possible that we have not seen stronger effects because our way of viewing those effects in field experiments are not sufficiently sensitive or attuned to the outcomes as would, for instance, more controlled studies using extensive behavioral observations and batteries of psychological tests, although O'Keefe, Klebe, Strucker, Sturm, and Leggett (2010) addressed many of these issues. Still, the research methods typically available to study isolation may be particularly out of phase with the phenomena we wish to study. Psychological research requires voluntary participation by subjects, and it is unethical to assign people involuntarily to isolation conditions, which could cause harm. It is also a violation of accepted ethical standards to test responses without subject permission. There are some exceptions, such as the use of institutional archival data sources, as used by Sestoff et al. (1998). Even so, studies like those of Andersen et al. (2001, 2003) have inherent subject self-selection issues that can affect outcome, even if there is a very high level of participation. In most studies, participation is much lower, and even well-designed studies like that of Zinger et al. (2001) inevitably suffer in their ability to generalize findings. More importantly, as noted earlier, it is likely that volition is a crucial factor in the degree to which isolation is stressful and potentially harmful, and research needs to distinguish voluntary from involuntary seclusion.

Careful and valid research is very hard to do in these highly restricted sites, even with cooperation of the controlling agencies and administrators. It is virtually impossible without it. Institutions and agencies are reluctant to support research by independent scholars – the results can be used in legal proceedings against them – and courts have not been active in mandating such research. Given these conditions, the clear and unassailable data some demand is unlikely to be available any time soon.

WHY SHOULD ISOLATION BE HARMFUL?

Most of the discussion in the research literature on isolation deals with the impact of solitary confinement – that is, how harmful is it? But these studies include curiously little discussion about why isolation could or should be harmful to inmates. Rather, it is often discussed in the manner of an assumed stressor, as if any explanation of why solitary confinement could be problematic is too basic to be necessary. Suedfeld (1982) suggests that there is a pervasive anti-solitary confinement bias common among correctional researchers that, in effect, causes them to start with the assumption that solitary confinement is harmful and then to seek to demonstrate that effect. One does not have to posit alternate motivations, however, to recognize that the context of most studies has been long-standing beliefs that solitary confinement is aversive and potentially harmful.

This attitude may come from several sources. First, much of the use of solitary confinement in prisons and other situations (such as for POWs) has been as a punishment. Logic suggests that a condition widely and commonly used as punishment has, by experience, shown itself to be at least unpleasant and probably stressful, aversive, and traumatizing in nature.[3] There have been many anecdotal reports of negative responses to solitary confinement, going back to reports indicating that prisoners "went crazy" or committed suicide as a response to the total isolation of nineteenth-century Pennsylvania-style penitentiaries (Toch, 2003).

Many authors cite research in psychological laboratories on sensory deprivation as justification for their assumptions that solitary confinement is harmful to prisoners and indicative of the need for further study (Grassian & Friedman, 1986; Haney, 2003; Liederman, 1962). Indeed, early research in sensory deprivation seemed to indicate that exposures to extreme isolation even of moderate duration (several hours) could lead to significant negative psychological reactions, including anxiety, agitation, and hallucinations

(Bexton, Heron, & Scott, 1954; Liederman, 1962; Lilly, 1956; Zubek, 1969; and others). Liederman, for example, suggested that extreme isolation, whether voluntary or otherwise, has deleterious effects on mood as well as on one's ability to perceive surroundings. The nervous system, he said, requires changing stimuli and responds badly to too much or too little stimulation. He argues, though, against using isolation as a punishment for prisoners and says it is ineffective as a tool for social control and potentially dangerous to some inmates who have poor control over their inner mental life.

Benjamin and Lux (1977) offer several explanations for the impact of isolation on mental stability. For instance, stimulus deprivation has effects on the nervous system that impact biochemical processes related to stress responses. The human nervous system requires stimulation and "*meaningful contact with the outside world*" (their italics) (p. 270). Lacking that, a syndrome of withdrawal and disinterest ensues. On a broader scale, they suggest that humans require normal sources of reinforcement (such as social interaction) and, lacking those, resort to abnormal sources (acting out).

As Suedfeld points out (1982), however, there are at least two problems with extending this research to prison isolation. First, the levels of sensory deprivation in these laboratory studies are quantitatively and qualitatively different from prison situations. Almost no cases of prison isolation reach the extreme levels of limitation of sensory input achieved in the laboratory. Laboratory sensory deprivation subjects are placed in a setting with no light and almost total sound attenuation. Significant efforts are made to reduce tactile and olfactory stimulation. Sensory deprivation research subjects are literally cut off from almost all sensory input. By comparison, however unpleasant solitary confinement may be, most inmates in isolation cells still experience significant sensory stimulation. Isolation cells commonly (and by court rulings) have artificial light and may have access to natural light. In fact, a common complaint of prison inmates who are in isolation is of too much rather than too little light (Suedfeld, 1982), because, in some solitary confinement situations, room lights are left on all the time, making sleep difficult. There are usually objects in the cell (furniture, books) and sound from external sources, as well. In some cases, cells defined as isolated may even have televisions or radios. "Isolated" inmates, then, experience touch, smells, and some, though limited, amounts of visual variety, and other forms of stimulation.

In addition, there are threats to internal validity that affect interpretation of the results of sensory deprivation laboratory research. Orne (1962) demonstrated that suggestion and expectation can play a large role in subject responses. Through placebo control studies, he found that elements of the experimental context (such as instructions, environmental cues, and the demeanor of the experimenter) could indicate to subjects that the experimenter thought there was reason for concern about harmful effects of the study. Those elements, independent of the actual level of deprivation, played a large role in the likelihood subjects would have a negative response to the situation. Whether there is an analogous impact of expectation effects in reaction to prison isolation is not known and has not been studied.

Sensory deprivation, then, may not be an appropriate model for describing most cases of solitary confinement in prisons, both because the original research itself is suspect and because it may not be an ecologically valid representation of actual prison solitary confinement conditions. It does not follow, however, that because laboratory research in sensory deprivation may not apply, prison solitary confinement is not harmful. The question is to discover whether solitary confinement environments cause harm and to identify a model that explains how and why. Explaining how solitary confinement works to affect inmates is important to identify the critical variables to be measured in research and addressed in design, policy, or legal reviews.

Indeed, why isolation might be harmful is not a trivial question. The elements of solitary confinement that could cause high levels of stress – beyond the questionable model of sensory deprivation – are not obvious, compared to, for example, the related question of crowding in prisons. There are several obvious candidates for crowding factors that could cause significant stress in inmates. Crowded situations, for instance, can lead to competition for scarce resources and such competition often results in aggressive behavior. In addition, sharing a cell with one or several inmates can place someone in a vulnerable position. Inmates in crowded conditions may be living with the continual threat of assault and with no options for privacy and retreat. It is not hard to imagine how such circumstances could lead to acute and chronic stress, which might result in physical and psychological problems.

Both of these issues, resource access and risk of assault, however, are very different for the inmate in isolation. The levels of resources available to the isolated inmate may be adequate or inadequate – important items can be provided or intentionally restricted, as a punishment or even as torture – but he or she is not in direct competition with other inmates for them. Similarly, however unpleasant the setting may be, threats from other inmates are not necessarily a problem for the inmate in true isolation. Risk of bodily harm is more likely to be from one's self, through suicide attempts. As Suedfeld (1982) and others have noted, the attitude and actions of those in charge can be critical in determining the level of stress experienced in isolation. If your well-being is completely in the hands of others, their beneficence or malevolence is crucial.

Several other explanations for negative effects of solitary confinement have been offered. Haney (2003) noted that inmates in confinement are removed from the "rhythms of life." This is likely to be especially true when there is no regular access to natural light and views. Understanding the importance of views, especially of nature, on stress and cognitive functioning is growing (see Kaplan, 1995; Ulrich, 1993) and is discussed in more detail in Chapter 10. Lack of window views reduces the ability of an inmate to cope with the oppressive feelings of incarceration and isolation by projecting one's self mentally into that distant situation and psychologically escaping.

Also, inmates in solitary confinement typically experience significant or total reduction of access to services, activities, and programs. Even though solitary confinement environments may not be "sensory or stimulus deprived" in the sense of laboratory studies, they clearly are, at the very least, environments in which inmates have a very limited variety of experiences and activities and environments that may lead to extremes of monotony and boredom. Even though monotony and boredom are usually thought of as minor and temporary inconveniences, they can have serious consequences, especially when magnified by being in a total institution. Boredom has been used to explain why inmates volunteer to be subjects in research programs (Moser et al., 2004) and has been linked to depression and hostility (Vodanovich, 2003).

Negative effect in response to boredom results from sensation seeking and attempts to achieve optimal levels of arousal (Berlyne, 1960; Fenichel, 1951; Zuckerman, 1994), although boredom itself may not result in increased levels of arousal (Thackray, 1981). Even segregation settings where inmates have access to books or other diversions have been reported to be excessively boring because of the lack of activities to occupy time (Conrad, 1977). Recently, boredom has been discussed as contributing to a variety of conditions both endemic to and dangerous in a prison situation, including substance abuse, impulsiveness, depression, hopelessness, anxiety, hostility (Harris, 2000), as well as mood disturbance, risk-taking, paranoia, and severe mental illness (Todman, 2003). We should note that monotony and boredom in prison are not limited to inmates in solitary confinement, even though it may be most exacerbated there. Inmates in general population settings also complain of the lack of variety of settings and experiences (Moser et al., 2004; Wener & Clark, 1977).

Inmates in solitary confinement are also likely to be under constant intrusive observation. Even though they may not have to share living space, the lack of control over access to one's self represents a significant loss of privacy. Goffman (1961) has cited loss of privacy as a means used by armies as well as prisons to help break down an individual's sense of identity, and others have suggested that loss of privacy, especially in the extreme condition, can be stressful (Altman, 1981; Margulis, 2003; Westin, 1967). This loss of privacy is, like boredom, a condition common to correctional settings, although it may be more extreme in some kinds of solitary confinement.

It may be that the most important condition that results from solitary confinement experiences is also the most obvious – the exclusion of contact with other people. Solitary confinement may not represent *sensory* deprivation, but it is almost always a setting of significant *social* deprivation. In solitary confinement, as Haney (2003) noted, there are few or no opportunities for experiences of affection, relationships, conversation, and other normal human interactions, so much so that Haney suggests that a common outcome of isolation is what he calls "social pathology," or a reduced ability to carry on normal social relationships. Life in the general population of prisons and jails may be awkward and dysfunctional, but close bonds can develop there (Toch, 1992). Because humans are social animals, these deprivations can be serious issues.

An appropriate conceptual approach for the experience of isolation, then, should address the issue of loss of contact with other people. Bennett (1980), in discussing problems with the elderly, defined *isolation* as a deprivation of social contact and context, in contrast to *loneliness*, which is more commonly viewed as an experiential state. Loss of contact and context may be the most damaging aspect of solitary confinement. Baumeister and Leary (1995) have posited that "human beings are fundamentally and pervasively motivated by a need to belong, that is, by a strong desire to form and maintain enduring interpersonal attachments" (p. 522). Connection to such social networks can help cope with and reduce stress (Cohen, Sherrod, & Clark, 1986), whereas deprivation of social attachment increases physical and psychological pathology.

Social comparison theory, for instance, proposes that it is through interaction and comparison with other people that we come to define and understand ourselves and develop or maintain our self-concept (Suls, 1977). Seen from this perspective, isolation in solitary confinement reduces the ability of the inmate to understand his or her own feelings and behaviors as reflected by the responses and behaviors of others, and makes it impossible to use social contact as a moderator for stress and anxiety. Social situations, to a significant extent, determine and are determined by the social roles we take on. We learn to understand who we are, and how we are doing through the reflection of the responses of others. "The meaning of one's behavior is in the response to it" by others (Burke 1996, p. 143).

For social comparison theory, an individual's identity evolves and is maintained through a "continuously operating, self-adjusting, feedback loop"

(Burke, 1996, p. 147). That is, individuals are constantly adjusting actions in accord with the responses of their local reference group. The roles we take on and evolve in these circumstances help us to define ourselves and to understand how we fit into social situations. Isolation eliminates those sources of reference and self-understanding. It can reduce the opportunity that an inmate has for "social reality testing" (Haney, cited in Arrigo & Bullock, 2008, p. 628). As seen through this lens, if we understand who we are, at least in part, through our interactions with others, then the nineteenth-century model of total solitary confinement at Eastern State Prison seems especially poorly suited for achieving its stated goals of helping inmates achieve greater insights and understanding of themselves.

High levels of anxiety tend to lead people to a greater desire for affiliation because of the need people have to compare themselves with others to determine the validity of their feelings. People are more likely to avoid isolation and increase social contact when stressed. Social affiliation is an important buffer or moderator for the effects of stressors (Burke, 1996). People who have social support seem to be much less vulnerable to the effects of stressors (Frone, Russell, & Cooper, 1991), and people under stress seek social support as a source of help. This may also help to explain why social isolation in prison is sometimes seen as more disturbing to female than male inmates (Freudenberg, 2002). When stressed, women count more on social contacts and are more likely to respond to stress and distress with affiliative behaviors. Toch (1992) notes that for women, much more than for men, "the prison kinship system helps to ward off the depersonalizing effects of confinement" (p. 230). Solitary confinement for women, then, would represent an even more direct assault on important behaviors for coping with the stresses of prison life.

These findings may also help to explain the particularly deleterious impact that isolation has on those with previously existing mental disorders (Brodsky & Scogin, 1988). The lack of social reference groups may be especially critical for those with prior mental illness. It is not unreasonable to think that isolation in these conditions could lead to or exacerbate ruminations, paranoia, delusions, and the like. It has also been suggested that isolation leads to greater focus on inner mental life to the degree that it makes the inmate more susceptible to suggestion (A. Barabasz, 1991; M. Barabasz, 1991).

The difference between voluntary and involuntary solitary confinement is clear and powerful (Haney, 2003; Nurse, Woodcock, & Ormsby, 2003). If sensory deprivation, as tested in laboratories, was the primary causal factor of stress in solitary confinement, one would not expect the voluntary nature to be critical, given that sensory deprivation in laboratory subjects, who were voluntary, seemed to show severe effects. If the harmful effects of solitary confinement are largely due to social deprivation, however, then one might expect that those who voluntarily choose isolation are from a subgroup that, at least at that point in time, specifically desires less contact with this group of people. It may be that the fear of assault, for example, makes the isolation more attractive and the lack of social contact, such as in protective custody, less onerous.

Involuntarily confined inmates may be more likely to be people who want to maintain contact with the other inmates. For them, then, isolation is a loss of important experiences. There is a New York City public radio host who regularly interviews celebrities and asks what they would take with them if they were given 6 months alone on a desert island. Time alone, for these interviewees, is almost invariably seen as an opportunity to learn, meditate, or relax. The level of choice and of resources turns this isolation into a vacation. The distinction between that circumstance and the prison, with its low resources and involuntary solitary confinement, could hardly be greater.

Altman's (1981) privacy model emphasizes the importance of volition in considering the impact of isolation. Choosing isolation is a very different situation from having it forced upon you. Inmates in voluntary solitary confinement have a significant degree of control over their deprivation and can often terminate the isolation when they feel too isolated or bored. Although some have suggested that voluntary solitary confinement in prisons is not really voluntary since the isolation serves as their escape from threats of violence, these inmates are clearly exercising some level of control over their condition, something others in solitary cannot do. The fact that they initiated the confinement through a request, and may be able to terminate the confinement, also on request, makes this a very different condition from that of those who are placed there against their will as a punitive measure or because of their security status.

CONCLUSION

In spite of the many studies cited here, it is fair to say that the nature, qualities, and impacts of prison isolation on inmate behavior, health, and mental functioning is an under-researched area. This is even truer for isolation than prison crowding, in part because those places with the most extreme conditions of isolation (such as supermax facilities) are precisely those least accessible to the researcher. Given the potential for bad publicity or lawsuits, prison systems seem to feel that research by external scholars is likely to lead to problems. The more extreme the level of isolation in prison, the less we know about it.

As we have shown, isolation in the correctional context takes many forms, is done for many reasons, and varies widely in severity, length, and setting. Some of these differences are likely to be critical in determining the level of impact on the inmate. Even though there are varieties of opinion and some diversity of findings, it seems clear that isolation, especially for longer terms and at more extreme levels, is a stressor that can and does elicit potentially significant negative psychological, social, and behavioral effects. Negative effects may not be inevitable – especially where isolation is brief, less severe, voluntary, or done for benign reasons. There may even be cases, as discussed by Suedfeld (1982), where isolation has therapeutic effects (e.g., REST). But such conditions (that is, "brief, less severe, voluntary, or done for benign reasons") are rarely found in prison isolation, even in facilities that are thoughtfully and efficiently managed.

We have noted before that the prison context makes almost all conditions more stressful. The cases of most concern are where the isolation is long term, strict, and involuntary, and therefore more likely to evoke negative emotional, behavioral, social, and/or cognitive responses. Others have pointed out that inmates, especially those likely to end up in isolation, are those most likely to suffer from mental conditions that make them most vulnerable to the negative effects of isolation (Arrigo & Bullock, 2008; Haney, 2003). As with most stressors, the severity of the impact depends on the specifics of the situation and the individual in question, but when the isolation is extreme and long term, and when the individual is mentally fragile, it seems likely that the impact can be significant and destructive.

Simple stimulus or *sensory deprivation*, as these terms have been used in psychological laboratories, are not likely to be the best models to explain the impacts of isolation stress in prisons. Most prison isolation situations allow far more sensory input than present in most laboratory studies. Furthermore, these studies, mostly decades old, are themselves methodologically suspect.

Rather, it makes more sense to think about prison isolation as removal from, as Haney (2003) suggests, "the rhythms of life," and as a form of social deprivation. As such, it is significant and is made different from the norm of prison life by the loss of quantity and variety of social contact, as well as the lack of access to close contacts, friendships, and social attachments. Altman (1981) has noted that although voluntary separation from others (solitude) may be beneficial, involuntary loss of social contact (isolation) is a form of deprivation. As noted at the beginning of this chapter, separation from society and social contacts defines prison life, but the isolation of solitary confinement from prison society takes this to another extreme.

There are, of course, other important elements of life that are lost in solitary, such as the lack of access to natural light and nature. There is no research, at this point, that describes how much more limited these are in typical isolation situations than normal prison life, and what the impact may be. Given the levels of restrictiveness in many segregation units, however, it is fair to assume that daylight and nature views are also severely limited from the already less-than-generous levels present in most general population prison units. There is evidence that loss of daylight and nature can have important psychological and psychophysiological effects, as discussed in Chapter 10.

There are several psychological perspectives that explain why loss of social contact can be so harmful. Social comparison theory suggests that it is through interaction with others that we learn about ourselves, gain context to assess our behavior and attitudes, and assess whether an idea, or thought, or response to a situation is reasonable or "crazy." By removing that perspective, creating distance from Haney's "rhythm of life," isolation can increase rumination, uncertainty, anxiety, and even paranoia. Because of the likelihood of these kinds of psychopathological effects, Arrigo and Bullock (2008) suggest that officials should be obliged to take special care to avoid placing those with mental illness in isolation, and should closely monitor inmates in isolation for harmful effects and staff abuses. They need to assure that environmental conditions are as humane as possible, with good lighting, space for exercise, access to personal effects, and social interaction.

There is considerable research and discussion of the use of social contact and affiliation as ways of dealing with stress (Bunk & Schaufei, 1993; Dijkstra, Gibbons, & Buunk, 2010; Suls, 1977; Suls & Wheeler, 2000). Toch (1992) has commented that isolation in prison removes inmates from their "normal" mechanisms for coping with the harshness of life behind bars. Recent research in noncorrectional settings has shown that monotony, boredom, and loneliness can be significant stressors. Studies on loneliness, in particular, have connected loss of important and primary social contact to neurological functions (Cacioppo et al., 2002).

In the end, it seems likely that isolation is stressful for the most basic and the most human reason of all. People are, for the most part, social animals and isolation removes them from the social contacts that make life meaningful, pleasant, and survivable.

References

Altman, I. (1981). *Environment and Social Behavior: Privacy, Personal Space, Territory, and Crowding.* New York: Irvington Press.

Andersen, H. S., Sestoft, D., Lillebaek, T., Gabrielsen, G., & Hemmingsen, R. H. (2003). A longitudinal study of prisoners on remand: Repeated measures of psychopathology in the initial phase of solitary versus nonsolitary confinement. *International Journal of Law & Psychiatry, 26*(2), 165–177.

Andersen, H. S., Sestoft, D., & Lillebaek, T. (2001). Ganser syndrome after solitary confinement in prison: A short review and a case report. *Nordic Journal of Psychiatry*, 55(3), 199–201.

Arrigo, B. A., & Bullock, J. L. (2008). The psychological effects of solitary confinement on prisoners in supermax units: Reviewing what we know and recommending what should change. *International Journal of Offender Therapy and Comparative Criminology*, 52(6), 622.

Azrin, N. H. (1961). Time-out from positive reinforcement. *Science*, 133, 382–383.

Barabasz, A. (1991). Effects of isolation on states of consciousness. In A. A. Harrison, Y. A. Clearwater & C. P. McKay (Eds.), *From Antarctica to Outer Space: Life in Isolation and Confinement* (pp. 201–208). New York: Springer-Verlag.

Barabasz, M. (1991). Imaginative involvement in Antarctica: Applications to life in space. In A. A. Harrison, Y. A. Clearwater & C. P. McKay (Eds.), *From Antarctica to Outer Space: Life in Isolation and Confinement* (pp. 209–216). New York: Springer-Verlag.

Baumeister, R. F., & Leary, M. R. (1995). The need to belong: Desire for interpersonal attachments as a fundamental human motivation. *Psychological Bulletin*, 117(3), 497.

Benjamin, T. B., & Lux, K. (1975). Constitutional and psychological implications of the use of solitary confinement: Experience at the Maine state prison. *Clearinghouse-Review*, (June), pp. 83–90.

Benjamin, T. B., & Lux, K. (1977). Solitary confinement as psychological punishment. *California Western Law Review San Diego, California*, 13(2), 265–296.

Bennett, R. (Ed.). (1980). *Aging, Isolation, and Resocialization*. New York: Van Nostrand Reinhold Company.

Berlyne, D. E. (1960). *Conflict, Arousal, and Curiosity*. New York: McGraw-Hill.

Bexton, W. H., Heron, W., & Scott, T. H. (1954). Effects of decreased variation in the sensory environment. *Canadian Journal of Psychology*, 8, 70–76.

Blatier, C. (2000). Locus of control, causal attributions and self-esteem: A comparison between prisoners. *International Journal of Offender Therapy & Comparative Criminology*, 44(1), 97–110.

Bonta, J., & Gendreau, P. (1990). Reexamining the cruel and unusual punishment of prison life. *Law & Human Behavior*, 14(4), 347–372.

Brodsky, S. L., & Scogin, F. R. (1988). Inmates in protective custody: First data on emotional effects. *Forensic Reports*, 1(4), 267–280.

Buunk, B., & Schaufeli, W. (1993). Burnout: A perspective from social comparison theory. *Professional Burnout: Recent Developments in Theory and Research*, 53–69.

Burke, P. J. (1996). Social Identities and Psychosocial Stress. In H. B. Kaplan (Ed.), *Psychosocial Stress: Perspectives on Structure, Theory, Life-Course, and Methods* (pp. 141–174). San Diego: Academic Press.

Cacioppo, J. T., Hawkley, L. C., Crawford, L. E., Ernst, J. M., Burleson, M. H., Kowalewski, R. B., et al. (2002). Loneliness and health: Potential mechanisms. *Psychosomatic Medicine*, 64, 407–417.

Canter, D. (2004, January 14). He knew he was just like the rest: A killer. *Times on Line*.

Clemmer, D. (1958). *The Prison Community*. New York: Rinehart.

Cohen, F. (1998). The right to treatment in the mentally disordered inmate and the law. Kingston, NJ: Civic Research Institute, Inc.

Cohen, S., and Spacapan, S. (1984). The social psychology of noise. In D. M. Jones & A. J. Chapman. (Eds.), *Noise and Society*. New York: John Wiley & Sons Ltd.

Cohen, S., Sherrod, D. R., & Clark, M. S. (1986). Social skills and the stress-protective role of social support. *Journal of Personality and Social Psychology, 50*(5), 963.

Conrad, J. (1977). The survival of the fearful. In J. P. Conrad & S. Dinitz (Eds.), *In fear of Each Other: Studies of Dangerousness in America* (pp. 119–132). Lexington, MA: Lexington Books.

Dickens, C. (1842). *American Notes and Pictures from Italy.* New York: Charles Scribner and Sons.

Dijkstra, P., Gibbons, F., & Buunk, A. (2010). Social comparison theory. In J. E. Maddux & J. P. Tangney (Eds.), *Social Psychological Foundations of Clinical Psychology* (pp. 195). New York: Guilford.

Evans, G. W. (Ed.). (1982). *Environmental Stress.* New York: Cambridge University Press.

Evans, G. W., Wener, R. E., & Phillips, D. (2002). The morning rush hour: Predictability and commuter stress. *Environment & Behavior, 34*(4), 521–530.

Fenichel, H. (1951). Review of the literature on boredom. *Psychoanalytic Quarterly, 20,* 345–346.

Freudenberg, N. (2002). Adverse effects of US jail and prison policies on the health and well-being of women of color. *American Journal of Public Health, 92*(12), 1895.

Frone, M. R., Russell, M., & Cooper, M. L. (1991). Relationship of work and family stressors to psychological distress: The independent moderating influence of social support, mastery, active coping, and self-focused attention. *Journal of Social Behavior & Personality, 6*(7), 227–250.

Gendreau, P., & Bonta, J. (1984). Solitary confinement is not cruel and unusual punishment: People sometimes are. *Canadian Journal of Criminology, 26*(4), 467–478.

Gendreau, P., & Theriault, Y. (2010). *Bibliotherapy for Cynics Revisited: Commentary on One Year Longitudinal Study of the Psychological Effects of Administrative Segregation.* Washington, DC: NIC Corrections and Mental Health Update.

Goffman, E. (1961). *Asylums.* New York: Anchor.

Grassian, S., & Friedman, N. (1986). Effects of sensory deprivation in psychiatric seclusion and solitary confinement. *International Journal of Law & Psychiatry, 8*(1), 49–65.

Haney, C. (2003). Mental health issues in long-term solitary and "supermax" confinement. *Crime and Delinquency, 49*(1), 124–156.

Harris, M. B. (2000). Correlates and characteristics of boredom proneness and boredom. *Journal of Applied Social Psychology, 30*(3), 576–598.

Hodgins, S., & Cote, G. (1991). The mental health of penitentiary inmates in isolation. *Canadian Journal of Criminology, 33*(2), 175–182.

Ignatieff, M. (1978). *A Just Measure of Pain: The Penitentiary in the Industrial Revolution, 1750–1850.* New York: Pantheon Books.

Jackson, M. (2001). Commentary #3: Psychological effects of administrative segregation. *Canadian Journal of Criminology, January,* 109–116.

Jones, A. (1986). Self-mutilation in prison: A comparison of mutilators and nonmutilators. *Criminal Justice and Behavior, 13*(3), 286–296.

Joseph, A. (2006). *The Impact of Light on Outcomes in Healthcare Settings.* Concord, California: Center for Health Design.

Kaplan, S. (1995). The restorative benefits of nature: Toward an integrative framework. *Journal of Environmental Psychology, 15,* 169–182.

Korn, R. (1988). Follow-up report on the effects of confinement in the High Security Unit at Lexington. *Social Justice, 15*(1), 20–29.

Kupers, T. A. (2008). What to do with the survivors? Coping with the long-term effects of isolated confinement. *Criminal Justice and Behavior, 35*(8), 1005.

Liederman, P. (1962). Man alone: Sensory deprivation and behavior change. *Correctional Psychiatry and Journal of Social Therapy, 8,* 64–74.

Lilly, J. C. (1956). Mental effects of reduction of ordinary levels of physical stimuli on intact healthy persons. *Psychological Research Reports, 5,* 1–9.

Lippke, R. L. (2004). Against supermax. *Journal of Applied Philosophy, 21*(2), 109–124.

Margulis, S. T. (2003). On the status and contribution of Westin's and Altman's theories of privacy. *Journal of Social Issues, 59*(2), 411–429.

Miller, H. A. (1994). Reexamining psychological distress in the current conditions of segregation. *Journal of Correctional Health Care, 1,* 39–51.

Moore, E. O. (1980). A prison environment: Its effect on healthcare utilization. *Dissertation Abstracts International, 41*(2), 437.

Morris, N. (2000). Prisons in the USA: Super Max – the bad and the mad. In L. Fairweather & S. McConville (Eds.), *Prison Architecture: Policy, Design, and Experience* (pp. 98–108). Oxford, UK: Architectural Press.

Moser, D. J., Arndt, S., Kanz, J. E., Benjamin, M. L., Bayless, J. D., Reese, R. L., et al. (2004). Coercion and informed consent in research involving prisoners. *Comprehensive Psychiatry, 45*(1), 1–9.

Newman, O. (1973). *Defensible Space: Crime Prevention through Urban Design.* New York: Macmillan Publishing Company, Inc.

Nurse, J., Woodcock, P., & Ormsby, J. (2003). Influence of environmental factors on mental health within prisons: Focus group study. *British Medical Journal, 327*(7413), 490–494.

O'Donnell, I., & Edgar, K. (1999). Fear in prison. *The Prison Journal, 79*(1), 90–99.

O'Keefe, M., Klebe, K. J., Stucker, A., Sturm, K., & Leggett, W. (2010). *One Year Longitudinal Study of the Psychological Effects of Administrative Segregation:* Colorado Department of Corrections, Office of Planning and Analysis.

Orne, M. (1962). On the social psychology of the psychological experiment. *American Psychologist, 17,* 776–783.

Paulus, P., & Dzindolet, M. (1993). Reactions of male and female inmates to prison confinement: Further evidence for a two-component model. *Criminal Justice and Behavior, 20*(2), 149–166.

Pizarro, J., & Stenius, V. M. K. (2004). Supermax prisons: Their rise, current practices, and effect on inmates. *The Prison Journal, 84*(2), 248–264.

Re: *Medley,* 134 160 (U.S. Supreme Court 1890).

Roberts, J. V., & Gebotys, R. J. (2001). Commentary #1: Prisoners of isolation: Research on the effect of administrative segregation. *Canadian Journal of Criminology, January,* 85–97.

Rogers, R. (1993). Solitary confinement. *International Journal of Offender Therapy & Comparative Criminology, 37*(4), 339–349.

Sestoft, D. M., Andersen, H. S., Lilleboek, T. (1998). Impact of solitary confinement on hospitalization among Danish prisoners in custody. *International Journal of Law and Psychiatry, 21*(1), 99–108.

Shalev, S. (2008). *A Sourcebook on Solitary Confinement* (No. ISBN 978-0-85328-314-0): Mannheim Centre for Criminology London School of Economics and Political Science Houghton Street, London WC2A 2AE, UK.

Shalev, S. (2009). *Supermax: Controlling Risk through Solitary Confinement.* Portland, OR: Willan Publishing.

Shalev, S., & Lloyd, M. (2010). *Though This Be Method, Yet There Is Madness in't: Commentary on One Year Longitudinal Study of the Psychological Effects of Administrative Segregation.* Washington, DC: NIC Corrections and Mental Health Update.

Suedfeld, P. (1982). Reactions and attributes of prisoners in solitary confinement. *Criminal Justice and Behavior, 9*(3), 303–340.

Suedfeld, P., & Roy, C. (1975). Using social isolation to change the behavior of disruptive inmates. *International Journal of Offender Therapy and Comparative Criminology, 19*(1), 90–99.

Suedfeld, P., Ramirez, C., Deaton, J., & Baker-Brown, G. (1982). Reactions and attributes of prisoners in solitary confinement. *Criminal Justice and Behavior, 9*(3), 303–340.

Suls, J. (1977). Social comparison theory and research: Overview from 1954. In H. Toch, (2003). The contemporary relevance of early experiments with supermax reform. *Prison Journal, 83*(2), 221–228.

Thackray, R. I. (1981). The stress of boredom and monotony: A consideration of the evidence. *Psychosomatic Medicine, 43*(2), 165.

Toch, H. (1992). *Mosaic of Despair: Human Breakdown in Prison.* Washington, DC: American Psychological Association.

Toch, H. (2003). The contemporary relevance of early experiments with supermax reform. *Prison Journal, 83*(2), 221–228.

Toch, H. Too little or too much: Activity and privacy. In H. Toch (ed.), *Living in Prison: The Ecology of Survival* (rev. ed.) (pp. 27). Washington, DC: American Psychological Association.

Todman, M. (2003). Boredom and psychotic disorders: Cognitive and motivational issues. *Psychiatry: Interpersonal & Biological Processes, 66*(2), 146–167.

Ulrich, R. (1993). Biophilia, biophobia, and natural landscapes. In S. Kellert & E. O. Wilson (Eds.), *The Biophilia Hypothesis* (pp. 138–172). Washington, DC: Island Press.

van Dierendonck, D., & Nijenhuis, J. T. (2005). Flotation restricted environmental stimulation therapy (REST) as a stress-management tool: A meta-analysis. *Psychology & Health, 20*(3), 405–412.

Vodanovich, S. J. (2003). Psychometric measures of boredom: A review of the literature. *Journal of Psychology: Interdisciplinary & Applied, 137*(6), 569–595.

Weinberg, M. M. (1967). Effects of partial sensory deprivation on involuntary subjects. *Dissertation Abstracts International, 28*(5), 2171–2172.

Wener, R. E., & Clark, N. (1977). *User Based Evaluation of the Chicago Metropolitan Correctional Center – Final Report.* Washington, DC: U.S. Bureau of Prisons.

Westin, A. (1967). *Privacy and Freedom.* New York: Atheneum.

Zinger, I., Wichmann, C., & Andrews, D. A. (2001). The psychological effects of 60 days in administrative segregation. *Canadian Journal of Criminology, 43*(1), 47–83.

Zubek, P. (1969). *Sensory Deprivation: 15 Years of Research.* New York: Meredith.

Zuckerman, M. (1994). *Behavioral Expressions and Biosocial Bases of Sensation Seeking.* New York: Cambridge University Press.

9

The Effects of Noise in Correctional Settings

Visit almost any large-scale prison or jail in the country and one of the first things that will strike you is the assault on your ears. Announcements blare over the PA, an officer yells across the dayroom to catch an inmate's attention, and a dozen inmates are carrying on conversations. Chairs and tables are being dragged across the floor, and TVs are playing. It is a relief for those wearing visitor passes to exit through the clanking heavy metal door to the relative quiet of the hallway.

But what about the staff who are there for all or most of 8-hour shifts or the inmates who live there? What is the impact of this constant cacophony on them? As with many stressors, it is obvious that noise is unpleasant, at best. But what are the concerns about noise beyond being an unpleasant background to everyday activities? How are individuals – staff and inmates – affected? Does noise change staff and inmate behavior in ways that are important to health, safety, and performance?

This chapter addresses physical as well as psychological definitions of noise, how noise is considered in research settings, as well as in correctional institutions and national standards for institutional design. The review of research on noise will consider both auditory and nonauditory effects of noise, such as those on behavior and stress.

Noise is usually defined as unwanted sound (Lipscomb, 1974; Schmidt, 2005; Stansfeld & Matheson, 2003). This definition carries with it, of course, both physical and psychological components including its loudness and discordant nature, how unpleasant it seems, the signal qualities of the sound relating to its content, and the information it carries.

Although the standard definition of *noise* includes an important psychological component (since "unwanted" implies evaluation or appraisal), psychological elements almost never play a role in the measurement of noise, at least as commonly taken to determine the acoustic properties of a space. Most assessments measure ambient sound – not noise. The most common form of measurement for spatial acoustics looks at the intensity or power of a sound, most typically using a sound meter that provides a reading on the decibel (db) scale. Measurements are usually made in dBA, which filters the input for sounds that are in the range of the human ear. The decibel scale is logarithmic, such that an increase in just three decibels represents a doubling of the power of the sound.

Acoustical experts often make use of a noise criteria curve (NC), which is similar to decibel readings but adjusts for the frequency as well as the intensity of the sound, providing ratings of acceptable levels of background noise to allow for conversation (Beranek, 1989).[1] Yet, power and frequency measures alone may not be sufficient even as measures of the critical physical aspects of sound in a setting. Although decibel level is reliable for measuring the power of constant sound, it may not be the best way of reporting the acoustic quality of the space as experienced over a period of time, for instance, in the way the intelligibility of speech is affected. For that purpose, it is important to take into account the reverberation time (RT), an index of sound decay that measures how long it takes a sound to bounce back to its source. Variance from optimal reverberation times can significantly affect speech intelligibility, and provides a better approximation of the psychological response to the acoustic environment (Bistafa & Bradley, 2000; Duquesnoy & Plomp, 1980; Steeneken & Houtgast, 1973).

The relationship between increases in the power of a sound and increases in the perception of loudness of the sound are not linear and are characterized by a power function. This psychophysical function, as described by Stevens (1955), demonstrated that perceived loudness doubles as the decibel level increases by 10 units. To address this relationship, Stevens developed a scale of rated perception of loudness – sones. There is, however, no such standard rating for the level of "unwantedness" or "annoyance" of a sound – and such ratings are rarely attempted, except in the cases of noise research conducted as part of psychological experiments (Fields, 1993). In most cases, then, measurements of the level of "noise" are actually reporting sound levels. The quality of "noise" is inferred.

NOISE IN CORRECTIONAL INSTITUTIONS

Noise is an important issue in prisons and jails in large measure because most correctional institutions are inherently difficult spaces in terms of their acoustic properties, because of their design and the multiple sources of sound that are constantly present, and because acoustics has received relatively little attention from correctional planners.

ACOUSTIC DESIGN ISSUES

Jail and prison living areas usually combine large, open interior spaces with ubiquitous use of hard materials and hard surfaces. Because of the cavernous dayrooms that are often created when living units have two or three flights of cells, large reverberation times (sometimes longer than 2 seconds) are a common problem in correctional settings, creating uncomfortable echoing, with waves of sounds reflecting around the space, even while new sounds are generated (Rostad & Christoff, 2006). Correctional institutions typically use hard materials and hard surfaces for economic and security purposes. Despite evidence of positive experiences with softer materials in some settings, as discussed in earlier chapters of this book, many correctional officials and designers assume that soft materials, such as carpeting, upholstered furniture, and wall fabric are too costly because they will be quickly worn out or intentionally damaged by the inmates. Floors, walls and ceilings, therefore, are typically constructed from concrete or similarly hard and reverberant materials and are covered with a minimum amount of sound-absorbing materials. Glass and metal are also commonly used. All of these are highly reflective of sound and, along with the very high ceilings and large open areas that are often present in these facilities, increase the reverberation time of a space. As can be seen in Figure 35, as reverberation time increases, holding dBA constant, sound intelligibility drops precipitously.

Multiple Sources of Sound

Correctional settings house large numbers of people engaged in many different formal and informal activities, resulting in a continuous mix of voices in varieties of conversations at different and variable levels of loudness. The sound that comes from dozens of voices, often fifty or more, occupying a large open space at the same time, and engaged in tasks or casual activity, can be considerable. On top of that, these settings have a number of mechanical

FIGURE 34. Jail dayrooms typically are large spaces with hard materials. Courtesy of Carter Goble Lee Associates.

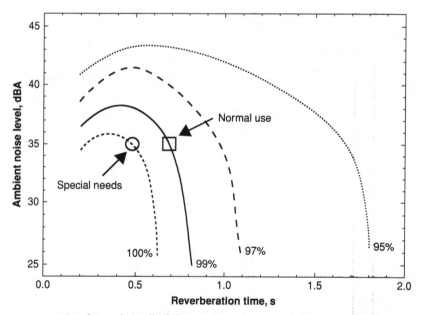

FIGURE 35. Equal speech intelligibility contours for 300-m³ (classroom-sized) room and RT design goals. http://irc.nrc-cnrc.gc.ca/pubs/ctus/51_e.html Bradley, J. S. (2002). *Acoustical Design of Rooms for Speech*. Ottawa: National Research Council of Canada.

sources of sound. Most correctional facilities have background sound that comes from mechanical systems, mostly including heating, cooling, and ventilation. These constant sources can add a significant background "hum" to the space.

Most correctional institutions also experience a significant amount of sound input from various electronic devices, such as one or more televisions, radios, or music systems,[2] and an intercom system that often has multiple speakers. Even though television sound levels are often limited mechanically or by rules, it is not uncommon for intercom speakers to blare at a very high level. In jails and prisons there is also the common sound of the opening and closing of doors, gates, cabinets, and so on, sometimes with a very loud bang.

Level of Attention

Though many recognize that acoustic properties of correctional settings are poor and, at the very least, irritating, this issue has typically not been a major priority for designers or managers. Current standards provided by the American Correctional Association limit ambient noise levels to 70 dBA during the day and 45 dBA at night (*Performance-Based Standards, 2004*). Standards that addressed the full range of auditory issues and placed stricter limits on acoustic design would necessarily involve more sophisticated measurement (such as of reverberation times) and would require significant expense to bring facilities into compliance.

Even though these are acoustically challenging spaces with many sources of input, there is little impetus or motivation to push forward significant improvements in acoustic design. Use of acoustic tiles on ceilings or walls can be helpful, but often makes only relatively small improvement to the overall acoustic quality of the space. In addition, although some of these noises are constant and predictable (mechanical noise), other sources are intermittent and unpredictable, properties that have reliably been found to increase annoyance. Moreover, most of the occupants of the spaces – inmates and officers – commonly perceive themselves as having little ability to control the level of these inputs or their own exposure. As has been noted in previous chapters predictability and control appear to be the most critical dimensions in determining how much damage is caused by noise.

THE EFFECTS OF NOISE ON OCCUPANTS OF A SPACE

Even though this review focuses mostly on the nonacoustic effects of noise, it is important to note that there is a significant medical literature on the impact on acoustic sensitivity to short- and long-term exposure to high levels of sound. Stated simply, with significant long-term exposure, people suffer hearing loss. Constant and long-term exposure to high levels of sound (85 dBA or more) results in permanent threshold shift, a loss of sensitivity to sounds (Stansfeld & Matheson, 2003). There is in fact, one report that indicates a high incidence of hearing loss among inmates in correctional settings (Jacobson, Jacobson, & Crowe, 1989), suggesting exposure in these institutions to sound levels that are much higher than would be found in other kinds of residential environments. Noise exposure has also been linked to other physical problems, including nausea and headaches (Stansfeld & Matheson, 2003) and possibly hypertension (Evans, 2001).

The nonacoustic impacts of noise, largely drawn from studies in noncorrectional settings, have implications on health and quality of life for inmates and officers relating to task performance, social behavior, and stress. One obvious nonacoustic effect of noise that can directly impact inmates is sleep deprivation (also referred to in the next chapter concerning nighttime light levels). Noise at night can cause sleep disturbance, and there is evidence that people do not easily habituate to these effects. That is, the effects may remain significant even after long periods of time and repeated exposures. Repeated exposure to noise (at 50 dBA or higher) can be sufficient to increase heart rate and blood pressure during sleep (Stansfeld & Matheson, 2003), adding to stress and presumably making sleep less restful. A recent World Health Organization report (Fritschi, Brown, Kim, Schwela & Kephalopoulos, 2011) concluded that "noise affects sleep in terms of immediate effects (e.g. arousal responses, sleep stage changes, awakenings, body movements, total wake time, autonomic responses), after-effects (e.g. sleepiness, daytime performance, cognitive function deterioration) and long-term effects (e.g. self-reported chronic sleep disturbance)" (p. 55).

A meta-analysis of 143 sleep deprivation studies by Pilcher and Huffcutt (1996) concluded that sleep deprivation has powerful negative effects on human functioning, in a way underestimated previously. They found that effects on mood were particularly strong (that is, much greater than on cognitive and motor performance effects) and that partial sleep deprivation (loss of some hours and stages of sleep) had the strongest detrimental effects. This analysis is supported by a recent study (Ireland & Culpin, 2006) that found a negative relationship between quantity and quality of sleep and aggressive behavior among incarcerated adolescent males. Noise has been shown to negatively affect sleep quality and stress levels among hospital patients, and contribute to burnout of nurses (Topf, 2000; Topf, Bookman, & Arand, 1996; Topf & Dillon, 1988; Topf & Thompson, 2001).

Performance Effects

Evidence from laboratory studies and from field research in a variety of non-correctional settings indicates that noise can have significant effects on the performance of tasks, particularly when the task is complex and demanding (Smith, 1989; Stansfeld & Matheson, 2003). Noise may affect task performance by means of a link between exposure, increased arousal, and impaired performance (Cohen & Weinstein, 1981). This increase in arousal level may cause workers to narrow their focus of attention, and therefore increase the chance that cues critical to the successful performance of the task will be missed (see Broadbent, 1979; Cohen & Weinstein, 1981; Evans & Hygge, 2007; and Smith, 1991, for detailed reviews).

The findings of several studies reinforce concerns for the effects of noise on the well-being and efficacy of prison staff. Noise may increase the likelihood of accidents on the job and this risk may persist after the noise itself is reduced (Cohen, 1973; Wilkins & Acton, 1982). High levels of noise may specifically impair the level of cognitive functioning, including memory, reading (Hygge, Evans, & Bullinger, 2002; Haines, Stansfeld, Job, et al., 2001), and vigilance (Smith, 1988). Noise may also make job stress worse, reduce job satisfaction, and reduce attachment to the organization (Leather, Beale, & Sullivan, 2003; Raffaello & Maass, 2002). These are factors that could affect turnover of officers and in turn can hinder the organization's ability to retain the experienced and motivated staff needed to support programs and security.

Social Behavior

Laboratory simulations indicate that uncontrollable or unpredictable noise can lead to increased aggressive behavior, although typically there are other factors involved. For example, Donnerstein and Wilson (1976) found that noise increased aggression if the subjects had been previously angered and had no sense of control over the noise source. Other studies also showed that, when they had no control over the noise, subjects were more aggressive when they also had been previously provoked or felt that they had been attacked (Gaur, 1988; Geen, 1978; Geen & McCown, 1984).

Although these studies have not been replicated in correctional institutions, potential implications for both staff and inmate behavior in such settings are easy to imagine. One might reasonably expect greater expression of anger in these settings where it is common to be exposed to loud, chronically present, unpredictable, and uncontrollable noise. It is also likely that in some of these noisy situations there will be people who are angry or feel otherwise attacked or provoked, or feel that those who had the power to reduce the noise level did not do so.

Other social effects of noise may also have implications for the correctional setting. For instance, research in laboratory and field settings indicates that when exposed to noise people are less likely to provide helping behavior. It appears that noise reduces the likelihood that someone will notice when others are in distress, and it also lessens the chances that they will choose to help out if they do notice the problem (Jones, Chapman, & Auburn, 1981; Mathews & Canon, 1975).

Noise and Stress

Many noise studies look at effects on human stress. The paradigmatic studies of stress from noise in humans were conducted by Glass and Singer (1972). Using noise as a model for what they considered to be a broader problem of urban stress, they found that controllability and predictability of the noise were the most important variables in determining responses to stress – more important even than loudness, particularly when measuring aftereffects. Exposure to unpredictable and/or uncontrollable noise led to increased stress and reduced motivation for completing the task, as shown in lower levels of persistence in the face of frustration. Glass and Singer (1972) interpreted these effects in terms of increases in learned helplessness induced by exposure to these uncontrollable, unpleasant environment effects. These effects have been replicated in both laboratory and field settings (schools) in studies suggesting significant behavioral, emotional, and mental health effects of noise (Evans & Stecker, 2004; Cohen, 1980).

Exposure to noise has also been found to affect psychophysiological indices of stress, such as increases in heart rate and cardiovascular responses. Prolonged exposure to noise levels similar to those commonly found in prisons and jails elevates blood pressure and may affect stress hormones like cortisol (Babisch, Fromme, Beyer, & Ising, 2001; Babisch et al., 2003; Evans, 2001; Evans & Johnson, 2000; Ising & Kruppa, 2004; Stansfeld & Matheson, 2003).

The Ecology of Noise

Only in the laboratory does noise exist as a single, isolated variable. In real and complex settings, such as correctional institutions, noise occurs in combination with other conditions that may be difficult in and of themselves. For instance, noise levels are likely to increase when there is significant crowding, because of the sheer growth in the number of voices and activities, as well as the heightened potential for arguments. Other environmental conditions, such as heat, cold, air quality (Anderson, Anderson, Dorr, DeNeve, & Flanagan, 2000; Anderson & DeNeve, 1992; Bell & Baron, 1977; Haertzen, Buxton, Covi, & Richards, 1993; Rotton, Frey, Barry,

Milligan, & Fitzpatrick, 1979; Wyon, Andersen, & Lundqvist, 1979), and general discomfort or boredom (James, 1982; Rupp & Vodanovich, 1997), may not cause more noise, but can co-exist with it in a jail or prison, adding to overall stress. Exposure to multiple stressors may increase their overall negative effect on the individual (Evans, Allen, Tafalla, & O'Meara, 1996; Evans & Stecker, 2004).

The level of control people feel they have over the noise is important in determining the amount of stress it causes, and in an institution this may be determined by the degree to which inmates feel they can escape the immediate situation or otherwise avoid high noise levels. Daffern, Mayer, and Martin (2004) noted, in another institutional context, that "the inability of... patients to retire to their rooms when irritated by the noise, teasing, insults, and intrusions into personal space by other patients may have contributed to the higher rate of aggression..." (p. 113). We (Wener & Olsen, 1980) also cited the ability inmates had to freely go into private rooms in the Metropolitan Correctional Centers as an important element in reducing tension levels in the face of many unit problems, including high noise levels. Stansfield and Matheson (2003) point out that noise can have broad effects on behavior, essentially altering the entire social ecology of a space. Because noise is both noxious and space related, people will alter their usual behavior patterns and move about a space in order to avoid or reduce exposure.

The population of jails and prisons is made up of people who often have had social and economic difficulties outside of the institution, and who, as a result, may suffer from poor self-image. It may also be useful, therefore, to note a study that found that people with low levels of perceived self-efficacy were more likely to experience stress when exposed to high levels of uncontrollable noise (Kuno, Yazawa, & Ohira, 2003). In addition, noise has a greater negative impact on people who experienced long-term and chronic unemployment, perhaps because of the increase in learned helplessness that comes from this condition (Weiss, 1997). These studies suggest that, if anything, the population of inmates comes from backgrounds and life experiences that may make them even more sensitive to noise effects than the general population.

SUMMARY AND CONCLUSION

There has been a distinct lack of research on the impact of noise on critical behaviors of interest for correctional settings, including task performance, learning, communication, social behavior, aggression, stress, and health, and even less research on noise in correctional settings themselves. This may be because other environmental issues (such as crowding) often seem to be more pressing. Moreover, noise is often confounded by crowding because much of the noise in correctional settings is generated by the people there. Nevertheless, there are several reasons to believe that noise should be addressed as part of jail and prison research programs. First, the noise level in these places can be very high. As Rostad and Christoff (2006) noted, the standards for minimally allowable noise levels adopted by the American Correctional Association (70 dBA daytime and 45 dBA at night) would not be considered reasonable in any white-collar setting – where similar behaviors (paperwork, meetings, discussion groups, classes) occur. For example, the ANSI standard for maximum school noise levels is 35 dBA and EPA standards for workplaces are more commonly in the 50 dBA range.

Even these ACA standards, however, are not easily met in many correctional facilities, including those in fairly new buildings. Rostad, Meister, and Wener (1996) measured noise levels and officer responses in state prisons and found that levels were high (commonly approaching the 70 dBA level). Reverberation times were often between 1.5 and 2 seconds and were perceived by officers to be very annoying and stressful. Moreover, officers rated the noise levels as a concern, and indicated that they felt that noise contributed to tension levels.

Rostad and Christof (2006) also noted that measurement of dBA levels was difficult to use as a standard because of the high degree of variability of sound levels over the course of a day in many prisons and jails. They proposed a revised standard that also addressed reverberation time, which can be reasonably estimated from plans, suggesting that standards should be set at levels as low as 0.5 seconds for one-floor institutions.

A second reason to believe that noise is an important issue for correctional institutions lies in the reviews of research in other settings showing that exposure to intermittent, uncontrollable, and unpredictable noise, over long periods of time, at sound levels considerably lower than those often found in prisons and jails, have a range of negative effects that could impact the welfare of inmates, smooth management and operation of institutions, and the well-being of those who work in them. These include the ability to successfully operate educational and rehabilitative programs, and changes in mood, motivation, and behavior that could affect levels of tension, stress, and health.

No single level of measurement of sound can be cited and defended by research that represents a clear threshold beyond which physical and psychological problems start. The nature of sound and noise is too complex and too embedded in the physical and social context for that to be true, although benchmarks have been found in past research that can be used as guideposts for planners and administrators. It is very clear, though, that having less exposure and more control over noise is better for all concerned. It is also likely that prisons and jails are places where the occupants are more rather than less sensitive to potential noise effects. They are settings where noise levels must be endured for long stretches of time (8-hour shifts for staff, 24-hour days for inmates) for days, weeks, months, and years; where residents are present involuntarily; and where all involved, inmates and staff, are likely to feel that they have little or no control over the sources of or amount of exposure to noise levels. They are also sites where those affected, inmates and staff, are likely to be exposed to multiple stressors (noise, crowding, boredom, fear, and so forth), which can multiply the impacts of any individual stressor.

Lastly, prisons and jails are places where we should be especially careful about noise effects, because of the potential for severe consequences from any situation that results in increases of stress, frustration, and anxiety. Any phenomenon with the potential to worsen the mood, increase argumentativeness, and levels of hostility and aggression among inmates or staff members should be of special concern to administrators, staff, and inmate advocates. In addition, the potential for noise to increase stress and cause health problems for officers should be troubling given the number of years many will be exposed to these workplace conditions. The physical and psychological consequences reviewed in this chapter suggest that correctional administrators and designers should consider noise an important issue in facility safety and security and for inmate and staff well-being.

References

Anderson, C. A., Anderson, K. B., Dorr, N., DeNeve, K., & Flanagan, M. (2000). Temperature and aggression. In M. P. Zanna (Ed.), *Advances in Experimental Social Psychology,* 32(pp. 63–133). San Diego, CA: Academic Press.

Anderson, C. A., & DeNeve, K. M. (1992). Temperature, aggression, and the negative affect escape model. *Psychological Bulletin,* 111(2), 347–351.

Arnsten, A., & Goldman-Rakic, P. (1998). Noise stress impairs prefrontal cortical cognitive function in monkeys: Evidence for a hyperdopaminergic mechanism. *Archives of General Psychiatry,* 55(4), 362–368.

Babisch, W., Fromme, H., Beyer, A., & Ising, H. (2001). Increased catecholamine levels in urine in subjects exposed to road traffic noise: The role of stress hormones in noise research. *Environment International,* 26(7–8), 475–481.

Babisch, W., Segal, S., Eviatar, E., Lapinsky, J., Shlamkovitch, N., Kessler, A., et al. (2003). Stress hormones in the research on cardiovascular effects of noise. *Stress,* 5(18), 1–11.

Bell, P. A., & Baron, R. A. (1977). Aggression and ambient temperature: The facilitating and inhibiting effects of hot and cold environments. *Bulletin of the Psychonomic Society,* 9(6), 443–445.

Beranek, L. L. (1989). Application of NCB noise criterion curves. *Noise Control Engineering Journal,* 33(2), 45–56.

Bistafa, S. R., & Bradley, J. S. (2000). Reverberation time and maximum background-noise level for classrooms from a comparative study of speech intelligibility metrics. *The Journal of the Acoustical Society of America, 107*, 861.

Bradley, J. (2002). Acoustical design of rooms for speech. *Construction Technology Update, 51*, 6.

Broadbent, D. E. (1979). Human performance and noise. *Handbook of Noise Control, 2*, 1–20.

Cohen, A. (1973). Industrial noise and medical, absence, and accident record data on exposed workers. In W. Ward (Ed.), *Proceedings of the 2nd International Congress on Noise as a Public Health Problem* (Report No. EPA 550/973-008), pp. 441–453.

Cohen, S. (1980). Aftereffects of stress on human performance and social behavior: A review of research and theory. *Psychological Bulletin, 88*, 82–108.

Cohen, S., & Weinstein, N. (1981). Nonauditory effects of noise on behavior and health. *Journal of Social Issues, 37*(1), 36.

Daffern, M., Mayer, M. M., & Martin, T. (2004). Environment contributors to aggression in two forensic psychiatric hospitals. *International Journal of Forensic Mental Health, 3*(1), 105–114.

Donnerstein, E., & Wilson, D. (1976). Effects of noise and perceived control on ongoing and subsequent aggressive behavior. *Journal of Personality and Social Psychology, 34*(5), 774–781.

Duquesnoy, A. J., & Plomp, R. (1980). Effect of reverberation and noise on the intelligibility of sentences in cases of presbyacusis. *The Journal of the Acoustical Society of America, 68*, 537.

Evans, G. W. (2001). Environmental stress and health. In A. Baum & T. Revenson (Eds.), *Handbook of Health Psychology* (pp. 365–385). Hillsdale, NJ: Erlbaum.

Evans, G. W., Allen, K., Tafalla, R., & O'Meara (1996). Multiple stressors. *Journal of Environmental Psychology, 16*, 147–154.

Evans, G. W., & Hygge, S. (2007). Noise and performance in children and adults. In L. Luxon & D. Prasher (Eds.), *Noise and Its Effects* (pp. 549–566). London: John Wiley Publishers.

Evans, G. W., & Johnson, D. (2000). Stress and open-office noise. *Journal of Applied Psychology, 85*(5), 779–783.

Evans, G. W., & Stecker, R. (2004). The motivational consequences of environmental stress. *Journal of Environmental Psychology, 24*, 143–165.

Fields, J. M. (1993). Effect of personal and situational variables on noise annoyance in residential areas. *Journal of the Acoustical Society of America, 93*, 2753–2763.

Fritschi, L., Brown, A. L., Kim, R., Schwela, D., & Kephalopoulos, S. (Eds.). (2011). *Burden of disease from environmental noise: Quantification of healthy life years lost in Europe.* Bonn, Germany: WHO European Centre for Environment and Health.

Gaur, S. D. (1988). Noise: Does it make you angry? *Indian Psychologist, 5*(1), 51–56.

Geen, R. G. (1978). Effects of attack and uncontrollable noise on aggression. *Journal of Research in Personality, 12*(1), 15–29.

Geen, R. G., & McCown, E. J. (1984). Effects of noise and attack on aggression and physiological arousal. *Motivation & Emotion, 8*(3), 231.

Glass, D., & Singer, J. (1972). *Urban Stress.* New York: Academic Press.

Haertzen, C., Buxton, K., Covi, L., & Richards, H. (1993). Seasonal changes in rule infractions among prisoners: A preliminary test of the temperature-aggression hypothesis. *Psychological Reports, 72*(1), 195–200.

Haines, M. M., Stansfeld, S. A., Job, R. F. S., et al. (2001). Chronic aircraft noise exposure, stress responses, mental health, and cognitive performance in school children. *Psychological Medicine, 31*, 265–277.

Hygge, S., Evans, G. W., & Bullinger, M. (2002). A prospective study of some effects of aircraft noise on cognitive performance in school children. *Psychological Science, 13*, 469–474.

Ireland, J. L., & Culpin, V. (2006). The relationship between sleeping problems and aggression, anger, and impulsivity in a population of juvenile and young offenders. *Journal of Adolescent Health, 38*(6), 649–655.

Ising, H., & Kruppa, B. (2004). Health effects caused by noise: Evidence in the literature from the past 25 years. *Noise and Health, 6*(22), 5–13(19).

Jacobson, C., Jacobson, J., & Crowe, T. (1989). Hearing loss in prison inmates. *Ear and Hearing, 10*(3), 178–183.

James, A. (1982). Boredom – The stress of predictability. *Journal of Physical Education, Recreation & Dance, 53*(7), 35–36.

Jones, D., Chapman, A., & Auburn, T. (1981). Noise in the environment: A social perspective. *Journal of Environmental Psychology, 1*(1), 43–59.

Kuno, M., Yazawa, H., & Ohira, H. (2003). Learned helplessness, generalized self-efficacy, and immune function. *Japanese Journal of Psychology, 73*(6), 472–479.

Leather, P., Beale, D., & Sullivan, L. (2003). Noise, psychosocial stress and their interaction in the workplace. *Journal of Environmental Psychology, 23*(2), 213–222.

Lipscomb, D. M. (1974). *Noise: The Unwanted Sounds.* Chicago: Nelson-Hall.

Mathews, K. E., & Canon, L. K. (1975). Environmental noise level as a determinant of helping behavior. *Journal of Personality and Social Psychology, 32*(4), 571–577.

Performance-Based Standards for Adult Local Detention Facilities (4th ed.). (2004). Alexandria, VA: American Correctional Association.

Pilcher, J. J., & Huffcutt, A. I. (1996). Effects of sleep deprivation on performance: A meta-analysis. *Sleep, 19*(4), 318–326.

Raffaello, M., & Maass, A. (2002). Chronic exposure to noise in industry: The effects on satisfaction, stress symptoms, and company attachment. *Environment & Behavior, 34*(5), 651.

Rostad, K., & Christoff, J. P. (2006). Negating noise: Study pushes for change to noise standard. *Corrections News, 12*(5), 34.

Rostad, K., Meister, W., & Wener, R. E. (1996). *Wisconsin Department of Corrections Noise Study.* Washington, DC: Committee on Acoustics in Corrections.

Rotton, J., Frey, J., Barry, T., Milligan, M., & Fitzpatrick, M. (1979). The air pollution experience and physical aggression. *Journal of Applied Social Psychology, 9*(5), 397–412.

Rupp, D. E., & Vodanovich, S. J. (1997). The role of boredom proneness in self-reported anger and aggression. *Journal of Social Behavior & Personality, 12*(4), 925–936.

Schmidt, C. W. (2005). Noise that annoys: Regulating unwanted sound. *Environmental Health Perspectives, 113*(1), A42.

Smith, A. (1989). A review of the effects of noise on human performance. *Scandinavian Journal of Psychology, 30*(3), 185.

Smith, A. P. (1988). Acute effects of noise exposure: An experimental investigation of the effects of noise and task parameters on cognitive vigilance tasks. *International Archives of Occupational and Environmental Health, 60*(4), 307–310.

Smith, A. T. (1991). A review of the non-auditory effects of noise on health. *Work & Stress, 5*(1), 49.

Stansfeld, S. A., & Matheson, M. P. (2003). Noise pollution: Non-auditory effects on health. *British Medical Bulletin, 68*(1), 243–257.

Steeneken, H. J. M., & Houtgast, T. (1973). The modulation transfer function in room acoustics as a predictor of speech intelligibility. *Acustica, 28*, 66–73.

Stevens, S. S. (1955). The measurement of loudness. *The Journal of the Acoustical Society of America, 27*, 815.

Topf, M. (2000). Hospital noise pollution: An environmental stress model to guide research and clinical interventions. *Journal of Advanced Nursing, 31*(3), 520–528.

Topf, M., & Dillon, E. (1988). Noise-induced stress as a predictor of burnout in critical care nurses. *Heart Lung, 17*(5), 567–574.

Topf, M., & Thompson, S. (2001). Interactive relationships between hospital patients' noise-induced stress and other stress with sleep. *Heart & Lung: Journal of Acute & Critical Care, 30*(4), 237.

Topf, M., Bookman, M., & Arand, D. (1996). Effects of critical care unit noise on the subjective quality of sleep. *Journal of Advanced Nursing, 24*(3), 545–551.

Weiss, L. J. (1997). Acute and chronic stress: The mediating effects of loss of control. *Dissertation Abstracts International: Section B: The Sciences & Engineering, 58*(5), 2756.

Welch, B. L. (1979). Extra-auditory health effects of industrial noise: Survey of foreign literature (AHRL-TR-79-41). *Aerospace Medical Research Laboratory, June*.

Wener, R. E. (2006). The Effectiveness of direct supervision correctional design and management: A review of the literature. *Criminal Justice & Behavior, 33*, 367–391.

Wener, R. E., & Olsen, R. (1980). Innovative correctional environments: A user assessment. *Environment & Behavior, 12*(4), 478–493.

Wilkins, P. A., & Acton, W. I. (1982). Noise and accidents – A review. *Annals of Occupational Hygiene, 25*(3), 249.

Wyon, D. P., Andersen, I., & Lundqvist, G. R. (1979). The effects of moderate heat stress on mental performance. *Scandanavian Journal of Work Environoronments & Health, 5*, 352–361.

10

Windows, Light, Nature, and Color

To the casual observer, the presence or absence of windows in a prison or jail may seem like a frill or a minor aesthetic concern – certainly not on the order of more well-known and highly publicized prison issues such as crowding or isolation as a stressful environmental problem. The same is true for the level of light, the presence of nature elements, or the kind and amount of color in the environment – hardly the things that become the focus of made-for-TV prison movies. But, as we have noted often before, incarceration acts to magnify and intensify experiences. Like a pebble in a shoe, even small irritants can become serious stressors after enough time and especially when there are few options to alleviate situations. Issues that are tolerable for brief periods in "the outside world," where there are other options for escape or avoidance and a measure of control, may become intolerable within the total institution. As we will see, research indicates that problems arising from the absence of windows, nature views, daylight, and color may not be small. In the United States, both the courts and standard-setting organizations, like the American Correctional Association, have, at various times and to varying degrees, recognized the importance of these issues as design elements. For example, the fourth edition of the American Correctional Association standards (*Performance-Based Standards*, 2004) requires that all inmates in adult local detention facilities (ALDF) have access to natural light. If confined 10 or more hours a day, that access must be via a window of at least 3 square feet. If the inmate is in the cell less than 10 hours a day, the cell does not have to have its own outside window. The institution has the option of providing natural light from an adjacent space. Recognizing that most inmates spend a great deal of time out of their cells and in dayrooms, the ALDF standard also requires windows in dayroom areas of at least 12 square feet, 2 additional square feet for each inmate who is likely to be in the dayroom at any one time and whose own cell does not have an outside window.

Earlier versions of these standards recommended specific lighting levels for interior spaces, such as a minimum of 20-foot candles in cells. These have been removed in later editions in favor of generic performance standards, as seen in statements indicating that overall lighting must be appropriate for specific tasks to be performed, taking into account available natural light, surfaces, and so on. As for view, some court rulings have indicated that inmates should have access to windows, though mostly for ventilation (*Hutchings* v. *Corum*, 1980).

Correctional environments are work environments for security and other staff, as well as for inmate–workers and students. There are tasks to be performed in offices and secure areas alike, including reading, writing, typing, and filing, among others. As such, they should conform to guidelines for lighting in the work environment such as those concerning levels of illumination and glare for proper use of computer workstations, as well as for classrooms, industrial facilities, recreational facilities, and public areas. These can be found in the *Handbook of the Illuminating Engineering Society of North America* (*Lighting Handbook*, 2000) as well as in guidelines supplied by the Occupational Safety and Health Administration (http://www.osha.gov/SLTC/etools/computerworkstations/wkstation_enviro.html#glare). These guidelines can also be useful for identifying needed quality and levels of illumination for inmates when they are in school and work situations, such as in educational programs or work assignments within the facility.

Because staff members spend considerable amounts of time within institution walls, any impacts that accrue from lack of access to daylight, view, and proper illumination may have psychological and physical consequences for their work-life and health. Moreover, in some cases, staff members may face even more extreme conditions than inmates. It is not unusual, for instance, for some officers to spend an entire shift in spaces with no outside windows, such as when they are assigned to interior central control rooms. It is hard to know just how harmful these situations may be, as little research has been conducted on these conditions in correctional institutions. Staff members in these enclosed spaces have tasks that require focused attention and high vigilance (such as attending to many video monitors and other security signals), likely leading to strain and mental fatigue, but they do not gain the benefit of relief and restoration that can be offered by window views, as demonstrated in studies described in this chapter.

The findings cited for this discussion come from research in laboratories, extreme and unusual environments, office spaces, and environments for

FIGURE 36. Interior central control room. Courtesy of Carter Goble Lee Associates.

critical care. The benefits and drawbacks of laboratory research on these issues are similar to those with crowding and isolation studies. They allow for a great deal of control of conditions (level of lighting, time of day, and so on), as well as choice of subjects and random assignment to experimental groups. Labs also make it easy to be very specific about the task to be performed and the selection of outcome measurements. As with research on other environmental issues, an inevitable trade-off exists between the level of control exerted ("internal validity") and the degree to which the conditions resemble, and hence can be generalized to real settings of concern ("external and ecological validity" – see Shadish, Cook, & Campbell, 2002, and Winkel, 1987, for discussion of these issues).

Unusual and extreme settings, such as arctic bases or space stations, have been the focus of some research and discussions on the impacts of windows, lighting, nature-views, and color because the results of design decisions in these spaces can be critically important to life and health. For instance, Haines (1988) noted the psychological value of windows in confined spaces in his paper on the design of space capsules. He observed that in designing these critical environments for space habitats, windows are often an afterthought, added only after all other considerations have been taken into account.

Engineers involved in the early design of space capsules opposed providing any windows at all, because they presumed windows created unnecessary
risks to the physical integrity of atmospheric containment. They yielded only
when the first astronauts insisted on having windows (Wolfe, 1979). In the
same context, Wise and Wise (1988) reviewed considerable work on color
for NASA designers of space environments addressing habitable settings for
long-duration flights.

A number of recent and valuable environment and behavior studies have
taken place in hospitals and other health care settings, where design can
have a powerful and quantifiable impact on health and behavior (for a fuller
discussion, see Zimring & Ulrich, 2004). The growth of evidence-based design
related to windows, light, and nature in healthcare facilities has provided great
opportunities for understanding and applying research to patient care, and
this research may, in some cases, be applicable to the correctional setting.

In this chapter I consider:

- The effects of light on human behavior and health, including both the kind
  of light (sunlight or electrical sources, including lamps of many different
  kinds in intensity and quality), amounts and timing of exposure to light,
  and special issues about the nature of and problems relating to shift work
  as connected to lighting.
- The importance and effect of windows (which in the correctional context
  includes the distinction between interior and exterior windows).
- The psychological effects of views. In addition to providing light, windows
  also provide views, both into and out of a space, with social, aesthetic,
  stimulation, and informational implications. Recent research, discussed
  later in this chapter, addresses the psychological impacts of views of natural
  versus built settings.
- Current understanding of the impact of color in interior design on behavior,
  particularly as relevant to the correctional setting.

Lighting, windows, view, and color are closely interconnected in ways that
make it easy to confuse, confound, and conflate key findings. For instance, a
finding of positive behavioral effects related to the presence of windows in a
given site might be due to the daylight coming in through a window or the
quality of view out of it. Especially in field settings, it is not easy to control or
account for which element is most important.

Moreover, any effects that are attributable to daylight might be related either
to the nature and quality of daylight or to the quantity of it. If the former,
it would be reasonable to ask if the use of electrical lights can provide the

same qualities and have a similar effect. If the latter, it raises the question of whether a similarly intense electrical light could produce similar results, albeit at significant costs in energy expenditure. Some researchers have suggested that color must also be considered, along with lighting and view (Heerwagen & Wise, 1997; Wise & Wise, 1988). Color is a function of, and not independent from, lighting conditions, and an integral element of the way we connect with nature.

EFFECTS OF LIGHT ON BEHAVIOR AND HEALTH

In most correctional settings, access to daylight is limited both by architecture and regimen. In addition, the 24-hour nature of the prison and jail setting means that a great deal of activity occurs in the evening and overnight. With respect to these settings, then, it is especially important to consider electrical light both as a compliment to and a substitute for natural light, and discuss the various kinds of lighting and their effects.

Kinds of Lights

There are several qualitatively different kinds of electrical lights, each with somewhat different physical properties (*Lighting Handbook*, 2000). The most common kinds of electrical lights are incandescent (light that comes from heating a filament) and fluorescent (light is emitted when current is passed through an ionized gas). Most fluorescent lighting uses white light, although the white light contains color tints. The nature of those *tints*, the wavelength emitted, depends on the chemical composition of the phosphor lining of the bulb. The kind of light that is appropriate for any given space will depend on a number of considerations, including the nature of the space and the kinds of activities that will take place (Karlen & Benya, 2004). A detailed discussion of lighting design for space, addressing issues of the nature of the space and activities, can be found in a report by the Illuminating Engineering Society of North America (*Quality of the Visual Environment Committee*, 2009).

Humans evolved in a daylit environment, and our bodies react to changes in lighting conditions such as occur over the course of a day or year (Lockley, 2009). The way we react to lighting depends on its intensity, the spectrum of the light, and the timing of our exposure (Veitch, 2004). Although there is a great deal of research on the impacts of light on human behavior, Veitch and McColl (2001) and Gifford (1994) suggest that many lighting studies are flawed by poor controls for intensity, color, bulb type, and time of exposure.

There has been considerable discussion of the potential benefits of so-called full-spectrum lights in both popular and professional literature. Full-spectrum fluorescent lamps are designed to mimic the qualities of daylight in the north sky. Full-spectrum bulbs emit light across the broad visible spectral range. Although these bulbs better approximate daylight than most other sources, it remains a less than perfect imitation of the sun. "The purported similarity between FSFL emissions and daylight is tenuous at best" (Boyce, 1994, p. 7).

The output of a full-spectrum lamp contributes to its good color rendering, so it is generally a good light source if fine color judgments are needed. Other benefits claimed in the literature for full-spectrum lamps, such as positive effects on perception, vision, cognition, physiology and health are generally inconsistent, in part because much of the research is of poor quality (Boyce, 1994; McColl & Veitch, 2001).

The most important difference between full-spectrum fluorescent light and daylight may be in the intensity of the light exposure. One study observed that occupants of buildings exposed to daylight often received 2,000 or more lux (lumens per meter), whereas those in electrically lit buildings rarely received more than 100 lux (Cawthorne, 1991, described in Baker, 2004). Full-spectrum bulbs are also different from daylight in other ways. Daylight, for instance, is polarized (Veitch, 1994).

Light intensity may be particularly important for maintaining circadian rhythms. Circadian refers the daily 24-hour cycle as reflected in the biological cycles of organisms (Takahashi & Zatz, 1982). These patterns are affected by light and dark cycles and can be changed by exposure to high-intensity light (Cajochen, Chellappa, & Schmidt, 2010; Pechachek, Anderson, & Lockley, 2008).

IMPACTS OF LIGHT

Preference

Office workers, who often believe that daylight is healthier (Heerwagen & Heerwagen, 1986; Veitch & Gifford, 1996; Veitch, Hine, & Gifford, 1993), say they prefer natural light to electric light (Galasiu & Veitch, 2006; Markus, 1967), and may tolerate lower levels of light when it is daylight from windows rather than electric lights (Baker & Steemers, 2002). People tend to overestimate the percentage of light on their desk that comes from the exterior source, and the further they are from the window, the more the daylight effect is overestimated (Heerwagen & Heerwagen, 1984; Wells, 1965).

Begemann, van de Beld, and Tanner (1997) suggested that indoor lighting preferences reflect natural cycles in that there is a preference for changes in luminance that follow daylight changes, rather than constant levels. Daylight is dynamic – changing in quality and quantity over the course of the day and year and with weather (Leslie, 2003). Lighting design that tries to mimic these effects can add to the quality of the setting and help break the monotony experienced in many electrically-lit places – especially in enclosed institutional environments. Some designers of windowless or underground spaces have tried to compensate for lack of daylight with lighting that attempts to imitate the way sunlight changes in direction and intensity over the course of the day (Carmody & Sterling, 1987; Scuri, 1995).

The level of preference for daylight appears so consistently in findings across places and situations that some suggest that these responses are universal and culture-free (Nagy, Yasunaga, & Kose, 1995). It is not a stretch, then, to propose that daylighting is an important issue in jails and prisons, where inmates and staff are often cut off from easy access to windows, views of nature, and daylight.

Effects of Light

Variations in indoor lighting levels and spectra can affect cognitive performance and mood (Baron, Rea, & Daniels, 1992; Boyce, Heerwagen, Jones, Veitch, & Newsham, 2003). Much of the research on the biological and psychological effects of light has studied daylight, per se, although the impact of light from other sources may have the same effects. The intensity, spectra involved and timing of light exposure, from whatever source, all play a role in determining the impact of light on biological systems.

Exposure to natural light, based on the planet's 24-hour cycle, plays an important role in setting and maintaining circadian rhythms – the body's biological clock (Boyce, Hunter, & Howlett, 2003; Burgess, Sharkey, & Eastman, 2002; Lockley, 2009). Recent findings indicate that this time-setting function does not respond only or uniquely to natural light, and may be significantly affected by artificial light in the blue-green range (Lockley, 2009).

Some experts believe that, because of the extraordinary amount of time spent indoors with only, or primarily, electric lighting, people in Western, developed countries are not exposed to sufficient amounts of high intensity light. Such inadequate exposure can have negative health consequences with respect to vitamin D deficiency (Joseph, 2006; Rasmussen et al., 2000) and depression (Begeman et al., 1997; Espiritu et al., 1994). "The people with the shortest daily exposure time to high light levels reported the lowest mood, with a moderate correlation between atypical SAD mood symptoms and time in bright light" (Veitch, 2011 p. 42).

Disruption of circadian rhythms affects hormone regulation (Burgess, Sharkey, & Eastman, 2002; Fu & Lee, 2003) and can have short-term and long-term health consequences (Fu & Lee, 2003; Kayumov, Lowe, Rahman, Casper, & Shapiro, 2007; Ma et al., 2007). Office workers not only prefer sunlight from windows; they may be depressed without it (Hollon, Kendall, Norsted, & Watson, 1980). A survey of office workers showed that there was a direct and positive effect of sunlight on job satisfaction, intent to quit, and well-being, although there was no effect for overall level of illumination (Leather, Pyrgas, Beale, & Lawrence, 1998).

A series of recent studies in health care settings have suggested that exposure to daylight can have important positive health effects. Patients in rooms with good exposure to natural light have been found to have reduced hospital stays and reduced mortality rates. Sunny rooms, especially in the morning (rooms with eastern-facing windows) were associated with reduced depression and better health outcomes (Beauchemin & Hays, 1996, 1998; Benedetti, Colombo, Barbini, Campori, & Smeraldi, 2001). In addition, intensive care units with windows were associated with lower levels of depression as well as reduced anxiety and postoperative delirium (Keep, James, & Inman, 1980; Parker & Hodge, 1976; Ulrich, 2001). Postoperative patients with rooms on the bright side of a hospital were found to feel less stress, less pain, and took more than 20 percent fewer pain medications than comparable patients housed on the other side of the building (Walch et al., 2005). These results may be supported by lab studies showing that exposure to bright lights increases levels of serotonin precursors, with effects on well-being and mood (aan het Rot, Benkelfat, Boivin, & Young, 2007). Effective use of windows in design can increase daylight exposure (broad-spectrum and high-intensity light) for these health benefits and also save energy costs (Leslie, 2003).

Daylight has the intensity and spectra to set circadian rhythms, and losing access to the intensity of daylight for significant periods of time can result in mood disorders, such as seasonal affective disorder (SAD) and fatigue (Leslie, 2003). Even so, it is not necessarily the case that, as has been suggested, that people who are in buildings without daylight are operating in "biological darkness" (Leslie, 2003, p. 383), as there is increasing evidence that electric lighting of appropriate intensity and wavelength can have powerful biological and psychological effects comparable or similar to daylight (Lockley, 2009).

Not all spectra of light have the same effect on setting circadian cycles. The body responds to light through receptors in the eye that operate independently of rods and cones, and that seem to be especially sensitive to light in the blue-green range (Lockley, 2009). Exposure to light during normal sleeping times (night-time) has the additional effect of inhibiting the production of melatonin, which affects sleepiness (see the shift work discussion later in this chapter). Although it may be possible to sufficiently address circadian needs with blue lights of sufficient intensity, such lights would likely be seen as unpleasant and insufficient for work needs (Pechacek, Andersen, & Lockley, 2008).

The timing of exposure to light is also important. Human sleep-wake cycles may be synchronized by regular exposure to light levels. Recent research indicates that maintaining good sleep cycles is not just a function of the amount, kind, and timing of light, but rather the balance of proper light-dark cycles (Burgess et al., 2002; Lockley, Arendt & Skene, 2007; Veitch, 2004). People need not just properly lit environments but also reasonably darkened settings, at the right times of day, for good sleep. "Healthy light is inextricably linked to healthy darkness" (Veitch, 2010, p. 2). People who do not have access to regular light-dark cycles, such as those in extreme environments (as in polar or space habitats) suffer "circadian desynchrony" (Lockley, Arendt & Skene, 2007) with potential short and long term health impacts. Even very low levels of light during sleeping hours can inhibit the release of melatonin, disrupting sleep (Veitch, 2004).

Shift Work and Sleep Deprivation

Lighting for night shift work is a concern for any 24-hour setting. Adapting to late shifts can be difficult in ways that impair both performance and judgment, and can have deleterious effects on life outside of work including mood and sleeping quality (Costa, 1996).

Exposure to very bright light during the night shift can be a two-edged sword. Working at night under high-intensity lamps can aid adjustment to night shifts and improve task performance, but can cause sleep disturbance (Doljansky, Kannety, & Dagan, 2005). Intermittent bright light, however, during night shift, can help with mood and sleep adjustment (Baehr, Fogg, & Eastman, 1999; Boivin & James, 2002; Crowley, Lee, Tseng, Fogg, & Eastman, 2003; Horowitz, Kendall, Norsted, & Watson, 2001; Iwata, Ichii, & Egashira, 1997; Leppamaki, Partonen, Vakkuri, Lonnqvist, Partinen, & Laudon, 2003). Veitch (2004) reports that exposure to high-intensity light is particularly important for night shift workers to improve performance on complex tasks, and suggests the use of task specific lighting for this purpose, rather than providing costly high levels of lighting throughout a space. Workers may do better on difficult tasks and be less sleepy if the workplace supplies high-intensity lighting of 1000 lux or greater (Veitch, van de Beld, Brainard, & Roberts, 2004). Shift workers also need darkness at home (through use of drapes or eye masks) to support daytime sleeping (Burgess et al., 2002). Exposure to bright light, such as sunlight, during the day can reduce some of the negative effects of high-intensity light exposure at night during a shift. High levels of light exposure in the day may reduce the tendency of night-time light to suppress melatonin production, improving sleep after the shift (Lockley, 2009).

Problems with sleep are widespread among middle-aged, male American workers (Millman, Redline, Carlisle, Assaf, & Levinson, 1991; National Commission on Sleep Disorders Research, 1992; Webb, 1995; Young, Palta, Dempsey, Skatrud, Weber, & Badr, 1993) and shift work adds to these difficulties. Sixty percent to 80 percent of shift workers show sleep disorders (Leger, 1994; Rosch, 1996). Workers who are on duty at night sleep fewer hours and less restfully, and it takes more than one night of good sleep to recover from accumulated sleep debt (Gordon, Cleary, Parker, & Czeisler, 1986; Van Dongen, Maislin, Mullington, & Dinges, 2003).

Barger, Lockley, Rajaratnam, and Landrigan (2009) note that alertness and performance are affected by, among other things, the phase in the daily (circadian) cycle and the amount of sleep (hours since last sleep, hours spent sleeping). Shiftwork directly affects these elements, by placing people on the job when their body expects sleep, and by setting up schedules that keep workers awake for long periods and disturb sleep patterns. Such conditions can "overpower an officer's ability to remain alert and to maintain a high level of performance, particularly for tasks requiring sustained vigilance" (p. 158). Risks go beyond reduced alertness and impaired performance because chronic sleep deprivation significantly increases the risk of accidents and injury and later cardiac disease.

Chronic sleep problems can make workers more susceptible to disease by increasing stress and social problems, and by leading to unhealthy behaviors (increased smoking, poor diet, and less exercise) (Kayumov et al., 2007; Knutsson, 2003). Shift workers may have as much as 40 percent increase in risk of cardiovascular disease (Bøggild & Knutsson, 1999). They have been reported to get more cluster headaches (Beck, Sieber, & Trejo, 2005) as well as gastrointestinal and metabolic disorders, possibly related to eating meals at odd hours (Costa, 1996).

When people work during the night they are more fatigued and less alert, especially just before normal waking time, leading to reduced performance on cognitive and manual tasks (Barger, Lockley, Rajaratnam, & Landrigan, 2009). People who are sleep deprived are more irritable and show fewer social inhibitions (Folkard, Lombardi, & Tucker, 2005).

Shift workers may be less effective on the job due to reduced cognitive performance, lower levels of mental alertness, and lower memory capacity. They may show less ability for self–regulation, self–control, and risk assessment and have poorer judgment, increased impulsiveness and poorer reasoning skills. (Alhola & Polo-Kantola, 2007; Kimberg, D'Esposito, & Farah, 1998).They may also have higher rates of absenteeism and staff turnover and make more use of sick time (Caruso, Hitchcock, Dick, Russo, & Schmit, 2004). Shiftwork also often results in increased use of overtime and greater reliance on less-experienced staff, because more senior staff members are likely to have a greater level of choice in their work hours and shifts (Shields, 2002).

Some of these problems can be lessened by the way shifts are managed. There may be increased levels of fatigue and reduced alertness, poorer performance on cognitive and vigilance tasks, as well as increased levels of injuries and health complaints when people work long shifts (such as shifts of 12 or 24 hours) in a 40 hour week Caruso et al., 2004; Dembe, Erikson, Delbos, & Banks, 2005). There is also a higher risk of accidents during night shifts (Folkhard, Lombardi, & Tucker, 2005). Level of alertness during overnight shifts can be improved with frequent short breaks (Swenson, Waseleski, & Hartl, 2008). While breaks and other countermeasures may help performance at work, however, there is no evidence that they reduce long-term negative health consequences of work during biological night (Pallesen et al., 2010).

The manner in which shifts are rotated can be important. When workers regularly change work hours, schedules that shift people forward in a clockwise direction (first work a day shift, then evening, then night) allow people to adjust more easily to the change (Knauth, 1995). Moreover, the number of days on the same shift matters. When people work longer periods on the same shift (several months or more) their circadian patterns have a chance to adjust, although long-term health problems may still occur (Knauth, 1995). Working a few weeks on a shift allows for very little adjustment, resulting in significant sleep disruption (Lockley, 2009).

Training to help shift workers learn to adjust their exposure to light at work and to dark at home can help reduce turnover rates (Delprino, n.d., cited in Swenson et al., 2008). Workers can also be taught ways to recognize the symptoms of sleep disorders in order to seek help, and make better use of caffeine to combat fatigue (Muehlbach & Walsh, 1985; Wyatt, Cajochen, Ritz-De Cecco, Czeisler, & Dijk, 2004).

WINDOWS

Windows serve multiple functions (Aries, Veitch, & Newsham, 2010; Heerwagen, 1990), some of which are no different now than they were in primitive structures when windows were simple holes cut into castle or cabin walls. They let in direct and reflected sunlight, and they aid ventilation and temperature control (though often less so in modern buildings with sealed windows and controlled environments). They also serve as a source of information about place, the environment, or weather. They provide stimulation, sensory change, and variability of visual field as remediation for isolation and boredom, and provide a source of activity and distraction from the monotony of activities and stimuli by giving outside views of people and landscapes. Windows provide a feeling of connection to the outside world and can offer views of nature with benefits for stress reduction, mental restoration, and recovery. Heerwagen (1990) suggests that, in addition to the above functions, windows unconsciously influence the level of satisfaction with an environment.

For space travelers, the importance of windows grows for longer missions (Haines, 1988). In the interior of a small capsule or room of a space vehicle, the eye might never have an object on which to focus that is more than a few meters away. At close focus the ciliary muscles in the eye contract to thicken the lens and shorten focal length for viewing. Windows allow for infinite focus of the eye. Long or infinite focus allows these muscles to relax, reducing muscle strain and possibly relieving tension that could lead to headaches (Wolff, Siberstein, Lipton, & Dalessio, 2001). Other discussions of space habitats suggest that "[w]indows, works of art, and other distracters which divert attention from other people can promote social distance" and reduce perceived crowding (Harrison, Caldweli, Struthers, & Clearwater, 1988, p. iii). Windows may also reduce perceived crowding by increasing perceived spaciousness (Desor, 1972; Schiffenbauer, Brown, Perry, Shulack, & Zanzola, 1977).

Windows in space vehicles offer visual stimuli and variety and provide an opportunity for psychological distancing and escape from others in these extremely close and confined situations. Although the differences between life in space capsules and prison cells are numerous and important, these findings may still hold some relevance for the confined environment of correctional settings, such as the function of windows in providing visual variety and the potential for psychological escape.

The Downside of Windows

Although there is a great deal in the environmental design and behavior literature about the benefits of windows, less has been written about perceived problems. Windows may be expensive additions to buildings (Boyce, Hunter, & Howlett, 2003), so it is important to be aware of their negative as well as positive impact, especially in correctional settings with respect to security;

heating, ventilation, and air-conditioning (HVAC); and exposure. Windows are, literally, punctures in otherwise solid and secure enclosures and as such represent risks of and opportunities for security breaches. In these secure settings it is common for windows to be designed to reduce the potential of escape, by making them too small to crawl through (approximately 5 inches wide or less) and/or by embedding them with devices that can trigger an alarm if cut or hit.

With respect to view, windows (at least those without special reflective coatings) represent a sword that cuts both ways. The view out (visual access) is highly valued, but being *on view* (visual exposure) usually is not (Appleton, 1975; Archea, 1984; Heerwagen, 1990). Especially where there are few options for movement or view control (such as the ability to adjust blinds), windows may make those near them feel exposed and on display, which can be uncomfortable and stressful. In correctional settings there is often a conflict between the need for security – for staff to be able to see into bedrooms, toilet areas, showers – and the culturally powerful desire for privacy in those spaces (Kira, 1976). In general, being in a "goldfish bowl" with high visual exposure but low visual access is a very unpleasant condition (Heerwagen, 1990; Archea, 1977).

Windows also affect HVAC systems. Facility managers often complain that operable windows, which are typically much appreciated by building users, make it difficult to control and balance HVAC systems. Modern enclosed systems operate on assumptions of controlled air flow and input. A window open to the outside brings in uncontrolled and unconditioned air, adding variability and unpredictability to HVAC systems. "Building occupants love [operable windows]. Mechanical engineers hate them. Operable windows, though simple and familiar, have not found widespread acceptance in modern commercial buildings in the United States" (Daly, 2002, p. 22). Daly points out, though, that this need not be true – with well-designed systems; operable windows can be efficient and energy saving.

Windows can also bring intense sunlight into a small, enclosed space, creating a local greenhouse effect that increases heat, or act as an opening for heat loss in cold weather, and thus be a source of unpleasant temperature fluctuation. This remains a concern even though materials (such as double- or triple-glazed windows) and designs (orientation, shading, and other options) can significantly mitigate these problems.

The view through a window may create hazards with respect to the local community surrounding a prison or jail. A window in an inmate area that faces outside public space is often seen as an opportunity for illicit communication between an inmate and a friend or relative, via gestures or signs. Such a window also creates privacy issues for the inmates (being seen or recognized by outsiders) or may provide an opportunity for an inmate to expose himself or herself. We heard reports of such situations in the Chicago Metropolitan Correctional Center where there were complaints of inmates exposing themselves to occupants of a nearby skyscraper.

Miller (1993) notes that windows are often seen as posing security and management problems in the form of risk of escape, contraband, vandalism, "view conflicts with persons outside the facility... (and) view conflicts between housing units" (p. 108). Correctional officials also point out that windows in inmate areas with views to areas outside the institution can represent a hazard for staff. If, for instance, an inmate can see staff vehicles and note license plates numbers, it becomes possible to harass them later on.

In classroom situations, windows can also be seen as a source of glare, which makes work difficult and causes discomfort, as well as a distraction that makes it more difficult to concentrate. Sometimes correctional designers address these problems by using interior rather than exterior windows (that is, cell windows to an interior hallway or dayroom rather than to the outside), with a subsequent loss of the potential for the kind of normalization of the living environment that improves conditions for inmates.

There are other options, though, by which view conflicts can be ameliorated, such as making use of the orientation and siting of windows; using a "heavily landscaped visual buffer" (Miller, 1993, p. 109); installing high windows, skylights, or clerestory windows (although skylights and clerestories may not support requirements for "view to the outside"); using smoked or reflective or translucent glazing (though not opaque because of lack of view out); and making use of visual screens. ACA standards require that a natural light source must be less than 20 feet away to serve as a light source for a cell.

User Preferences

Discussions of the benefits of windows often assume positive health and mood effects of daylight. Considerable research suggests that, at the very least, most people have strong preferences for windows in most circumstances and in many kinds of settings (Christoffersen, Peterson, Johnsen, & Valbjorn, 1999; Finnegan & Soloman, 1981; Heerwagen, 1990; Keep, James, & Inman, 1980; Markus, 1967; Nagy et al., 1995; Ruys, 1970; Wineman, 1982). Patients in acute care units attach a high importance to windows – especially when they provide a nature view (Verderber, 1986). Given options, people most often choose window spaces to sit or work at over those without or further from windows, and will report a desire for window spaces on surveys (Wotton & Barkow, 1983).

Office workers indicate a dislike for windowless work spaces (Aries, Veitch, & Newsham, 2010; Collins, 1976; Farley, Veitch, & Institute for Research in Construction, 2001) and have lower job satisfaction in windowless settings (Finnegan & Solomon, 1981), even though they are likely to overestimate the percentage of light on their desk that comes from the exterior source (Heerwagen & Heerwagen, 1984; Wells, 1965). Students and parents seem to prefer classrooms with windows, even when teachers consider them a distraction (Edwards & Torcellini, 2002). People in settings without any or many windows or easy access to windows may experience feelings of being cut off from the world (Kim & Wineman, 2005) and will choose window seats when they can. People in spaces without windows often seem to compensate for the lack of light and/or view by using additional decoration and by placing art with an outdoor theme in their rooms (Heerwagen & Orians, 1986).

The relationship of windows to satisfaction may not be simple. In some cases, satisfaction has been found to be higher when one could see a window but was not right next to it presumably because it provided some of the benefits, such as light and view, without some of the negative effects, such as glare and temperature fluctuation (Charles, Veitch, Newsham, Marquardt, & Geerts, 2003).

There are no similar studies of preference for windows in correctional settings. We found behavioral indications that windows in a jail were highly valued for activity and distraction (Wener & Olsen, 1980). As noted in Chapter 4 (and shown in Figure 26, p. 83), inmates in the Chicago MCC spent long periods standing on chairs in the unit exercise room in order to be able to see out of the only window on the unit that had a panoramic view (all others were 5 inches wide). West (1986) found that inmates commented on how much they enjoyed having a window view of nature and watched animals as an activity, which Heerwagen (1990) attributed to an ability of a view to redirect attention from current concerns. Even Eastern State Prison, which isolated inmates to an extraordinary degree, had cells with windows and small individual courtyards providing visual access to nature, albeit mostly a view up to the sky.

Impact of Views of and Contact with Nature

Many people have long been convinced that contact with nature is critical to human physical and mental health. Such was, in part, the motivation of Frederick Law Olmsted for the design of Central Park, which he conceived as a place for the diverse population of New York City to have access to nature (Rybczynski, 1999). Serious research on the effect of exposure to nature and nature views on behavior, mood, and health, however, is a relatively recent phenomenon. Several conceptual models explain why nature and nature views can be important to humans – the biophilia stress model and the attention restoration model. The biophilia hypothesis (Kellert & Wilson, 1993) is evolution-based (Ulrich, 1993), and assumes that there is a survival advantage conferred from direct contact with nature. It suggests that exposure to nature reduces stress and that there is an evolutionary advantage conferred by rapid stress recovery. These psychological and psychophysiological effects, it proposes, are direct and immediate and not mediated by cognition.

Guided by this theory, Ulrich's classic study of views in hospitals (1984) launched a body of work on view and health care. He found that patients with views of trees had easier, faster recoveries from surgery than those with views of a brick wall. In other work, he and his colleagues also found faster recovery from stress with exposure to nature scenes, and that exposure to nature images led to lower blood pressure and reduced anxiety (Ulrich et al., 1991). Other studies have shown that nature views make for faster recovery from stress (Parsons Tassinary, Ulrich, Hebl, & Grossman-Alexander, 1998). Heerwagen (1990) reported in an unpublished study that adding nature scenes to a dental waiting room produced positive effects in physiological measures of stress (heart rate) that were not seen in self-report measures. There is evidence from research in hospital settings that the presence of windows in intensive care settings can significantly reduce depression, anxiety, and post treatment delirium (Keep et al., 1980; Parker & Hodge, 1976; Wilson, 1972). Nature scenes, combined with nature sounds, were successfully used to reduce pain in patients undergoing flexible bronchoscopy (Diette, Lechtzin, Haponik, Devrotes, & Rubin, 2003). For Ulrich (1991), windows are important in providing "positive distractions" from the stress of the situation. Views, especially of nature scenes, may reduce boredom and stress from deprivation of stimuli, but also offset overload due to a surfeit of inputs.

The second theoretical approach is based on a cognitive explanation offered by Kaplan and Kaplan (1989), related to attention and depletion of attention, harkening back to early writings of William James. Focusing on scenes, mental tasks, and situations that are not inherently fascinating and pleasant requires concentration and is mentally fatiguing (S. Kaplan, 1995). Scenes and situations that provide easy fascination can be restorative, in that exposure to them can speed recovery from mental fatigue. They allow a person to rest the inhibitory mechanism on which concentration depends. Nature scenes are relatively fascinating. Kaplan (1995) notes that fascination, alone, is insufficient for restorative experiences. To be restorative an environment must also allow the observer to "be away" (mentally travel into the scene), have extent (scope and distance – "be rich enough and coherent enough so that it constitutes a whole other world," p. 173), and be compatible with their needs. Access to or views of nature have been found to lead to less frustration, more satisfaction, and fewer self-reported ailments (R. Kaplan, 1993). Nature vacations provide more recovery and restoration than urban trips (Hartig, Mang, & Evans, 1991) and nature exposure improves performance on mentally challenging tasks (Hartig, Evans, Jamner, Davis, & Gärling, 2003). Nature experienced in a walk or through photographs significantly improved cognitive performance, as measured by digit span backwards[1] and other attentional tasks (Berman, Jonides, & Kaplan, 2008). Digit span has been related to attentional capacity, cognitive performance, and anxiety (Hodges & Spielberger, 1969; Moldawsky & Moldawsky, 1952), and found responsive to nature scenes in other studies (Ottosson & Grahn, 2005; Tennessen & Cimprich, 1995). Heerwagen (1990) suggested that views of nature not only affect situational satisfaction, but broader life satisfaction as well (see R. Kaplan, 1993).

There is growing evidence in this literature that exposure to nature may also reduce aggressive behavior. For instance, Mooney and Nicell (1992) found that gardens reduced aggressive behavior in Alzheimer patients, and Rice and Remy (1998) found that inmates in prison reported less aggressive feelings when working in a garden. Gardens have also been effective in reducing the emotional distress of hospitalized children (Sherman, Varni, Ulrich, & Malcarne, 2005).

Even though most prisons in the United States and elsewhere present inmates with settings of concrete, steel, and stone, it is not unusual to find prison settings that offer access to nature. Some early prisons had extensive landscaping and gardens and prison farms became commonplace in the American South after the Civil War. These farms arose in part as a response to the end of convict leasing (a form of involuntary servitude) and advocates often cited their benefits of fresh air and healthy environments. Still, they were often seen as harsh and exploitative environments (Zimmerman, 1951). In modern times, many (though not all) prison farms have been closed, such as one in Connecticut where the women inmates worked picking fruit and vegetables until it was replaced in the late twentieth century with a modern maximum security building (Rierden, 1997).

Modern proponents for gardens and farms on prison grounds base their advocacy on research of the psychological benefits of biophilia and also note the potential rehabilitative effects of meaningful garden work (Sullivan, 2011). The new Justice Center in Leoben, Austria, has mixed outdoor space with small amounts of plantings and displays of art to try to create a more aesthetically comfortable and stress-reducing setting.

FIGURE 37. Auburn State Penitentiary. Courtesy of Cayuga Historical Museum.

Both theoretical models may be useful in explaining the link of nature to aggressive behavior. Mental fatigue can lead to emotional outbursts, anger, irritability and aggressive behavior, poorer thought process, and reduced control over impulses (Kuo & Sullivan, 2001a, 2001b). Stressful situations have also been shown to reduce tolerance of frustration (Glass & Singer, 1972).

FIGURE 38. http://ccpl.lib.co.us/pictures/cd-1/87-077-028-1.JPG Colorado Prison Farm. Courtesy of Royal Gorge Regional Museum & Historical Center, Canon City Historical Society.

FIGURE 39. Radishes growing in the organic garden of the Danville Correctional Center. The garden, an outgrowth of the University of Illinois' Education Justice Project in collaboration with the prison and the Danville Area Community College. Courtesy of William Sullivan.

FIGURE 40. Rikers island Greenhouse. Courtesy of John Jiler, from *Doing time in the garden*, p. 31.

FIGURE 41. Justizzentrum, Leoben, Austria. R. Wener

A study of the impact of nature on aggression in low-income housing projects found that even relatively small amounts of green space on a building site was associated with improved attention span and lower rates of aggressiveness, as measured by self-report and rates of incidents (Kuo & Sullivan, 2001a). There was also a significant negative correlation between attention span and aggressiveness.

Leather et al. (1998) found that the view of nature in an office setting served as a buffer for negative effects of job stress. Research with adolescents and adults (Korpela, 1992; Korpela & Hartig, 1996; Korpela, Hartig, Kaiser, & Fuhrer, 2001) indicates that nature views may be especially useful when people seek to restore calm after experiencing "threatening or emotionally negative events" (Korpela et al., 2001, p. 576). Placing nature art scenes on the wall in office settings has reduced anger, mediated by reductions in levels of stress (Kweon, Ulrich, Walker, & Tassinary, 2008).

These positive effects of nature on behavior may also be seen in prisons in two studies with findings similar to research on light and view in health care settings. West (1986) looked at stress-related illness reports and found that a view of nature had a positive effect on health in a prison. Inmates commented on how much they enjoyed nature views and watching animals, which seemed

FIGURE 42. Justizzentrum, Leoben, Austria. Courtesy Paul Ott

to serve as a way to forget current concerns and mentally project themselves into another scene (Heerwagen, 1990). In West's study, the positive effect of nature views was strongest where inmate turnover was highest. As noted in our discussion of "Territoriality" (Chapter 6), population turnover in a total institution can add stress to the social system of a living unit and may lead to increased aggression.

Another study by Moore (1985) showed that inmates with external views of nature had reduced blood pressure and used lower levels of institutional health care facilities when compared to inmates who had only internal views of courtyards. Others (Lindemuth, 2007) have suggested that creating prison gardens in which inmates could work might have significant stress reduction effects.

Ulrich (2001) proposes that, in a health care context, windows can and should play a role in "supportive design," that is, design that helps achieve

FIGURE 43. Justizzentrum, Leoben, Austria. R. Wener

the goals of the organization. For health care this means design that reduces negative or iatrogenic responses to treatment and supports recovery. In a correctional setting it could mean design that helps to reduce stress, agitation, irritation, and aggression and increases positive interaction.

We introduced a large nature mural on the wall of a county jail's open booking area and collected data from correctional officers who worked there before and after the change (Farbstein, Farling, & Wener, 2009). Although the mural did not affect reported mood or stress, it significantly improved cognitive performance (digit span backwards) and had a positive effect on psychophysiological measures of stress (heart rate variability) in officers. These data are supported by the results of a number of studies also indicating that some of the positive effects of contact with or view of nature can be achieved by views of simulated nature, such as photos or art work. Findings have shown benefits for stress reduction, dealing with pain, recovery from health problems, and reduction of blood pressure and heart rate from views of nature scenes in art, photographs, and film (Nanda, Eisen, & Baladandayuthapani, 2008; Ulrich, 1999).

COLOR

Many people, when they muse on questions of environmental design and behavior, think first about the effects of color. This is unsurprising because we often have strong preferences for and powerful emotional associations with colors. A great deal of attention is paid to color in environmental design, especially in interior spaces. Color plays an important role in room lighting and the lightness or darkness and the reflectance of wall surfaces can enhance or counteract lighting systems (Veitch 2004).

Color in designed spaces is clearly apparent and easily noticed. Moreover, color, if effective in changing mood or behavior, would be an inexpensive and easy fix for behavioral problems, a magic bullet. This is precisely why it is tempting to use color to try to change attitude or behavior in correctional settings, where there is often little leeway for more extensive improvements to existing buildings, and also why there is a need for great care in considering research findings.

For all the interest in color and behavior as a concept, there is relatively little research and less theory that addresses this issue, and little can be said with confidence about the psychological and behavioral effects of color. Several researchers who have conducted thorough literature reviews have commented that the number of well-controlled studies are few and most of the work is purely empirical with very little theoretical basis (Elliot, Maier, Moller, Friedman, & Meinhardt, 2007; Kaye, 1975; Wise & Wise, 1988). Elliot et al. note that "a significant portion of the research on color and performance represents a direct attempt to discover which colors, if any, boost worker, student, or athlete performance or productivity" (p. 154). Much work is based on conceptions from the 1940s suggesting that blue-green colors are calming and colors at the red-orange-yellow end of the spectrum are arousing (Goldstein, 1942). There is, however, little data indicating a broad and general relationship between color and mood (Stone, 2003; Wise & Wise, 1988).

The assessment of a number of these literature reviews is that a simple and direct relationship between color and human response is, at best, unclear (Elliot et al., 2007; Stone, 2003) or does not exist (Wise & Wise, 1988). Elliot et al. (2007) report that "almost nothing is known at present regarding how the different colors that people perceive impact their affect, cognition and behavior" (p. 166). His literature review goes on to point out that most studies have found no effect of red versus blue on task performance, and that those that have may show opposite results (red leads to better performance in some, worse in others). Stone (2003) notes, for example, that even though some studies have found red and yellow to be stimulating and blue and green calming, others have had mixed results.

Some studies suggest a difference between colors (red-orange-yellow versus blue-green, for instance) in level of arousal or relaxation (Elliot et al., 2007; Krames & Flett, 2000), although results here also vary and are, in some cases, contradictory. Color effects, to the degree they are found, may interact with individual differences, in particular with stimulus screening (Dijkstra, 1983; Kwallek & Lewis, 1990). Low stimulus screeners are people who are more easily aroused and who are also more easily distracted by environmental stimulation than are high-stimulus screeners (Mehrabian, 1977). Consistent with that definition, Kwalleck, Soon, and Lewis (2007) and Dijkstraa, Pieterseb, and Pruyna (2008) found that low wavelength colors were more arousing for low-stimulus screeners.

Studies that have found some color-behavior connections vary in approach and ecological validity. In some cases, for instance, subjects are exposed to a limited view of colors for very brief periods (such as looking at color swatches while performing a task).

Wise and Wise (1988), in a particularly useful review, argue that the evidence for physiological effects, such as arousal, is unconvincing. Where they exist the effects seem to be reactive and brief – transitory – and thus unlikely to have any lasting effects on performance or reaction to real environments. This, they say, makes sense if one considers ecological context and views red as a signal condition that usually exists in nature to elicit a reflexive response, such as to danger. There are "no 'hard-wired' linkages between environmental colors and particular judgmental or emotional states" (p. 110), they say, and using them prescriptively in this way is simplistic.

To say that there is no simple relationship between pure colors and behavior, however, is not to suggest that colors have no impact at all. As Wise and Wise (1988) point out, this is partly because of the complexity of color. First, color has multiple dimensions – hue, as well as saturation and brightness. In addition, how a pigment color on a wall is perceived will also be affected by lighting conditions, including the brightness and quality of the light, as well as the color spectrum of the light itself.

One reason why these studies are inconclusive, they suggest, is that many have looked at color as a unitary concept, that is, the effects of an individual color, in and of itself, independent of situation and context. Color may be more likely to have a significant impact when considered within its appropriate place in the environment. Wise and Heerwagen (1997) note that "'contextual' use of color . . . produced occupant effects, and not the explicit color of certain single elements" (p. 2).

Color, then, needs to be viewed as an ecological construct, relevant as both signal and symbol (Küller, Ballal, Laike, Mikellides, & Tonello, 2006) in the way we respond to the environment, as part of the ecological niche in which humans evolved. Its role is similar to and integrated with that of nature as described in the growing literature on biophilia.

The clear message from these reviews is that managers should not expect that doing something as simple as painting a room one specific color will generate a powerful response. This, however, describes much of the history of discussions of color in prisons and jails. There are two main threads concerning the use of color as a behavior change agent in prisons and/or jails. First is the suggestion that the colors of blue and green can be used to help create a calming atmosphere in institutional settings. Such, apparently, was the case in at least one area of Alcatraz when a cell block and solitary confinement area were painted green in an attempt to calm inmates, although there is no data on its effectiveness (Fehrman & Fehrman, 2004). Similarly, Krames and Flett (2000) recommend a similar use of colors in order to have a calming effect in Canadian jails.

The other example is the use of Baker-Miller pink as a means of providing emergency calming to an aroused or out-of-control inmate. This was first suggested by Schauss (1979) as a means of reducing aggressive behavior through short-term exposure to a specific shade of pink (160 nanometers). There were a number of promising anecdotal reports in the 1970s and early 1980s (Chapman, 1981; Johnston, 1981), and quasi-experimental studies (Caudill, 1981; Pellegrini, Schauss, & Miller, 1981) following its use in naval brigs and, at one point the use of pink "time-out" cells spread widely within correctional and psychiatric institutions. More recent studies, including some with better controls, have had mixed or negative effects (Gilliam, 1991; Gilliam & Unruh, 1988; Profusek & Rainey, 1987), and use of this color in holding or "time-out" cells seems to have faded. Elliot et al. (2007) note that though a few studies showed reduced muscle strength in pink rooms (Schauss, 1985), most have not. In fact, Pelligrini, Schauss, and Miller (1981) proposed that a Hawthorne Effect is operating in that the effect of Baker-Miller pink may be as much related to presenting inmates with a newly painted space as the specific color used.

It would be a mistake to take this review as a mandate to ignore color as unimportant or insufficiently powerful for attention and use in correctional contexts. Every aspect of facility design, of course, involves color decisions – even in absentia. Design in institutions often results in the use of dull, mono-chromatic surfaces of traditional institutional shades. Although it is clear that one cannot reasonably use color to fine-tune mood or behavior, or radically change space perception (such as by making a small room look large), colors can and should be part of an overall design plan that can counteract the monotony and boredom of a place – a potentially positive and stimulating effect for all users, inmates, as well as staff (Wise & Wise, 1988). The key to the successful use of color is placing it in an appropriate environmental context, considered with patterns and textures, used to reflect natural elements that can have positive psychological effects (Wise & Heerwagen, 1997; Wise & Wise, 1988).

CONCLUSION

The use of light, windows, nature views, and color are profoundly important for life inside total institutions. These elements represent much of what is lost with incarceration, in the denial of control over ones' setting, including the ability to raise or lower lighting levels, change colors, and gain access to the natural environment. There are some facilities in which inmates receive daylight and have some contact with or broad views of natural settings in their cells, or in recreation yards, but those are few and the number is not increasing as new institutions come online. The situation in jails, where it is not uncommon for inmates to spend almost all their time in limited, interior spaces, is commonly worse than that in prisons, where inmates often have more extended opportunities in yards. Even so, many prisons have limited access to daylight and nature and poor interior lighting.

The problem with lighting for inmates, as described here, is both too little light and too little darkness. Research indicates that the absence of daylight or other intense light during waking hours, and sufficient darkness at night can affect circadian rhythms and impair the quality of sleep, leading to health and behavioral problems. Providing "biologically active lighting" (Veitch et al., 2004, p. 17) has the potential to improve performance and to reduce health problems and on-the-job accidents.

The inability to be part of and touch nature, or even to view it, eliminates yet one more important option for adapting to and reducing stress and mental fatigue. Not only do inmates suffer from exposure to many sources of stress, they also are denied many or most of the means the rest of us use to deal with stress.

Staff members may be similarly affected by an inability to relieve stress and mental fatigue with nature access or views. Poor lighting can affect not only their ability to do their job, but can also add to the difficulty associated with shift work. The type, quality, and level of electrical lights, the amount and availability of sunlight, and the number, kind, and view content of windows may all play a more important role in the behavior and attitudes of inmates and staff than has been previously believed.

Nature views and daylight can affect satisfaction, health, irritability, aggressiveness, mental function, problem solving, stress responses and recovery, and even levels of violence – all factors that can be critical for operations and staff functioning, for inmate success in education and rehabilitation, and for maintaining a calm and safe environment on living units. Lack of daylight and insufficient darkening at night can affect the quality of inmate sleep, with myriad ramifications for physical and mental health and behavior. Poor access to daylight and inadequate electrical lighting may affect staff alertness and mood, especially given the increased stresses of changing shifts. Providing better quality settings that do not severely isolate people from nature and daylight – through windows, lighting, views, colors, and design – is important if we want to reduce hostility and stress in inmates and support their attempts to help themselves through education, therapy, or training. It is also important in providing safe and healthy environments for those who work there. The fact that some of these benefits may be available through the use of art that provides nature scenes provides some options for retrofitting institutions with modest budgets.

This review does not propose that anything as simple as switching the kinds of bulbs in lamps will have a major impact on institutions and the inhabitants. Nor does it indicate that these issues should be addressed only as a response to simple creature comforts. Rather, it suggests that designers should address lighting, view, and color in a broad and holistic fashion, using all the elements at their disposal to create settings that are less oppressive, less stress producing and more restorative for those experiencing stress, and more supportive of prosocial behavior and productive activity. The benefits could be significant in reducing elements that trigger irritability, frustration, and aggressive responses in inmates, and reducing stress and increasing positive responses to problems among staff.

Good design, as always, has a myriad of benefits. Architecture that promotes significant levels of daylight provides lighting without the energy costs of electric lights. Facilities that rely solely on electric lighting for most or all their lighting needs experience initial and ongoing costs from installation, replacement, and repair of light fixtures. High levels of electric illumination can have positive effects on performance but also increase cooling loads and energy costs (Pechacek et al., 2008).

There is also a need for standard-setting agencies to pay more attention to research in the development of standards and guidelines for prisons and jails. There are, for instance, sophisticated ways to measure daylight from windows that may be more useful for promoting use of windows in new institutions than mandating square feet of window space, without attention of design, orientation, and actual penetration of daylight (Mardaljevic, Heschong, & Lee, 2009). Standards might also address the level of darkness available to inmates for sleeping.

Paid staff represents the largest ongoing and long-term cost to any facility. Scheduling systems that take into account the ability of people to adjust to shift changes and provide training to help people adjust to night shifts (Landrigan, Czeisler, Barger, Ayas, Rothschild, & Lockley, 2007) should provide benefits in healthier, more satisfied, and more effective employees.

References

Alhola, P., & Polo-Kantola, P. (2007). Sleep deprivation: Impact on cognitive performance. *Neuropsychiatric Disease and Treatment, 3*(5), 553–567.

aan het Rot, M., Benkelfat, C., Boivin, D. B., & Young, S. N. (2007). Bright light exposure during acute tryptophan depletion prevents a lowering of mood in mildly seasonal women. *European neuropsychopharmacology, 18*(1), 14–23.

Appleton, J. (1975). *The Experience of Landscape.* New York: John Wiley & Sons Inc.

Archea, J. A. (1977). The place of architectural factors in behavioral theories of privacy. *Journal of Social Issues, 33*(3), 116–137.

Archea, J. (1984). *Visual Access and Exposure: An Architectural Basis for Interpersonal Behavior.* Unpublished Ph.D. Dissertation, Pennsylvania State University.

Aries, M. B. C., Veitch, J. A., & Newsham, G. R. (2010). Windows, view, and office characteristics predict physical and psychological discomfort. *Journal of Environmental Psychology, 30*(4), 533–541.

Baehr, E. K., Fogg, L. F., & Eastman, C. I. (1999). Intermittent bright light and exercise to entrain human circadian rhythms to night work. *American Journal of Physiology-Regulatory, Integrative and Comparative Physiology, 277*(6), 1598.

Baker, N. (2004). Human nature. In K. Steemers & M. A. Steane (Eds.), *Environmental Diversity in Architecture* (pp. 47–64). Abingdon, UK: Spon Press.

Baker, N., & Steemers, K. (2002). *Daylight Design of Buildings.* London: James & James Science Publishers Ltd.

Barger, L. K., Lockley, S. W., Rajaratnam, S. M. W., & Landrigan, C. P. (2009). Neurobehavioral, health, and safety consequences associated with shift work in safety-sensitive professions. *Current Neurology and Neuroscience Reports, 9*(2), 155–164.

Baron, R. A., Rea, M. S., & Daniels, S. G. (1992). Effects of indoor lighting (illuminance and spectral distribution) on the performance of cognitive tasks and interpersonal behaviors: The potential mediating role of positive affect. *Motivation and Emotion*, 16(1), 1–33.

Baulk, S. D., Fletcher, A., Kandelaars, K. J., Dawson, D., & Roach, G. D. (2008). A field study of sleep and fatigue in a regular rotating 12-h shift system. *Applied Ergonomics*.

Beauchemin, K. M., & Hays, P. (1996). Sunny hospital rooms expedite recovery from severe and refractory depressions. *Journal of Affective Disorders, 40*(1–2), 49–51.

Beauchemin, K. M., & Hays, P. (1998). Dying in the dark: Sunshine, gender and outcomes in myocardial infarction. *Journal of the Royal Society of Medicine, 91*(7), 352.

Beck, E., Sieber, W. J., & Trejo, R. (2005). Management of cluster headache. *American Family Physician, 71*(4), 717–724.

Begemann, S. H. A., Van den Beld, G. J., & Tenner, A. D. (1997). Daylight, artificial light and people in an office environment, overview of visual and biological responses. *International Journal of Industrial Ergonomics, 20*(3), 231–239.

Benedetti, F., Colombo, C., Barbini, B., Campori, E., & Smeraldi, E. (2001). Morning sunlight reduces length of hospitalization in bipolar depression. *Journal of Affective Disorders, 62*(3), 221–223.

Berman, M. G., Jonides, J., & Kaplan, S. (2008). The cognitive benefits of interacting with nature. *Psychological Science, 19*(12), 1207–1212.

Bøggild, H., & Knutsson, A. (1999). Shift work, risk factors and cardiovascular disease. *Scandinavian Journal of Work Environment and Health, 25*, 85–99.

Boivin, D. B., & James, F. O. (2002). Phase-dependent effect of room light exposure in a 5-h advance of the sleep-wake cycle: Implications for jet lag. *Journal of Biological Rhythms, 17*(3), 266.

Boyce, P. R. (1994). *Is Full-Spectrum Lighting Special?* (No. IRC Internal Report No. 659): Lighting Research Center Rensselaer Polytechnic Institute.

Boyce, P., Hunter, C., & Howlett, O. (2003). *The Benefits of Daylight through Windows.* Troy, NY: Lighting Research Center (published at LRC-website).

Boyce, P. R., Heerwagen, J. H., Jones, C. C., Veitch, J. A., & Newsham, G. R. (2003). *Lighting Quality and Office Work: A Field Simulation Study.* Richland, WA: Pacific Northwest National Laboratory.

Burgess, H. J., Sharkey, K. M., & Eastman, C. I. (2002). Bright light, dark and melatonin can promote circadian adaptation in night shift workers. *Sleep Medicine Reviews, 6*(5), 407–420.

Cajochen, C., Chellappa, S., & Schmidt, C. (2010). What Keeps Us Awake? – the Role of Clocks and Hourglasses, Light, and Melatonin. *International Review of Neurobiology, 93*, 57–90.

Carmody, J. C., & Sterling, R. L. (1987). Design strategies to alleviate negative psychological and physiological effects in underground space. *Tunnelling and Underground Space Technology, 2*(1), 59–67.

Caruso, C. C., Hitchcock, E. M., Dick., R. B., Russo, J. M., & Schmit, J. M. (2004). *Overtime and Extended Work Shifts: Recent Findings on Illnesses, Injuries, and Health Behaviors.* U.S. Dept. of Health and Human Services, Centers for Disease Control and Prevention, National Institute for Occupational Safety and Health.

Caudill, C. (1981). *Pink Room – A Color and Aggression Study in a Correctional Environment.* Rockville, MD: National Criminal Justice Reference Service.

Cawthorne, D. (1991). *Buildings, Lighting and the Biological Clock, Martin Centre for Architectural and Urban Studies.* University of Cambridge, Cambridge.

Chapman, J. p. (1981). Pink rooms: Can they alter behavior? *IMPACT, January,* 11–13.

Charles, K., Veitch, J., Newsham, G. R., Marquardt, C., & Geerts, J. (2003). *Environmental Satisfaction in Open-Plan Environments: 5.* Workstation *and Physical Condition Effects.* Ottowa: Institute for Research in Construction, National Research Council Canada.

Christoffersen, J., Peterson, E., Johnsen, K., & Valbjorn, O. (1999). *Windows and Daylight – A Post-Occupancy Evaluation of Offices* (No. Report 318). Horsholm, Denmark: Statens Byggeforskningsinstitut.

Collins, B. L. (1976). Windows and human satisfaction. *Solar Radiation Considerations in Building Planning and Design: Proceedings of a Working Conference.*

Costa, G. (1996). The impact of shift and night work on health. *Applied Ergonomics,* 27(1), 9–16.

Crepeau, L. J., Steele, C. T., & Duplessis, C. A. (2006). At-Sea Evaluation of an Alternative Submarine Watchstanding Schedule. Rubicon Foundation. http://archive. rubiconfoundation.org/3763.

Crowley, S. J., Lee, C., Tseng, C. Y., Fogg, L. F., & Eastman, C. I. (2003). Combinations of bright light, scheduled dark, sunglasses, and melatonin to facilitate circadian entrainment to night shift work. *Journal of Biological Rhythms,* 18(6), 513.

Daly, A. (2002). Operable windows and HVAC systems. *HPAC Engineering,* 74(12), 22–30.

Dembe, A. E., Erickson, J. B., Delbos, R. G., & Banks, S. M. (2005). The impact of overtime and long work hours on occupational injuries and illnesses: New evidence from the United States. *British Medical Journal,* 62(9), 588–597.

Desor, J. A. p. (1972). Toward a psychological theory of crowding. *Journal of Personality and Social Psychology,* 21(1), 79–83.

Diette, G. B., Lechtzin, N., Haponik, E., Devrotes, A., & Rubin, H. R. (2003). Distraction therapy with nature sights and sounds reduces pain during flexible bronchoscopy: A complementary approach to routine analgesia. *Chest,* 123(3), 941–948.

Dijkstra, A. (1983). *Personal Functioning, Health, and Absenteeism in a Public Transport Company.* Paper presented at the Working Environment in Urban Public Transport. Stockholm: University of Stockholm.

Dijkstraa, K., Pieterseb, M. E., & Pruyna, A. T. H. (2008). Individual differences in reactions towards color in simulated healthcare environments: The role of stimulus screening ability. *Journal of Environmental Psychology,* 28(3), 268–277.

Doljansky, J. T., Kannety, H., & Dagan, Y. (2005). Working under daylight intensity lamp: An occupational risk for developing circadian rhythm sleep disorder? *Chronobiology International,* 22(3), 597–605.

Edwards, L., & Torcellini, P. (2002). *A Literature Review of the Effects of Natural Light on Building Occupants* (No. NREL/TP-550-30769). Golden, CO: National Renewable Energy Laboratory, U.S. Dept of Energy.

Elliot, A. J., Maier, M. A., Moller, A. C., Friedman, R., & Meinhardt, J. (2007). Color and psychological functioning: The effect of red on performance attainment. *Journal of Experimental Psychology: General,* 136(1), 154–168.

Espiritu, R. C., Kripke, D. F., Ancoli-Israel, S., Mowen, M. A., Mason, W. J., Fell, R. L., et al. (1994). Low illumination experienced by San Diego adults: Association with atypical depressive symptoms* 1. *Biological Psychiatry,* 35(6), 403–407.

Farbstein, J., Farling, M., & Wener, R. E. (2009). *Effects of a Simulated Nature View on Cognitive and Psycho-physiological Responses of Correctional Officers in a Jail Intake Area.* Washington, DC: National Institute of Corrections.

Farley, K. M. J., Veitch, J. A., & Institute for Research in, C. (2001). *A Room with a View: A Review of the Effects of Windows on Work and Well-being.* Institute for Research in Construction, National Research Council Canada.

Fehrman, K., & Fehrman, C. (2004). *Color: The Secret Influence.* Prentice Hall.

Finnegan, M., & Solomon, L. (1981). Work attitudes in windowed versus windowless environments. *Journal of Social Psychology, 115*, 291–292.

Folkard, S., Lombardi, D. A., & Tucker, P. T. (2005). Shiftwork: Safety, sleepiness and sleep. *Industrial Health, 43*(1), 20–23.

Fu, L., & Lee, C. C. (2003). The circadian clock: Pacemaker and tumour suppressor. *Nature Reviews Cancer, 3*(5), 350–361.

Galasiu, A. D., & Veitch, J. A. E. (2006). Occupant preferences and satisfaction with the luminous environment and control systems in daylit offices: A literature review. *Energy and Buildings, 38*(7), 728–742.

Gifford, R. (1994). *Scientific Evidence for Claims about Full-Spectrum Lamps: Past and Future* (No. IRC Internal Report No. 659). Troy, NY: Lighting Research Center, Rensselaer Polytechnic Institute.

Gilliam, G. E., & Unruh, D. (1988). The effects of Baker-Miller pink on biological, physical and cognitive behaviors. *Journal of Orthomolecular Medicine, 5*, 202–206.

Gilliam, J. E. (1991). The effects of Baker-Miller pink on physiological and cognitive behavior of emotionally disturbed and regular education students. *Behavioral Disorders, 17*(1), 47–55.

Glass, D., & Singer, J. (1972). *Urban Stress.* New York: Academic Press.

Goldstein, K. (1942). Some experimental observations: The influence of colors on the functions of the organism. *Occupational Therapy, 2*, 147–151.

Gordon, N. P., Cleary, P. D., Parker, C. E., & Czeisler, C. A. (1986). The prevalence and health impact of shiftwork. *American Journal of Public Health, 76*(10), 1225–1228.

Haines, R. (1988). Space station proximity operations and window design. *Space Station Human Factors Research Review, 4*, 1–18.

Harrison, A., Caldweli, B., Struthers, N. J., & Clearwater, Y. A. (1988). *Incorporation of Privacy Elements in Space Station Design.* Washington, DC: NASA.

Hartig, T., Evans, G. W., Jamner, L. D., Davis, D. S., & Gärling, T. (2003). Tracking restoration in natural and urban field settings. *Journal of Environmental Psychology, 23*(2), 109–123.

Hartig, T., Mang, M., & Evans, G. W. (1991). Restorative effects of natural environment experiences. *Environment and Behavior, 23*(1), 3–26.

Heerwagen, J. H. (1990). The psychological aspects of windows and window design. In R. I. Selby & K. H. Anthony (Eds.), *Coming of Age* (pp. 269–280). Oklahoma City, OK: Environmental Design Research Association.

Heerwagen, J. H., & Heerwagen, D. R. (1986). Lighting and psychological comfort. *Lighting Design and Application, 6*, 47–51.

Heerwagen, J. H., & Heerwagen, R. (1984). Energy and psychology: Designing for a "state of mind." *Journal of Architectural Education, 37*(3/4), 34–37.

Heerwagen, J. H., & Orians, G. (1986). Adaptations to windowlessness: A study of the use of visual decor in windowed and windowless ffices. *Environment & Behavior, 19*(5), 623–639.

Heerwagen, J. H., & Wise, J. A. (1997). *The ecoLogic of color, pattern and texture: A synthesis of research for the design of office environments.* Herman Miller, Inc.

Hodges, W. F., & Spielberger, C. D. (1969). Digit span: An indicant of trait or state anxiety? *Journal of Consulting and Clinical Psychology, 33*(4), 430–434.

Hollon, S. D., Kendall, P. C., Norsted, S., & Watson, D. (1980). Psychological responses to earth-sheltered, multilevel and aboveground structures with and without windows. *Underground Space, 5*, 171–178.

Horowitz, T. S., Cade, B. E., Wolfe, J. M., & Czeisler, C. A. (2001). Efficacy of bright light and sleep/darkness scheduling in alleviating circadian maladaptation to night. *American Journal of Physiology – Endocrinology and Metabolism, 281*(2), E384.

Hughey, J., & Speer, P. (1990). Psychological response to underground work environments: A conceptual model and preliminary tests. In R. I. Selby & K. H. Anthony (Eds.), *Coming of Age* (pp. 281–290). Oklahoma City, OK: Environmental Design Research Association.

Hutchings v. Corum. (1980). 501 F. Supp. 1276, 1296 (W.D. Mo. 1980).

Iwata, N., Ichii, S., & Egashira, K. (1997). Effects of bright artificial light on subjective mood of shift work nurses. *Industrial Health, 35*(1), 41–47.

Johnston, D. (1981). Is it merely a fad, or do pastel walls stop jail house brawls? *Corrections Magazine New York, 7*(3), 28–32.

Joseph, A. (2006). *The Impact of Light on Outcomes in Healthcare Settings*. Princeton, NJ: Robert Wood Johnson Foundation.

Kaplan, R. (1993). The role of nature in the context of the workplace. *Landscape and Urban Planning, 26*(1–4), 193–201.

Kapan, R., & Kaplan, S. (1989). *The Experience of Nature*. New York: Cambridge University Press.

Kaplan, S. (1992). The restorative environment: Nature and human experience. In D. Relf (Ed.), *The Role of Horticulture in Human Well-being and Social Development: A National Symposium* [Proceedings of Conference Held 19–21 April 1990, Arlington, VA] (pp. 134–142). Portland, OR: Timber Press.

Kaplan, S. (1995). The restorative benefits of nature: Toward an integrative framework. *Journal of Environmental Psychology, 15*, 169–182.

Karlen, M., & Benya, J. (2004). *Lighting design basics*. Hoboken, NJ: Wiley.

Kaye, S. M. (1975). Psychology in relation to design: An overview. *Canadian Psychological Review, 16*, 104–110.

Kayumov, L., Lowe, A., Rahman, S. A., Casper, R. F., & Shapiro, C. M. (2007). Prevention of melatonin suppression by nocturnal lighting: Relevance to cancer. *European Journal of Cancer Prevention, 16*(4), 357.

Keep, P., James, J., & Inman, M. (1980). Windows in the intensive Therapy Unit. *Anaesthesia, 35*(13), 257–262.

Kellert, S. R., & Wilson, E. O. (Eds.). (1993). *The Biophilia Hypothesis*. Washington, DC: Island Press.

Kim, J., & Wineman, J. (2005). *Are Windows and Window Views Really Better? A Quantitative Analysis of the Economic and Psychological Value of Views*. Troy, NY: Daylight Dividend Program – Lighting Research Center, RPI.

Kimberg, D. Y., D' Esposito, M., & Farah, M. J. (1998). Cognitive functions in the prefrontal cortex – Working memory and executive control. *Current Directions in Psychological Science, 6*(6), 185–194.

Kira, A. (1976). *The bathroom*. New York: Viking Press.

Knauth, P. (1995). Speed and direction of shift rotation. *Journal of Sleep Research*, 4(s2), 41–46.

Knez, I. I. (2001). Effects of colour of light on nonvisual psychological processes. *Journal of Environmental Psychology*, 21, 201–298.

Knutsson, A. (2003). Health disorders of shift workers. *Occupational Medicine*, 53(2), 103–108.

Korpela, K. M. (1992). Adolescents' favourite places and environmental self-regulation. *Journal of Environmental Psychology*, 12(3), 249–258.

Korpela, K., & Hartig, T. (1996). Restorative qualities of favorite places. *Journal of Environmental Psychology*, 16(3), 221–233.

Korpela, K. M., Hartig, T., Kaiser, F. G., & Fuhrer, U. (2001). Restorative experience and self-regulation in favorite places. *Environment and Behavior*, 33(4), 572.

Krames, L., & Flett, G. L. (2000). *Jail/Holding Cell Design: Proposals for Modification and Design Changes to Jail/Holding Cells* (No. TR–03–2000). Canadian Police Research Center.

Küller, R., Ballal, S., Laike, T., Mikellides, B., & Tonello, G. (2006). The impact of light and colour on psychological mood: A cross-cultural study of indoor work environments. *Ergonomics*, 49(14), 1496–1507.

Kuo, F. E., & Sullivan, W. C. (2001a). Aggression and violence in the inner city: Effects of environment via mental fatigue. *Environment and Behavior*, 33(4), 543.

Kuo, F. E., & Sullivan, W. C. (2001b). Environment and crime in the inner city: Does vegetation reduce crime? *Environment & Behavior*, 33(3), 343–367.

Kurumatani, N., Koda, S., Nakagiri, S., Hisashige, A., Sakai, K., Saito, Y., et al. (1994). The effects of frequently rotating shiftwork on sleep and the family life of hospital nurses. *Ergonomics*, 37(6), 995–1007.

Kwallek, N., & Lewis, C. M. (1990). Effects of environmental colour on males and females: A red or white or green. *Applied Economics*, 21, 275–278.

Kwallek, N., Soon, K., & Lewis, C. M. (2007). Work week productivity, visual complexity, and individual environmental sensitivity in three offices of different color interiors. *Color Research and Application*, 32(2), 130–143.

Kweon, B.-S., Ulrich, R. S., Walker, V. D., & Tassinary, L. G. (2008). Anger and stress: The role of landscape posters in an office setting. *Environment and Behavior*, 40, 355–381.

Landrigan, C., Czeisler, C., Barger, L., Ayas, N., Rothschild, J., & Lockley, S. (2007). Effective implementation of work-hour limits and systemic improvements. *Joint Commission Journal on Quality and Patient Safety*, 33(Supplement 1), 19–29.

Leather, P., Pyrgas, M., Beale, D., & Lawrence, C. (1998). Windows in the workplace: Sunlight, view, and occupational stress. *Environment and Behavior*, 30(6), 739.

Leger D. (1994). The cost of sleep-related accidents: A report for the national commission on sleep disorders research. *Sleep*, 17(1), 84–93.

Leppämäki, S., Partonen, T., Vakkuri, O., Lönnqvist, J., Partinen, M., & Laudon, M. (2003). Effect of controlled-release melatonin on sleep quality, mood, and quality of life in subjects with seasonal or weather-associated changes in mood and behaviour. *European Neuropsychopharmacology*, 13(3), 137–145.

Leslie, R. P. (2003). Capturing the daylight dividend in buildings: Why and how? *Building and Environment*, 38(2), 381–385.

Lighting Handbook: Reference & Application (9 ed.). (2000). New York: Illuminating Engineering Society of North America (IESNA).

Lindemuth, A. L. (2007). Designing therapeutic environments for inmates and prison staff in the United States: Precedents and contemporary applications. *Journal of Mediterranean Ecology, 8,* 87–97.

Lockley, S. W. (2009). Circadian rhythms: Influence of light in humans. *Encyclopedia of Neuroscience,* 971–988.

Lockley, S. W., Arendt, J., & Skene, D. J. (2007). Visual impairment and circadiam rhythm disorders. *Dialogues in clinical neuroscience, 9*(3), 301.

Ma, W. P., Cao, J., Tian, M., Cui, M. H., Han, H. L., Yang, Y. X., et al. (2007). Exposure to chronic constant light impairs spatial memory and influences long-term depression in rats. *Neuroscience Research, 59*(2), 224–230.

Mardaljevic, J., Heschong, L., & Lee, E. (2009). Daylight metrics and energy savings. *Lighting Research & Technology, 41*(3), 261.

Markus, T. (1967). The significance of sunshine and view for office workers. In R. G. Hopkinson (Ed.), *Sunlight in Buildings.* Rotterdam: Boewcentrum International.

McColl, S. L., & Veitch, J. A. (2001). Full-spectrum fluorescent lighting: A review of its effects on physiology and health. *Psychological Medicine, 31*(6), 949–964.

Mehrabian, A. (1977). Individual differences in stimulus screening and arousability. *Journal of Personality, 45*(2), 237–250.

Miller, R. (1993). *Design Guide for Adult Local Detention Facilities.* Washington, DC: National Institute of Justice.

Millman, R. P., Redline, S., Carlisle, C. C., Assaf, A. R., & Levinson, P. D. (1991). Daytime hypertension in obstructive sleep apnea. Prevalence and contributing risk factors. *Chest, 99*(4), 861–866.

Mitchell, R. J., & Williamson, A. M. (2000). Evaluation of an 8 hour versus a 12 hour shift roster on employees at a power station. *Applied Ergonomics, 31,* 83–93.

Moldawsky, S., & Moldawsky, P. C. (1952). Digit span as an anxiety indicator. *Journal of Consulting and Clinical Psychology, 16*(2), 115–118.

Mooney, P., & Nicell, P. L. (1992). The importance of exterior environment for Alzheimer residents: Effective care and risk management. *Health Manage Forum, 5*(2), 23–29.

Moore, E. (1985). *Environmental Variables Affecting Prisoner Health Care Demands.* Paper presented at the Proceedings of the American Institute of Architect, Los Angeles.

Muehlbach, M. J., & Walsh, J. K. (1995). The effects of caffeine on simulated night-shift work and subsequent daytime sleep. *Sleep, 18*(1), 22–29.

Nagy, E., Yasunaga, S., & Kose, S. (1995). Japanese office employees' psychological reactions to their underground and above-ground offices. *Journal of Environmental Psychology, 15*(2), 123–134.

Nanda, U., Eisen, S. L., & Baladandayuthapani, V. (2008). Undertaking an art survey to compare patient versus student art preferences. *Environment and Behavior, 40*(2), 269.

National Commission on Sleep Disorders Research. (1992). *Wake Up America: A National Sleep Alert.* Palo Alto, CA: Stanford University Sleep Disorders Clinic and Research Center.

Ottosson, J., & Grahn, P. (2005). A comparison of leisure time spent in a garden with leisure time spent indoors: On measures of restoration in residents in geriatric care. *Landscape Research, 30*(1), 23–55.

Pallesen, S., Bjorvatn, B., Magerøy, N., Saksvik, I. B., Waage, S., & Moen, B. E. (2010). Measures to counteract the negative effects of night work. *Scandinavian journal of work, environment & health, 36*(2), 109–120.

Parker, D. L., & Hodge, J. R. (1976). Delirium in a coronary unit. *Journal of the American Medical Association, 201*, 132–133.

Parsons, R., Tassinary, L. G., Ulrich, R. S., Hebl, M. R., & Grossman-Alexander, M. (1998). The view from the road: Implications for stress recovery and immunization. *Journal of Environmental Psychology, 18*, 113–140.

Pechacek, C. S., Andersen, M., & Lockley, S. W. (2008). Preliminary method for prospective analysis of the circadian efficacy of (day) light with applications to healthcare architecture. *LEUKOS – The Journal of the Illuminating Engineering Society of North America, 5*(1), 1–26.

Pellegrini, R. J., Schauss, A. G., & Miller, M. E. (1981). Room color and aggression in a criminal detention holding cell. A test of the "tranquilizing pink" hypothesis. *Journal of Orthomolecular Psychiatry, 10*(3), 8.

Performance-Based Standards for Adult Local Detention Facilities (4th ed.). (2004). Alexandria, VA: American Correctional Association.

Profusek, P. J., & Rainey, D. W. (1987). Effects of Baker-Miller pink and red on state anxiety, grip strength, and motor precision. *Perceptual & Motor Skills, 65*(3), 941–942.

Quality of the Visual Environment Committee: Light + Design: A Guide to Designing Quality Lighting for People and Buildings (DG-18). (2009). New York: Illuminating Engineering Society of North America.

Rasmussen, L. B., Hansen, G. L., Hansen, E., Koch, B., Mosekilde, L., Mølgaard, C., et al. (2000). Vitamin D: Should the supply in the Danish population be increased? *International Journal of Food Sciences and Nutrition, 51*(3), 209–215.

Rice, J. S., & Remy, L. L. (1998). Impact of horticultural therapy on psychosocial functioning among urban jail inmates. *Journal of Offender Rehabilitation, 26*(3–4), 169–191.

Rierden, A. (1997). *The farm: Life inside a women's prison*. Amherst, MA: University of Massachusetts Press.

Rosch, P. J. (1996). Editorial. Stress and sleep: Some startling and sobering statistics. *Stress Medicine, 12*(4).

Ruys, T. (1970). *Windowless Offices*. Seattle, WA: University of Washington.

Rybczynski, W. (1999). *A Clearing in the Distance: Frederick Law Olmsted and America in the Nineteenth Century*. New York: Scribner.

Schauss, A. G. (1979). Tranquilizing effect of color reduces aggressive behavior and potential violence. *Journal of Orthomolecular Psychiatryy, 8*(4), 218–221.

Schauss, A. G. (1985). The physiological effect of colour on the suppression of human aggression: Research on Baker-Miller pink. *International Journal of Biosocial Research, 2*(7), 55–64.

Schiffenbauer, A. I., Brown, J. E., Perry, P. L., Shulack, L. K., & Zanzola, A. M. (1977). The relationship between density and crowding: Some architectural modifiers. *Environment and Behavior, 9*(1), 3.

Schmidt, D. E., Goldman, R. D., & Feimer, N. R. (1979). Perceptions of crowding. Predicting at residence, neighborhood, and city levels. *Environment and Behavior, 11*(1), 102–130.

Scuri, P. (1995). *Design of Enclosed Spaces*. London: Chapman & Hall.

Shadish, W. R., Cook, T. D., & Campbell, D. T. (2002). *Experimental and Quasi-Experimental Designs for Generalized Causal Inference.* Boston, MA: Houghton Mifflin.

Sherman, S. A., Varni, J. W., Ulrich, R. S., & Malcarne, V. L. (2005). Post-occupancy evaluation of healing gardens in a pediatric cancer center. *Landscape and Urban Planning,* 73(2–3), 167–183.

Shields, M. (2002). Shift work and health. *Health Reports,* 13(4), 11–33.

Stone, N. J. (2003). Environmental view and color for a simulated telemarketing task. *Journal of Environmental Psychology,* 23(1), 63–78.

Sullivan, W. (2011). *Bringing out the best in people: Can urban greening help?* Paper presented at the Make no little plans: Proceedings of the 43rd annual conference of the Environmental Design Research Association.

Swenson, D. X., Waseleski, D., & Hartl, R. (2008). Shift work and correctional officers: Effects and strategies for adjustment. *Journal of Correctional Health Care,* 14(4), 299.

Takahashi, J., & Zatz, M. (1982). Regulation of circadian rhythmicity. *Science,* 217(4565), 1104–1111.

Tennessen, C. M., & Cimprich, B. (1995). Views to nature: Effects of attention. *Journal of Environmental Psychology,* 15, 77–85.

Thomas, F., Hopkins, R. O., Handrahan, D. L., Walker, J., & Carpenter, J. (2006). Sleep and cognitive performance of flight nurses after 12-hour evening versus 18-hour shifts. *Air Medical Journal,* 25(5), 216–225.

Ulrich, R. (1984). View through a window may influence recovery from surgery. *Science,* 224(April 27), 420–421.

Ulrich, R. S. (1991). Effects of interior design on wellness: theory and recent scientific research. *Journal of Health Care Interior Design,* 3, 97–109.

Ulrich, R. (1993). Biophilia, biophobia, and natural landscapes. In S. Kellert & E. O. Wilson (Eds.), *The Biophilia Hypothesis* (pp. 138–172). Washington, DC: Island Press.

Ulrich, R. (1999). Effects of gardens on health outcomes: Theory and research. *Healing Gardens: Therapeutic Benefits and Design Recommendations,* 27–86.

Ulrich, R. S. (2001). *Effects of Healthcare Environmental Design on Medical Outcomes.* Paper presented at the Design and Health: Proceedings of the Second International Academy for Health and Design Stockholm, Sweden.

Ulrich, R. S., Simons, R. F., Losito, B. D., Fiorito, E., Miles, M. A., & Zelson, M. (1991). Stress recovery during exposure to natural and urban environments1. *Journal of Environmental Psychology,* 11(3), 201–230.

Van Dongen, H. P. A., Maislin, G., Mullington, J. M., & Dinges, D. F. (2003). The cumulative cost of additional wakefulness: Dose response effects on neurobehavioral functions and sleep physiology from chronic sleep restriction and total sleep deprivation. *Sleep,* 26(2), 117–126.

Veitch, J. A. (1994). *Full Spectrum Lighting Effects on Performance, Mood and Health.* Ottawa: NRC Institute for Research in Construction; National Research Council Canada.

Veitch, J. (2004). *Final Report – the 5th International LRO Lighting Research Symposium – Light and Human Health* (No. 1009370). Palo Alto, CA: Electric Power Research Institute.

Veitch, J. (2010). *Principles of healthy lighting: highlights of CIE TC 6-11's report.* Paper presented at the The 5th International LRO Lighting Research Symposium – Light and Human Health, Orlando, FL.

Veitch, J. A. (2011). Workplace Design Contributions to Mental Health and Well-being. *HealthcarePapers, 11,* pp. 38–46.

Veitch, J. A., & Gifford, R. (1996). Assessing beliefs about lighting effects on health, performance, mood, and social behavior. *Environment and Behavior, 28*(4), 446.

Veitch, J. A., & McColl, S. L. (2001). A Critical examination of perceptual and cognitive effects attributed to full-spectrum fluorescent lighting. *Ergonomics, 44*(3), 255–279.

Veitch, J. A., van den Beld, G., Brainard, G., & Roberts, J. E. (2004). *Ocular Lighting Effects on Human Physiology and Behaviour.* Vienna, Austria: CIE – International Commission on Illumination.

Veitch, J. A., Hine, D. W., & Gifford, R. (1993). End users' knowledge, beliefs, and preferences for lighting. *Journal of Interior Design, 19*(2), 15–26.

Verderber, S. (1986). Dimensions of person-window transactions in the hospital environment. *Environment and Behavior, 18,* 450–466.

Walch, J. M., Rabin, B. S., Day, R., Williams, J. N., Choi, K., & Kang, J. D. (2005). The effect of sunlight on postoperative analgesic medication use: A prospective study of patients undergoing spinal surgery. *Psychosomatic Medicine, 67*(1), 156–163.

Webb, W. B. (1995). The cost of sleep-related accidents: A reanalysis. *Sleep, 18,* 276–280.

Wells, B. W. P. (1965). Subjective responses to the lighting installation in a modern office building and their design implications. *Building Science, 1,* 57–68.

Wener, R. E., & Olsen, R. (1980). Innovative correctional environments: A user assessment. *Environment & Behavior, 12*(4), 478–493.

West, M. J. (1986). *Landscape Views and the Stress Response in the Prison Environment.* Unpublished Master of Landscape Architecture, University of Washington, Seattle, WA.

Wilson, L. M. (1972). Intensive care delirium. The effect of outside deprivation in a windowless unit. *Archives of Internal Medicine, 130*(2), 225–226.

Wineman, J. (1982). The office environment as a source of stress. In G. Evans (Ed.), *Environmental Stress* (pp. 105–132). New York: Cambridge University Press.

Winkel, G. (1987). Implications of environmental context for validity assessments. In D. Stokols & I. Altman (Eds.), *Handbook of Environmental Psychology* (Vol. 1, pp. 71–97). New York: John Wiley.

Wise, B. K., & Wise, J. W. (1988). *The Human Factors of Color in Environmental Design: A Critical Review.* (No. NASA CR-177498). Moffett Field, CA: NASA, Ames Research Center.

Wise, J. A., & Heerwagen, J. H. (1997). *The EcoLogic of Color, Pattern and Texture: A Synthesis of Research for the Design of Office Environments.* Herman Miller, Inc.

Wolfe, T. (1979). *The Right Stuff.* New York: Farrar Straus & Giroux.

Wolff, H. G., Silberstein, S. D., Lipton, R. B., & Dalessio, D. J. (2001). *Wolff's Headache and Other Head Pain.* New York: Oxford University Press, USA.

Wotton, E., & Barkow, B. (1983). *An Investigation of the Effects of Windows and Lighting in Offices.* Proceedings of the International Daylighting Conference, Phoenix, Washington, DC: American Institute of Architects, 405–411.

Wyatt, J. K., Cajochen, C., Ritz-De Cecco, A., Czeisler, C. A., & Dijk, D. J. (2004). Low-dose repeated caffeine administration for circadian-phase-dependent performance degradation during extended wakefulness. *Sleep, 27,* 374–381.

Young, T., Palta, M., Dempsey, J., Skatrud, J., Weber, S., & Badr, S. (1993). The occurrence of sleep-disordered breathing among middle-aged adults. *New England Journal of Medicine, 328*(17), 1230–1235.

Zimmerman, J. (1951). The penal reform movement in the South during the Progressive Era, 1890–1917. *The Journal of Southern History, 17*(4), 462–492.

Zimring, C., & Ulrich, R. (2004). *The Role of the Physical Environment in the Hospital of the 21st Century: a Once-in-a-lifetimeOpportunity.* Concord, CA: The Center for Health Design.

SECTION THREE

A MODEL AND CONCLUSIONS

11

An Environmental and Contextual Model of Violence in Jails and Prisons

Violence – whether actual events or fear of potential action – is a critical theme in the life of a correctional institutional. The violent act is often the force that drives administrative decisions and inmate behavior. The effort, time, personnel, and resources that are allocated to maintain safety are not available for counseling, education, or rehabilitation. Moreover, "fear of violence or riots can dominate the thinking of the warden to the point where he/she contributes to its occurrence" (McDougal, 1985, p. ix). The hardest barriers do not necessarily reduce prison violence in and of themselves. The most secure settings may have among the highest level of assaults (Atlas, 1982) and even "supermax" design does not necessarily reduce assaults and increase safety for inmates or staff (Briggs, Sundt, & Castellano, 2003).

Violence can shape policy and design. Critical incidents, such as escapes, serious assaults, and group disturbances, demand visible responses. At times correctional institutions seem to take on an onion-like quality as they develop layer after layer of features, each created in response to a real incident or a perceived threat. Additional hardware, cameras, or staff positions may appear as an answer to events that are statistically unlikely but would be highly embarrassing, such as putting a screen over the rooftop to reduce the chance of helicopter-aided escapes.

It is not surprising that many people believe that physical and sexual assault are widespread in correctional institutions. In the history of correctional settings, cruelty and aggression, sanctioned or not, have been common. Although assault rates are significant,[1] however, most inmates are not afraid most of the time, and some researchers have argued that even though sexual harassment may be frequent (Robertson, 1999), the incidence of traumatic events like homosexual rape may be vastly overstated (Cohen, Cole, & Bailey, 1976; Lipscomb, Muram, Speck, & Mercer, 1992; Nacci & Kane, 1984; Toch, 1985).

Whatever the reality is of prison and jail violence, its image has been magnified by media representations. From newspaper stories and periodic exposés, factual or sensationalized accounts are regularly presented to the public describing prison violence. Film and television shows with vivid images of riots, stabbings, and homosexual rape have become part of our shared consciousness (Mason, 2003).

Moreover, we expect these institutions to be violent places because they are, after all, the places where we send our most violent people. The justice system, at successive levels, filters out many of the least dangerous criminals. Nonviolent offenders are less likely to be arrested, charged, tried, convicted, and sentenced to prison (Bowker, 1980). The population that is finally incarcerated is likely to include the most violent individuals. In the United States of the over 2 million persons held in local and federal prisons and jails (Sabol & Couture, 2008), about half were serving time for violent offenses (*Prisoners in 2001*, 2002).

This inference – that jails are violent places because inmates are violent people – is also bolstered by the *fundamental attribution error*, a tendency to give more weight to intrapersonal or dispositional factors and underestimate the impact of situational factors (Ross, 1977; Ross & Nisbett, 1991). Given no clear evidence to the contrary, people assume that the behaviors they observe are caused by factors internal to the individual (such as character and personality) rather than by the nature of the situations those people are in. The fundamental attribution error may be strongest when the behavior in question is dangerous or threatening (Haney & Zimbardo, 2009). Moreover, because personal attributes are difficult to change (more difficult than altering the physical environment), such beliefs limit motivation to support programs that might reduce the level of aggression.

In this chapter, I review research and theory on the nature of violent behavior in jails and prisons and present a contextual model of institutional violence that includes past research and also addresses the experiences in direct supervision facilities as documented in previous chapters. The model and its various parts will be described and explained, and then used to explain the observed success of direct supervision institutions.

RESEARCH AND THEORY ON VIOLENT BEHAVIOR IN CORRECTIONAL SETTINGS

Research in corrections has focused on several models that attempt to organize explanatory factors for violence in institutions. The importation model proposes that aspects of the inmate's life before prison (including age, race, socioeconomic status) that relate to violent behavior are "imported" into the institution (Irwin & Cressey, 1962; McCorkle, Miethe, & Drass, 1995). That is, how inmates behave and the nature of social systems within the confines of the institution are largely dependent on their behavior and place in society prior to institutionalization, including roles, behavior patterns, and cultural norms. As an alternative, the deprivation model suggests that inmate behavior within the institution is a response to prison conditions, which significantly deprive them of valued aspects of normal life, including the ability to make one's own choices, form heterosexual relationships, and insure their own safety. Overcrowding, inadequate staffing, and poor management can be among the deprivations that lead to violence (Hochstetler & DeLisi, 2005). Other approaches include an administrative control model that focuses on the quality of governance, (Hochstetler & DeLisi, 2005), a situational model that addresses issues such as where assaults take place (Jiang & Fisher-Giorlando, 2002), and a model that focuses on how inmates cope with prison hardships (Toch, 1977).

All these models have found some levels of support. Hochstetler and DeLisi (2005) noted that "the most convincing case for importation obviously was that pre-incarceration characteristics, such as arrest history and prison history, predicted prison offending" (p. 258). There are also findings that support the impacts of deprivation factors such as crowding, security level, and racial makeup of staff (McCorkle, Miethe, & Drass, 1995). The way management responds to violence (coercive versus remunerative) also seems to have had an impact (Huebner, 2003).

Several reviews have noted that many who discuss prison violence presume that it relates to personality or dispositional factors, even in the absence of convincing data (Bottoms, 1999; Cooke, 1991; Wortley, 2003). Bottoms (1999) commented that even while many have given "lip service" to the relevance of environmental factors in prison violence, the focus on intrapersonal causes predominates. For example, Megaree (1976) presents a taxonomy of six kinds of violent offenders, only one of which has a situational element (that is, people who commit violence as an instrumental act).

Inmate age has been consistently found to be one of the best predictors of institutional violence. Younger inmates are more likely to engage in violent acts than are older inmates (Bennet, 1976; Cohen et al., 1976; Cooke, 1991; Lahm, 2008).[2] Cooke (1991) comments that age is the only variable that has consistently served as a useful predictor of prison violence. Reports on youth violence also cite a maturation effect, showing that serious violence declines sharply as adolescents reach adulthood (Grotpeter, Menard, Gianola, & O'Neal, 2008).

Some researchers have also reported correlations between the level of violent behavior and race or ethnicity, with some suggesting that Hispanic "machismo" culture or African American violent subcultures carry over to violence in institutions (Cohen et al., 1976; Harer & Steffensmeier, 1996). Additionally, offenders who had experienced physical or sexual abuse as a child were more likely to victimize other inmates when they were incarcerated (Kury & Smartt, 2002).

On the other hand, there is also evidence for the effect of a variety of situational elements on violence (Jiang & Fisher-Giorlando, 2002). The famous Stanford simulated prison experiment (Haney, Banks, & Zimbardo, 1973), though not without its critics (Carnahand & McFarland, 2007; Haslam & Reicher, 2006) provides support for the power of the situation – that adopting guard and prisoner roles can rapidly evoke aggressive responses. Sommer (1976) suggested that the very nature of the dominant/submissive relationship between the guard and the inmate is likely to create resentment and lead to violent actions.

Institutional violence has been related to crowding (Gaes & McGuire, 1985; Megaree, 1976; Sechrest & Crim, 1989), gang affiliation (Gaes, Flanagan, Motiuk, & Stewart, 1999), the amount of time that has been served (violent acts are more likely to be committed by inmates at the early stages of a sentence) (Bottoms, 1999), psychopathology (for example, Park, 1976), the nature of the social structure and dominance hierarchies (Cohen et al., 1976; Park, 1976; Rochman, 1991), quality of management (Deland, 1993; McCorkle, Miethe, & Drass, 1995), and frustration (Toch, 1992). Environmental factors have also been related to prison violence, including privacy and territoriality (Flynn, 1976), hard architecture (Nagel, 1976), and scarcity (Ellis, 1984). Suedfeld, Ramirez, Deaton, and Baker-Brown (1980) suggested that violence results from increased arousal due to spatial intrusion (noting Kinzel's [1970] data on body buffer zones and inmates), monotony (due to restricted environments), and lack of external control and predictability.

Scharf (1983) offered that violence stems from the crisis of meaning inmates experience in jails and prisons. The lack of an adequate metaphor for institutional life (that is, prison as monastery or as hospital) creates a situation in which inmates lead boring and empty lives. Gangs, he says, represent efforts "to create a meaningful community in an anomic prison environment" (p. 139).

Other factors that have been discussed as relating to prison violence include desegregation (although after an initial increase in violence when Texas prisons were first integrated, violence returned to earlier levels) (Trulson & Marquart, 1968), and lack of conjugal contact. Hensley and Koscheski (2002), however, found no relationship between participation on conjugal visit programs and violent acts.

Toch (1992) offered a more contextual model. He notes that violence is not a random event and suggests that it is related to its setting and context. He views the dyadic interchange between inmates as the basic unit of the violent act, and focusses on the experiences and motivations of both parties. His person–environment congruence model of prison violence suggests that violence is the result of the interplay between what the individual needs and what the environment affords. For example, some inmates may have a greater need for privacy (need to control overstimulation) or safety (need for protective settings) than others. They will, therefore, respond differently to the privacy and safety afforded by the setting. Toch suggests that assault can be reduced by creating settings that are tailored to meet these varying needs.

In institutions where violence is a constant threat, it is reasonable to ask why there is so much assault and who commits the violent acts. As noted previously, the answers offered often focus on the characteristics of the inmates. By contrast, many new direct supervision jails and prisons (Chapter 3) succeeded dramatically in reducing tension, fear, and levels of violent behavior, even while housing the full range of types of inmate, as described in detail in earlier chapters. The more salient questions for my work instead have been "why is there not more violence?" in these closed institutions that are crowded with inmates, many of whom have violent histories; and "why have these settings been so successful?" These studies have pointed toward the nature of the setting for the answers.

The power of the setting to influence behavior was demonstrated in Barker's (1968) research in ecological psychology. He found that behavior could be predicted more accurately by knowing about the nature of a behavior setting than by knowing details of the personalities of individuals in the setting. In many daily situations, Barker observed that the settings we are in limit, guide, enable, and proscribe our actions and determine much of the variability of our behavior.

ASSUMPTIONS FOR AN ENVIRONMENTAL
AND CONTEXTUAL MODEL

The model for institutional violence described in this chapter addresses a range of variables and attempts to place them in a broader context (see Figure 44). There are several assumptions basic to this model that should be made clear at the outset. First, I assume that the potential for violence in an institution is affected by organizational and social as well as environmental factors.

Each variable has its meaning within and, in part, because of the way it fits into the larger context. Being in a prison changes the nature and meaning of all behaviors, whether minor and seemingly insignificant (asking someone for a cigarette) or more obviously provocative (demanding someone give up their place in a line).

Including such a broad array of factors that may affect and influence one another hopefully adds verisimilitude to a model, even though it also increases complexity. As in most aspects of life, there are few simple, one-directional causal relationships in institutional violence. One can tease out and separate the psychological and organizational aspects of the setting, for example, but each is important and mutually dependent. To pull them apart for analysis or theory is artificial from the perspective of the user's setting, as a situation is typically perceived as a unity, not in isolated parts. "People react to environments globally and affectively before they analyze them or evaluate them in more specific terms" (Rapoport, 1982, p. 14). Social situations may determine behavior, but the environment provides the clues. The situation's various aspects inevitably affect one another in the sense that no behavior occurs in isolation and is always best understood as part of its broader context.

Second, the impact of setting on violent behavior is viewed in a probabilistic, not deterministic, sense. Changes in environment or organizational style, for example, are not likely to cause or eliminate violent acts per se. The changes may affect the violent acts directly, but more often they set in motion a series of events that affect the likelihood of the violent acts occurring.

Third, the model is built on the assumption of interaction among characteristics of people and aspects of the environment. Sometimes individual characteristics of inmates, such as personality and psychopathology, can lead directly to violent behavior (Buffington-Vollum, Edens, Johnson, & Johnson, 2002). Even where this is true, however, these dispositionally linked acts affect and are affected by the setting. For example, there is evidence from other kinds of settings of a link between stress and violence (Moffat, 1994; Nijman, a Campo, & Ravelli, 1999; Terpstra, Gispen-De Wied, & Broekhoven, 2003; Umberson, Anderson, & Williams, 2003). In a psychiatric institution, "repeated inpatient aggression may be the result of a vicious circle, whereby a patient's violent behavior is often followed by an increase in stress on the patient caused by environmental or communication factors, heightening the risk of another outburst of violence" (Nijman et al., 1999, p. 832).

It is not difficult to imagine, then, that in a tense correctional environment – one where inmates feel at risk for their own personal safety – stress can exacerbate the kinds of psychopathologies that can lead to violent outbursts.

A tense and dangerous place, for instance, could make someone already exhibiting paranoid-like qualities more likely to be fearful and to act on that fear. The pathologies and behavior of inmates act also upon the ambience of the environment. If there are inmates in a setting who have personalities and/or pathologies that make their behavior especially unpredictable, the overall level of fear and tension in the setting is likely to increase, as will the responses that are triggered by fear and tension.

Fourth, this model is focused specifically on the ordinary day-to-day behavior and routines of institutional life as they relate to violent acts. It does not purport to specifically address or explain special cases of violence, such as riots, terrorist activity, paid "hits," or carryover of gang activity from conflicts outside prison. These special cases may be driven by other outside forces and are less affected directly by the situational context as described here.[3] It is appropriate, of course, for prison officials to be concerned about these situations. This model, however, primarily addresses the kinds of day-to-day violent activity that makes up the majority of incidents officers and inmates experience, and are most likely to be affected by policy or design changes.

My goal here is to provide a conceptual framework that is inclusive and comprehensive, including environmental, organizational, and social facets of the system, and to suggest how they directly or indirectly lead toward or away from violent behavior. The framework provides an explanation of behavior that is consistent with current findings, makes predictions about other settings and situations, and has heuristic value in suggesting research directions.

ELEMENTS OF THE MODEL

The major components of this model, which will be discussed in detail in the following sections and which is presented in Figure 44, are as follows:

1. The *institutional context* in which the staff and inmates exist and function. By institutional context I am casting a very broad net and mean all the conditions that determine the nature of the institution, including the physical environment (architecture, environmental conditions, and so on), the organizational environment (management systems, regime, and so on), the social environment (makeup of inmate population – age, gender, security level, and so on) – and aspects of staffing (number, training, and so on).

2. *Mediating conditions* that determine how inmates will respond to the context, including fear and risk, perceived adequacy of resources, and stress and mental fatigue. A mediator is a variable that "accounts for

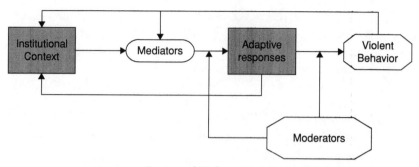

FIGURE 44. Contextual Violence Model – simplified

the relation between the predictor and the criterion (and) . . . explain(s) how external physical events take on internal psychological significance . . . " (Baron & Kenny, 1986; p. 1176).

3. Behaviors that represent *adaptive responses* to these contextual conditions (such as responding to fear by getting weapons, forming gangs, and so on).

4. *Violent behavior* including assaultive acts on individuals or objects with intent to do harm.

5. *Moderating factors* that may change the relationship between adaptive responses and violent behavior (and consequently the institutional context), such as the likely consequences of violent behavior. A moderator is a "qualitative (e.g., sex, race, class) or quantitative (e.g., level of reward) variable that affects the direction and/or strength of the relation between an independent or predictor variable and a dependent or criterion variable" (Baron & Kenny, 1986, p. 1174).

Each of these is considered in turn in the following sections.

Institutional Context

Institutional context refers to all the physical, organizational, and social factors that define the setting and create the environment to which the user will be responding and adapting (see Figure 45). These include aspects of the physical design and institutional resources; the goals, style, and efficiency of the organization; the number, history, and nature of the inmates; and the number, training, and focus of the staff. The person in the setting may not experience these as distinctly different realms. The individual might perceive experiences in a setting as pleasant or unpleasant, for instance, without dissecting the experience into specific features.

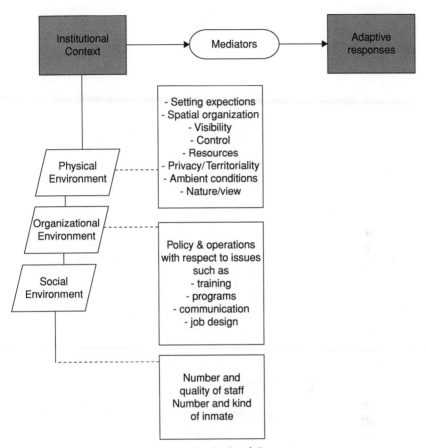

FIGURE 45. Institutional Context

Our response upon entering a new situation is initially global (Ittleson, 1970; Rapoport, 1982). We don't discriminate between organizational, design, and social aspects of the situation, at least at first, as we react to them. Altman and others have suggested a transactional model (Altman & Rogoff, 1987; Stokols, 1987) in which these elements are part of a system of continuous transactions between the environment and people. For example, spatial design reflects organizational structure even while it is affected by it. Organizations are regularly creating or modifying settings to fit their needs and goals, as in the way corporations choose open office systems when they want to improve communications or have better visual access to watch what workers are doing. The number of doorways or other barriers through which a person must pass to reach an executive reflects the horizontal or vertical structure of the organizational flowchart, but the way the organization works may also be modified and shaped by the physical setting it has created or inherited. The design and the organizational structure of a correctional institution, as it is created, and as it evolves, affects and is affected by the nature of the inmates and the staff.

Physical Environment

SETTING EXPECTATIONS. The way the facility is designed, furnished, decorated, and maintained can affect behavior at a number of levels. Some are obvious – such as the number of barriers, doors, and locks an inmate has to pass to reach a resource. Access can be easy – such as in open living areas where inmates use TVs, water fountains, canteens, showers, and phones without restriction; or difficult – as when an inmate is locked in a cell and must make a request for virtually any need.

Other design issues are more subtle, like the way the aesthetic quality of a space may change mood and expectations. As noted earlier, the impact of the appearance of the setting is immediate and global in nature. When people enter a new place, they pull from it an immediate sense of the situation, provided by physical cues but interpreted through their own cultural history (Rapoport, 1982). The visual quality of the setting (including layout, decor, colors, furnishings, materials and finishes, and upkeep) creates an immediate global impression that sets expectations and may have a powerful impact on behavior. "Settings somehow communicate expected behavior if the cues can be read and understood" (Rapoport, 1982, p. 57).

Qualities of a setting along a continuum from "homelike to institutional" have been shown to influence global evaluations in institutions for the developmentally disabled (Egli, Feuer, Roper, & Thompson, 2002; Egli, Roper, Feuer, & Thompson, 1999; Thompson, 1990; Thompson, Robinson, Dietrich, Farris, & Sinclair, 1996). Moreover, settings rated as "homelike" for the kind and quality of furniture, surfaces, textures, layout, lighting, and acoustics had more staff–resident interaction and increased levels of community participation (Thompson et al., 1996; Egli et al., 2002).

The interiors of living units in the first direct supervision jails were designed with a goal of creating less institutional and more residential-like appearances. My colleagues and I (Wener, 2006; Wener, Farbstein, & Frazier, 1985) and others (Nelson, O'Toole, Krauth & Whitemore, 1983) have suggested that the interior appearance of the jail affects behavioral expectations and norms, including what the occupants of the space (staff and inmates) perceive to be the normal and accepted actions in that place. Inmates entering a correctional space for the first time are unlikely to arrive tabula rasa. They bring a set of understandings about "going to jail" from their own past, from what they have heard and been told by others, and/or from what they have seen in books, films, television, or newspapers. As they enter the institution, these expectations may be quickly confirmed or disconfirmed by the physical features they encounter, as well as by the behavior and demeanor of others. Inmates gain an instant impression of how they are expected to respond to requests, commands, threats, and challenges. Physical features such as the level of noise or visual signs of vandalism may provide a sense of whether the setting is controlled or chaotic. The hard architecture of traditional jail designs may encourage vandalism by the mere presence of "vandal-proof" fixtures that challenge the user ("break me if you can") and communicate an expectation of destructive behavior, what Sommer (1974) has called "hard architecture." Creating a physical setting with less traditional décor is one way to break those expectation sets.

This is similar to the notion of incivilities – the "broken window hypothesis" – which has been much discussed in terms of street crime and vandalism. It proposes that a sense of disorder and physical evidence of damage can create the impression that uncivil behavior is tolerated, accepted, or at least unpunished, making it more likely that such behavior will continue (Keizer, Lindenberg, & Steg, 2008; Taylor, 2005; Wilson & Kelling, 1982). Disorder can also indicate that authorities are not in control, which might make inmates feel that they need to take action to defend themselves. Moreover, traditional jail or prison layouts with barred, graffiti-stained walls, concrete and iron surfaces, and a detached attitude from the staff may provide a message that staff and inmates are expected to exist in a state of opposition rather than cooperation. If bars, walls, and locks are needed to separate inmates from each other and from staff, this must indeed be a dangerous place.

A more normalized setting, on the other hand, such as those created for the first Metropolitan Correctional Center (MCC), may send another message and set very different expectations, indicating that the inmates and staff are expected to behave in ways consistent with external civilized standards. The soft colors and materials, open layout, and casual behavior of staff and inmates imply a norm of cooperation, and that opportunities for contact are not seen as chances for assault. The presence of breakable, even fragile objects announces that rough and destructive handling is not anticipated (see the subsection "Vandalism" later in this chapter for a discussion of the design factors that affect violence to objects).

Layout – Physical Organization of Space
The kinds of decisions an architect makes concerning layout and the general organization of space can influence perception and social behavior in a

number of ways. Layout affects the options for the kind of management or supervision style that can be used. The degree of physical openness of the design sets limits on the effectiveness of visual surveillance. Poor site-lines can force reliance on closed circuit TV to observe spaces, which is rarely as good an option as actual staff presence (see Allard, Wortley, & Stewart, 2008; Benton & Obenland, 1975). In this respect, direct supervision is like community policing (Trojanowicz & Bucqueroux, 1990), bringing the uniformed officer into direct and personal contact with potential offenders in ways that reduce the chances of an offense occurring. Officers, like a cop on the beat, need to see and be seen. The open unit goes beyond simple visual access, though, to include social access and contact. Not only can inmates and staff see and be seen, they can interact, allowing staff to quickly respond to an inmate who is being assaulted. First and second generation jail designs (see discussion in Chapter 3; Nelson, 1988) distinctly limit contact. They rely heavily on physical barriers and visual surveillance as opposed to personal contact and communication. As a result, inmates or staff members in a first or second generation institution, if assaulted, do not benefit from an immediate staff response (Farbstein & Wener, 1989), and hence are less likely to trust their safety to staff intervention.

An open design provides the opportunity to make use of a direct supervision management model in an institution. Some officers and inmates have told us that the presence of bars and hard physical separations of traditional institutions often seem to encourage oppositional behavior. In a way, it is the opposite of "good fences make good neighbors." Rather, forced separation by hard barriers frees people from the usual social civilities that come into play when they have to deal with someone face to face. Direct contact forces both to deal with each other as individuals in a social situation, and by so doing to reduce perfunctory cruelty and casual unpleasantness.

Layout and design also affect the degree to which inmates have access to key services. Can inmates get to TVs, phones, food, bathrooms, medical help, or counselors on their own, or do they need staff to escort, unlock doors, or schedule use? Designs that force reliance on staff for large and small needs may reduce the sense of control, increase frustration for inmates and staff, and multiply the opportunities for irritation and conflict. The organization of space also affects how officers are able to do their job and the quality of staff–inmate interaction. In many new facilities, for example, officers are required to manage many tasks (open doors, answer phones, log activities) that force them to stay near a control panel. This can anchor the officer to the control station and therefore reduce opportunities to move around the living area, observe behavior, and have contact with inmates.

In design, of course, the devil is often in the details. For instance, even though officers at the Manhattan House of Detention had tasks to do that kept them at or near the station more than might otherwise be desired, the problem there was not so severe. The living unit was small and visually open, and inmate activities (such as eating, playing cards, watching television) were grouped in spaces that were immediately adjacent to the station. Even though the officer was often stuck at the open station, "popping" doors, answering phones, or filling out paperwork, he or she was still within a comfortable distance for easy and frequent interaction with inmates (Wener, 1985). Some other institutions we have studied, however, have created living areas with much bigger spaces where inmate activities are more spread out. There, an officer who is anchored to the station by his or her duties is effectively cut off from many opportunities for communication and supervision (Bogard & Wener, 2007).

Visibility
As noted in Chapters 3 and 4, direct supervision is based, in part, on the notion that visibility, however complete, is not in itself sufficient to maintain security and control. That does not mean, however, that visibility is not useful. Indeed, having spaces that are open and visually available, even if not panoptic, supports an officer's ability to see what is going on within a living unit, and increases the likelihood that consequences will apply to bad behavior, such as violence or vandalism (see "Moderating Influence of Consequences – Risk of Being Apprehended").

Level of Control
Providing inmates with features that allow them to have some control over contact, resources, and exposure to stressors can be useful in many ways that affect violence and vandalism. For example, being able to avoid contact with others by going into your room and closing the door, especially when those others are annoying or threatening, eliminates situations that can escalate into violence. Being able to adjust systems (such as by turning off lights) reduces the likelihood that they will be broken in order to turn them off. Control reduces stress, lowers irritability, and increases tolerance for frustration, all of which help to reduce violence.

RESOURCE LEVELS. The restrictive nature of total institutions turns most of the amenities of daily life into scarce resources, including items as simple and basic as food, soap, toilet paper, telephones, and TVs. Relative scarcity results from the availability of desired elements, such as the number of telephones in the living area, as well as policy, which sets how often one has access to the telephones. As noted in Chapter 4, design differences between the Chicago and New York MCCs affected the relative availability of televisions, from a sufficient number in Chicago to half as many in New York, where arguments over channel selection were common. Seating near the television or in the dining area for a meal can also become a sought-after commodity. Scarcity breeds competition, which often leads to aggression (Mesquida & Weiner, 1996).

PRIVACY AND TERRITORIALITY. As discussed at length in Chapter 6, layout and design affect the level of privacy an inmate can attain and the way in which territorial behaviors are expressed, both of which can influence aggressive behavior. Privacy in this context does not just refer to being alone, but rather to being able to connect to and interact with the right or desired number of people at any given moment. It is all too clear in corrections that being alone can be either the most positive condition or the most punitive. It depends on the level of choice and control experienced.

Privacy can affect violence in correctional settings in several ways, most directly by giving inmates "access control," options and choices about their degree of contact with others and the means for regulating that contact, as well as providing them with the ability to avoid contact, such as by going into a room and closing the door when they wish. Retiring to a room can be a way to avoid difficult situations that can otherwise escalate into an argument or fight. Encountering another person who is acting in an aggressive, odd, or otherwise unpredictable way in a public space leaves an inmate with limited choices. Some options (such as confrontation) make violence more likely. Withdrawing to a bedroom to wait until the other person leaves, cools down, or is dealt with by staff is the least aggressive response possible.

Privacy can also reduce aggressive behavior in less direct ways, by providing inmates with a sense of control over aggravating conditions. Control can significantly reduce the amount of stress those conditions produce, cutting the response chain through which stress can lead to aggressive behavior (Evans, 1982).

AMBIENT CONDITIONS. There is a panoply of ambient conditions that can directly or indirectly affect violent behavior, such as noise, lighting, temperature, and air quality. The considerable literature on noise, reviewed in Chapter 8, and light, reviewed in Chapter 10, showed effects on mood, irritability, and stress related to aggressive behavior. Although relatively little research has addressed air quality and aggressive behavior, many studies looking at temperature effects in the general population suggests a relationship between heat and aggression (Anderson, 1989; Anderson, Anderson, Dorr,

DeNeve, & Flannagan, 1998, 2000; Anderson & DeNeve, 1992; Bell & Barron, 1977; Haertzen, Covi, & Richards, 1993; Wyon, Anderson, & Lundqvist, 1979). "It may be more cost-effective (as well as humanitarian) to cool prison environments as a means of reducing inmate violence rather than to increase the supervision and segregation of prisoners" (Anderson, 1989, p. 94).

NATURE AND VIEW. As described in Chapter 10, experimental findings indicate that access to and views of nature can have a strong impact on stress and mental functioning in ways that have been related to aggression and self-reports of anger in other contexts (Hartig, Mang, & Evans, 1991; Hartig et al., 2003; Kuo & Sullivan, 2001a, 2001b; Ulrich et al., 1991). Inmates inevitably encounter many sources of stress in an institution, and the inability to be in or even view scenes of nature removes an important option for coping that is available to the non-incarcerated public.

Organizational Environment

The organizational environment is addressed in less detail here, because it is not the major focus of this book. It is presented, however, to acknowledge not only its effects but the close interconnections of the organizational and physical contexts (see Figure 45). The impact of the physical environment can be magnified or weakened by formal or informal organizational policies or understandings. Privacy is a good example. The physical design may provide opportunities for inmates to gain privacy, for instance, in individual rooms with accessible doors. Policy, however, determines whether these choices can be exercised. Some juvenile detention institutions, for instance, have rules that do not allow residents to reenter their rooms once they have left in the morning, in which case the design of the room or the presence of a door make little difference, when there is no choice or control over access and essentially no ability to use the room for privacy.

The adequacy or scarcity of resources is similarly connected to policy. For example, the number of telephones in a living area may define the upper limit of use, but policy determines the number of calls each person is allowed in a period of time, the length of time per call, the manner of queuing for phone use, and the kind and level of supervision of inmates in the telephone area. These rules all set the real level of accessibility of the resource.

However open the living unit design or how good the line of sight may be, organizational factors, such as the quality of staff training, ultimately determine the kind and quality of communication between staff and inmates – and for that matter between staff and administrators. Direct supervision facilities work, to a large degree, because managers are intensely committed to principles that demand officers be around and in control of the living areas. They need to know and interact with the inmates (Zupan, 1991). The degree to which inmates perceive rules and enforcement as "just and fair" (one of the nine principles of direct supervision [Nelson, 1990]) is key to maintaining the general expectation of reasonable behavior on the part of all (Bottoms, 1999). This philosophy determines what kinds of rehabilitation or educational programs will be offered and how they will be maintained.

The principles of direct supervision reflect a concern for systems that provide for open communication, not only between officers and inmates, but also between officers and management (Davis, 1987a). Officers need to be well trained, feel supported from above, and empowered to make decisions on the living unit.

Organizational context also includes programs that can determine the quality of time spent in an institution. Many kinds of programs are available for use in correctional settings that are meant to support personal growth and change, such as group therapy or addiction treatment; education, such as high school equivalency or college courses; or vocational training, such as prison industries or classes in employable industries like gardening or computer repair. Programs fill the day, reduce boredom, and can give the inmate a sense of doing something constructive with incarcerated time. Correctional philosophy, policy, and allocation of staffing and resources determine whether such programs will exist at all and how available they will be.

Social Environment
The social environment refers to the number, nature, roles, and group dynamics of the people in the setting (see Figure 45). The quality of the correctional context is significantly connected to the makeup of the staff and the inmates as they interact with the physical and organizational environments.

STAFF CHARACTERISTICS. The atmosphere in the institution is critically related to the kind, quality, and quantity of the staff. The staff–inmate ratio and number of staff per living unit can play a large role in determining the kind and quality of staff–inmate contact. One example that has been much discussed concerns staffing of direct supervision jails (Bogard & Wener, 2007) where staff–inmate ratios have proven to be more flexible than originally thought, ranging from thirty-six inmates per one officer up to seventy inmates per officer at planned capacity, and even higher in conditions of overcrowding. At the high end of this spectrum, most administrators agree that the ability of the officer to know the inmates and deal proactively with problems is diminished. Assaults by inmates on staff are more likely when staff-inmate ratios are larger (Lahm, 2009a).

Some facilities have developed rules of thumb that place an additional officer in a living unit when the population exceeds certain limits. Operationally, however, having two officers in a 100-person living area is not the same as having one for fifty inmates. In higher densities, each officer has a reduced capacity to know and meet with all the inmates, increasing the likelihood of conflict among inmates. Whether there are one, two, or three officers for 100 inmates, for example, each officer still needs to recognize and be familiar with all 100 inmates for a direct supervision system to work properly.

In addition, adding more officers to the living unit changes the dynamics of the situation (Bogard & Wener, 2007). A study of the Contra Costa County Detention Center (Zimring, 1989) showed that when two officers are present, they tend to spend more time talking to one another, and less time with the inmates. When two officers are on a living unit together, the natural tendency will be for them to associate with each other, limiting the effectiveness of staff–inmate contacts.

Staff selection, supervision, and training are critical to safe institutional operation (Van den Heuval, 1986; Zupan, 1991). Zupan (1991) notes that "officers (in direct supervision settings) are effective when they produce an environment that is free from conflict among inmates and between inmates and staff" (pp. 105–106). Because they can't rely on physical separation, they are forced to make use of "sophisticated management and leadership skills to maintain order" (p. 106). Critical issues include whether staff are selected for characteristics that support positive staff–inmate communication, are given a clear and unambiguous message about their job function and responsibilities, and are committed to supporting the goals and missions of the facility.

Inmate Characteristics

As noted earlier in this chapter, the qualities of the inmate population that influence violent behavior have been a primary focus of much past research. Demographic factors such as age, gender, race/ethnicity, nature of the offense, and behavioral history are important predictors of violence (Bennet, 1976; Cohen et al., 1976; Harer & Steffensmeier, 1996). For instance, younger inmates tend to be more aggressive than older ones (Cooke, 1991; Lahm, 2009b).

It is also useful to ask if inmates have psychological or other problems requiring special attention and whether treatment is provided. Do inmates come from a culture with special emphasis on violence (such as for retribution)? Much of the literature on assault in jails and prisons has focused on individual psychopathology, such as the assaultive nature of sociopathic personalities and problems arising from paranoia. Such conditions can affect assaults, independently of other environmental factors. Individual psychopathologies, however, do not exist in a vacuum. The level of stress and tension in an institution can affect the quantity and quality of psychopathologies. If an abundance of weapons can make most inmates and staff concerned, it is easy to imagine a greater impact on those who are already clinically paranoid or anxious.

The quality of management and its policies, as well as staff training and interaction, can play an important role in the way psychopathologies manifest themselves. Are staff members aware of inmate problems so that they can predict and proactively deal with them? Are there screening and treatment programs to identify and help those inmates? Research from psychiatric settings indicates that some psychological pathologies may in themselves increase the chances of aggressive behavior, and also that these conditions affect and are affected by the environment (Ng, Kumar, Ranclaud, & Robinson, 2001; Nijman et al., 1999; Whittington & Whykes, 1996). That is, stressful situations exacerbate psychological conditions, and the expression of these conditions through aggressive behavior increases tension in the living area. If these individual psychopathologies are left to express themselves, staff and inmates will become more uncomfortable. The unpredictability of an assault from an unstable inmate can be especially stressful to the individual and to the system.

Mediating Responses to and Perception of the Institutional Context

The situational context, circumscribed by the nature and interaction of the physical, organizational, and social environments, will affect the way in which inmates and staff respond to and perceive their situation. There are many layers of response one could address, but for this model, I focused on three situations and responses that have particular relevance to the chances of a violent outcome. These act as mediating variables, explaining the impact of physical, organizational, and social context on violence:

1. The degree to which inmates feel safe or fearful and see themselves at a risk of being assaulted;
2. The perceived level of adequacy of important resources; and
3. The level of stress and mental fatigue that inmates and staff experience (see Figure 46).

In general, mediating variables explain or account for the relationship between a predictor (in this case, environmental context) and an outcome (violence) (see Baron & Kenny, 1986, and Evans & Lepore, 1997, for thorough

FIGURE 46. Mediating factors

discussions of mediation and moderation). Perceptions of fear, scarcity, and stress, in turn, may lead to specific adaptive or maladaptive actions that can increase or reduce the likelihood of aggressive and violent acts.

Context Affects Fear and Perceived Risk

Central to this model is the relationship of fear and perceived risk to inmate behavior (see Figure 47). Perceived risk is especially interesting as an issue related to violence because risk is the result of clearly identifiable forces, because it has several obvious effects, and because it is amenable to interventions. Our investigations in various settings have led us to believe that when inmates feel that they have a real chance of being physically or sexually assaulted and that staff cannot or will not protect them, they will take steps to protect themselves. In a total institution there is only a small set of options available to inmates as protective and coping responses, and unfortunately most of these have consequences that add to the overall levels of tension and fear in the institution.

The connections and interactions between the contextual factors and perceived risk are presented in Figure 47. The physical setting affects safety and perceptions of risk in several direct and less direct ways. As noted in earlier discussions of the designs of indirect and direct supervision facilities, architecture can make it difficult for staff to provide protection by creating physical barriers between staff and inmates, or by placing staff at a greater physical (and social) distance, thus reducing visual contact and awareness of problems. Linear prisons and jails are prototypical of this situation. Staff cannot readily see or hear inmates much of the time, except when they are on tours of the cellblocks. Those tours tend to be predictable, allowing an assailant to wait until the officer has passed out of sight and hearing. The ability of staff to protect an inmate is low.

In many traditional jails where inmates and staff are separated by hard barriers, officers appear anxious when they enter inmate spaces, and vandalism and graffiti are common. The overall impression of such a place is more like

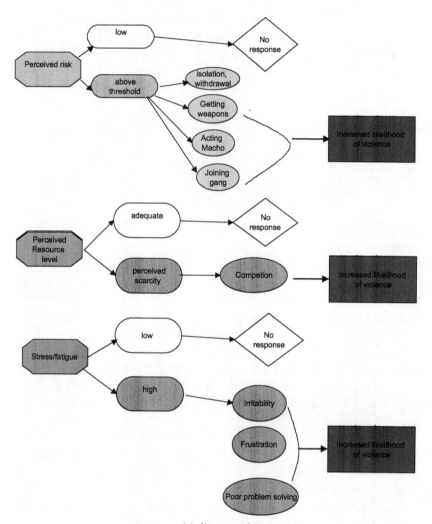

FIGURE 47. Mediators and responses

a cage for wild animals than housing for people. For an inmate entering the system, the clear message is that "this place is dangerous – to staff and also to me." It suggests that the facility is not controlled by staff. Unpredictability and perceived lack of control – chaos – is uncomfortable, stressful, and even terrifying.

Although design creates the opportunity, policy ultimately determines the degree to which staff will interact with inmates and the manner in which staff will respond to an assault of one inmate upon another. In some institutions, staff members rarely enter living units. In others, an officer must wait for backup before responding in order to help a threatened inmate. In these situations inmates may feel left to fend for themselves. If, because of policy, staff selection, training, or lack of supervision, officers appear to be unconcerned about inmate welfare, inmates will feel obliged to ensure their own safety.

Social factors also set the context. The nature of the inmate population is clearly important for the level of the real and perceived risk. Some people are more predisposed than others toward responding violently to social conflict and frustration, whether because of age, culture, personality, or pathology (Blonigen & Krueger, 2007). Younger inmates and those with violent histories are the most dangerous, and risk is highest when fellow inmates are perceived as being unpredictable. Inmates who are mentally unstable or especially predisposed to violence are a special and obvious threat. The threat to order is increased when diagnostic and classification schemes fail to screen these inmates out of general living units in favor of more controlled settings.

The high turnover rate in most jails (many inmates stay less than 48 hours) keeps the social order in turmoil and makes life in the institution unpredictable. New inmates are less likely to know the informal rules that help govern institutional life. They may be more likely to feel the need to show how tough they are or to impress other residents. Turnover leads to higher rates of violence (Ellis, 1984), when unpredictability is increased and previously stable dominance hierarchies may be challenged (Sundstrom & Altman, 1974).

If, for the above or other reasons, inmates perceive that their safety is threatened, they will search for strategies to cope with the threat and protect themselves. One relatively benign strategy is to try and isolate themselves, by retreating to a locked secure space, or by asking to be placed in protective custody, for example. Some institutions allow inmates to enter their cells and close the door behind them on request, but this may only serve as a response to a short-lived threat and is rarely a viable option over the long term. Protective custody, for instance, is typically available only for special cases and for a limited time.

Other means of self-protection are more problematic for other inmates, staff, and for the general well-being and equilibrium of the institution. Inmates may seek weapons as a means of self-defense, manufacturing them out of materials at hand or having them smuggled into the institution.

In conversations, correctional officials concede that inmates can often obtain some sort of weapon if the motivation is strong enough. As seen through this lens, weapons in an institution are largely defensive in nature. Their presence is a good index of the level of fear. Absence of weapons is a sign of lack of desire or need more than lack of opportunity.

Alternatively, inmates may seek the support and protection of others, individually or in a group. The group could be a preexisting "gang" or simply an ad hoc coalition. Like a gem that splits at the fault lines when struck, inmate populations under stress tend to break down into coalitions based on the most obvious commonalities – race and ethnicity. Inmates in the Manhattan House of Detention told us that friendships and conversations between members of different racial and ethnic groups were common there because general fear of assault was low. This was in contrast, they pointed out, to other institutions, such as Riker's Island, where fear of assault was endemic. In that case, they said that inmates remained in their common groups for protection and intergroup interaction was rare (Wener, 1985). The safety of a group comes, of course, because someone who might pick on a lone inmate may hesitate when that assault would bring a response from many others. In this case, clearly, a single incident can quickly spread to a large-scale fight.

As a third protective option, inmates may try to preempt an attack by acting tough, crazy, or "macho" (Toch, 1992). An inmate will pick a fight with another inmate or an officer to demonstrate that he is not to be fooled with. One inmate wrote, "(w)hen I entered Walpole State Prison in June of 1969, it was clear I would have to devise a strategy for my survival. . . . When I beat (the guard) . . . I made a reputation for myself as a fearless fighter who would stand up to repressive guards. I later used this persona to protect myself from attacks from both guards and prisoners . . . " (Bissonette, 2008, p. 1). Bowker (1985) recalls an inmate who "carefully cultivated his reputation as a crazy loner who would fight against impossible odds if challenged" (p. 14) to scare off potential threats.

All of these defensive tactics have unfortunate consequences for the setting. Objective danger for other inmates and for staff increases when weapons proliferate, when racial/ethnic cliques or gang activity increase, or when inmates posture, threaten, and "act tough." The culture of correctional institutions is such that backing off a fight may be difficult and retaliation often becomes the norm. A dangerous cycle can be set into place. Staff members, sensing the danger and tension, tend to back off, and feel less comfortable and less able to freely interact with and among inmates. With staff more distant and less available, inmates feel even less protected, forcing even more reliance on other options – weapons, protective groups, or intimidation – and so on in an increasingly negative spiral.

Perceived Scarcity of Resources

The perceived adequacy of resources available to inmates is another important mediator of violence in institutions. When resources are scarce, competition increases, leading to friction and conflict. In several cases, a review of prison records has revealed, for example, that many arguments erupt over access to telephones (Wener & Olsen, 1978). Often there are only one or two telephones for fifty or more inmates. Inmates typically must sign up for calling times and/or get in line to make outgoing calls. As one can imagine, these lines are not always as orderly as a London bus queue. Arguments are not uncommon over whose turn it is or how long someone has spent on the phone. Conflict is less common when more phones are available (LaVigne, 1994; Wener & Olsen, 1978).

Similar conflicts can arise over what TV channel to watch, access to food or snacks or any of a number of other resources. In our studies, arguments over TV watching were somewhat common in a jail with two TVs for forty-eight persons, but rare in a similar facility with four TVs for forty-four inmates (Wener & Olsen, 1980). In total institutions, small events can become critical concerns.

The effect of increases in population density on assaults (see Chapter 7, "Prison Crowding") may be due in part to the effect on the distribution of resources. The entire range of institutional resources is affected by over-crowding. As population density rises, access to counseling and other staff, recreation and medical services, educational, job training, and therapeutic programs may become much more difficult. The best response to overcrowding may be to increase the level of these services, but few institutions are given the budget to do so (Bogard & Wener, 2007). A larger population, of course, also adds pressure by increasing time spent waiting for food or telephone calls, showers, use of outdoor or exercise facilities, ability to gain any access to privacy, and choice of TV shows.

Stress and Mental Fatigue

I have already noted a variety of environmental conditions in correctional settings that can lead to increases in stress and mental fatigue, including noise, temperature fluctuations, poor air quality, and crowding. The presence of several or many stressors at once, and the absence of restorative features, such as nature views or the ability to cope by regulating privacy, makes the situation even worse. These conditions can cause responses of perceived helplessness and reduced tolerance for frustration, anxiety, and irritability, all of which may increase the chance that encounters will become conflicts rising to the level of violent acts. Evans, Allen, Tafalla, and O'Meara (1996) noted that "one of the costs of coping with a stressor may be diminished capability to deal effectively with (a) ... subsequent source of stress" (p. 147). Mental fatigue can affect aggressive behavior, such as by increasing irritability (Kuo & Sullivan, 2001a).

Moderating Influence of Consequences – Risk of Being Apprehended

The issues described above provide the preconditions and motivators for assaultive behaviors, but these behaviors can be moderated by the way their consequences are addressed (see Figure 48). While mediating variables explain the relationship between a predictor and an outcome, a moderating variable influences the strength or direction of that relationship (Baron & Kenny, 1986; Evans & Lepore, 1997). Even though fear, resource scarcity, and stress may generate aggressive behavior, the likely consequences – chances of being seen or apprehended – may dampen the frequency with which that behavior will occur. Wortley (2003), in a somewhat analogous fashion, discusses control by prompts and control by consequences as the primary factors affecting violent behavior. He cites increasing risks, increasing anticipated punishments, and reducing rewards as prompts and consequences that reduce aggressive responses.

Wortley (2003) observed that situational factors can both precipitate and regulate violent behavior. In particular, greater surveillance increases the risk to the inmate of being caught misbehaving and hence reduces its frequency. Allard et al. (2008) found supportive evidence indicating that the presence of closed circuit television (CCTV) reduced some kinds of misbehaviors in prisons. Specifically, they found that CCTV surveillance had a greater effect on planned than on unplanned or spontaneous behaviors, and hence led to less reduction of spontaneous violence than other kinds of problem behaviors.

In general, then, conditions that increase the risk of being observed or apprehended will also increase inhibitions to violence, although less so for violence that erupts from emotional outbursts. The likelihood of being seen and punished is connected to both design and operational factors. The physical and visible openness of the space, the number of inmates, the operating model and actions of officers (in the unit and touring versus off the unit or stationary), all make it harder for an assault to go undetected. When the scale of the setting is small and staff–inmate interaction is high, it is more likely that officers will know what is going on.

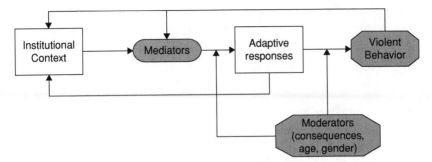

FIGURE 48. Moderator – Consequences

VANDALISM

The issues that arise when considering aggression to objects are similar to those involved in violence against people. While there is a victim to tell the story of an assault, though, vandalism can often be assessed only in retrospect, viewed from its outcome and impact (encountering a broken object), leading to presumptions of causes and intent. Like violence, acts of vandalism commonly evoke the fundamental attribution error, suggesting that causes are related to personal attributes of the vandal, such as maliciousness.

Also like violence, vandalism can be viewed as a sign and symptom of other problems, representing many different kinds of situations, causes, and intentions – only a subset of which includes the malicious intention to harm. The different kinds of vandalism are likely to respond to different interventions.

Not only is vandalism a problem in itself because of the damage that is done, but the visual residue of vandalism (the unsightly remains of broken objects, damaged furniture or walls, graffiti, and so on) may lead to more and worse behavior, as with broken windows on the street (Wilson & Kelling, 1982). The vandalized spaces and objects are, themselves, taken as a sign that such behavior is normative in that setting, that it is accepted (by not having been stopped or at least quickly repaired) and is unlikely to be punished. Cleaning up litter in a park reduces the rate of future littering (Reiter & Samuel, 1980). Litter left in the park seems to attract more new instances of littering. Littering or vandalism can become, in effect, the new standard and accepted norm.

Fisher and Baron (1982) indicate that vandalism carries both individual and social meaning and can be viewed from the perspective of a social equity model in which the act, for the vandal, is seen as "a meaningful response to what are perceived as unfair conditions" (p. 185). Goldstein (1996) describes vandalism from an interactionist perspective of person–environment relations, indicating that each situation involves both situational and personal aspects. His review of vandalism literature includes descriptions of many different typologies of vandalism, often with overlapping categories. In some cases, vandalism types are described as the result largely of personal and interpersonal issues including:

- Instrumental vandalism – acts of aggression causing damage to property and objects for some kind of monetary or other gain. This includes what has been called predatory vandalism (Martin, 1961), acquisitive and tactical vandalism (Cohen, 1971), and vandalism for financial gain (Coffield & Fundação Calouste, 1991).
- Vindictive vandalism – vandalism that seems to have as its primary motive the intent to damage or destroy, including malicious vandalism (Cohen, 1971), hostility directed and thoughtless vandalism (Thaw, 1981), wanton vandalism (Zeisel, 1976), and, at least in some cases, ideologically inspired vandalism (Cohen, 1971). Attempts to address inequities (Fisher & Baron, 1982) might also fall into this category.

In other situations "vandalism" appears to be a mislabeled response of the individual or group to the design of the setting and/or interaction of situation and design:

- Overuse – poorly placed or badly thought-out design or materials that cannot withstand appropriate but heavy use – as described by Weinmayr (1969). This kind of damage has been described as hidden maintenance-related damage that is misnamed as vandalism (Thaw, 1981; Zeisel, 1976).
- Conflicting uses – use of one facility leads to damage to another (such as a ball field near breakable windows) or use of an object needed to achieve another goal, leading to damage (climbing a tree to watch a game) – called leverage vandalism or "no-other-way-to-do-it" vandalism by Weinmayr (1969).
- Curiosity – vandalism caused by use stemming from behaviors triggered by excitement and interest, which has also been called vandalism from play (Cohen, 1971) or irresistible temptation (Weinmayr, 1969). It is similar to what Sommer (1974) has called the challenge of hard design (Sommer, 1974).

Clearly environmental design plays a strong role in vandalism, affecting the availability of the place or object to be damaged and the motivation to do so. Many of the issues noted in the typologies above can be seen in examples of vandalism, or lack thereof, in correctional settings.

The plan for the Metropolitan Correctional Centers (see Chapter 3) involved the use of "soft" non-institutional design in a conscious attempt to alter aggressive behavior, including aggression toward objects. The Bureau of Prisons presumed that soft design would evoke better caretaking. This included the presence of furniture, fixtures, and objects of the sort used in normal homelike settings (see Thompson et al., 1996, for a discussion of homelike qualities) as opposed to objects chosen to resist expected wanton destruction. Hence, the use of bright colors, fabric-covered furniture, porcelain toilets, and fragile light fixtures in the three original MCCs. The planners of the MCCs also presumed that the same open design that brought staff into easy, regular, and informal contact with inmates to deter violent behavior would also reduce vandalism. As I described in Chapters 3, 4, and 5, the level of breakage in all of the MCCs, and in similar jails, like CCMDF, was astonishingly low. Even the most fragile items, such as the frosted bare bulbs used in the Chicago MCC, were hardly ever broken (see Figure 24 as shown on p. 76). Porcelain toilets rarely needed replacing.

As mentioned in Chapter 4, in the case of the MCCs, the exceptions seemed to prove the rule. For instance, we found that the few places to experience serious breakage in the MCCs, such as the intake holding rooms, were the only places that violated these principles (see Figure 25, p. 82). That is, these holding areas had spare, hard rooms with hard surfaces that appeared to be designed to resist vandalism. Inmates in these holding cells were out of easy view of staff work stations, eliminating constant informal surveillance.

The MCCs also provided examples of "vandalism" from misplacement and overuse. In preparing to study the Chicago MCC, we were asked by the head administrator to look into damage in the TV lounge areas. Maintenance staff complained of vandalism in these areas, in the form of cigarette burns in the carpet and broken TV knobs. Both inmates and the unit officers told us that the TV sets were broken by overuse and not by angry or malicious vandalism. The sets were on constantly, and channel changing was continuous. The sets were apparently not designed for such heavy use and channel changing knobs commonly broke – little else did.

The cigarette burns presented a different situation. These burns occurred when many men smoking cigarettes sat in the TV lounge areas with few ashtrays (these were days well before correctional institutions were declared smoke-free). The behavioral norm seemed to be that someone within an arm's reach of an ashtray would use it, but those who were not simply crushed their cigarettes on the floor or furniture. They simply were not motivated to make the effort to get up to use an ashtray if one wasn't near (especially since getting up might result in a loss of a seat or at least an argument over the right to that seat). This did not demonstrate good caretaking of the facility and was not what would be considered polite behavior in other settings, but it also, clearly, was not malicious vandalism – there was no intent to destroy. When more ashtrays were added, people used them and burns were reduced or eliminated.

Other forms of breakage seemed related to level of control ("no other way to do it"). According to Fisher and Baron (1982), control moderates how the individual will cope with perceived inequity. In many correctional institutions, breakage of room lighting is common, as can be verified by the extraordinary expense involved in producing, marketing, and installing so-called vandal-proof lighting fixtures. Inmates we interviewed told us that in many settings cell lighting, which is constantly on and controlled by staff, is seen as a major disturbance. An inmate who is having trouble sleeping and who wants the room dark (see Chapter 10 on the importance of light–dark cycles) may see covering or disabling the light as the only option. Again, this is not behavior that would be considered acceptable in most settings, but the goal is often not malicious destruction but, rather, control of conditions. We found that in the MCCS, where there were light switches in the room allowing inmates control over most local lighting, lights were rarely damaged.

A similar example concerned air vents. One common vandalism complaint from facility maintenance staff was that inmates often stuffed towels in air vents, causing problems maintaining proper temperature and air flow. When we inquired, we were told by both officers and inmates that this was the only way to control air flow. Inmates complained that rooms often became cold at night when they were trying to sleep, an uncomfortable situation that people thought contributed to catching colds. The facility's maintenance staff's concerns may have been real, but again, this did not appear to be malicious vandalism. Rather, it was an attempt to control the local environmental conditions. Our report on the Chicago MCC suggested that new facilities should provide louvers in inmate rooms to allow control of air flow. The CCMDF, which adopted a number of the design changes we suggested, did not add louvers of this sort. On the week before the official opening of the facility, the sheriff's office had a VIP night during which many local officials and politicians slept in the new jail. Our colleague was working in the facility that night and reported that the next morning many of the VIP-occupied rooms had towels stuffed in the vents.

USING THE MODEL TO EXPLAIN THE SUCCESS OF
DIRECT SUPERVISION

If this model is useful (an important criterion for any model in environment-behavior research), it should help us identify and explain the factors that affect perceived risk, perceived scarcity, stress, and the likelihood of being apprehended in correctional facilities. In this, the model can help us to discover the reasons for the low level of assaults in direct supervision institutions.

The first experience with the institution, where perceptions are initially formed, usually comes in the intake or reception area in which new inmates are processed and assigned to living units. In the direct supervision jail at Contra Costa County, California, inmates wait for processing in an open lounge, not unlike a physician's waiting room. Locked cells are available for any inmates who are a threat to themselves or others. Inmate seating is located near the processing desk so that staff can see and constantly interact with them and supervise their behavior.

The classification systems at most direct supervision jails try to screen out inmates who appear to need tighter controls. Many jails send inmates first to a specially staffed orientation unit, before they are assigned to a longer-term living area. Because many inmates are released within 48 hours, the use of the orientation unit drastically reduces turnover on most living units.

This open, relaxed space and the professional, nonhostile behavior of staff suggest a whole different context for the inmate – one that both overtly and subtly indicates that normal, nonviolent behavior is typical and expected. In Contra Costa County, this initial impression is reinforced by the use of open, noninstitutional design and colors, moveable furniture, and available privacy on the living units. Most importantly, the officer is constantly present and by proximity to the inmates obviously in control of the setting. All of this reinforces the image of a setting in which "normal" behaviors are expected and encouraged.

Interviews with inmates in many of these of facilities indicate that the constant contact with and availability of staff helps to convince inmates that they are unlikely to be assaulted. They expect that the officer is available, ready, and able to protect them should they be threatened by another inmate. The relative absence of weapons is an index of how safe most inmates feel, as is increased intergroup interaction.

Direct supervision jails also succeed by providing access to important resources. This has been as simple as adding more TV lounges and telephones, or meeting basic needs (providing toilet paper, opening doors, getting appointments with counseling or medical staff, etc.). The basic principles of direct supervision (Davis, 1987a; Nelson, 1983, 1990) emphasize the need to create an environment that is calm, controlled, and seen as just and fair by the inmates (Bottoms, 1999), which includes, in part, assuring that the necessities of institutional life are available.

Direct supervision designs increase the likelihood that assaultive behavior will be noticed and dealt with. The presence of staff and openness of the design

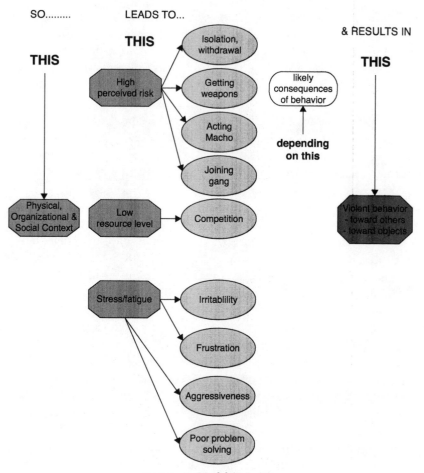

FIGURE 49. Model Overview

make for effective surveillance. The scale of the facility and high levels of staff–inmate contact increase the flow of information and reduce the chance that assaults will go unnoticed.

SUMMARY

The model presented in this chapter shows several aspects of the nature and causes of violence in institutional settings. First, although specific features of a place or a person can directly set off conflict, violence is influenced by a response to a broad array of contextual features. The model suggests that contextual features can act, in part, by affecting the degree to which inmates feel safe, the level at which they perceive important resources to be scarce, and the level of stress and mental fatigue (see Figure 48). The influences of these mediators on violence are moderated by the physical and organizational characteristics that determine the likelihood of being caught and punished for violent acts, depending on the impulsiveness of the moment.

References

Allard, T. J., Wortley, R. K., & Stewart, A. L. (2008). The effect of CCTV on prisoner misbehavior. *The Prison Journal, 88*(3), 404.

Altman, I., & Rogoff, B. (1987). World views in psychology: Trait, interactional, organismic, and transactional perspectives. *Handbook of Environmental Psychology, 1,* 7–40.

Anderson, C. A. (1989). Temperature and aggression: Ubiquitous effects of heat on occurrence of human violence. *Psychological Bulletin, 106*(1), 74–96.

Anderson, C., Anderson, K. B., Dorr, N., DeNeve, K., & Flannagan, M. (1998). Temperature and aggression: Paradox, controversy, and a (fairly) clear picture. In R. Geen & E. Donnerstein (Eds.), *Human Aggression: Theories, Research, and Implications for Social Policy* (pp. 247–298). San Diego, CA: Academic Press, Inc.

Anderson, C., Anderson, A., Dorr, K. B., DeNeve, N., & Flanagan, K. M. (2000). Temperature and aggression. In M. P. Zanna (Ed.), *Advances in Experimental Social Psychology, 32*(pp. 63–133). San Diego, CA: Academic Press, Inc.

Anderson, C., DeNeve, A., & M., K. (1992). Temperature, aggression, and the negative affect escape model. *Psychological Bulletin, 111*(2), 347–351.

Atlas, R. (1982). Violence in prison: Architectural determinism. *Dissertation Abstracts International, 43*(3), 933.

Barker, R. G. (1968). *Ecological Psychology: Concepts and Methods for Studying the Environment of Human Behavior.* Stanford, CA: Stanford University Press.

Baron, R. M., & Kenny, D. A. (1986). The moderator-mediator variable distinction in social psychological research: Conceptual, strategic, and statistical considerations. *Journal of Personality and Social Psychology, 51*(6), 1173–1182.

Beck, A., & Harrison, P. (2007). *Sexual Victimization in State and Federal Prisons Reported by Inmates, 2007.* U.S. Dept. of Justice, Office of Justice Programs, Bureau of Justice Statistics.

Bell, P. A., & Baron, R. A. (1977). Aggression and ambient temperature: The facilitating and inhibiting effects of hot and cold environments. *Bulletin of the Psychonomic Society, 9*(6), 443–445.

Bennet, L. (1976). A study of violence in California prisons: A review with policy implications. In A. K. Cohen, G. F. Cole, & R. G. Bailey (Eds.), *Prison Violence* (pp. 3–22). Lexington, MA: Lexington Books.

Benton, F. W., & Obenland, R. (1975). *Prison and Jail Security.* Champaign, IL: National Clearinghouse for Criminal Justice Planning and Architecture, Illus.

Bissonette, J. (2008). *When the Prisoners Ran Walpole.* Boston, MA: South End Press.

Blonigen, D. M., & Krueger, R. F. (2007). Personality and violence: The unifying role of structural models of personality. In D. J. Flannery, A. T. Vazsonyi, & I. D. Waldman (Eds.), *The Cambridge Handbook of Violent Behavior* (pp. 288–305). New York: Cambridge University Press.

Bogard, D., & Wener, R. E. (2007). *Assessment of Strategies Used to Manage Crowding in Direct Supervision Jails.* Washington, DC: National Institute of Corrections Jail Center.

Bottoms, A. E. (1999). Interpersonal violence and social order in prisons. In M. Tonry & J. Petersilia (Eds.), *Prisons* (Vol. 26, pp. 205–283). Chicago, IL: University of Chicago Press.

Bowker, L. H. (1980). *Prison Victimization.* New York: Elsevier.

Bowker, L. H. (1985). An essay on prison violence. In M. Braswell, S. Dillingham, & R. Montgomery (Eds.), *Prison Violence in America* (pp. 7–18). Cincinnati, OH: Anderson Publishing Co.

Briggs, C. S., Sundt, J. L., & Castellano, T. C. (2003). The effect of supermaximum security prisons on aggregate levels of institutional violence. *Criminology, 41*(4), 1341–1376.

Buffington-Vollum, J., Edens, J., Johnson, D., & Johnson, J. (2002). Psychopathy as a predictor of institutional misbehavior among sex offenders. *Criminal Justice and Behavior, 29*(5), 497.

Carnahan, T., & McFarland, S. (2007). Revisiting the Stanford Prison experiment: Could participant self-selection have led to the cruelty? *Personality and Social Psychology Bulletin, 33*(5), 603.

Coffield, F., & Fundação Calouste, G. (1991). *Vandalism and Graffiti: The State of the Art.* Calouste Gulbenkian Foundation.

Cohen, A. K., Cole, G. F., & Bailey, R. G. (1976). *Prison Violence.* Lexington, MA: D.C. Heath and Company.

Cohen, S. (1971). Direction for research on adolescent school violence and vandalism. *British Journal of Criminology, 9*, 319–340.

Cooke, D. (1991). Violence in prisons: The influence of regime factors. *The Howard Journal, 30*(2), 95–109.

Davis, R. (1987a). *Using the Principles of Direct Supervision as an Organization Management System.* Paper presented at the Second Annual Conference on New Generation Jails, Clearwater, FL.

Davis, R. (1987b). Direct supervision as an organization management system. *American Jails, Spring*, 50–53.

Deland, G. (1993). Violence is a product of the quality of management. *Corrections Compendium, 18*(3), 4.

DeLisi, M., Trulson, C., Marquart, J., Drury, A., & Kosloski, A. (2010). Inside the prison black box: Toward a life course importation model of inmate behavior. *International Journal of Offender Therapy and Comparative Criminology, 55*(8), 1186–1207.

Egli, M., Feurer, I., Roper, T., & Thompson, T. (2002). The role of residential home-likeness in promoting community participation by adults with mental retardation. *Research in Developmental Disabilities, 23*(3), 179–190.

Egli, M., Roper, T., Feurer, I., & Thompson, T. (1999). Architectural acoustics in residences for adults with mental retardation and its relation to perceived homelikeness. *American Journal of Mental Retardation, 104*, 53–66.

Ellis, D. (1984). Crowding and prison violence: Integration of research and theory. *Criminal Justice and Behavior, 11*(3), 277–308.

Evans, G. W., & Cohen, S. (Eds.). (1987). *Environmental Stress.* New York: Wiley.

Evans, G. W. (Ed.). (1982). *Environmental Stress.* New York: Cambridge University Press.

Evans, G. W. & Lepore, S. J. (1997). Moderating and mediating processes in environment-behavior research. In G. T. Moore and R. Marans (Ed.), *Advances in Environment, Behavior, and Design: Toward and Integration of Theory, Methods, and Design* (Vol. 4, pp. 256–286). New York: Springer.

Evans, G. W., K. M. Allen, Tafalla, R, & O'Meara, T. (1996). Multiple stressors: Performance, psychophysiological and affective responses. *Journal of Environmental Psychology*, 16(2): 147–154.

Farbstein, J., & Wener, R. E. (1989). *A Comparison of "Direct" and "Indirect" Supervision Correctional Facilities.* Washington, DC: National Institute of Corrections.

Fisher, J. D., & Baron, R. M. (1982). An equity-based model of vandalism. *Population & Environment*, 5(3), 182–200.

Flynn, E. (1976). The ecology of violence. In A. K. Cohen, G. F. Cole, & R. G. Bailey (Eds.), *Prison Violence* (pp. 115–133). Lexington, MA: Lexington Books.

Gaes, G., Flanagan, T. J., Motiuk, L., & Stewart, L. (1999). Adult correctional treatment. In M. Tonry & J. Petersilia (Eds.), *Prisons* (Vol. 26, pp. 361–426). Chicago: University of Chicago Press.

Gaes, G., & McGuire, W. J. (1985). Prison violence: The contribution of crowding versus other determinants of prison assault rates. *Journal of Research in Crime and Delinquency*, 22, 41–65.

Goldstein, A. P. (1996). *The Psychology of Vandalism.* New York: Plenum Press.

Grotpeter, J., Menard, S., Gianola, D., & O'Neal, M. (2008). *Sexual Violence: Longitudinal, Multigenerational Evidence from the National Youth Survey* (No. NCJ 223284). Rockville, MD: National Institute of Justice.

Haertzen, C., Buxton, K., Covi, L., & Richards, H. (1993). Seasonal changes in rule infractions among prisoners: A preliminary test of the temperature-aggression hypothesis. *Psychological Reports*, 72(1), 195–200.

Haney, C., & Zimbardo, P. (2009). Persistent dispositionalism in interactionist clothing: Fundamental attribution error in explaining prison abuse. *Personality and Social Psychology Bulletin*, 35(6), 807.

Haney, C., Banks, C., & Zimbardo, P. (1973). Interpersonal dynamics in a simulated prison. *International Journal of Criminology and Penology*, 1(1), 69–97.

Harer, M. D., & Steffensmeier, D. J. (1996). Race and prison violence. *Criminology*, 34(3), 323–355.

Hartig, T., Evans, G. W., Jamner, L. D., Davis, D. S., & Gärling, T. (2003). Tracking restoration in natural and urban field settings. *Journal of Environmental Psychology*, 23(2), 109–123.

Hartig, T., Mang, M., & Evans, G. W. (1991). Restorative effects of natural environment experiences. *Environment and Behavior*, 23(1), 3–26.

Haslam, S. A., & Reicher, S. (2006). Stressing the group: Social identity and the unfolding dynamics of responses to stress. *Journal of Applied Psychology*, 91(5), 1037.

Hensley, C., & Koscheski, M. (2002). Does participation in conjugal visitations reduce prison violence in Mississippi? *An Exploratory Study. Criminal Justice Review*, 27(1), 52–65.

Hochstetler, A., & DeLisi, M. (2005). Importation, deprivation, and varieties of serving time: An integrated-lifestyle-exposure model of prison offending. *Journal of Criminal Justice*, 33(3), 257–266.

Huebner, B. M. (2003). Administrative determinants of inmate violence: A multilevel analysis. *Journal of Criminal Justice, 31*(2), 107–117.

Huesmann, L. R., & Kirwil, L. (2007). Why observing violence increases the risk of violent behavior in the observer. In D. J. Flannery, A. T. Vazsonyi, & I. D. Waldman (Eds.), *The Cambridge Handbook of Violent Behavior and Aggression* (pp. 545–570). New York: Cambridge University Press.

Irwin, J. (1985). *The Jail: Managing the Underclass in American Society.* Berkeley, CA: University of California Press.

Irwin, J., & Cressey, D. (1962). Thieves, convicts and the inmate culture. *Social Problems, 10*(2), 142–155.

Ittelson, W. H. (1970). Perception of the large-scale environment. *Transactions of the New York Academy of Sciences, 32*(7), 807.

Jiang, S., & Fisher-Giorlando, M. (2002). Intimate misconduct: A test of the deprivation, importation, and situational models. *The Prison Journal, 82*(3).

Keizer, K., Lindenberg, S., & Steg, L. (2008). The spreading of disorder. *Science, 322*(5908), 1681.

Kinzel, A. F. (1970). Body-buffer zone in violent prisoners. *American Journal of Psychiatry, 127*(1), 59–64.

Kuo, F. E., & Sullivan, W. C. (2001a). Environment and crime in the inner city: Does vegetation reduce crime? *Environment & Behavior, 33*(3): 343–367.

Kuo, F. E., & Sullivan, W. C. (2001b). Aggression and violence in the inner city: Effects of environment via mental fatigue. *Environment and Behavior, 33*(4), 543.

Kury, H., & Smartt, U. (2002). Prisoner-on-prisoner violence: Victimization of young offenders in prison. *Some German findings. Criminal Justice, 2*(4), 411–437.

Lahm, K. F. (2008). Inmate-on-inmate assault: A multilevel examination of prison violence. *Criminal Justice and Behavior, 35*(1), 120.

Lahm, K. (2009a). Inmate assaults on prison staff. *The Prison Journal, 89*(2), 131.

Lahm, K. (2009b). Physical and property victimization behind bars. *International Journal of Offender Therapy and Comparative Criminology, 53*(3), 348.

LaVigne, N. (1994). Rational choice and inmate disputes over phone use on Riker's Island. In R. V. Clark (Ed.), *Crime Prevention Studies* (pp. 109–126). Monsey, NY: Criminal Justice Press.

Lee, R., & Coccaro, E. F. (2007). Neurobiology of impulsive aggression: Focus on serotonin and the orbitofrontal cortex. In D. J. Flannery, A. T. Vazsonyi, & I. D. Waldman (Eds.), *The Cambridge Handbook of Violent Behavior and Aggression* (pp. 170–186). New York: Cambridge University Press.

Lipscomb, G. H., Muram, D., Speck, P. M., & Mercer, B. M. (1992). Male victims of sexual assault. *JAMA, 267*(22), 3064–3066.

Martin, J. M. C. (1961). *Juvenile Vandalism: A Study of Its Nature and Prevention.* Thomas.

Mason, P. (2003). *The Prison in Cinema.* Images. 2003, from http://www.imagesjournal.com/issue06/features/prison.htm

McCorkle, R., Miethe, T., & Drass, K. (1995). The roots of prison violence: A test of the deprivation, management, and "not-so-total" institution models. *Crime & Delinquency, 41*(3), 317.

McDougal, E. (1985). Forward. In M. Braswell, S. Dillingham & R. Montgomery (Eds.), *Prison Violence in America* (pp. vii–xi). Cincinnati, OH: Anderson Publishing Co.

Megaree, E. (1976). Population density & disruptive behavior in a prison setting. In A. K. Cohen, G. F. Cole, & R. G. Bailey (Eds.), *Prison Violence* (pp. 135–144). Lexington, MA: Lexington Books.

Mesquida, C. G., & Wiener, N. I. (1996). Human collective aggression: A behavioral ecology perspective. *Ethology and Sociobiology, 17*(4), 247–262.

Moffat, G. K. (1994). A checklist for assessing risk of violent behavior in historically nonviolent persons. *Psychological Reports, 74*(2), 683–688.

Mumola, C. (2005). *Suicide and Homicide in State Prisons and Local Jails.* Washington, DC: U.S. Department of Justice, Office of Justice Programs.

Nacci, P. I., & Kane, T. R. (1984). Inmate sexual aggression: Some evolving propositions, empirical findings, and mitigating counterforces. *Journal of Offender Counseling, Services and Rehabilitation, 9*, 1–20.

Nagel, W. (1976). Environmental influences in prison violence. In A. K. Cohen, G. F. Cole, & R. G. Bailey (Eds.), *Prison Violence* (pp. 3–22). Lexington, MA: Lexington Books.

Nelson, W. R. (1983). New generation jails. *Corrections Today, April,* 108–112.

Nelson, W. R. (1988). The origins of direct supervision: An eyewitness account. *American Jail, Spring,* 8–14.

Nelson, W. R. (1990, May 20). *Revisiting the Principles of Direct Supervision.* Paper presented at the 5th Annual Symposium on Direct Supervision, Reno, NV.

Nelson, W. R., O'Toole, M., Krauth, B., & Whitemore, C. (1983). *New Generation Jails.* Rockville, MD: National Institite of Corrections.

Ng, B., Kumar, S., Ranclaud, M., & Robinson, E. (2001). Ward crowding and incidents of violence on an acute psychiatric inpatient unit. *Psychiatric Services, 52*(4), 521–525.

Nijman, H. L. I., a Campo, J. M. L. G., & Ravelli, D. P. (1999). A tentative model of aggression on inpatient psychiatric wards. *Psychiatric Services, 50*(6), 832–834.

Park, J. (1976). The organization of prison violence. *Prison Violence.* Lexington, MA: Lexington Books.

Paulus, P., V. Cox, et al. (1975). Some effects of crowding in a prison environment. *Journal of Applied Social Psychology, 5*(1), 86–91.

Prisoners in 2001. (2002). Washington, DC: Department of Justice, Bureau of Justice Statistics.

Rapoport, A. (1982). *The Meaning of the Built Environment.* Beverly Hills, CA: Sage Publications.

Reiter, S. M., & Samuel, W. (1980). Littering as a function of prior litter and the presence or absence of prohibitive signs 1. *Journal of Applied Social Psychology, 10*(1), 45–55.

Rhee, S. H., & Waldman, I. D. (2009). Genetic analysis of conduct disorder and antisocial behavior. In Y.-K. Kim (Ed.), *Handbook of Behavior Genetics* (pp. 455–471). New York: Springer.

Robertson, J. (1999). Cruel and unusual punishment in United States prisons: Sexual harassment among male inmates. *American Criminal Law Review, 36*(1).

Rochman, S. (1991). Alternatives to prison violence. *Corrections Compendium, 16*(6), 1–8.

Ross, L. (1977). The intuitive psychologist and his shortcomings: Distortion in the attribution process. In L. Berkowitz (Ed.), *Advances in Experimental Social Psychology* (Vol. 10). New York: Academic Press.

Ross, L., & Nisbett, R. (1991). *The Person and the Situation: Perspectives of Social Psychology.* New York: McGraw-Hill.

Sabol, W. J., & Couture, H. (2008). *Prison Inmates at Midyear 2007.* Washington, DC: U.S. Department of Justice, Office of Justice Programs, Bureau of Justice Statistics.

Scarpa, A., & Raine, A. (2007). Biosocial bases of violence. In D. J. Flannery, A. T. Vazsonyi, & I. D. Waldman (Eds.), *The Cambridge Handbook of Violent Behavior and Aggression* (pp. 151–169). New York: Cambridge University Press.

Scharf, P. (1983). Empty bars: Violence and the crisis of meaning in the prison. *The Prison Journal, 63*(1), 114–124.

Sechrest, D. K., & Crim, D. (1989). Population density and assaults in jails for men and women. *American Journal of Criminal Justice, 14*(1), 87–103.

Sommer, R. (1974). *Tight Spaces: Hard Architecture and How to Humanize It.* Englewood Cliffs, NJ: Prentice-Hall, Inc.

Sommer, R. (1976). *The End of Imprisonment.* Oxford: Oxford University Press.

Stokols, D. (1987). Conceptual strategies of environmental psychology. In I. Altman &. D. Stokols (Eds.), *Handbook of Environmental Psychology* (Vol. 1, pp. 41–70). New York: Wiley.

Suedfeld, P., Ramirez, C., Deaton, J., & Baker-Brown, G. H. (1980). Environmental effects on violent behavior in prisons. *International Journal of Offender Therapy and Comparative Criminology, 24,* 209–215.

Sundstrom, E., & Altman, I. (1974). Field study of territorial behavior and dominance. *Journal of Personality and Social Psychology, 30,* 115–124.

Taylor, R. B. (2005). The incivilities or "broken windows" thesis. In L. E. Sullivan, *Encyclopedia of Law Enforcement.* Thousand Oaks, CA: Sage.

Terpstra, J., Gispen-De Wied, C. C., & Broekhoven, M. H. (2003). Attenuated stress responsiveness in an animal model for neurodevelopmental psychopathological disorders. *European Neuropsychopharmacology, 13*(4), 249–256.

Thaw, I. (1981). *An Acts-against-Property Model: A Case Study: An Extension of the Traditional Vandalism Model.* Univ. Microfilms International.

Thompson, T. (1990). Home-like architectural features of residential environments. *American Journal on Mental Retardation, 95*(3), 328–341.

Thompson, T., Robinson, J., Dietrich, M., Farris, M., & Sinclair, V. (1996). Architectural features and perceptions of community residences for people with mental retardation. *American Journal on Mental Retardation, 101*(3), 292–313.

Toch, H. (1977). *Living in Prison: The Ecology of Survival.* New York: Free Press.

Toch, H. (1985). Social climate and prison violence. In M. Braswell, S. Dillingham, & R. Montgomery (Eds.), *Prison Violence in America* (pp. 37–46). Cincinnati, OH: Anderson Publishing Co.

Toch, H. (1992). *Violent Men: An Inquiry into the Psychology of Violence.* Washington, DC: American Psychological Association.

Trojanowicz, R. C., & Bucqueroux, B. (1990). *Community Policing: A Contemporary Perspective.* Cincinnati, OH: Anderson Publishing Co.

Trulson, C., & Marquart, J. (1968). Racial desegregation and violence in the Texas prison system. *Criminal Justice Review, 27*(2), 233–255.

Umberson, D., Anderson, K. L., & Williams, K. (2003). Relationship dynamics, emotion state, and domestic violence: A stress and masculinities perspective. *Journal of Marriage and the Family, 65*(1), 233–247.

Van den Heuval, R. (1986). The training needs of mid-level managers in direct supervision jails. In J. Farbstein & R. E. Wener (Eds.), *Proceedings of the First Annual Symposium on New Generation Jails* (pp. 8–10). Boulder, Co.: National Institute of Corrections, U.S. Department of Justice.

Weinmayr, V. M. (1969). Vandalism by design. *Landscape Architecture, 59*, 286.

Wener, R. E. (2006). Direct supervision – Evolution and revolution. *American Jails, March-April,* 21–26.

Wener, R. E. (1985). *Environmental Evaluation: Manhattan House of Detention.* New York: NYC Department of Corrections.

Wener, R. E., Frazier, W., & Farbstein, J. (1985). Three generations of evaluation and design of correctional facilities. *Environment & Behavior, 17*(1), 71–95.

Wener, R. E., & Olsen, R. (1978). *User Based Assessment of the Federal Metropolitan Correctional Centers – Final Report.* Washington, DC: U.S. Bureau of Prisons.

Wener, R. E., & Olsen, R. (1980). Innovative correctional environments: A user assessment. *Environment & Behavior, 12*(4), 478–493.

Whittington, R., & Wykes, T. (1996). Aversive stimulation by staff and violence by psychiatric patients. *British J of Clinical Psychology, 35*, 11–20.

Wilson, J. Q., & Kelling, G. L. (1982). Broken windows. *Atlantic Monthly, 249*(3), 29–38.

Wortley, R. (2003). *Situational Prison Control: Crime Prevention in Correctional Institutions.* New York: Cambridge University Press.

Wyon, D. P., Andersen, I., & Lundqvist, G. R. (1979). The effects of moderate heat stress on mental performance. *Scandinavian Journal of Work, Environment, & Health, 5*, 352–361.

Youth Violence: A Report of the Surgeon General. (2001). Washington, DC: U.S. Public Health Service. Office of the Surgeon General.

Zeisel, J. (1976). *Stopping School Property Damage: Design and Administrative Guidelines to Reduce School Vandalism.* Boston: American Association of School Administrators and Educational Facilities Laboratories.

Zimring, C. (1989). Post Occupancy Evaluation: Contra Costa County Main Detention Facility, Kaplan/McLaughlin/Diaz, San Francisco, CA.

Zupan, L. L. (1991). *Jails: Reform and the New Generation Philosophy.* Cincinnati, OH: Anderson Publishing Co.

12

Conclusion

The research described in this book provides ample reason to pay close attention to the physical setting of a correctional institution for the good and
welfare of the inmates, the staff, and society as a whole. Most of us can
agree that there is institutional and social value in keeping the people who
live and work in these settings safe and involved in useful programs. The
conditions in the institution can have a significant impact on the individual, the group, and the organization. Crowding can lead to social withdrawal
and reduced cooperative behavior, cause stress-related effects on physical and
mental health, and increase aggressiveness that can overwhelm services and
programs and can affect almost every aspect of institutional functioning. It
is also clear that the impact of crowding can be moderated by physical design
and management approach. On the other end of the spectrum, isolation can,
at the very least, produce or exacerbate social and psychological disturbances,
reduce the ability of individuals to function well once they return to the general population (and possibly to society), and increase the chances of self-
harm.

Lack of privacy makes it hard for those inmates who have an interest in
change to be engaged in reflection and self-evaluation. Exposure to uncontrollable noise results in reduced tolerance for frustration, increased irritability
and argumentativeness, and greater likelihood of responding aggressively to
provocations. Lack of access to nature can increase stress and irritability, can
decrease the ability to recover from attentional fatigue, and can increase the
likelihood of aggressive behavior. Reduced exposure to daylight can affect
mood and health and can reduce sleep quality.

Sleep, in fact, may be a signal issue for residents of total institutions that
is little discussed or studied in correctional contexts even though it can have
vast effects. It is well known that sleep deprivation affects physical and mental
health, mood, and behavior. There may be a negative relationship between

sleep and aggressive behavior. Moreover, sleep is an example of an issue that is affected by many of the conditions we have discussed in these chapters – privacy, crowding, lighting (and darkening), and noise. Trying to get a good night's sleep when regularly exposed to the full view of and shared tight space with others, in an environment that is too bright and noisy, would be challenging to most people.

As we have pointed out numerous times, most of the issues described here affect staff as well as inmates. Exposure to environmental stressors such as crowding, noise, lack of daylight and nature views, on top of the tension that often goes along with corrections work, will reduce the ability of staff members to deal with problems and conflicts, increase their levels of stress, and reduce job satisfaction.

Most importantly, these stresses do not exist out of context or in isolation. The effects of all of them are probably worse when experienced in prison or jail because of the nature of involuntary confinement. This includes high levels of exposure and extremely low levels of control over the setting, along with few possible adaptive responses in a context that may include pervasive anxiety, fear, and hostility. In this setting, each stressor, individually and together, can have greatly magnified effects. Environmental stresses, multiply experienced, can take a toll on inmates' behavior and health, can affect the ability of staff to adequately do their job, and can alter the capacity of an institution to fulfill its mission. These are not trivial issues and involve much more than just whether people are comfortable or happy. They go to the core of institutional missions, to the ability to maintain a safe and secure environment, and, in some cases, to the ability to provide a setting that does not fail the test of the Eighth Amendment to the U.S. Constitution, which prohibits cruel and unusual punishment.

This book is about the environment of correctional institutions, but, as we tried to show in Chapter 11 through a model of violent behavior in institutions, the physical setting is only one piece of that. The facility should, and eventually usually does, reflect how the organization defines itself – what its goals and missions are, and what it is trying to accomplish. Architecture is, to a significant extent, a tool that is used to meet those goals. Violence is far from the only concern to be addressed, but it can be a defining issue. Once violence is under control, other things become possible. An example comes from Tom Allison who managed the Orange County (Florida) Jail and was responsible for several successful direct supervision units within that massive system. He noted (personal communication, 1994) that once violence was under control, as it was in his Genesis facility (Wener & Farbstein, 1994), staff had the time and energy to focus on more productive activities, such as overseeing therapeutic, educational, and vocational programs. It was these programs in the Genesis facility that Applegate, Surette, and McCarthy studied (1999) when they found that time spent in a direct supervision facility could reduce recidivism.

This book was meant to be a general review of environments in jails and prisons – and not a tome on the effects of direct supervision, per se. Even so, it seems that the discussion seems to keep coming around to direct supervision. As was noted in the introduction, this may have been inevitable given my experience with these settings.

More importantly, direct supervision has much to say about the nature of people in settings and about possibilities for behavior change in jails and prisons. It is, in some ways, a placeholder for the larger discussion of the way design can affect behavior. It provides a vivid example of dramatic change in atmosphere, ambience, and potential, which is important, not as an end unto itself, but as a demonstration of what else may be possible. The first direct supervision jails represented a paradigm shift in correctional design and operations, not just by changing behavior, but more importantly by forcing managers and designers to reevaluate basic assumptions of how correctional settings need to operate.

This paradigm shift has widened the gulf between what correctional professionals know and what the public assumes about institutional life. Maybe that is why, when professionals talk about the design of these kinds of settings to a class, or at a public forum, they often wait for one inevitable question. You can try to guess who is going to ask it – maybe the one who looks quizzical and uncertain, or that guy with the slight grin who just knows he is going to put you on the spot. "Don't you think," he might start, "that these places are just too nice for criminals?" They might add "won't they want to stay – for a vacation?" or more modestly "they won't deter crime, will they?"

The one thing that is certain is that it comes from someone who thinks they know about life "inside" from TV or movies – but hasn't been there. It is always a tricky question to answer. One can respond that researchers don't advocate – they just study the impacts of the setting on behavior – but that is both a "cop-out" and incomplete. I, for one, have been convinced by years of research that the design and management style that underpins direct supervision makes an important difference. I do advocate, though hopefully from an empirical base.

There is, of course, the legalistic answer. Many of these people, in jails at least, are not technically guilty at all. They are incarcerated before trial and hence, in our system, presumed innocent. Don't innocent people deserve a decent and safe environment? True enough, but then what about the millions who live in prisons post conviction? Why do we advocate for such facilities there?

Then there is the economic response. Direct supervision institutions are, at the very least, no more expensive to build, and, in fact, are often less costly to construct and to operate. When Contra Costa County, California (West County Detention Facility), decided to build a second direct supervision facility, they tried to see how far they could stretch this notion.[1] If inmates don't need to be locked in their rooms all night (after all, open dorms have worked[2]), then why spend considerable sums on plumbing for each cell? Instead "dry cells" were built, with bathrooms outside of the cells, saving money and creating a better sleeping environment. If inmates don't damage their cells with malicious vandalism, if officers have clear control over activity in units, and if the barriers between cells aren't needed to provide high security containment (where would an inmate go under the unlikely circumstance that they managed to break through a wall into the next cell), why spend the money for steel-reinforced concrete between cells – so plaster board was used instead. Each of these decisions was controversial then and remains so now, but they show the potential for savings at the extreme end of the spectrum.

Still, these answers are also inadequate in themselves. Most of those who are the strongest proponents would be in favor of direct supervision even if "innocent until proven guilty" was not the appropriate standard, and many would remain advocates even if it were more costly. The best response to that inevitable question may be to parse its implicit assumptions. One implication is that harsh, unpleasant, scary, and dangerous institutions deter crime. If that were the case, the problem of crime should have been solved many years ago. There is little evidence to suggest that past use of the most spare, barren, and dangerous institutions has affected the mental calculus of the criminal. Quick and certain punishment may influence criminal behavior, but imprisonment is rarely quick or, at the time of the crime, seems certain. Pickpockets, after all, famously worked the crowd at London hangings of pickpockets (Anderson, 2002).

Direct supervision, as conceived and practiced, is not about being nice to inmates. To the contrary, direct supervision was "invented" by corrections professionals who had many years of line experience and were looking for ways to run facilities that were safer, better, cheaper, and, if possible, more effective. It is about trying to change behavior by changing conditions and norms. The original goal was to create more humane environments for all (inmates and staff) and, in so doing, to reduce the negative effects of incarceration ("first do no harm"), while creating a setting where behavior change through programming was at least possible.

Another part of the response must be to look at the reasons for the use of detention in the first place. There are many such models and they are often confused in what Sommer (1976) has called "the model muddle." Is imprisonment simply a means to get people who have done and will do crimes off of the street and out of harm's way? For that goal, warehousing may be sufficient. Is someone sentenced to prison *as* punishment (that is, where loss of freedom is the penalty) or *for* punishment (when the harshness of conditions is the deterrent)?

Or, is imprisonment sought as a means to "correct" – to change, to reform, to educate, to treat, to rehabilitate on the understanding that most individuals will someday leave the institution? Then conditions clearly matter. Which model is adopted remains a policy issue to be decided by lawmakers, elected officials, and, eventually, the voting public. Unfortunately, most often there is no clear statement of models of corrections, and many systems function as if several, all, or none are in force.

The choice of a model for a jail or prison is partly an empirical one (what works?) and partly a moral and ethical one (what is right?). Direct supervision is a humane response in a system where being humane is often a goal but one that is not always achieved. Being humane is no small, simple, or secondary thing. It may be a measure of our society and its ability to move beyond vengeance to effective action. Humane action, in this case, comes with very little penalty – it is not more expensive, is not less effective in deterrence or operation, and likely only helps in creating positive outcomes of programs. Supporting humane settings should not require an explanation or apology.

There is, actually, one penalty. The sad fact is that negative publicity is possible and often feared by elected and appointed officials for advocating building a humane jail or prison. There are no surveys I know of that identify the number of officials who have declined to use direct supervision, or who have watered down the model and chosen harder fixtures and furnishings, even if more costly, because of the risk of a news story about "codling criminals," but everyone who has worked in this field has heard such tales. Sheriffs know that they will rarely lose votes for being labeled tough and won't come within miles of any system that might be called soft. Psychologists can coin the term "soft architecture" (Sommer, 1974), but no elected official will touch it. Humane should be value enough, and when it comes with better outcomes and not extra expense, it should not be a hard sell. But it is.

On a personal note, even after four decades, I still discuss the larger implications of this research with some trepidation, acutely aware that I only occasionally walk into correctional living space, and then always walk out again in a short time. I neither suffer the stresses of an inmate nor shoulder the responsibilities and risks of an officer. I regularly do reality checks to assure myself that these results reflect the actual situation, and not some distant academic perspective. Who am I to tell the men and women who put themselves on the line as officers what will make them more or less safe? What always brings me back to acceptance of these principles are the data themselves – the source of which are many hundreds of officers and administrators and thousands of inmates who have been surveyed and interviewed.

Echoes from the history of jails and prisons, as discussed in Chapter 2, provide reason for concern over the status of this innovation. As we pointed out, the history of corrections is replete with examples of innovations that were thoughtful, humane, effective, and, at least in some cases, appeared to be successful, but were eventually (more often sooner than later) consigned to the dustbin of correctional history. These reforms and reformers were overcome by economics and crowding or by politics. Seemingly good ideas were crushed when agencies were no longer willing or able to continue the program.

It certainly is possible that direct supervision will be just one more trend that will fade with time, even though it seems at the moment to have some staying power. Prison populations tend to grow disproportionately to general population size and maybe even to crime rates, and the most certain effect of overcrowding is that it threatens progressive philosophies and programs. Direct supervision can be such a victim, too. A look at the *NIC Direct Supervision Sourcebook* for 2006 shows that there are hundreds of such institutions, and the number continues to grow. The most important professional organizations recognize direct supervision as the state of the art. If the history of corrections tells us anything, though, it is that all successes are fragile. Schneiger said as much in his study of the Manhattan House of Detention (1985) when he noted that the smooth and safe operation there was not inevitable and could be lost without continued effort and focus.

Some disturbing signs suggest that this fragility is real. First, the large number of institutions listed in the *Direct Supervision Directory* may be deceiving. Several researchers (Farbstein & Wener, 1989; Tartaro, 2006) have suggested that many of these jails do not seem to fully implement the principles of direct supervision. Even more disconcerting are reports from many in the field of "backsliding." Some institutions that started out as early and successful examples of direct supervision jails have seen their founders and chief administrator's turnover, sometimes several times. These may be interesting case studies in organizational practices – how policies and procedures get passed on and handed down from one generation of leadership to another. Emphasis on full-scale training seems to be the first to go, because cutting back the number of weeks of training given to new officers is an easy way to reduce expenses, and several facilities have had difficulty after skimping in this way.

It is commonplace, almost trite, to use the conclusion of a book to call for more research, but the circumstances in correctional facilities would seem to justify, if not demand, just that. It is not just scientific curiosity that suggests we need to know more. The impacts of corrections systems are huge by almost any measure. These facilities house millions of people in the United States and worldwide. The systems drain societies of people, effort, and resources. The immediate economic costs are obvious, but the long-term costs have to take into account what impact inmates will have on society once released and the costs of dealing with the high percentage who will eventually be reincarcerated.

There has probably been more research on crowding than any other issue addressing the psychological impact of correctional environments, mostly because of the many court cases addressing crowding, but even here there are many open questions, as illustrated by the divergent views in the literature discussed in Chapter 7. The negative impacts of incarceration are felt on the individuals who are locked up, but also on their families. Improving the physical conditions in institutions is not a solution to these problems. Real solutions need to be addressed at a broader level of social values and operation of the entire criminal justice system. But better conditions can help to ameliorate some of negative effects.

A call for better facilities does not argue against those who want a moratorium on construction, or an emphasis on alternatives to corrections, but it does recognize the likelihood that millions will remain locked up for years to come. There is plenty of evidence that it is possible to do so in ways that reduce or eliminate the most serious risk to safety and health, both physical and mental. Addressing these issues has many additional benefits. It can make corrections work less oppressive dangerous and stressful; it creates the setting and atmosphere within which programs that might reduce recidivism can work, which, in turn, would lower populations and reduce cost in the long term.

References

Anderson, D. A. (2002). The deterrence hypothesis and picking pockets at the pickpocket's hanging. *American Law and Economics Review, 4*(2), 295–313.

Applegate, B. K., Surette, R., & McCarthy, B. H. (1999). Detention and desistance from crime: Evaluating the influence of a new generation jail on recidivism. *Journal of Criminal Justice, 27*(6), 539–548.

Farbstein, J., & Wener, R. E. (1989). *A Comparison of "Direct" and "Indirect" Supervision Correctional Facilities.* Washington, DC: National Institute of Corrections – Prison Division.

Schneiger, F. (1985). *Organizational Assessment of Manhattan House of Detention.* New York City: New York Department of Corrections.

Sommer, R. (1974). *Tight Spaces: Hard Architecture and How to Humanize It.* Englewood Cliffs, NJ: Prentice-Hall, Inc.

Sommer, R. (1976). *The End of Imprisonment.* Oxford: Oxford University Press.

Tartaro, C. (2006). Watered down: Partial implementation of the new generation jail philosophy. *The Prison Journal, 86*(3), 284.

Wener, R. E., & Farbstein, J. (1994). *Genesis Facility: Post-Occupancy Evaluation, Final Report* (No. 154459). Washington, DC: National Institute of Corrections.

Wyon, D. P., Andersen, I., & Lundqvist, G. R. (1979). The effects of moderate heat stress on mental performance. *Scandinavian Journal of Work, Environment, & Health, 5,* 352–361.

Notes

Chapter 1: Introduction

1   I have chosen to use the plural personal pronoun (we, our) when I discuss research projects because I was almost always part of a team in conducting these studies.

2   We learned later, after our study was completed, that this case was eventually decided in the U.S. Supreme Court (*Bell* v. *Wolfish*, 1977).

Chapter 2: Historical View

1   This is true, by the way, for zoos as well, which have evolved greatly in response to modern views of their functions as research facilities, educational institutions, and protectors of endangered species (Coe, 1985; Maple & Finlay, 1989; Rothfels, 2002).

2   This could amount to a life sentence as average life expectancy for white males in 1870 was about 45 years, less for black males (Haines, 2002).

3   England shipped approximately 30,000 prisoners to America before 1776. Throughout the eighteenth and nineteenth centuries, approximately 160,000 prisoners were shipped to Australia. [McConville, S. (1995). "The Victorian prison: England, 1865–1965." *The Oxford History of Prisons*. N. Morris & D. J. Rothman (pp. 177–150). New York: Oxford University Press.]

4   A review of the list of executions at London's Newgate Prison between 1606 and 1895, however, suggests that even though many capital offenses were on the books, the vast majority of executions were for murder or treason (Vincent, 1895).

5   "They believed that all the guards would have to do is watch the prisoners from the guard station and make rounds every so often to make sure there was silence. It sounded simple, but in reality, the prisoners had to be supplied with work, bathed, fed, and allowed in the exercise yards for an hour a day." One of the biggest problems in the early years of Eastern State was keeping the guards, who were given a ration of alcoholic beverages during the workday, sober during working hours. Prison commissioners were forced to pass a rule that stated that anyone found drunk on the job would be "dismissed immediately" (Phillips, 1996, para. 13).

6   Eastern State Penitentiary had flush toilets before these were installed in the White House (Woodham 2008).

7   Rothman (1995) is less cynical about motives and argues that reform goals held significant sway over planning decisions in the early nineteenth century. He suggests that the building boom of that era could not have been explained any other way, because inmates could have been set to work or simply detained less expensively. It was the reform goals, he says, that spurred legislatures to allocate significant sums for prisons that otherwise might not have been forthcoming.

8   "The jail has to be formed out of rough stones in order to appear fearsome, but in such a manner that the prisoners are not deprived of light from the sky" (Cadalso y Manzano, 1922, as cited in Johnston, 2000, p. 6).

9   Captured soldiers developed intricate hidden ways of communicating despite threats of torture (*American Experience*, "Vietnam Online," 1983).

Chapter 3: The Development of Direct Supervision as a Design and Management System

1   These facility plans have also been variously called "podular direct supervision" and "new generation." I have chosen to eschew the former as cumbersome and the latter as too generic.

2   This presumption was modified somewhat by the Supreme Court ruling in *Bell* v. *Wolfish* (1979). The Court ruled that pretrial inmates are not entitled to greater rights than sentenced inmates. "*Bell* v. *Wolfish* abandoned the old rule that the presumption of innocence entitle to pretrial detainees meant that their conditions of detainment must be the least restrictive alternative" ("Civil Liabilities, Unconstitutional Jail and Planning of New Institutions Part I," 1997, p. 9).

Chapter 4: Post-Occupancy Evaluations of the Earliest DS Jails

1   The fit was so good that once approached, the BOP agreed to fund these studies almost immediately. It helped that at the time we made a proposal to study the MCC, Congress was asking the BOP to justify the expense of these jails.

2   Harry Weese and Associates for the Chicago MCC, Jordan Gruzen and Associates for the New York MCC, and Thomas Tucker and Associates for the San Diego MCC.

3   Although the term "direct supervision" was coined sometime later, the concept was completely implemented in the MCCs.

4   The evolution of the triangle design is revealing – both about the way in which designs respond to programs and the intermingling of the creative process with programmatic practicality. I interviewed the designers at Harry Weese & Associates, who were responsible for the Chicago plan, and asked them why the triangular form was used. Several staff architects noted that the triangle allowed them to provide all cells with an external view, while maintaining an open interior space on a compact building footprint. Mr. Weese, in response to that question, leaned back and rather wistfully noted that he had always wanted to create a triangular high-rise building, and it was this commission that gave him the opportunity. For years the triangular plan was seen as emblematic of direct supervision and was copied in many other sites.

5   Detailed results and analysis can be found in a series of final reports and published papers (Wener, 1977; Wener & Clark, 1977; Wener & Olsen, 1978; Wener & Olsen, 1980; Wener, Frazier, & Farbstein, 1985).

6   *This noise standard was used in the 2nd addition of ACA standards for Adult Local Detention Facilities* (Performance-based Standards, 2004).
7   On some occasions, New York officers told us, they locked themselves in the linen closet – not for safety but so that they could complete their paperwork in privacy.
8   By double-bunking all beds.

Chapter 5: Effectiveness of Direct Supervision Models

1   Although case studies are inherently descriptive in nature and not appropriate for testing causal relations, there has been a reassessment and resurgence of interest in their value as a research tool (see Yin, 1994).
2   Cross-sectional refers to research that looks at two or more groups or places at the same point in time (for instance, two different kinds of jails), whereas longitudinal research looks at the same group or place at different points in time (for instance, at a jail population before and after conversion to direct supervision).
3   It is hard to find an exact number of institutions included in these studies because not all studies name their sites and there is some overlap of sites among the studies.
4   The Eighth Amendment to the U.S. Constitution forbids "cruel and unusual punishment" and this proscription has been used as the basis of inmate suits against poor conditions in jails and prisons.

Chapter 7: Prison Crowding

1   Rated capacity refers to the number of inmates identified as the appropriate maximum by some operating rating agency.
2   The case was known as *Bell* v. *Wolfish* (1979) and eventually went to the U.S. Supreme Court where a landmark jail crowding decision was issued, stating that placing two inmates in a single cell does not constitute cruel and unusual punishment.

Chapter 8: The Psychology of Isolation in Prison Settings

1   Video arraignment can substitute for some court visits; video visiting may replace seeing a loved one in person.
2   In the United States, at least, court rulings have led to policies in almost all settings that require at least 1 hour out-of-cell time per day.
3   That is not the same as saying that isolation is effective as a punishment. By classical Skinnerian definition, punishment is an action following a behavior that causes that behavior to decrease in frequency. It is not at all clear that isolation is an effective form of discipline. In any case, long periods of isolation are hardly Skinnerian in principle.

Chapter 9: The Effects of Noise in Correctional Settings

1   Noise criteria evaluate sound levels by taking measurements at the loudest locations in a room at ear level.
2   In many prisons (but not jails), inmates have their own radios and televisions, with headsets to reduce noise.

Chapter 10: Windows, Light, Nature, and Color

1   The subject is read random numbers in increasingly long strings and asked to repeat the numbers in reverse order.

Chapter 11: An Environmental and Contextual Model of Violence in Jails and Prisons

1   In 2007, 4.5 percent of all state and federal inmates reported experiencing one or more incidents in which they were sexually victimized (assaulted or pressured for sex) by inmates or staff (Beck & Harrison, 2007). Homicide rates were reported to be between 3 and 4 per 1,000 inmates in jails and prisons in 2002 (Mumola, 2005).

2   Findings that youth are more likely to commit violent offenses seem also to be true outside of institutional life (*Youth Violence: A Report of the Surgeon General*, 2001).

3   They are not totally unaffected, however. A planned assault driven by factors that are external to the institution may still be easier to detect and stop with appropriate management systems, design, and staffing.

Chapter 12: Conclusion

1   Jail administrator Larry Ard was an early advocate for direct supervision and responsible for their ground breaking new facility in Martinez, California. He was willing to push the model further than most.

2   We studied an excellent DS facility in Orange County, Florida – Genesis – that only had open dorms. The loss of privacy was significant, but still, this facility was safe and effective, and very inexpensive to build (Wener & Farbstein, 1994).

Index